T0366150

# Generational Income Mobility in North America and Europe

Labor markets in North America and Europe have changed tremendously in the face of increased globalization and technical progress, raising important challenges for policy makers concerned with equality of opportunity. This book examines the influence of both changes in income inequality and of social policies on the degree to which economic advantage is passed on between parents and children in the rich countries. Standard theoretical models of generational dynamics are extended to examine generational income and earnings mobility over time and across space. Over twenty contributors from North America and Europe offer comparable estimates of the degree of mobility, how it has changed through time, and the impact of government policy. In so doing, they extend the analytical tool kit used in the study of generational mobility, and offer insights for not only the conduct of future research but also directions for policies dealing with equality of opportunity and child poverty.

MILES CORAK is Director of Family and Labour Studies at Statistics Canada. He is also adjunct professor with the Department of Economics at Carleton University, a Research Fellow at the Institute for the Study of Labor (Bonn), and during 2003/04 was a visiting researcher at the UNICEF Innocenti Research Centre. He is the editor of *Government Finances and Generational Equity* (1998) and *Labour Markets, Social Institutions, and the Future of Canada's Children* (1998).

# Generational Income Mobility in North America and Europe

EDITED BY

MILES CORAK

CAMBRIDGE
UNIVERSITY PRESS

# CAMBRIDGE
## UNIVERSITY PRESS

University Printing House, Cambridge CB2 8BS, United Kingdom

Cambridge University Press is part of the University of Cambridge.

It furthers the University's mission by disseminating knowledge in the pursuit of
education, learning and research at the highest international levels of excellence.

www.cambridge.org
Information on this title: www.cambridge.org/9780521827607

© Cambridge University Press 2004

First published 2004
First paperback edition 2011

*A catalogue record for this publication is available from the British Library*

*Library of Congress Cataloguing in Publication data*
Generational Income Mobility in North America and Europe / edited by Miles Corak.
  p.  cm.
Includes bibliographical references and index.
ISBN 0 521 82760 4
1. Income distribution – North America.  2. Income distribution – Europe.  3. Social
mobility – North America.  4. Social mobility – Europe.  I. Corak, Miles.
HC95.Z9I514  2004
339.2´2 – dc22  2004045659

ISBN 978-0-521-82760-7 Hardback

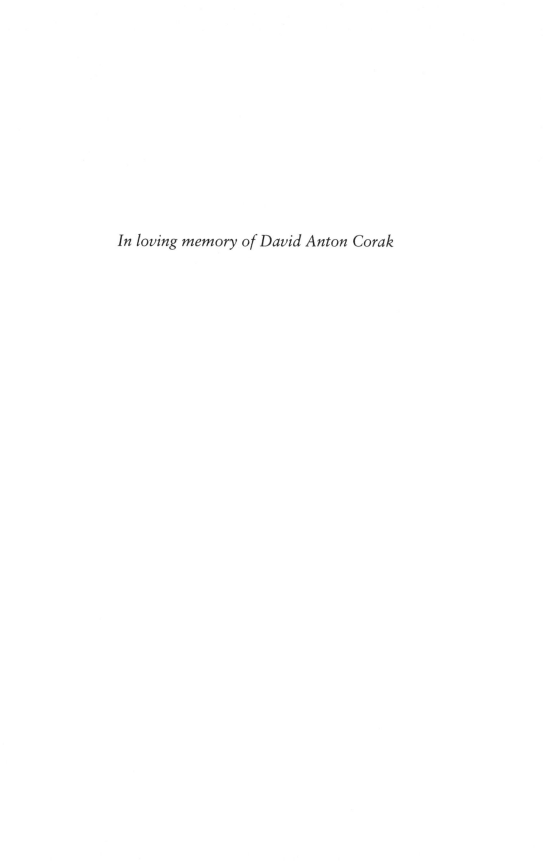

*In loving memory of David Anton Corak*

# Contents

# Figures

# Tables

# Contributors

ANDERS BJÖRKLUND is Professor of Economics at the Swedish Institute for Social Research (SOFI) at Stockholm University. He was visiting professor at the University of Michigan in 1995/96. In recent years his research has focused on intergenerational income mobility, economics of education, and earnings and income inequality.

JO BLANDEN is a Research Officer at the Centre for Economic Performance at the London School of Economics.

MILES CORAK is Director of Family and Labour Studies at Statistics Canada and a Research Fellow of the Institute for the Study of Labor (IZA), Bonn, Germany. During 2003/04 he was a visiting researcher at the UNICEF Innocenti Research Centre, Florence, Italy.

KENNETH A. COUCH is an Associate Professor in the economics department at the University of Connecticut. His research interests include inequality, intergenerational mobility, and the analysis of government programs designed to assist the poor.

TOR ERIKSSON is a Professor in Economics at the Aarhus School of Business and a Research Director at the Center for Corporate Performance in Aarhus, Denmark. His research interests include intergenerational mobility and topics in personnel and labor economics.

JOHN ERMISCH is a Professor at the Institute for Social and Economic Research at the University of Essex and a Fellow of the British Academy. His research deals with how markets interact with household and demographic decisions. His latest book is *An Economic Analysis of the Family* (Princeton University Press, 2003).

GØSTA ESPING-ANDERSEN is Professor of Political and Social Sciences at the University of Pompeu Fabra in Barcelona. His recent books include *Social Foundations of Postindustrial Economies* (Oxford, 1999) and *Why We Need a New Welfare State* (Oxford, 2003).

MARCO FRANCESCONI is Principal Research Officer at the Institute for Social and Economic Research at the University of Essex. His current research interests include economic analyses of labor market dynamics, intergenerational links, and public policy evaluations.

ALISSA GOODMAN is the Programme Director of the Education, Employment, and Evaluation Sector at the Institute for Fiscal Studies, London.

NATHAN D. GRAWE is Assistant Professor of Economics at Carleton College, Northfield, Minnesota. His research examines the transmission of economic inequalities within the family and in particular the role of educational financing.

PAUL GREGG is a Reader in the Economics Department at the University of Bristol. He has research associations with the Centre for Market and Public Organisation at Bristol, the Centre for Economic Performance at the London School of Economic, and is a member of the Council of Economic Advisers at HM Treasury.

BJÖRN GUSTAFSSON is Professor at the Department of Social Work, Göteborg University, Sweden, and a Research Fellow of the Institute for the Study of Labor (IZA), Bonn, Germany.

MARKUS JÄNTTI is a Professor in the Department of Economics and Statistics at Abo Akademi University in Finland. His research interests include inequality, poverty, and socio-economic mobility, particularly in a comparative context.

DEAN R. LILLARD is Senior Research Associate in the Department of Policy Analysis and Management at Cornell University. His research interests include intergenerational mobility, the economics of education, and health economics.

LEONARD M. LOPOO is an Assistant Professor of Public Administration at the Maxwell School of Citizenship and Public Affairs at Syracuse University. His research focuses on the economics of the family.

STEPHEN MACHIN is Professor of Economics at University College London, Director of the Centre for the Economics of Education, and Research Director of the Centre for Economic Performance at the London School of Economics. He is a co-editor of the *Economic Journal*, and has been visiting Professor at Harvard University (1993/4) and at the Massachusetts Institute of Technology (2001/2).

SUSAN E. MAYER is Dean and Associate Professor at the Harris School of Public Policy Studies at the University of Chicago.

MARIANNE E. PAGE is Associate Professor of Economics at the University of California, Davis. Her research interests include intergenerational mobility and the behavioral effects of education and welfare programs.

EVA ÖSTERBACKA is Assistant Professor at the Department of Economics and Statistics, Åbo Akademi University. Her main research deals with the relationship between family background and economic outcomes.

TORUN ÖSTERBERG is affiliated with the Department of Social Work, Göteborg University, Sweden.

ODDBJØRN RAAUM is a Senior Research Fellow at The Ragnar Frisch Centre for Economic Research, University of Oslo. His research deals with wage formation, labor market policies, economic return to education, labor market performance among immigrants, and the impact of family background on adult socio-economic outcomes.

JOHN E. ROEMER is Elizabeth S. and A. Varick Stout Professor of Political Science and Economics at Yale University. He currently works on issues at the intersection of political philosophy, economics, and politics.

GARY SOLON is Professor of Economics at the University of Michigan.

# *Preface*

This volume contains twelve essays from twenty-three collaborators, and spans – to varying degrees – ten countries in North America and Europe, as well as touching upon the experience of a further five with lower levels of per capita income. It grew out of a substantive concern with the need for internationally comparable results in the analysis of generational income mobility. The early 1990s witnessed a number of data and methodological developments that revitalized research on this topic in labor economics, and which began to complement a long-standing literature in sociology. As more and more studies of the relationship between parental income and the adult labor market success of children became available, concerns about the comparability of the findings both within and across countries began to be expressed. The idea for this volume springs from this concern, and it is intended to present the major findings and methods to researchers in the area but also to a broader audience concerned with mobility across the generations from both a research and policy perspective.

The initial idea and planning for the project sprang from conversations between Anders Björklund, Marco Francesconi, Susan Mayer, and myself. I am, in the first instance, grateful for their collaboration and to the former Canadian International Labour Network for supporting the initial planning by sponsoring our participation at one of its conferences. I would also in particular like to thank Statistics Canada for funding and hosting a workshop that brought the majority of the collaborators together in Ottawa during February 2001 to present and discuss initial drafts of the chapters. Christopher Jencks and Sascha Becker also participated in this workshop and their input to the discussions is much appreciated. Thanks are also due to Gert Wagner and the staff of the Deutsches Institut für Wirtschafts-forschung (DIW) for sponsoring and hosting a follow-up workshop in Berlin in June 2001 at which a number of revised chapter drafts were reviewed. Finally, I thank Chris Harrison, Patricia Maurice, Alison Powell, and their colleagues at the Cambridge University Press for their review of the project and work in shepherding it through the production process.

# 1 | Generational income mobility in North America and Europe: an introduction

MILES CORAK

D URING the 1990s, a number of countries in both North America and Europe set explicit targets for the reduction of child poverty, including the United Kingdom, Ireland, and Canada. In the United Kingdom, the pledge, announced in 1999, was to eliminate child poverty in a generation; in Canada, the ambition, made clear a decade earlier, was to seek to do the same by the year 2000. And even in countries less explicit about their goals, reducing child poverty has been an important public policy concern. This, for example, is as true in the United States, where child poverty rates have historically been among the highest relative to other rich countries, as it is in Sweden, where they have been among the lowest. Clearly, this issue has a strong resonance in public policy discourse, and reflects a growing concern over the welfare of all children regardless of their place in the income distribution. But why should societies care more about children than any other group? One possible reason is that children have certain rights as citizens, but are dependent upon others for the defense of their rights. This may certainly be the case, but another reason – one often explicitly made by advocates – is instrumental: children should be thought of as investments in the future. This argument suggests that in the long run the productivity of the economy and the well-being of all citizens would be higher if the well-being of children were improved, and in particular if child poverty were reduced. UNICEF (2000), for example, clearly states this view. The premise is that if children are raised in a state of low income there will be long-term consequences,

I would like to thank Gaspar Fajth, Nathan Grawe, Susan Mayer, and Gary Solon for comments on a previous draft of this chapter, which was completed while I was on leave from Statistics Canada and visiting the UNICEF Innocenti Research Centre in Florence, Italy. An early and abridged version has appeared as Corak (2003). The responsibility for the content as well as for any errors or omissions is entirely mine, and in particular should not be attributed to either Statistics Canada or to UNICEF.

they will become less than they otherwise could be, indeed may grow up to be poor adults who in turn raise poor children.

This rationale has had increasing relevance because of the growing importance of human capital to economic growth, which in turn has created unprecedented pressures for more inequality in the rich countries. In fact, the move from resource extraction and manufacturing as the sources of prosperity, to service economies relying upon human capital has not only placed a premium on education and skills, it has also led in some countries to an outright decline in the earnings of the less skilled. Further, important institutions – including labor market regulations, family policy, unionization, and minimum wages – have changed dramatically. In some countries the pressures for more inequality are also associated with increased integration of product, capital, and labor markets influencing earnings and take-home pay. In all countries, however, individuals and families face a different and perhaps growing set of risks, and in some cases have experienced dramatic changes in wage rates, access to good jobs, and ultimately to their relative standing in the income distribution. Among others, Gottschalk and Smeeding (1997) and Katz and Autor (1999) have reviewed an explosion of research documenting changes in the economic returns to education and skills, the level and structure of wages, and the distribution of income. The latter argue that all rich countries seem to have been confronted with similar changes in the demand for labor that placed increasing importance on education and skills. Katz and Autor also argue that the consequences are very different according to variations in supply-side responses and differences in labor market institutions. In North America, but principally in the United States, the wage structure has changed tremendously, the gap between those in the top of the distribution and those in the bottom growing significantly since the late 1970s and early 1980s. But this is not primarily or uniquely a North American phenomenon: similar changes, while still significant, were much more muted in Canada, but they were just as dramatic in the United Kingdom and at the same time not as notable in other European economies (Katz and Autor 1999, Tables 9 and 10).

In short, the world in which children in the rich countries have been growing up is very different than it was a generation ago. In this context, it is quite reasonable to imagine that policy makers are concerned with their well-being. But just what is known about the long-term consequences of childhood experiences? What is the relationship between family background, particularly family income, and the long-term outcomes of children? How has this relationship changed over time, and how does it differ across countries? In particular, do increased globalization and higher returns to education lead to a weaker or a stronger tie between parental income and the long-term labor market success of children? It is very hard to find definitive answers to these questions, which all have to do with generational mobility. In contrast to the substantial and sustained efforts social scientists have made in documenting and trying to understand the nature of earnings inequality and particularly its relationship to changes in technology and globalization, there is markedly less research addressing generational income mobility.

"Generational mobility" refers to the relationship between the socio-economic status of parents – more particularly to their income – and the status and income their children will attain in adulthood. Solon (1999) illustrates the importance of this concept by imagining two societies with the same income distribution, the fraction of low-income families and the fraction of high-income families – however these terms are defined and measured – being exactly the same, as are any other measures of inequality one could devise. In the first society, individuals inherit their economic position entirely from their parents: children born to parents at the very bottom of the income distribution grow up to be adults at the very bottom of the income distribution; those born to parents at the top go on to have incomes placing them at the top. In this society there is no generational income mobility. Knowing the parents' place in the income distribution exactly predicts the position the child will occupy in the next generation's income distribution. In contrast, in the second society there is no relationship between family background and the adult outcomes of children. Those born to parents at the bottom of the income distribution are as likely to end up at the bottom, or as likely to end up at the top, as those born to parents at the top. In this society, there is complete generational income mobility. Knowing the parents' position in the income distribution offers no information about where the children will end up. At any point in time the two societies are equally unequal, but they differ very much in the character of their inequality. These are clearly polar cases, and one would not expect any advanced economy to be at either extreme, but it is easy to imagine that the consequences of income inequalities will be influenced by the situation of societies between them. It may not

also be hard to imagine – and indeed Benabou and Ok (2001) offer a
formal model – that individuals living in a society characterized by a
good deal of generational income mobility may be much more tolerant
of existing inequalities than those living in a society with very little
generational mobility. They may believe that even if their efforts and
skills are not fairly rewarded, their hopes for and investments in their
children will be.

Understanding the extent of generational mobility is, in other words,
a first step in understanding the consequences of income inequalities,
as well as the extent of 'equality of opportunity.' As such, it is also
important to understand the mechanisms that determine the degree of
income mobility across the generations as they are related to a host
of pressing policy concerns. Education policy – dealing with access to
higher education but also with early childhood care – access to health
care, and immigration policy are all motivated or informed by this
issue. In fact, there is a well developed literature on the generational
dynamics of social status, this topic being a mainstay of sociological research, as evidenced in the surveys by Erickson and Goldthorpe
(2002, 1992), and by Treiman and Ganzeboom (1990). However, the
aspects of generational dynamics dealing with income have been relatively less explored, and certainly less explored than studies of income
inequalities at a point in time. Even so, important steps have been made,
particularly since the early 1990s, with the work of Altonji and Dunn
(1991), Solon (1992), and Zimmerman (1992), and subsequently by
a significant number of other researchers as reviewed in, for example,
Björklund and Jäntti (2000), Mulligan (1997, chapter 7), and Solon
(1999). Researchers in this field now have a well-charted theoretical
map of the terrain, as well as an appreciation of both the empirical
challenges and the methods to deal with them. While there is a growing consensus on the broad sweep of the major empirical findings for
some countries, it is fair to say that this literature stands at a cross-
roads. More and more results are being produced for more and more
countries, but with different sorts of data, with variations in sometimes
subtle methodological choices, and covering different time periods. As
a result, it may be difficult to draw meaningful cross-national comparisons that shed light on the underlying causes and the role and
importance of policy and institutional differences.

The research presented in this book contributes to this agenda. In
this first chapter, I offer background on the theoretical and empirical

methods used in this field, summarize the major findings of the book and their relationship to other aspects of the existing literature, and draw general lessons for future research and policy consideration. The objectives of collecting these essays under one cover are three in number: first, to offer analyses of the degree of generational income mobility in the rich countries and a framework for their interpretation both across time and space; second, to highlight empirical concerns in deriving and comparing these estimates as well as to illustrate new methods and data to deal with them; and finally, to highlight the scope and challenges of policy interventions and how they can make a difference to outcomes. To put it another way, collectively the contributors offer insights on the theory and interpretative framework for the study of generational income mobility, offer – along a number of different dimensions – methodological contributions associated with measurement and estimation, and, finally, offer findings that may help to inform policy discussions.

The story line of the chapters unfolds along these three themes. The analyses in Chapters 2 and 3 deal exclusively with the theory of generational mobility motivating the central estimation techniques. In different ways, both authors offer a structure for framing and interpreting the empirical results. The research in Chapter 2 focuses exclusively on an extension of the standard economic theory of generational income mobility – as presented in Becker and Tomes (1979) – to concerns dealing with changes through time and comparisons across space. It also offers an interpretation of the linear model of regression to the mean used in many of the subsequent chapters. The relationship between equality of opportunity and generational income mobility is formally discussed in Chapter 3 by a focus upon another mainstay in the empirical analysis of generational dynamics in both economics and sociology: the transition matrix. Chapter 4 marks the transition from theory to measurement. A number of innovative empirical techniques are used in order to implement the ideas of both of the preceding chapters, while at the same offering a series of cross-country comparisons of generational income mobility in developed and developing countries. The threads of many of the issues and findings discussed in Chapter 4 extend through the following four chapters of the book. These chapters, 5 through 8, offer a series of country studies examining the degree of generational income mobility in the United States, the United Kingdom, and Germany. In some cases this research emphasizes changes through time within the particular country, in others the focus is on measurement issues and the use of occupational status, while in others the findings from alternative empirical techniques are highlighted. In all cases these chapters begin to shift attention from the practical concerns of accurately measuring the degree of generational mobility, to the investigation of underlying causes. Chapters 9, 10, and 11 travel further along this line by highlighting the importance of the family in determining the degree and pattern of generational mobility, and by examining the generational consequences of social policy. In these chapters the focus is on the family in Norway, Sweden, and Finland, the welfare system in the United States, and unemployment insurance in Canada and Sweden. The final chapter summarizes the major messages of the book, but in a manner that attempts to extend the analyses and draw out more explicit directions for the conduct of policy promoting equality of opportunity.

## 1 Major findings

Taken as a whole, the chapters offer results and lessons of a general nature for the direction of future research and policy, particularly if the frame of reference is an international one. The major contributions might be summarized as follows. First, with respect to theory and a framework to guide empirical investigation, the analyses suggest that in an economy emphasizing human capital as the basis for sustained growth – one in which the economic returns to education have gone up – more challenges will be placed in the way of equality of opportunity. This happens in the basic model of generational mobility used by economists because rich parents have an increased opportunity to invest in their children, and the efficacy of these investments goes up. But this is not to say that governments are impotent. On the contrary, the design of policy can have an important role to play in tempering or reversing market forces. This said, deciphering the extent to which the degree of equal opportunity has been attained from the kinds of indicators generally proposed is not straightforward. Equality of opportunity requires a more subtle understanding of the influence of the family on child outcomes and the motivations that will ultimately govern adult behaviour. It should not be equated with complete generational mobility in incomes. A broader understanding of the social context is necessary and the indicators offered in this book are only a first step.

Second, with respect to methodological developments, the most significant way to advance knowledge in this field involves the development of appropriate data. Ideal data sets for the study of long-term processes, those playing out over the course of a generation or more, rarely exist. Researchers and practitioners often imagine the ideal data source as being a long-standing longitudinal survey that captures young people in their early years while still in the parental home, follows them through time, and eventually obtains information from them in adulthood. A survey of this sort must be based upon a representative sample of individuals and accurately measure both parental income but also the adult income of children. In addition, these income measures must represent the long-term economic well-being of the family and the resources available to invest in children, not simply annual income for a limited number of years. There are many challenges in bringing such an ideal to fruition: maintaining the representative nature of the sample through long periods of time and the entire income distribution, and obtaining accurate reporting of incomes are but two, to say nothing of the necessarily long lags between implementation and release dates. The advantages and limitations of a number of longitudinal surveys are illustrated in this book. In some cases the advantages of these data are clearly evident, but in other cases researchers are forced to tease results from rather small samples.

However, an important alternative worthy of more consideration is information from administrative sources. These data are collected as part of the conduct of a government program, like income taxation, and are linked through time into appropriate units of analysis. Many of the usual drawbacks of administrative data – that the concepts measured and the units of analysis do not correspond to theoretical constructs, that the sample is not representative, and that only a limited number of co-variates are available – are not always applicable to studies of generational income dynamics, or at least are not insurmountable. The development of these data continues to represent an important way forward in the advancement of knowledge, and they are used advantageously in the studies dealing with the Nordic countries and Canada in the pages that follow. These chapters illustrate the advantages of administrative data, which can offer samples measured in the tens – if not hundreds – of thousands, contain information on incomes orders of magnitudes more accurate than that available from household surveys, and may contain a surprising amount of supplementary

information useful for focusing an analysis of income correlations or
transition matrices on finely defined population groups. It is decades
since Atkinson, Maynard, and Trinder (1983, pp. 20–23) outlined the
difficulties of obtaining similar data for the United Kingdom, yet for
many countries their lament continues to remain appropriate. Some of
the research in the following chapters suggests that the development
of administrative data for research purposes and their dissemination
in a way that respects issues of confidentiality and privacy has offered
an extremely cost- and time-effective way of promoting knowledge on
generational issues in a number of countries. These countries should
stand as examples for future work in others.

All of this said, longitudinal data, from either survey or administrative sources, are not the *sine qua non* of generational research.
Researchers, including the contributors to this book, have made creative use of empirical methods to overcome limitations in the quality
of available data. The most notable illustration in the following chapters involves the use of cross-sectional surveys containing retrospective
information. Obtaining information from a sample of adults on the
incomes their parents earned decades ago in the past is fraught with
difficulties and generally avoided by statistical agencies. It is, however,
much easier to obtain retrospective information on parental education
and occupation; information that is often used in sociology and from
which estimates of parental income can be derived using instrumental variables or two sample split instrumental variables. This does not
come without a cost in terms of potentially biased results, but the nature
and direction of these biases are understood and the method opens up
the possibility of examining the degree of generational income mobility
in a comparable way when longitudinal data are not available. Including retrospective information of this sort in more data sets would offer
a cost-effective way of more fully understanding generational dynamics
in North America and Europe, and especially in developing countries.

There are a number of illustrations of these and other empirical
techniques in the following chapters, but the major implications do
not deal with methodological developments in their own right. Rather,
new methods – both with respect to empirical techniques and with
respect to data development – are used to obtain new and hopefully
robust results. Accordingly, the third contribution has to do with the
empirical findings, particularly in a cross-national context. Principal
among these is that the United States and Britain appear to stand out

as the least mobile societies among those rich countries under study. In the United States and the United Kingdom at least 40 percent of the economic advantage high-income parents have over low-income parents is passed on to the next generation. The Nordic countries and Canada seem to be the most mobile societies, with less than 20 percent of an income advantage being passed on between parent and child. Germany resembles the United States and the United Kingdom more closely than it does the other countries. The experience in the United States and the United Kingdom also illustrates that the degree of generational income mobility is not immutable. Progressive education policies have increased mobility across the generations in the United States during the post-war period, while changes to the schooling system in the United Kingdom dating back to the 1980s have had the opposite effect.

Further, the underlying processes may differ across the income distribution, which highlights the need for a more subtle understanding of the causal factors at work. This is as true within North American and European countries as it is between them and countries with lower levels of per capita income. In North America, children with above average potential experience more generational mobility than their European counterparts, while below average children experience less. Further, the extent of the differences between the rich countries may well be important, but it pales in significance when a comparison is made with poorer countries. In the several developing countries studied there appears to be significantly less generational mobility and in at least one case possibly none at all. The causes of these differences are beyond the scope of the present analysis, but surely have to do with the structure of property rights, the operation of labor markets, and the nature of, and access to, schooling at all levels. As such, policy makers dealing with developing countries need to be conscious not only of combating poverty at any point in time, but with structural changes that will have generational consequences.

Causal concerns are more explicitly raised in the analyses of some of the rich countries. A deeper understanding of the processes determining generational mobility will follow from a focus on the family and the allocation of resources within the family – as opposed to neighborhood influences – and on the interaction between the family and social policy. Even in the Nordic countries, where the degree of generational mobility is the greatest, there are important differences in

outcomes according to family size. Children raised in larger families
are more likely to have inferior earnings outcomes than their counterparts in smaller families. Further, transfer programs may have unintended generational consequences. The design of income transfers and
social insurance, as illustrated in the differences between the unemployment insurance programs in Sweden and Canada, may influence
the likelihood that children will also rely on transfer payments in their
turn as adults. More broadly, this suggests that future research needs to
understand not just how much money the family has but also how these
funds are obtained. It also suggests that future directions for social
policy may not be so much in the area of further increasing access to
higher education, but on the circumstances much earlier in life that put
individuals in the fortunate situation of being able to choose whether
to continue on to higher education. In particular, this refers to early
childhood education and investment that may have an important non-
monetary dimension. Parenting style and the social resources available
to parents will become an increasingly important concern if rich countries are to continue to promote an agenda of equality of opportunity,
and indeed to counter some of the likely market tendencies that may
erode or challenge the degree they have attained.

## 2 Theory and an empirical framework

Much of economic analysis uses a simple empirical model to measure generational income mobility. This is usually done in percentage, or equivalently logarithmic terms, and refers to the fraction of
income differences between parents that on average is observed among
their children in adulthood. For example, if the incomes of two sets
of parents differ by 50 percent and the incomes of their children differ by 30 percent, the generational persistence of incomes is said to be
60 percent since six-tenths of the difference in parental income is passed
on to the children. Equivalently if $Y$ represents permanent income and
$t$ is an index of generations, this way of thinking can be captured by
the following expression:

$$ln\, Y_{i,t} = \alpha + \beta\, ln\, Y_{i,t-1} + \varepsilon_{i,t} \tag{1.1}$$

In this equation the adult income (in natural logarithms) of family $i$'s
child, $ln\, Y_{i,t}$, is expressed as the average adult income of the children

of generation $t$, as represented by $\alpha$, plus two factors determining the deviation from this average: a fraction of parental permanent income ($\beta \ ln \ Y_{i,t-1}$) and other influences not associated with parental income ($\varepsilon_{i,t}$). In one way or another, equation (1.1) is the starting point for the analyses in many of the subsequent chapters.

The average income of generations will evolve through time, and it may be that many or all members of a generation will have incomes higher than those their parents had at a similar age in the past. This is captured in equation (1.1) by the value of $\alpha$. However, and more importantly, the equation reflects the idea that an individual's income is nonetheless related to his or her parents' income. This is captured by the value of $\beta$, which represents the fraction of income that is on average transmitted across the generations. In other words, $\beta$ summarizes in a single number the degree of generational income mobility in a society. It is often referred to as the generational income elasticity, and could conceivably be any real number. A positive value would indicate generational persistence of incomes in which higher parental income is associated with higher child incomes; a negative number would indicate generational reversal of incomes in which higher parental income is associated with lower child incomes. In fact empirical studies in the rich countries have always found $\beta$ to lie between the values of zero and one. A value of one would indicate complete generational persistence of incomes, a value of zero complete generational mobility. If, as above, 60 percent of the difference in parental incomes were passed on to the children, $\beta$ would have the value of 0.6. When $\beta$ is greater than zero but less than one there is some generational mobility of income, so that parents with incomes above (or below) the average will have children who grow up to have incomes above (or below) the average. However, the deviation from the average will not be as great in the children's generation. That this is the case in the rich economies should not be too surprising.

However, depending upon the degree of inequality in parental incomes, even small values of $\beta$ can confer substantial advantages to the children of the well off. For example, using data from the United States, Harding, Jencks, Lopoo, and Mayer (2001, Table A.1) report that, in 1999, households with children under the age of 18 at the top income quintile had 12 times as much money (when corrected for household size) as those at the bottom quintile. The generational income elasticity directly translates this ratio into the economic advantage a child from the higher-income family can expect to have in the next generation over one from the lower-income family.[1] For different values of $\beta$ this is:

| $\beta$ | 0 | 0.2 | 0.4 | 0.6 | 0.8 | 1.0 |
|---|---|---|---|---|---|---|
| Income advantage | 1.0 | 1.64 | 2.70 | 4.44 | 7.30 | 12.0 |

With a generational elasticity as high as 0.6, children born to the higher-income parents will earn, when no other influences are at work (that is, when $\varepsilon_{i,t} = 0$), almost four and a half times as much as children born to the lower-income parents. A four-and-a-half fold income advantage is no small matter. Lower values of $\beta$ translate into smaller advantages. With a $\beta$ of 0.2 the income advantage falls to about one and two-thirds. This is still considerable, but it pales in comparison to the fact that the higher-income parents started off earning twelve times the income of the lower-income families, and implies that there will be virtually no association between the incomes of grandparents and their grandchildren.

Equation (1.1) is more than simply the starting point for empirical analyses producing a summary measure of generational mobility; it is also motivated by economic theory, specifically the model of Becker and Tomes (1979). Mulligan (1997, Chapters 2 and 3) offers a clear exposition of this and other related economic models of generational income dynamics. A central point of the Becker and Tomes model is that income mobility across the generations and inequality within generations can be understood in a unified way by recognizing that parents care about and can influence the earnings capacity of their children. Parents do this by allocating their time and money between current consumption and investments in the human capital of their children, investments that will increase their future economic well-being. Human capital is broadly defined to refer to those aspects of the child's earning potential that parents can influence. Certainly other things beyond parental control will determine a child's earnings, including market

---

[1] This is derived by taking the antilog of equation (1.1) so that $Y_{i,t} = \exp(\alpha)$ $\times \exp(\beta \ln Y_{i,t-1}) = \exp(\alpha)(Y_{i,t-1})^{\beta}$ if $\varepsilon_{i,t}$ is ignored. This implies that the ratio of incomes for children from high income ($H$) and low income ($L$) backgrounds is $Y_{H,t}/Y_{L,t} = (Y_{H,t-1}/Y_{L,t-1})^{\beta}$, that is, the ratio of their parents' incomes raised to the $\beta$ power.

luck and inherited ability. Further, the degree to which these are passed on through the generations and the impact on earnings will in part be determined by social institutions. The distinction, however, is that these influences are not explicitly the domain of parental choice, and this is what makes human capital different. Human capital investment is often equated with monetary investments in education and particularly higher education, but it also means investments in the physical health of children as well as investments in their mental health and social development. Parental choices are determined by preferences and by constraints, and as such parents face a trade-off between current consumption and future consumption of the child. They can increase the child's consumption in the future by investing in the child's earnings capacity or by outright income transfers. Their propensity to do so will be determined by their preferences and by the rate of return on these investments. $\beta$ is an amalgam of these two factors, but also of the degree to which other endowments from the family – its culture and family connections are two examples – are inherited by the children. The degree of inheritability of these endowments is also influenced by the structure of the society and markets into which children grow up and find their way. The greater the parental preference for the future, the greater the return to any investments, and the greater the inheritability of other aspects of family background important for earnings, the greater $\beta$.

Gary Solon in Chapter 2 takes this perspective as his starting point and extends it in a way that explicitly offers a framework for comparative analysis either over time within a country, or over space between different countries. As such, the chapter sets out the major themes explored in the empirical sections of the book, and offers a structure, broadly speaking, for interpreting the results. Two important questions motivate the analysis: what is the role of the market in determining income mobility across the generations; what is the role of public policy? The first relates to the fact that there have been very significant changes in the returns to higher education in the United States and some other rich economies since the late 1970s and early 1980s. These changes have not occurred to the same degree in all the rich countries. Chapter 2 assesses the consequences of these labor market changes for the investments families make in children, and for the ability of children to get ahead in life. The second issue has to do with the fact that the nature and amount of public investment in children has changed tremendously during the post-war era and varies just as much across countries. The consequences of these differences for generational mobility are also a part of the story behind the Becker–Tomes model, but are explicitly addressed by Solon. The author shows that increases in the return to education will tighten the link between parent and child incomes, while increases in progressive public investments – those of relatively greater benefit to the less well off – will loosen it. An era of rising returns to education or declining progressivity in public invest- ment is an era of declining generational mobility. The analysis shows that this relationship is determined by the degree to which endowments are transmitted across the generations, the efficacy of human capital investment in increasing the earnings of the next generation, and the returns to investments of this sort. Temporal differences in generational mobility within a country or cross-country differences could arise from differences in any of these factors, but also from the structure of public investments.

The use of $\beta$ as a summary measure of generational mobility is appro- priate in responding to questions about the fraction of parental differ- ences reflected in the outcomes of children.[2] Questions of this sort are appropriate because the outcome – income or earnings – is a continu- ous and readily interpretable measure. However, generational mobility is also a relative concern and there may be interest in understanding the relationship between the parents' ranking in the income distribution and the ranking children will occupy in their turn as adults. Empirically this is often addressed with the use of transition matrices, a method that is the natural fallout of sociological concerns with social hierarchies as measured, for example, by occupational status, measures that are not necessarily continuous and for which cardinal differences make little sense or are less relevant. But transition matrices are also used with continuous cardinally measurable variables like income, particularly to reflect the view that an income above or below a particular thresh- old – like a line distinguishing the poor from the non-poor or the rich from the non-rich – is of substantive interest. Transition matrices can be summarized in a single number as a correlation coefficient and this

---

[2] This paragraph is based on the presentation by Christopher Jencks at the Statistics Canada workshop on generational income mobility held in Ottawa, February 2001 and on Harding, Jencks, Lopoo, and Mayer (2001).

helps to make clear their association with the generational elasticity. As numerous researchers have made clear, $\beta$ is related to the correlation between parent and child incomes ($\rho$) according to the ratio of the standard deviation of incomes ($\sigma$) in the child's generation to that of the parent's, that is $\beta = \rho[\sigma(\ln Y_{i,t})/\sigma(\ln Y_{i,t-1})]$. When the dispersion of income is not changing through time, so that this ratio is equal to one, the two measures will be the same, and it is a straightforward task to convert the information reflected in the intergenerational elasticity into a transition matrix using the bi-variate normal distribution. The transition matrix is also used repeatedly in the following chapters to describe patterns of generational mobility across specified quantiles of the income or earnings distribution.

In Chapter 3, however, John E. Roemer uses it as the basis for a theoretical discussion on the meaning of equality of opportunity and its relationship to empirical findings. As suggested, this discussion could just as easily have been framed in terms of the elasticity between generational incomes. Its main concern is to define what is meant by equality of opportunity and to sketch out implications for the interpretation of intergenerational transition matrices. Just how are the results from these measures to be interpreted? Does equality of opportunity imply that the generational elasticity is zero, that the entries in the transition matrix are identical? According to the author the belief in equality of opportunity would imply that inequities of outcome are indefensible when they are due to differential circumstances. The chapter offers a hierarchy of "circumstances" through which parents influence their children. These are four in number: through social connections that facilitate access to education and jobs; through family culture and investments that influence beliefs and skills; through the genetic transmission of ability; and through the formation of preferences and motivations in children. These are the successively broader fields – each corresponding to a successively broader definition of equality of opportunity – that policy makers could potentially seek to level. Roemer makes explicit that equating equality of opportunity with complete generational mobility implies that not only should the influence of social connections and also of family culture and investment be eliminated, but so should the genetic transmission of ability and the influence of family on the formation of preferences and goals among children. The author argues that this is "a view that only a fraction of those who consider the issue would, upon reflection, endorse." As such, his research is a cautionary note to readers of generational income mobility studies and suggests that there are subtleties in the interpretation of these findings requiring a finer understanding, a theme that recurs in a number of the other chapters. He also suggests that there is need for analyses focusing on aspects other than parental income. Parental education, for example, may offer a more appropriate indicator of the influence parents may have on the aspirations and personality of their children.

## 3 From theory to measurement

The research in Chapter 4 offers an empirical analysis of generational mobility in a set of four rich countries – the United States, Canada, Germany, and the United Kingdom – and five developing countries – Ecuador, Malaysia, Nepal, Pakistan, and Peru – in a way that accounts for a host of measurement issues that often confound cross-country comparisons, but also by proposing and using an estimation strategy meant to reflect the issues raised by Roemer. Nathan Grawe argues that Roemer's clarification of the meaning of equality of opportunity requires an estimation strategy explicitly addressing the extent to which the outcomes of the highest-earning sons of low-income families fall short of the highest earning sons from high-income families. These are presumably individuals who make the same types of choices, reflecting similar motivations and preferences, and equality of opportunity would imply no difference in their outcomes. The argument also holds for the lowest-earning sons from low- and high-income families. Grawe looks at both high- and low-earning sons for all nine countries by relying on quantile regression methods rather than just least squares estimation of equation (1.1). By examining the degree of generational mobility at different levels of child outcomes, the analysis also sheds light on the extent to which less than perfect equality of opportunity is due to higher-income parents passing on advantages to their most able children, or to keeping their least able children from suffering disadvantage; or from another perspective, the inability of low-income parents to pass advantages on to their most able children that they would have received had they been born to higher-income parents, as well as support to their least able children falling short of what higher income parents would have been able to provide. Similar concerns also motivate the analysis by O'Neill, Sweetman, and Van de gaer (2000), though they use different empirical methods.

The implementation of this perspective in a comparative way requires careful attention to a number of data issues. It is difficult to draw valid inferences about cross-country differences in generational income mobility by comparing independently completed studies. While the results may differ for substantive reasons, they may also differ because of a host of data and methodological decisions made by researchers. These are now well known in this literature, having been clearly delineated by Atkinson, Maynard, and Trinder (1983) and more formally through subsequent research by, for example, Jenkins (1987), Solon (1989, 1992), Reville (1995), Zimmerman (1992), and Grawe (2003). The first of these issues concerns the appropriate measurement of $Y_{i,t-1}$ in equation (1.1), parental 'permanent' income. Permanent income must be derived by the researcher from information available in the data set, often annual measures of income or earnings. This inevitably implies that it will be measured with error so that researchers actually observe, $\tilde{Y}_{i,t-1} = \lambda Y_{i,t-1} + v_i$, where $v_i$ represents a transitory shock to income and $\lambda$ is a parameter that may possibly vary over the course of an individual's life cycle. If $\lambda$ is equal to one the classical errors in variables problem arises and leads the estimated coefficient $(\tilde{\beta})$ to differ from the true coefficient according to a factor determined by the ratio of the variance of $v_i$ to that of $Y_{i,t-1}$, so that $\tilde{\beta}(1 + \sigma_v^2/\sigma_Y^2) = \beta$. In other words, the estimated coefficient will be an understatement of the true value if no correction is made for measurement error in permanent income.[3] The common corrections include using an average of a number of annual measures of parental income in order to reduce the influence of transitory variations, or instrumental variable estimates of permanent income using supplemental information on the determinants of parental income independent of child outcomes. This concern also in part motivates the use of parental occupation in many sociological studies of generational dynamics, occupation being assumed to be less subject to variation and measurement error. Indeed,

---

[3] This takes as its starting point a view of the world offered in the Becker–Tomes model, that parents are able to smooth their income over time and it is their permanent income that matters when investment decisions are made for their children's future, not the actual income they earned during the period the child was raised. Also it might be noted that this measurement error is aggravated if the sample used is not representative of the underlying population of parents. If this is the case the sample variance understates the true variance, $\sigma_Y^2$, and the attenuation bias is larger as a result.

instrumental variables corrections are often based on occupation as an instrument for parental income. If the objective is to estimate (1.1) it is often assumed important to correct for measurement error of this sort in parental income, but not necessarily for child income. A less than accurate measurement of the child's permanent income will lend imprecision to the results without introducing a bias to the coefficient estimate. This, as O'Neill, Sweetman, and Van de gaer (2002) formally illustrate, is not the case if transition matrices are being derived. If this is the objective, analysts must correct both parental and child outcomes for measurement errors. However, Haider and Solon (2003) suggest that it is also not the case for regression analysis in a more general errors in variable model where $\lambda \neq 1$, that is when the relationship between a child's current and permanent income, that between $\tilde{Y}_{i,t}$ and $Y_{i,t}$, is not one-for-one and varies over the life cycle. This lesson has yet to permeate the literature.

The second measurement issue is a related concern associated with the age at which incomes are obtained for the parents. Individual annual incomes tend to rise rather steeply between the ages of twenty and thirty, and then flatten out during the prime working years in the forties and fifties, before finally declining. This pattern is not identical across individuals and is subject to more variance at older ages (Grawe 2003). Consequently, the importance of measurement error will vary depending upon which part of the life cycle is captured. The analysis in Chapter 4 is very conscious of measurement errors problems and, in particular, points out that a simple comparison of independently completed research published on the average degree of generational mobility reveals as much about the age of the parent as it does about substantive differences between countries. Studies based upon measures of income when the parent is fifty years of age or older yield much lower estimates of $\beta$ than those when the parent is younger (Figure 4.2).[4] These issues motivate Grawe, following examples by

---

[4] Haider and Solon (2003) suggest that this observation should also be directed to the age at which the child's income is observed. There is a tendency to obtain lower estimates of $\beta$ when the child's income is measured early in the life cycle. This is because $\lambda$, at least in the data from the United States that they use, is as low as 0.6 when children are in their late twenties and early thirties. There is a possibility that $\beta$ will be overstated if child incomes are measured at later ages since $\lambda$ rises during the late thirties and early forties, and is as high as 1.2 after the mid to late forties.

Björklund and Jäntti (1997) and Couch and Dunn (1997), to make a series of comparisons between the United States and the other countries, each based upon similarly constructed data sets.

Grawe finds, first, that there is uncertainty in the results for the United States, stemming from the fact that two alternative surveys – the National Longitudinal Survey (NLS) and the Panel Study of Income Dynamics (PSID) – lead to different findings. The estimates from the PSID do in fact reproduce previous research using this data, and find $\beta$ from the least squares estimation of equation (1.1) to be between 0.4 and 0.5: the actual result offered in Table 4.2 is 0.47. But those from the NLS are considerably lower. The tendency for estimated elasticities derived from the NLS to be lower than those from the PSID is also observed in the compilation of findings from previous research by Solon (1999, Tables 3 and 4), the NLS-based estimates by Zimmerman (1992) being an exception. Grawe's research makes clear that Zimmerman's results are due to sample selection rules focusing the analysis on full-time and, for the most part, full-year workers. He draws the conclusion that definite answers on the relative standing of the United States *vis-à-vis* other rich countries requires a stance on which data set is closer to the truth. In both cases the analyses are based on rather small sample sizes, never more than about 350 father–son pairs and often substantially fewer. The development of richer data sources, particularly those relying on administrative data, would be important in resolving this ambiguity. In fact, since Grawe undertook his research, this has happened. Mazumder (2001) uses data from the Survey of Income and Program Participation linked to earnings data from administrative sources. His analysis is able to reproduce the PSID-based estimates but goes on to suggest that the elasticity could even be as high as 0.6 when measurement error is corrected by averaging father's income over horizons longer than the five years commonly used as a maximum in the literature. If on this basis Grawe's findings from the PSID are taken as a starting point, they suggest that the United States and the United Kingdom are on average the least generationally mobile societies under study. The generational earnings elasticity in Canada is less than half of the United States estimate, in Germany it is about two-thirds, but in the United Kingdom it is about the same or even a little larger.

These differences in the average, however, mask important differences at the upper and lower ends of the child's distribution. Grawe finds that the generational cycle of low income is both less and more severe in North America. Again, the picture is not entirely in focus because of uncertainties associated with the data from the United States. With this caution in mind, the author suggests that the United States and Canada display less generational persistence in the higher quantiles than in the lower, and that the opposite is the case in the United Kingdom and Germany. In other words, children with above average potential from low-income North American families experience more generational mobility than their European counterparts, but below average North American children from low-income families experience less. To put it perhaps too simply, if somehow low-income children in North America develop the motivations and preferences to get ahead in life they are likely to do so in spite of their economic background, while the odds of this happening are less in the United Kingdom and Germany. On the other hand if they do not, they are much more likely to fall into a generational cycle of low income; the odds of this happening are also less likely in the United Kingdom and Germany. In a sense, the policy concern directed to equality of opportunity in Canada and the United States becomes one of focusing on the aspects of family background, besides money, influencing the development of motivations and preferences; but in Europe, policy must also address the societal barriers that maintain the tie between family income and adult income in spite of preferences and motivation. Once again these statements should in a sense be considered as much hypotheses for future research as they are summaries of fact. Given the limitations of the data from the United States, progress might be made along these lines by using the methods proposed by Grawe on data from more European countries in comparison with the Canadian data.

But Grawe is able to expand the set of comparisons greatly by using information from five developing countries, including cross-sectional data containing retrospective parental information. His application of two-sample split instrumental variables opens an avenue of research in countries lacking longitudinal data spanning two generations. He finds much less generational mobility, and in one country – Ecuador – the possibility that the generational elasticity is actually greater than one cannot be rejected. Further, it appears that while the elasticity is high throughout the child's distribution it tends to be significantly higher at the lower end than at the upper end. Dunn (2003) and Ferreira and Veloso (2003) use the methods outlined in Chapter 4, and both report estimates of $\beta$ for a sixth country – Brazil – higher than those in the rich countries, about 0.7 or even higher depending upon the age of fathers and sons. Grawe suggests that the higher association between parent and child outcomes reflects a much tighter correlation between parental education and child outcomes than in the rich countries. The challenges facing policy makers addressing equality of opportunity in these countries may be of a different nature than in the rich countries, and may reflect, in Roemer's terms, differential outcomes associated with access to schooling and jobs. This certainly requires more research and institutional knowledge, but at the least suggests that policies directed to poverty alleviation in the developing countries should address structural changes informed by a generational perspective on the labour market and not simply inequalities at a point in time.

## 4 Country studies

The cost of explicitly undertaking cross-country comparisons of the sort presented in Chapter 4 is that the organization of data to ensure comparability perforce leads to a loss of information. All of the data sets used by Grawe contain more information than his comparative research is able to exploit, and as a result, there is value in pursuing detailed country studies. This is done in Chapters 5 through 8, which highlight developments in the United States, the United Kingdom and Britain, and also in Germany.

Chapters 5 and 6 focus on changes in generational mobility over time in, respectively, the United States and the United Kingdom. Susan E. Mayer and Leonard M. Lopoo examine trends in the generational income elasticity at age thirty for cohorts of Americans born between 1949 and 1965. They document important increases in public spending on children in the United States during the post-war period, noting that they have been of relatively more benefit to lower-income families. This has been accompanied by an increase in the degree of generational mobility. The authors find that the generational income elasticity has trended downward, but also note that this has happened in a slightly different way for women than for men. Explaining these gender differences is one of the major objectives of the chapter. For both men and women the elasticity rises and then falls, but the rise happens later for women. For men the elasticity is greater than 0.4 and rising for cohorts born from 1949 to about the early or mid-1950s, but then falls for all subsequent cohorts and eventually reaches 0.3 or even lower for those born in the mid-1960s. In contrast, the elasticity for women rises from just over 0.3 to peak much later. It rises to between 0.4 and 0.5 for cohorts born in the late 1950s and early 1960s, before then falling for subsequent cohorts back to a value of about 0.3 (Figure 5.1).

Mayer and Lopoo echo the discussion in Chapter 2 on the possible causes of changes in generational mobility, but focus their examination on two demographic factors associated with changing gender roles: the decline in the rate of marriage at age thirty, and the increase in women's participation in paid employment. The major implication they draw concerns the interpretation of changes in generational elasticities as signaling changes in equality of opportunity. Social or policy changes that clearly promote equality of opportunity may result in a tighter – not a weaker – tie between parent and child incomes. The argument, in brief, is as follows. Depending upon the structure of society and the nature of labor markets, parental investments in children may have different payoffs across gender. If traditional gender roles have become less binding then trends in the generational income elasticity may well differ for sons and daughters. In the parlance of Chapter 2, the rates of return to parental investments differ by gender, and changes in the labor market opportunities for women during the post-war period have increased the rate of return for girls relative to boys. These changes are reflected in delays in marriage and higher employment rates for women. The rise in the generational elasticity for women over most of the post-war period reflects increases in the rate of return, and more, not less, equality of opportunity. All this said, the analysis is based on the Panel Study of Income Dynamics and the authors are also mindful of limitations in the sample size and add, as do Levine and Mazumder (2002) who examine the same issue using three different data sets, that caution is needed before definitive conclusions can be made about trends in the generational elasticity in the United States.

The quality of the data available to Jo Blanden, Alissa Goodman, Paul Gregg, and Stephen Machin in their analysis of trends in the United Kingdom is much higher and they draw more definitive conclusions. They examine differences in generational income mobility between children growing up in the 1960s and 1970s and those growing up a decade later, using the National Child Development Study which surveyed all children born in the United Kingdom during a given week in 1958 and the British Cohort Survey which did the same in 1970.

The authors begin by underscoring the fact that this was a period of widening wage and income disparities. It was also a period in which the educational attainments of the young increased significantly, but in a way that was of relatively greater benefit to those from higher-income parents. They find, as would be predicted from the model in Chapter 2, that the generational income elasticity rose significantly between these two groups, even though they were born only twelve years apart. The changes in $\beta$ were such that the income advantage of having parents in the top fifth of the income distribution over having parents in the bottom fifth went from 20 percent to 40 percent in this short time. Chapter 6 relates these changes to the expansion of the university system. Differences in educational attainment account for almost one fifth of the change in $\beta$ for men and fully 40 percent for women. An analysis of transition matrices also verifies these findings, and on this basis the authors conclude by stating that "this fall in mobility can be accounted for by the fact that a greater share of the rapid educational upgrading of the British population has been focused on people with rich parents." By implication and in light of the findings in Chapter 5, it would seem that women from higher-income families were best positioned to capture the opportunities afforded by the education reforms.

Chapter 7 by John Ermisch and Marco Francesconi complements and extends the analysis of the United Kingdom in Chapters 4 and 6 by offering the first results from the British Household Panel Survey addressing intergenerational mobility. The authors argue for a closer integration of economic and sociological modeling of mobility and focus their attention on generational patterns in occupational prestige, as measured by the Hope–Goldthorpe index. This index is highly correlated with earnings but at the same time may offer an alternative measure of the permanent status of the parents. Ermisch and Francesconi exploit the retrospective information provided by all adult respondents to the survey on their parents' occupation when they, the respondents, were fourteen years of age. In this way, they offer an alternative estimate of the average degree of generational mobility, but also are able to examine non-linear patterns and trends over periods of time covering the post-war era. They find, first, that this indicator is in fact not immune to measurement error, probably stemming from recall errors but also from fundamental changes in the occupational structure of the labor market. They offer a number of alternative corrections and suggest that a best estimate of the average degree of generational mobility in occupational prestige is between 0.45 and 0.75. Estimates of this magnitude imply that about 40 percent of children born to fathers in the bottom quarter of occupational prestige will also be in the bottom quarter in their turn. These children have less than a five percent chance of attaining the top quartile. But the authors also find a general downward trend in the degree of persistence over the course of the last fifty years. Just as importantly, the data also permit the authors to move beyond these types of estimates to examine non-linear patterns in mobility. They find the linear model in fact obscures differential patterns of mobility between children born to parents in the lower and upper part of the occupational distribution. Their findings suggest that Britain is characterized by a higher degree of upward occupational mobility from the bottom than downward mobility from the top.

This underscores an important limitation of the research agenda embodied in equation (1.1), namely that the focus is on an overall outcome with one value of $\beta$ characterizing the entire income distribution. The policy focus on families in low income, however, reveals a concern that the pattern of generational mobility may change across the income distribution: those with lower incomes may not have the same opportunities to invest in their children as middle and upper income groups. This theme is the backdrop of the analysis by Kenneth A. Couch and Dean R. Lillard in Chapter 8, which takes the focus off the average and examines different degrees of income persistence at different points in the parental income distribution in Germany and the United States.

This is a natural perspective to adopt in sociology because of a view that labor markets are in some way segmented and prevent generational movement across categories associated with parental occupation and education. But non-linear models can also be motivated by models of human capital as the consequence of credit constraints in the capacity of parents to invest in the optimal levels of education for their children. Becker and Tomes (1986) and Mulligan (1997) offer formulations, but the discussions in Corak and Heisz (1999) and Grawe (2001) make explicit that the nature of the non-linear relationship between parent and child incomes is the outcome of an interaction between the resources available to the parent and the ability/predisposition of the child. In these models, parents wishing to increase the adult incomes of their children are better off to invest in their education if the expected rate of return for human capital investments is greater than that for financial assets. They will do so until the rate of return on the former falls to the level of the latter, at which point they will leave bequests or directly pass on assets. However, the expected rate of return to human capital investments varies with the child's ability, and whether a child receives the optimal amount of human capital investment may depend upon the parent's current resources. This will particularly be the case for low-income parents of high-ability children. Such parents are unlikely to be able to borrow the needed funds from financial institutions. These children will be less mobile than those with equal ability but born to parents of sufficient means.

Grawe (2001) shows that this model may imply any pattern in the generational elasticity of parent–child incomes depending upon the way in which child ability varies with parental income. For example, Corak and Heisz (1999) use non-parametric methods and find an inverted U pattern in the generational elasticity for Canada. They suggest that over the lower half of the income distribution $\beta$ is rising not only because parental income is rather low but also because child ability, and hence the optimal amount of human capital investment, is increasing. As a result, a larger and larger fraction of families are unable to make sufficient investments in the schooling of their children. Over the upper half of the income distribution the elasticity is falling because parental income gradually becomes high enough to finance post-secondary education. Regardless of the child's ability, there are sufficient resources to fund the desired level of schooling. The factors determining a child's 'ability' and its relationship to parental income are left entirely unaddressed. Non-linear patterns have not been uncovered in other countries in part because of a lack of attention, but also in part because of data limitations. Eide and Showalter (1999), Hertz (2003), Mulligan (1997, p. 193), and Solon (1992) explore this issue with data from the United States, with Hertz offering the most complete discussion and convincing evidence. Hertz also offers a clear illustration of the relationship between the generational income elasticity and the total expected degree of total income mobility. The analysis in Chapter 8 offers new information on non-linear patterns in the generational elasticity, using data on fathers and sons from the National Longitudinal Survey for the United States and the German Socio-Economic Panel for Germany. Non-linearities are modeled by augmenting measures of father's earnings in equation (1.1) with the square and cube of this information. The authors find that the degree of mobility is about the same in the two countries, and do not uncover strong evidence for differential effects of father's earnings across the distribution in either country.

## 5 Causality and policy concerns

Collectively these country studies illustrate both the advantages and limitations of currently available longitudinal surveys for the study of generational mobility. Just as importantly, however, they begin to hint at some of the possible causes of the differences between countries and of changes within them over time. At one level the causal factors are certainly societal, dealing with the structure of labor markets and access to schooling. In this sense they fall into the first set of circumstances delineated by Roemer. The elimination of overt discrimination in the access to jobs and the setting of wage rates, ensuring open access to higher learning and to all fields of study are important institutional changes representing both the major accomplishments and the major challenges in the rich countries, and likely distinguish them from some of the developing countries. But at another level the causes also have to do with the other sets of circumstances Roemer describes and are associated with the skills, preferences, and motivations of children. There is considerably more uncertainty as to the relative roles of society and family in determining these, and a more subtle research design – one that goes beyond the estimation of generational elasticities and their juxtaposition with important policy changes – is needed to offer convincing evidence.

One step in this direction involves the use of sibling and neighbor correlations in long-run outcomes. A broad indicator of the influence of family and community on the adult attainments of children can be derived from the extent to which sibling attainments are correlated. For example, to borrow from the discussion in Solon (1999, p. 1,767), if the subscripts $i$ and $j$ refer to the $j^{\text{th}}$ sibling in family $i$, then the natural logarithm of the permanent income $Y_{ij}$ of sibling $j$ can be represented as $ln\ Y_{ij} = a_i + b_{ij}$, where $a_i$ represents the influence of all things pertinent to the determination of income that are common to siblings, while $b_{ij}$ represents the influence of those specific to sibling $j$. These two sets of influences are assumed to be independent so that the variance in the outcome is just the sum of the variances of the two components, $\sigma_Y^2 = \sigma_a^2 + \sigma_b^2$. This assumption of independence also implies that the covariance in the outcomes of two siblings from the same family is $\sigma_a^2$. The correlation in outcomes for siblings $j$ and $j'$ is the indicator of interest and can be expressed as:

$$r = \text{covariance}(ln Y_{ij}, ln Y_{ij'})/\text{variance}(ln Y_{ij}) = \sigma_a^2/(\sigma_a^2 + \sigma_b^2) \qquad (1.2)$$

In other words, equation (1.2) represents the proportion of the total variation in child outcomes due to factors siblings have in common. These factors include common family influences but also common neighborhood influences. They do not include influences associated with genetic differences, nor family traits that are not held in common. The family environment could be very different for siblings if family resources were allocated differently by, for example, birth order, or if siblings spent different fractions of their lives growing up in a family of varying size.

In Chapter 9, Anders Björklund, Markus Jäntti, Oddbjørn Raaum, Eva Österbacka, and Tor Eriksson take this empirical framework as their starting point in an analysis of the earnings of young men and women in Norway, Finland, and Sweden. They use detailed administrative data to show that the sibling correlation is rather small in these countries, varying from about 0.15 to 0.25 for men, and from about 0.12 to 0.15 for women. In other words community and family influences account for at most and likely significantly less than 25 percent of the variation in earnings. This accords with their earlier work summarized in Björklund *et al.* (2002), which also includes the finding that in the United States about 40 percent of the variation is due to factors siblings share in common. As such the results do not offer evidence on the relative roles of these two very broad forces. Further, all of these findings refer to a set of influences that include both family and neighborhood. The impact of neighborhoods and peers on children is a subject of much interest in a number of disciplines, and is beyond the scope of the essays in this book. But the research design expressed in equation (1.2) can be extended to parse out the influence of neighbors by also including information on the adult earnings of children who grew up in the same community. Solon (1999) offers an exposition and literature review. Page and Solon (2003a, b) present evidence from the United States, Corak and Oreopoulos (2003) from Canada, and Raaum, Salvanes, and Sørensen (2001) from Norway using this framework. The general tone of this stream in the literature seems to be that family influences are central to understanding the determinants of long-run outcomes, while neighborhoods are of secondary, if any, importance. The common perception that neighborhoods matter reflects the tendency of individuals from similar family backgrounds to live in similar neighborhoods, and an appropriate research design to uncover causal effects must account for this sorting. Oreopoulos (2003) offers a convincing approach, mimicking that of a controlled experiment, by examining the long-run outcomes of children living in public housing in Toronto. He finds virtually no influence on a number of labor market outcomes in adulthood. With this as a backdrop, the authors of Chapter 9 exploit the detail and size of their information base to place an emphasis on family structure, exploring the influence of family size, birth order, and the gender composition of siblings on adult earnings.

They find, first, that sibling correlations do not vary much for either boys or girls by the number of children in the family or by their gender composition. However, alongside this is the finding that adult earnings do vary strongly by family size. The differential between the adult earnings of men raised in a family of five or more children relative to those raised in a family of two is as high as 18 percent in Finland, 14 percent in Sweden, and about 10 percent in Norway, with the differentials being comparable for women (13, 12, and 18 percent respectively). At the same time, the association between earnings and birth order or gender composition of the children is not large and often statistically insignificant. In sum, these findings, when interpreted as a whole, imply that the within-family allocation of resources important for long-run labor market success, both monetary and non-monetary, is not differentiated by birth order or gender. Parents in these Nordic countries invest in their children without discrimination, but what does matter is the overall magnitude of the time and money available as indicated by family size. It is an interesting question for future research as to whether this result also applies to other countries, but this may have to await the development of equally rich data sources.

This result, it should be noted, is subject to competing interpretations that have contrasting implications for policy. For example, it may be that family size matters because the per capita resources available to children are lower, there being simply less money and less time to go around in a larger family. In some circles this might be interpreted as suggesting that policy should offer larger families – or, for that matter, single-parent families – more support, whether monetary or non-monetary. On the other hand it may be that family size, in and of itself, does not matter. It could be that the characteristics or circumstances that lead to large families are also characteristics or circumstances relevant to labor market success, and these are also passed on to children. Parents choosing smaller families may also be parents who place greater emphasis on monetary success, and it is these preferences and priorities that are transmitted to the children and influence their adult attainments. In this case the policy directions are not as clear cut, and increases in monetary transfers, whatever their desirability in the short term, may not have an impact on the long-term success of children or, even worse, discourage it.

Considerations of this sort motivate the analyses in Chapters 10 and 11, which deal with how the interaction between social policy and the family may influence the directions children take in the labor market. It is sometimes argued that parental participation in transfer programs increases the likelihood that children will also participate when they reach adulthood, and that in this way transfer programs somehow prevent the development of self-sufficiency and perpetuate an intergenerational cycle of poverty. Marianne E. Page notes in the beginning of Chapter 10 that so-called "culture of poverty" arguments of this kind formed, to some degree, the backdrop for the 1996 reform of the welfare system in the United States. Theorists have offered different rationales for such arguments. One deals with preferences. Living in a family that relies on welfare may erode any stigma attached to the receipt of payments and cause the child to view the program as a legitimate income source. Another argument deals with perceptions or information. Living in a family that relies on welfare gives the child information about the program and its rules and thereby makes it easier to collect in turn. These theories are rarely rigorously tested in empirical research, which focuses on the comparatively simpler task of estimating the correlation in welfare receipt between parent and child. Page's contribution is at this level, and she stops short of offering a causal interpretation. She finds that the previous literature has in fact understated the extent of the intergenerational correlation, and examines the underlying reasons associated with measurement errors. Using Panel Study of Income Dynamics data up to 1993 she also finds that about 47 percent of women whose mothers received welfare went on to also rely on the program at least once, compared with 16 percent of those whose mothers did not use the program. These estimates imply a correlation of just over 0.3 in the use of welfare across the generations. Further, this correlation has moved up and down over the years with only a slight, if any, tendency to trend downward.

In Chapter 11 these issues are examined more directly through a comparison of the generational consequences of having a parent who collected unemployment insurance in Canada and Sweden. These two countries make a fitting comparison because their economies and expenditures on unemployment insurance are broadly similar, but at the same time the two programs differ in important aspects of their design. Using administrative data, Miles Corak, Björn Gustafsson, and Torun Österberg begin by noting that a rather significant fraction of young men in Canada and Sweden receive unemployment insurance benefits in at least one year between the ages of sixteen and about thirty, but also that there are significant differences according to whether their fathers had also received benefits. Just over 80 percent of young Canadians and almost 70 percent of young Swedes used unemployment insurance if their fathers had also done so, compared respectively to 70 percent and 58 percent of those whose fathers had not. These high incidence rates likely reflect high job turnover among young people as they settle into permanent/career employment. They also reflect the turbulent macro-economic climate in both of these countries during the early 1980s and 1990s that disproportionately affected the young. However, the major concern examined in Chapter 11 is the extent to which the differences between the two groups of young men in each country are causal. Do young people "learn" about the program from their parents and somehow have their preferences and opportunities shaped in a way that increases the likelihood they will collect unemployment insurance? Or is the difference simply due to characteristics, which may or not be observed by the analysts, that parents and children share in common? These questions are answered, in part, by using longitudinal data spanning the ages of fifteen to thirty to examine the role of both a father's past and future use of unemployment insurance on the probability that a son will begin using the program in any given year. The argument is that past use reflects both the causal role of parental participation and the role of unobserved characteristics, while future use reflects only the latter. This assumes the future cannot cause the past and implies that the difference between the estimated impacts of these two variables identifies the causal role. In Canada about a third of the approximate 12 percentage point difference between the two groups of sons is found to be causal, but in Sweden none of the gap can be attributed to parent–child interactions of a causal nature. At the same time, the authors point out that in Sweden the learning about the program that does go on occurs through an individual's own interaction with unemployment insurance, a son's past benefit receipt raising the likelihood of his future receipt. They interpret these differences in terms of the different structure of unemployment insurance in the two countries. In Canada, unemployment insurance offers 'passive' income support during periods of job loss; in Sweden, it is a labor market adjustment policy that offers retraining in the hope of promoting long-term job attachment. It may be that what children "learn" about the program by virtue of their parents' participation is different under these two regimes, and in this sense there are generational consequences to aspects of program design. All this said, it is important to keep the magnitude of the effects being explored in mind; there is a good deal influencing the generational correlation in program use, most notably the level of parental income.

## 6 Conclusion

No published research on the subject of generational income mobility since the early 1990s has reported an estimate for $\beta$ greater than 0.4 in any of the rich countries other than the United States and the United Kingdom, the chapters of this book being no exception. On the one hand, this could mean that the appropriate information sources are not yet in place in all countries. Certainly, a particular strength of the data from the United States is the length of the time horizon covered in the longitudinal surveys that are the major sources for generational studies. The United Kingdom also has particularly long time horizons embedded in some of the surveys available to researchers. Estimates of generational elasticities are sensitive to the point in the life cycle that income and earnings are measured, being much lower if a long enough time horizon is not available to accurately estimate permanent income. It may well be the case, for example, that in Germany – where the panel data are just beginning to mature – the generational elasticity rivals that for the United States and the United Kingdom. On the other hand, the much higher elasticities reported in these two countries may also reflect substantive differences. The picture is not entirely in focus, yet some of the broad contours of country differences are visible. Generational elasticities higher than 0.2 are rarely, if ever, reported in Canada and the Nordic countries, the data in these countries offering both long time horizons and accurate reports of income. Higher quality data in more countries, possibly from administrative sources, may offer a sharper image and permit an unambiguous statement that the United States and the United Kingdom stand out as the least generationally mobile countries. But whatever the differences in the average degree of mobility among the rich countries, the differences between them and countries with lower levels of per capita income are much clearer. This may reflect the fact that the rich countries have, at least in part and possibly to varying degrees, leveled the playing field associated with the most basic tenets of equality of opportunity: the elimination of nepotism in employment, universal primary and secondary education, no barriers in the choice to pursue post-secondary education nor in the choice of field of study and occupation, and no differentiation in all of these matters by gender. Changes in the degree of generational mobility have occurred, and are associated with important shifts in policy and the structure of public spending. But the sense that economic changes associated with increases in the demand for skilled labor and higher returns to education will tilt the playing field to the detriment of children from lower-income families creates a greater urgency for progressive policy than perhaps a generation ago.

Along which avenues should public policy move in order to continue to promote generational mobility? Gøsta Esping-Andersen takes up the challenge of addressing this question in Chapter 12 in a way that summarizes the major findings of the previous chapters, but also in a way that suggests new directions for research. His argument is based on three interrelated points. First, in spite of a focus on different outcomes and the use of different methods, economic and sociological analyses of generational dynamics are addressing similar phenomena. The focus on earnings and income differs little from a focus on occupational status, the two sets of outcomes being two sides of the same coin. Occupational attainment and often-used indices of occupational status are highly correlated with income. Further, whether the methods address an average individual derived from a linear model of generational mobility or are more concerned with non-linearities and distinct divisions between groups, they both view educational attainment as the major locus of parental influence and the major determinant of adult outcomes. In this sense, both disciplines have offered a backdrop to the major policy thrust of the post-war era addressed to equality of opportunity: increases in the access to higher and higher levels of schooling.

The second point is that the benefits for public policy of continuing to adopt analytical perspectives focusing on the monetary resources of parents, their investments in the schooling of their children, and monetary outcomes in the next generation, may have reached its limits. For one thing societies vary a good deal in the levels of public spending for education with no discernable relationship with the degree of generational mobility. It is not further changes in the overall spending on education that will matter, but the structure of the system and the cognitive capacities of children that permit them to take advantage of the available opportunities. A system based on early tracking is detrimental to equality of opportunity, but it is those children with high levels of cognitive skills that will be able to take most advantage of whatever systems are in place. In an analysis of data from the International Adult Literacy Survey and the Programme for International Student Assessment that includes Canada, the United States, the United Kingdom, Sweden, Norway, Denmark, Germany, and the Netherlands, Esping-Andersen shows first, that cognitive skills are an important determinant of long-run earnings; second, that they are only loosely correlated with educational attainment; and third, that cognitive performance is more closely related to the "cultural capital," or, more broadly put, the parenting style of the family, than it is to its material wealth. The decisive kinds of parental investments are not the monetary kind. The inheritance of education, occupation, and income is influenced in the first instance by the impact parents have on a child's cognitive performance, and societies that have leveled the playing field with respect to these circumstances have had the most success in promoting generational mobility.

The third point in Esping-Andersen's argument is that research and policy should focus on the family, and particularly the role played in the development of cognitive abilities among children. The important window of opportunity is during the early years, up to about six years of age. The author shows that cognitive abilities are much more unequally distributed in some societies than others. Further, the degree of this inequality is strongly and positively correlated with the degree to which parental education is linked with the cognitive performance of children. Societies in which parental education is closely related to child cognitive outcomes are also societies in which these outcomes are less equally distributed. Understanding the reasons for this is important in setting the appropriate direction for public policy, and should be a priority for research. Certainly there are basic educational reforms that could be pursued – delaying or abolishing tracking, standardizing curricula, and extra support for less privileged children – but, on the whole, attention should shift to the family. The appropriate policy will involve more than simply offering financial support to low-income families, to include the public provision of social services. Universal access to affordable day care permits mothers to work and explains the absence of child poverty in countries like Sweden. When coupled with the appropriate school setting and organized after-school activities this shifts the source of cognitive stimulation from parents to social institutions, and begins to ultimately offset inequities in long-run outcomes.

This is not to say that money is of no consequence. Policy makers are increasingly claiming that child poverty in economies of plenty should be no more tolerated than poverty among the elderly, the elimination of which has been one of the important accomplishments of the more progressive welfare states. This claim is often buttressed by the fact that children differ from other groups because current circumstances are important not just for their well-being in the present but also decades into the future. However, the capacity of children to become self-sufficient and successful adults is compromised not only by monetary poverty, but by poverty of experience, influence, and expectation. This argument calls for broader thinking on the mechanisms and causes of generational mobility, and will inevitably draw governments into broader areas of social and labor market policies. Money is of consequence, but it is not enough.

### References

Altonji, Joseph G., and Thomas A. Dunn (1991). "Family Incomes and Labor Market Outcomes of Relatives." In Ronald G. Ehrenberg (editor). *Research in Labor Economics*. Vol. 12, pp. 269–310. Greenwich, CT: JAI Press.

Atkinson, A. B., A. K. Maynard, and C. G. Trinder (1983). *Parents and Children: Incomes in Two Generations*. London: Heinemann.

Becker, Gary S. and Nigel Tomes (1979). "An Equilibrium Theory of the Distribution of Income and Intergenerational Mobility." *Journal of Political Economy*. Vol. 87, no. 6, pp. 1153–89.

(1986). "Human Capital and the Rise and Fall of Families." *Journal of Labor Economics*. Vol. 4, no. 3, pp. S1–S39.

Benabou, Roland, and Efe A. Ok (2001). "Social Mobility and the Demand for Redistribution: The POUM Hypothesis." *Quarterly Journal of Economics*. Vol. 116, pp. 447–87.

Björklund, Anders, Tor Eriksson, Markus Jäntti, Oddbjörn Rauum, Eva Österbacka (2002). "Brother Correlations in Earnings in Denmark, Finland, Norway and Sweden Compared to the United States." *Journal of Population Economics*. Vol. 15, pp. 757–72.

Björklund, Anders, and Markus Jäntti (1997). "Intergenerational Income Mobility in Sweden Compared to the United States." *American Economic Review*. Vol. 87, pp. 1009–18.

(2000). "Intergenerational Mobility of Economic Status in Comparative Perspective." *Nordic Journal of Political Economy*. Vol. 26, no. 1, pp. 3–32.

Corak, Miles (2003). "Is the Playing Field Level? Family Background and the Life Chances of Children." *Renewal*. Vol. 11, pp. 69–77.

Corak, Miles, and Andrew Heisz (1999). "The Intergenerational Earnings and Income Mobility of Canadian Men: Evidence from Longitudinal Income Tax Data." *Journal of Human Resources*. Vol. 34, no. 3, pp. 504–33.

Corak, Miles, and Philip Oreopoulos (2003). "Intergenerational Mobility and Sibling Correlations of Canadian Men." Family and Labour Studies, Statistics Canada, unpublished.

Couch, Kenneth A., and Thomas A. Dunn (1997). "Intergenerational Correlations in Labor Market Status: A Comparison of the United States and Germany." *Journal of Human Resources*. Vol. 27, pp. 575–601.

Dunn, Christopher (2003). "Intergenerational Earnings Mobility in Brazil and its Determinants." University of Michigan, unpublished.

Eide, Eric R. and Mark H. Showalter (1999). "Factors Affecting the Transmission of Earnings Across Generations: A Quantile Regression Approach." *Journal of Human Resources*. Vol. 34, no. 2, pp. 253–67.

Erickson, Robert and John H. Goldthorpe (1992). *The Constant Flux: A Study of Class Mobility in Industrial Societies*. Oxford: Clarendon Press.

(2002). "Intergenerational Inequality: A Sociological Perspective. *Journal of Economic Perspectives*. Vol. 16, pp. 31–44.

Ferreira, Sergio Guimarães, and Fernando A. Veloso (2003). "Intergenerational Mobility of Earnings in Brazil." BNDES Brazil, unpublished.

Gottschalk, Peter, and Timothy M. Smeeding (1997). "Cross-National Comparisons of Earnings and Income Inequality." *Journal of Economic Literature*. Vol. 35, pp. 633–87.

Grawe, Nathan D. (2001). "In Search of Intergenerational Credit Constraints Among Canadian Men: Quantile Versus Mean Regression Tests for Binding Credit Constraints." Family and Labour Studies, Analytical Studies Branch Research Paper No. 158. Ottawa: Statistics Canada. Forthcoming in *Journal of Human Resources*.

(2003). "Life Cycle Bias in the Estimation of Intergenerational Earnings Persistence." Family and Labour Studies, Analytical Studies Branch Research Paper No. 207. Ottawa: Statistics Canada.

Haider, Steven, and Gary Solon (2003). "Life-Cycle Variation in the Association between Current and Lifetime Earnings." University of Michigan, unpublished.

Harding, David J., Christopher Jencks, Leonard M. Lopoo, and Susan E. Mayer (2001). "Trends in Intergenerational Economic Mobility: Theories and Estimates for the US since 1960." Unpublished.

Hertz, Tom (2003). "Rags, Riches and Race: The Intergenerational Economic Mobility of Black and White Families in the United States." Forthcoming in Samuel Bowles, Herbert Gintis, and Melissa Osborne (editors). *Unequal Chances: Family Background and Economic Success*. Princeton: Princeton University Press and Russell Sage.

Jenkins, Stephen (1987). "Snapshots versus Movies: 'Lifecycle Biases' and the Estimation of Intergenerational Earnings Inheritance." *European Economic Review*. Vol. 31, pp. 1149–58.

Katz, Lawerence F., and David H. Autor (1999). "Changes in the Wage Structure and Earnings Inequality." In Orley C. Ashenfelter and David Card (editors). *Handbook of Labor Economics, Volume 3A*. Amsterdam: North-Holland.

Levine, David I., and Bhashkar Mazumder (2002). "Choosing the Right Parents: Changes in the Intergenerational Transmission of Inequality – Between 1980 and the Early 1990s." Federal Reserve Bank of Chicago, Working Paper 2002-08.

Mazumder, Bhashkar (2001). "Earnings Mobility in the US: A New Look at Intergenerational Inequality." Federal Reserve Bank of Chicago, Working Paper No. 2001-18.

Mulligan, Casey B. (1997). *Parental Priorities and Economic Inequality*. Chicago: University of Chicago Press.

O'Neill, Donal, Olive Sweetman and Dirk Van de gaer (2000). "Equality of Opportunity and Kernel Density Estimation: an Application to Intergenerational Mobility." In T. B. Fomby and R. C. Hills (editors). *Advances in Econometrics*. Vol. 14, pp. 259–74. Greenwich, CT: JAI Press.

(2002). "Consequences of Specification Error for Distributional Analysis With an Application to Intergenerational Mobility." Universiteit Gent, Faculteit Economie en Bedrijfskunde, Working Paper No. 2002/156.

Oreopoulos, Philip (2003). "The Long-Run Consequences of Living in a Poor Neighbourhood." *Quarterly Journal of Economics.* Vol. 118, pp. 1533–75.

Page, Marianne E., and Gary Solon (2003a). "Correlations between Brothers and Neighboring Boys in the Adult Earnings: The Importance of Being Urban." *Journal of Labor Economics.* Vol. 21, pp. 831–56.

(2003b). "Correlations between Sisters and Neighboring Girls in Their Subsequent Income as Adults." *Journal of Applied Econometrics.* Vol. 18, pp. 545–62.

Rauum, Oddbjørn, Kjell G. Salvanes, and Erik Ø. Sørensen (2001). "The Neighbourhood is Not What it Used To Be: Has There Been Equalization of Opportunity Across Families and Communities in Norway?" Department of Economics, University of Oslo, Memorandum No. 36/2001.

Reville, Robert T. (1995). "Intertemporal and Life Cycle Variation in Measured Intergenerational Earnings Mobility." RAND Working Paper.

Solon, Gary R. (1989). "Biases in the Estimation of Intergenerational Earnings Correlations." *Review of Economics and Statistics.* Vol. 71, pp. 172–74.

(1992). "Intergenerational Income Mobility in the United States." *American Economic Review.* Vol. 82, no. 3, pp. 393–408.

(1999). "Intergenerational Mobility in the Labor Market." In Orley C. Ashenfelter and David Card (editors). *Handbook of Labor Economics, Volume 3A.* Amsterdam: North-Holland.

Treiman, Donald J., and Harry B. G. Ganzeboom (1990). "Cross National Comparative Status Attainment Research." *Research in Social Stratification and Moblity.* Vol. 9, pp. 105–27.

UNICEF (2000). *The State of the World's Children 2001.* New York: United Nations Children's Fund.

Zimmerman, David J. (1992). "Regression Toward Mediocrity in Economic Structure." *American Economic Review.* Vol. 82, no. 3, pp. 409–29.

# 2 | A model of intergenerational mobility variation over time and place

GARY SOLON

A rapidly growing literature, surveyed in Solon (1999), is examining the empirical association between the incomes of parents and their children. With the acquisition of new data, researchers recently have begun to explore the ways in which intergenerational income mobility varies between countries and over time. Solon (2002) summarizes the new international evidence, which is substantially expanded by several of the chapters in this book. In addition, Reville (1995), Fertig (2001), and the authors of Chapter 5 have begun to study temporal change in intergenerational mobility in the United States, and the authors of Chapter 6 address that subject for the United Kingdom. This new research on intergenerational mobility variation over time and place is important both because it documents important features and trends in income inequality and because it may produce valuable clues about *how* income status is transmitted across generations.

The purpose of this chapter is to present a theoretical framework for interpreting the evidence from this newly emerging literature. I begin by modifying the Becker–Tomes (1979) model in a way that rationalizes the log-linear intergenerational income regression commonly estimated by empirical researchers. Analysis of the model shows that the steady-state intergenerational income elasticity increases with the heritability of income-related traits, the efficacy of human capital investment, and the earnings return to human capital, and it decreases with the progressivity of public investment in human capital. Cross-country differences in both intergenerational mobility and cross-sectional income inequality could arise from differences in any of these factors.

The author is grateful for helpful comments from Anders Björklund, Miles Corak, John Laitner, Robert Willis, and participants in the Statistics Canada workshop on intergenerational mobility. The author also gratefully acknowledges grant support from the National Institute on Aging (2-P01 AG10179).

The model also can be used to understand intergenerational mobility changes over time. For example, should we expect that the recent era of increasing earnings inequality in the United States and other countries also has been an era of decreasing intergenerational mobility? To address such questions, I use the model to examine how the intergenerational elasticity changes when the steady state is perturbed by an innovation to either the earnings return to human capital or the progressivity of public investment in human capital. The results suggest that an increase in the earnings return to human capital tends to decrease intergenerational mobility, and a shift to more progressive public investment in human capital tends to increase it.

## 1 Assumptions

Assume for simplicity that family $i$ contains one parent of generation $t-1$ and one child of generation $t$. The family must allocate the parent's lifetime after-tax earnings $(1-\tau)y_{i,t-1}$ between the parent's own consumption $C_{i,t-1}$ and investment $I_{i,t-1}$ in the child's human capital. The resulting budget constraint,

$$(1-\tau)y_{i,t-1} = C_{i,t-1} + I_{i,t-1}, \tag{2.1}$$

assumes that the parent cannot borrow against the child's prospective earnings and does not bequeath financial assets to the child. See Becker and Tomes (1986) for an analysis that relaxes this assumption. Given the simplifying assumption of proportional taxation at rate $\tau$, redistributive government policy will be represented in this analysis solely by progressive public investment in children's human capital.

The technology translating the investment $I_{i,t-1}$ into the child's human capital $h_{it}$ is

$$h_{it} = \theta \log(I_{i,t-1} + G_{i,t-1}) + e_{it} \tag{2.2}$$

where $G_{i,t-1}$ is the government's investment in the child's human capital (for example, through public provision of education or health care), $\theta > 0$ represents a positive marginal product for human capital investment, the semi-log functional form imposes decreasing marginal product, and $e_{it}$ denotes the human capital endowment the child receives regardless of the investment choices of the family and government. This endowment represents the combined effect of many child attributes influenced by nature, nurture, or both. In the words of Becker and Tomes (1979, p. 1158), children's endowed attributes "are determined by the reputation and 'connections' of their families, the contribution to the ability, race, and other characteristics of children from the genetic constitutions of their families, and the learning, skills, goals, and other 'family commodities' acquired through belonging to a particular family culture. Obviously, endowments depend on many characteristics of parents, grandparents, and other family members and may also be culturally influenced by other families."

With this characterization of the sources of the endowment, it is natural to assume that the child's endowment $e_{it}$ is positively correlated with the parent's endowment $e_{i,t-1}$. I follow Becker and Tomes (1979) in assuming that $e_{it}$ follows the first-order autoregressive process

$$e_{it} = \delta + \lambda e_{i,t-1} + v_{it} \tag{2.3}$$

where $v_{it}$ is a white-noise error term and the heritability coefficient $\lambda$ lies between 0 and 1.[1]

Finally, the child's income $y_{it}$ is determined by the semi-log earnings function

$$\log y_{it} = \mu + p h_{it} \tag{2.4}$$

where $p$ is the earnings return to human capital. Following Juhn, Murphy, and Pierce (1993), I will characterize an era of greater earnings inequality as an era of higher $p$. This era need not exhibit higher *levels* of earnings because the higher $p$ might be accompanied by a lower $\mu$.

## 2 Family investment behavior

Suppose the parent divides her or his after-tax income $(1 - \tau)y_{i,t-1}$ between own consumption $C_{i,t-1}$ and investment $I_{i,t-1}$ in the child's

---

[1] Although this heritability is partly biological, even the genetic aspect of the process interacts with social behavior in various ways including assortative mating. Lam and Schoeni (1994) and Chadwick and Solon (2002) emphasize the importance of assortative mating for research on intergenerational mobility. The present model, with its single-parent families, sheds no light on the role of assortative mating.

human capital so as to maximize the Cobb–Douglas utility function

$$U_i = (1 - \alpha) \log C_{i,t-1} + \alpha \log y_{it}. \tag{2.5}$$

The altruism parameter $\alpha$, which lies between 0 and 1, measures the parent's taste for $y_{it}$ relative to $C_{i,t-1}$. If the parent is cognizant of equations (2.1) through (2.4) and the variables therein, this utility function can be rewritten as

$$\begin{aligned} U_i = &(1 - \alpha) \log[(1 - \tau)y_{i,t-1} - I_{i,t-1}] \\ &+ \alpha\mu + \alpha\theta p \log(I_{i,t-1} + G_{i,t-1}) + \alpha p e_{it}. \end{aligned} \tag{2.6}$$

Equation (2.6) expresses the objective function in terms of the choice variable $I_{i,t-1}$.

Assuming an interior solution (that is, the level of public investment in the child's human capital is sufficiently low that the parent wishes to augment it with private investment), the first-order condition for maximizing utility is

$$\begin{aligned} \partial U_i / \partial I_{i,t-1} = &-(1 - \alpha)/[(1 - \tau)y_{i,t-1} - I_{1,t-1}] \\ &+ \alpha\theta p/(I_{i,t-1} + G_{i,t-1}) = 0. \end{aligned} \tag{2.7}$$

Solving for the optimal choice of $I_{i,t-1}$ yields

$$I_{i,t-1} = \left[ \frac{\alpha\theta p}{1 - \alpha(1 - \theta p)} \right] (1 - \tau)y_{i,t-1} - \left[ \frac{1 - \alpha}{1 - \alpha(1 - \theta p)} \right] G_{i,t-1}. \tag{2.8}$$

This remarkably simple result has several intuitive implications. First, holding public investment constant, higher-income parents invest more in their children's human capital. Second, holding taxes constant, higher public investment in a child's human capital partly crowds out the parent's private investment. Third, parents' investment in their children's human capital is increasing in parental altruism $\alpha$. Fourth, parental investment also is increasing in $\theta p$, which is the earnings return to human capital investment. In other words, parents are more inclined to invest in their children's human capital when the payoff is higher.

## 3 Implications for steady-state mobility and inequality

With these assumptions and results, it is straightforward to derive the implications for the intergenerational income association between $y_{it}$

and $y_{i,t-1}$, and also for the degree of cross-sectional inequality within a generation. Substituting equation (2.2) into equation (2.4) yields

$$\log y_{it} = \mu + p[\theta \log(I_{i,t-1} + G_{i,t-1}) + e_{it}]. \tag{2.9}$$

Then substituting in equation (2.8) for $I_{i,t-1}$ and rearranging produce

$$\log y_{it} = \mu + \theta p \log\left[\frac{\alpha\theta p}{1 - \alpha(1 - \theta p)}\right]$$

$$+ \theta p \log[(1 - \tau)y_{i,t-1} + G_{i,t-1}] + p e_{it}$$

$$= \mu + \theta p \log\left[\frac{\alpha\theta p(1 - \tau)}{1 - \alpha(1 - \theta p)}\right]$$

$$+ \theta p \log\left\{y_{i,t-1}\left[1 + \frac{G_{i,t-1}}{(1 - \tau)y_{i,t-1}}\right]\right\} + p e_{it}. \tag{2.10}$$

If the ratio $G_{i,t-1}/[(1 - \tau)y_{i,t-1}]$ is small, this equation can be approximately re-expressed as

$$\log y_{it} \cong \mu + \theta p \log\left[\frac{\alpha\theta p(1 - \tau)}{1 - \alpha(1 - \theta p)}\right] + \theta p \log y_{i,t-1}$$

$$+ \theta p\{G_{i,t-1}/[(1 - \tau)y_{i,t-1}]\} + p e_{it}. \tag{2.11}$$

Equation (2.11) suggests that intergenerational mobility is influenced by the government's policy for public investment in children's human capital. Suppose that this policy can be characterized as

$$G_{i,t-1}/[(1 - \tau)y_{i,t-1}] \cong \varphi - \gamma \log y_{i,t-1}. \tag{2.12}$$

A positive value of $\gamma$ would signify a sort of *relative* progressivity in public investment in children's human capital. With $\gamma > 0$, the absolute public investment may or may not be greater for children from high-income families, but the *ratio* of public investment to parental after-tax income decreases with parental income. The more positive $\gamma$ is, the more progressive is the policy.

Substituting equation (2.12) into equation (2.11) yields the regression equation

$$\log y_{it} \cong \mu^* + [(1 - \gamma)\theta p] \log y_{i,t-1} + p e_{it} \tag{2.13}$$

with intercept $\mu^* = \mu + \varphi\theta p + \theta p \log\{\alpha\theta p(1 - \tau)/[1 - \alpha(1 - \theta p)]\}$.

At first glance, equation (2.13) looks like the log-linear intergenerational income regression frequently estimated by empirical researchers. Viewed as the error term, however, $pe_{it}$ is not well behaved. It is correlated with the regressor $\log y_{i,t-1}$ because the child's endowment $e_{it}$ and the parent's log income $\log y_{i,t-1}$ both depend on the parent's endowment $e_{i,t-1}$.

In fact, equation (2.13) is a familiar entity in introductory econometrics textbooks. It is the first-order autoregression of $\log y_{it}$ with a serially correlated error term that itself follows a first-order autoregression, as shown in equation (2.3). In steady state, in which $\log y_{it}$ and $\log y_{i,t-1}$ have the same variance, the slope coefficient in the population regression of $\log y_{it}$ on $\log y_{i,t-1}$ is equivalent to the correlation between $\log y_{it}$ and $\log y_{i,t-1}$. In the present context, this quantity, which I will denote as $\beta$, is the steady-state intergenerational income elasticity. As shown in Greene (2000, pp. 534–35), this quantity is the sum of the two autoregressive parameters, the slope coefficient in equation (2.13) and the serial correlation coefficient in equation (2.3), divided by 1 plus their product. Thus, the steady-state intergenerational income elasticity is

$$\beta = \frac{(1 - \gamma)\theta p + \lambda}{1 + (1 - \gamma)\theta p \lambda}. \tag{2.14}$$

This is the estimand in most of the empirical literature on intergenerational income mobility.

Equation (2.14) shows the connection between the commonly estimated intergenerational income elasticity and the structural parameters of this chapter's model. The intergenerational elasticity $\beta$ is an increasing function of $\lambda$, $\theta$, $p$, and $1 - \gamma$. In other words, the intergenerational elasticity is greater as: (1) the heritability coefficient $\lambda$ is greater; (2) human capital investment is more productive ($\theta$ is greater); (3) the earnings return to human capital is greater ($p$ is greater); and (4) public investment in children's human capital is less progressive ($\gamma$ is less positive). The implications for cross-country comparisons are immediate. If country A displays less intergenerational mobility than country B, this could be because country A has stronger heritability, more productive human capital investment, higher returns to human capital, or less progressive public investment in human capital.

The steady-state implications for cross-sectional income inequality also are straightforward to derive. A familiar result from time-series analysis is that the first-order autoregression with a first-order autoregressive error term in equation (2.13) can be rewritten as a second-order autoregression with a "white noise" error term:

$$\log y_{it} = (1 - \lambda)(\mu^* + p\delta) + [(1 - \gamma)\theta p + \lambda] \log y_{i,t-1}$$
$$- [(1 - \gamma)\theta p\lambda] \log y_{i,t-2} + pv_{it}. \tag{2.15}$$

Then, the standard result on the variance of a variable following a stationary second-order autoregression[2] can be used to derive the cross-sectional variance of log income within a generation:

$$Var(\log y_{it}) = \frac{[1 + (1 - \gamma)\theta p\lambda] p^2 Var(v_{it})}{[1 - (1 - \gamma)\theta p\lambda](1 - \lambda^2)\{1 - [(1 - \gamma)\theta p]^2\}} \tag{2.16}$$

where $Var(v_{it})$ is the variance of the innovation in equation (2.3), the process for heritability of endowments.

Like the intergenerational elasticity $\beta$, this expression for $Var(\log y_{it})$ is an increasing function of $\lambda$, $\theta$, $p$, and $1 - \gamma$. Thus, like the intergenerational elasticity, cross-sectional income inequality is greater in the presence of stronger heritability, more productive human capital investment, higher returns to human capital, and less progressive public investment in human capital. This connection between intergenerational mobility and cross-sectional inequality accords with Björklund and Jäntti's (1997) conjecture that the contrasts between Sweden and the United States in both intergenerational mobility and inequality may be related to each other. The mapping between intergenerational mobility and cross-sectional inequality, however, is not exact because the expression for $Var(\log y_{it})$ in equation (2.16) also depends on $Var(v_{it})$, which does *not* appear in the expression for $\beta$ in equation (2.14). Thus, two countries with approximately the same intergenerational elasticity might differ in cross-sectional inequality because they differ in their heterogeneity of endowed income-related traits.

## 4 Departures from the steady state

Numerous writers have raised the question of whether the increase in earnings inequality that has occurred since the late 1970s has been

---

[2] See Box, Jenkins, and Reinsel (1994, p. 62). I thank Shinichi Sakata, Matthew Shapiro, and Phil Howrey for pointing me to this result.

accompanied by a decline in intergenerational mobility. While this ultimately is an empirical question, interpretation of the empirical evidence will benefit from a theoretical perspective. It is straightforward to use this chapter's model to examine how the intergenerational elasticity responds to perturbations from the steady state.

Suppose that society is in steady state in generation $t-1$, but earnings inequality increases in generation $t$. Following Juhn, Murphy, and Pierce (1993), I represent the increased earnings inequality as an increase from $p$ to $p_t$ in the earnings return to human capital. As Chapter 5 points out, however, at the same time that earnings inequality increased in the United States, public investment in human capital arguably became more progressive. Chapter 6 suggests that the progressivity of public investment moved in the opposite direction in the United Kingdom. I represent a change in the progressivity of public investment as a shift from $\gamma$ to $\gamma_t$ that is known by the parents in generation $t-1$ at the time that they choose how much of their own income to invest in the children of generation $t$.

The intergenerational income elasticity between generations $t$ and $t-1$ is

$$\beta_t = Cov(\log y_{it}, \log y_{i,t-1})/Var(\log y_{i,t-1}). \tag{2.17}$$

This no longer is equivalent to the intergenerational correlation because $y_{it}$ and $y_{i,t-1}$ have different variances. Some tedious algebra shows that

$$\beta_t = \frac{p_t}{p}\left[\frac{(1-\gamma_t)\theta p + \lambda + (\gamma - \gamma_t)(1-\gamma)\theta^2 p^2 \lambda}{1 + (1-\gamma)\theta p \lambda}\right]. \tag{2.18}$$

Although equation (2.18) is cumbersome, it yields very straightforward results for two special cases.

First, suppose that earnings inequality increases, but the progressivity of public human capital investment stays constant with $\gamma_t = \gamma$. Then equation (2.18) simplifies to

$$\beta_t = \frac{p_t}{p}\left[\frac{(1-\gamma)\theta p + \lambda}{1 + (1-\gamma)\theta p \lambda}\right]. \tag{2.19}$$

This is simply the steady-state elasticity $\beta$ from equation (2.14) inflated by the factor $p_t/p$. This result provides formal support for the common intuition that, other things being equal, an increase in earnings inequality might be expected to result in a higher intergenerational elasticity. It is worth noting that equation (2.19) holds regardless of whether the parents anticipate the change from $p$ to $p_t$.

Second, suppose that public human capital investment becomes more progressive, but the return to human capital stays constant with $p_t = p$. Then $\beta_t$ equals just the bracketed expression in equation (2.18). If one subtracts the steady-state elasticity in equation (2.14) from this new elasticity, one finds that the change in the intergenerational elasticity is

$$\beta_t - \beta = (\gamma - \gamma_t)\theta p. \tag{2.20}$$

Thus an increase in the progressivity of public human capital investment leads to a decrease in the intergenerational income elasticity.

## 5 Conclusion

In this chapter, I have developed a simple model in which optimizing behavior by families leads to the log-linear intergenerational income regression equation commonly estimated by empirical researchers. The steady-state intergenerational income elasticity turns out to be a straightforward function of parameters representing four key factors: the strength of the "mechanical" (for example, genetic) transmission of income-generating traits, the efficacy of investment in children's human capital, the earnings return to human capital, and the progressivity of public investment in children's human capital. The implication is that if country A displays less intergenerational mobility (a higher intergenerational income elasticity) than country B, this could be because country A has stronger heritability, more productive human capital investment, higher returns to human capital, or less progressive public investment in human capital. These same factors also tend to increase cross-sectional income inequality. In addition, an analysis of perturbations of the steady state suggests that an era of rising returns to human capital or declining progressivity in public human capital investment is also an era of declining intergenerational mobility.

## References

Becker, Gary S., and Nigel Tomes (1979). "An Equilibrium Theory of the Distribution of Income and Intergenerational Mobility." *Journal of Political Economy*. Vol. 87, no. 6, pp. 1153–89.

(1986). "Human Capital and the Rise and Fall of Families." *Journal of Labor Economics.* Vol. 4, no. 3, pp. S1–S39.

Björklund, Anders, and Markus Jäntti (1997). "Intergenerational Income Mobility in Sweden Compared to the United States." *American Economic Review.* Vol. 87, pp. 1009–18.

Box, George E. P., Gwilym M. Jenkins, and Gregory C. Reinsel (1994). *Time Series Analysis: Forecasting and Control.* Third Edition. Englewood Cliffs: Prentice Hall.

Chadwick, Laura, and Gary Solon (2002). "Intergenerational Income Mobility among Daughters." *American Economic Review.* Vol. 92, pp. 335–44.

Fertig, Angela R. (2001). "Trends in Intergenerational Earnings Mobility." Princeton, NJ: Center for Research on Child Wellbeing, Princeton University, Working Paper No. 2001-23.

Greene, William H. (2000). *Econometric Analysis.* Fourth Edition. Upper Saddle River: Prentice Hall.

Juhn, Chinhui, Kevin M. Murphy, and Brooks Pierce (1993). "Wage Inequality and the Rise in Returns to Skill." *Journal of Political Economy.* Vol. 101, pp. 410–42.

Lam, David, and Robert F. Schoeni (1994). "Family Ties and Labor Markets in the United States and Brazil." *Journal of Human Resources.* Vol. 29, pp. 1235–58.

Reville, Robert T. (1995). "Intertemporal and Life Cycle Variation in Measured Intergenerational Earnings Mobility." RAND Working Paper.

Solon, Gary (1999). "Intergenerational Mobility in the Labor Market." In Orley C. Ashenfelter and David Card (editors). *Handbook of Labor Economics, Volume 3A.* Amsterdam: North-Holland.

(2002). "Cross-Country Differences in Intergenerational Earnings Mobility." *Journal of Economic Perspectives.* Vol. 16, pp. 59–66.

# 3 | Equal opportunity and intergenerational mobility: going beyond intergenerational income transition matrices

JOHN E. ROEMER

POLICY makers in both Europe and North America often imagine a "new" economy – an economy based upon human capital and skills – as the source of economic growth, and are increasingly concerned with the extent to which all members of their societies are able to participate and experience a rising standard of living. "Access," "social inclusion," and "equality of opportunity" are the terms by which public policy changes are often judged, and there is as a result a strong need for indicators of the extent to which social institutions embody these characteristics and lead to "fair" outcomes. This has long been the case and in fact is one of the principal reasons the degree of intergenerational income mobility is viewed as being policy relevant. If the tie between the adult outcomes of children and their family background is rather loose then in some sense the playing field might be thought of as level, children's position in the income distribution being the result of their own efforts rather than accidents of birth. As such, the degree of intergenerational mobility is perceived as being closely related to social inclusion and equality of opportunity, ethics that are widely accepted, often legitimize public institutions, and as a result are central to a sense of shared destiny.

In this chapter, I will formally discuss the relationship between equality of opportunity and intergenerational income mobility. Many of the subsequent chapters document difficulties in obtaining accurate estimates of the correlation between parent and child incomes, offer new estimates, or offer comparisons between countries or across time. It may well be that the intergenerational correlation of incomes is higher in one country than previously thought because of measurement issues, or higher than in some other country, or has changed through time, but how ultimately are we to interpret a "high" or "low" correlation? How "high" is too "high"? When have we reached a situation that can be described as reflecting equality of opportunity? The empirical literature never explicitly addresses these questions with the result that readers may implicitly begin to assume that equality of opportunity holds if the rows of the intergenerational income transition matrix are identical, if an individual's chances of occupying the various income levels are independent of the income of their parents. I will argue that this desideratum is associated with a quite special view of equality of opportunity, a view that only a fraction of those who consider the issue would, upon reflection, endorse.

## 1 A framework for conceptualizing equality of opportunity

My starting point is a conceptualization of equality of opportunity that formalizes the "level the playing field" view that I have presented in Roemer (1998, 2002). Five words comprise the language of this approach. The *objective* is the aspect of well-being that the policy maker wants to equalize opportunities for – in the current project, this is for the most part income. *Circumstances* are the aspects of the environments of individuals that affect their achievement of the objective, *and* for which the society in question does not wish to hold individuals responsible. Generally, circumstances are thought to be environmental influences that are beyond the control of individuals. A *type* is the set of individuals in the society who share the same circumstances. *Effort* comprises the totality of actions of the individual that affect his or her achievement of the objective, and for which society *does* hold the individual responsible. Finally, the *instrument* is the policy that can be manipulated in order to change the value of the objective. The equal-opportunity policy is the value of the instrument such that the achievement of the objective of individuals shall be a function only of their efforts, not of their circumstances. In other words, the instrument is used to compensate those with disadvantageous circumstances so that in the end they have the same chances of acquiring high values of the objective as do those with advantageous circumstances. To be more precise, "equality of opportunity" has been achieved when all those who expend the same *degree of effort*, regardless of their type, have the same chances of achieving the objective.

In particular, equality-of-opportunity (EOp) views inequalities of outcome as indefensible, ethically speaking, when and only when they are due to differential circumstances. Inequalities due to differential effort are acceptable. In this way, EOp differs from "equality of outcome," which treats all inequalities in the achievement of the objective as ethically indefensible. Equality of opportunity could be achieved, perhaps, by starving everyone, so that everyone achieves a zero level of the objective. To be a palatable approach, EOp, as I have just defined it, must be combined with some conception of efficiency. I will discuss this briefly toward the end of the chapter.

In applications of this approach, one usually specifies a small set of circumstances that are measurable in the population under consideration. One then partitions the population into types according to these circumstances, and then attributes the observed variation within types of the objective to differential effort. Thus, effort is treated as the residual. It is therefore important to try and capture the most important circumstances in the set of "circumstances."

For the most part there is a unique circumstance in all of the following chapters of this volume: the income of a person's parent. The objective is the income of the child in adulthood. The relationship between the circumstance and the objective can be described in terms of an intergenerational correlation, or more specifically as an intergenerational transition matrix. For the sake of exposition I focus on the latter. The intergenerational transition matrix is a table whose $ij^{\text{th}}$ entry is the fraction of children whose parent or parents earned income level $i$, and who in turn earn income level $j$. The implicit social goal is to achieve a transition matrix whose rows are identical. The fact that children end up in all positions of the income distribution rather than always occupying the same position as their parents – that the rows of the transition matrix are positive vectors and not unit vectors – is due to differential effort, or perhaps differential abilities. In the latter case, the policy maker or society would not oppose differential rewards to those of differential ability, even if ability were something beyond the control of the individual. I do not focus on the instrument through which this would be achieved, but this is discussed more explicitly in other chapters, particularly Chapter 12: presumably educational investment would play a large role.

How do parents affect the chances for acquisition of income of their children? This is certainly a matter for some discussion, and while some of the issues are also discussed in many of the other chapters, I will assume that the influence of parents occurs through at least the following four channels: (C1) provision of social connections; (C2) formation of beliefs and skills in children through family culture and investment; (C3) genetic transmission of ability; (C4) formation of preferences and aspirations in children. I have listed these in the order that I think most readers would choose as the right order for inclusion in the set of circumstances for EOp policy: that is, most people think that equality of opportunity requires "leveling the playing field" with regard to inequalities of opportunity due to differential family connections; a somewhat smaller number of people would endorse a policy that would also count individuals as disadvantaged due to their being raised in families that inculcated them with pessimistic beliefs about what they could become, or did not invest in their skills; a smaller number still would compensate individuals not only for C1 and C2 but also for low innate ability; and the smallest number would compensate individuals in addition for the influence of family upbringing on their preferences. I am not sure about the ordering of the last two channels. As an economist, I differentiate between beliefs and skills on the one hand, and preferences/aspirations on the other. A sociologist might not parse the characteristics in this manner. The chief preference with which I am concerned is the income-leisure preference, or income-occupational choice preference.

When it is said that applicants for positions in social institutions (firms, universities) should be considered *only on their merits*, we are explicitly ruling out "social connections" as a legitimate characteristic for candidates. Thus, the practice of nepotism – of hiring relatives of incumbent members of the firm – is an anti-EOp policy, as is admitting preferentially to Ivy League schools the children of alumni. But merit might include ability, in which case a meritocratic view would not endorse counting C3 as circumstances. When education is focused upon as an instrument for equalizing opportunities, the hope is that public educational investment will compensate for inadequacies of family culture, mainly through channel C2. (Education can also work through compensation of disadvantage in channels C3 and C4.) Because the meritocratic view usually encompasses the legitimacy of returns to ability, it is in conflict with some versions of equality of opportunity – I think this is an important point.

Why do I place "family influence on preferences" as the last channel? Clearly, we do want to counteract preferences that we think are self-defeating in children, which may be a consequence of their upbringing. The reason this channel is listed last is that most people would say adults should be responsible for their preferences – in particular, with regard to pursuit of economic opportunities – even if those preferences are in large part the consequence of upbringing. The key here is that, even though one's preferences may have been instilled to a large extent in childhood, one acquires responsibility for them if one comes to identify with them. As Ronald Dworkin writes, a person should be held responsible for his preferences if and when he is glad he has them (Dworkin 1981). This excludes addictions and compulsions, which are preferences one would prefer not to have, but not income-occupational choice preferences.

## 2 Equality of opportunity and intergenerational mobility

For the sake of argument, let us accept two things: first, the four kinds of circumstance listed exhaust the set of parental influences on child incomes; and second, the set of parental influences is "nested" in this order, with regard to arguable inclusion in the set of circumstances for EOp policy. If so, then we have four associated conceptions of equality of opportunity, each associated with four possible sets of circumstances:

EOp1: Circumstances $= C1$
EOp2: Circumstances $= C1 \cup C2$
EOp3: Circumstances $= C1 \cup C2 \cup C3$
EOp4: Circumstances $= C1 \cup C2 \cup C3 \cup C4$

Before inquiring how the study of intergenerational income transition matrices (IITM) is related to equality of opportunity, it will be useful to describe how one would ideally study equality of opportunity, with regard to the above conceptions.

Let me suggest an amendment of the objective in the IITM studies, which is taken to be market income or, as I will refer to it, "pre-fisc" income. Arguably, "post-fisc" income – that is income after taxes and government transfers – is a more attractive objective since it is a more proximate measure of consumption opportunities. With the choice of pre-fisc income in the IITM approach, one is implicitly thinking of the instrument as public educational investment; with post-fisc income as the objective, one also includes income taxation and transfer as possible instruments.

Denote the relevant characteristics as follows: a person's type, as characterized by the characteristics of his or her parents is $t$, preferences are $p$, and ability is $a$. Effort is viewed as the consequence of the exercise of preferences. Furthermore, suppose that it can be established (through econometric analysis) that an individual's preferences are the sum of parental influences and an element of autonomous preference formation: namely, $p = p^f + p^s$, where $f$ is for *family* and $s$ is for *self*. The instrument is $\varphi$, and it can include both education and tax policy. The individual's post-fisc income is $y = y\,(a, p, \varphi, t)$. (Econometrically, there will be an error term as well.) Thus, we suppose that once ability, preferences, and policy are fixed, the only predictable variation in income is due to type, as indicated by characteristics of family upbringing. Finally, I propose the following assumption, which will probably be necessary to identify the distribution of $p^f$ in the various types: ($\mathbf{A^*}$) The distribution of $p^s$ is the same in all types.

Let me first describe how to test whether **EOp2**, which I conjecture is the view of equal opportunity that most citizens in democratic societies endorse today, has been achieved. Denote by $F_{\varphi^*}^{t,a,p^f}$ the distribution function of income $y$, at the observed policy $\varphi^*$, of those with characteristics $(t, a, p^f)$. A necessary condition for the achievement of **EOp2** is that, for every pair $(a, p^f)$, the distributions are the same for all types: formally,

$$\mathbf{EOp2} \cap \mathbf{A^*} \Rightarrow \left[(\forall a,\, p^f, t^1, t^2)(\forall \gamma)\big(F_{\varphi^*}^{t^1 a p^f}(\gamma) = F_{\varphi^*}^{t^2 a p^f}(\gamma)\big)\right]. \qquad (3.1)$$

Why would the distributions of income for those in different types, and with the same preferential components $p^f$ and abilities differ? This would only happen because of features **C1** and **C2**, and because of differential $p^s$. If we have equalized opportunities with respect to **C1** and **C2**, and if **A\*** holds, then the distributions of income in different types conditional upon $(a, p^f)$ should be identical. This is what (3.1) states.

What is the analogous exercise with regard to **EOp3**? Personally, I do not see why some individuals should have fewer consumption opportunities than others because of possessing inferior native ability. With **EOp3**, it becomes particularly important that we include fiscal policy as an instrument, because a market economy cannot be expected to deliver pre-fisc incomes that are insensitive to ability. But fiscal policy can compensate, in principle at least, for ability disadvantage. The ideal of **EOp3** will be achieved when

$$\mathbf{EOp3} \cap \mathbf{A}^* \Rightarrow \big[(\forall a^1, a^2, p^f, t^1, t^2)(\forall \gamma)\big(F_{\varphi^*}^{t^1 a^1 p^f}(\gamma)$$
$$= F_{\varphi^*}^{t^2 a^2 p^f}(\gamma)\big)\big]. \tag{3.2}$$

In other words, the distribution of income is independent of parental characteristics and ability of individuals, but not of the parental component of preferences.

Finally, it is worthwhile to present the necessary condition for the achievement of **EOp4**. It is defined as:

$$\mathbf{EOp4} \cap \mathbf{A}^* \Rightarrow \big[(\forall a^1, a^2, p^{f1}, p^{f2}, t^1, t^2)(\forall \gamma)\big(F_{\varphi^*}^{t^1 a^1 p^{f1}}(\gamma)$$
$$= F_{\varphi^*}^{t^2 a^2 p^{f2}}(\gamma)\big)\big]. \tag{3.3}$$

That is to say, the policy should compensate individuals for their types, their abilities, and the influence of family on their preferences. Only the income consequences of the autonomous part of preferences are left uncompensated. Individuals are held responsible for these and they will generate inequalities in the objective. Autonomous preferences determine the effort of individuals, which determines their income, given type, ability, the parental preference factor, and policy.

Thus, in general, equality of specified income-distribution functions is a necessary condition for various conceptions of equal opportunity, given the assumption **A***. But what is the relationship between these three versions of equality of opportunity? It is immediately clear that the conclusion of inference (3.3) implies the conclusion of inference (3.2), which in turn implies the conclusion of inference (3.1). On this basis it is now possible to examine how IITM studies can be understood. The ideal in these studies is that for each parental-characteristic-type, the distributions of income of children should be the same, namely:

$$(\forall t^1, t^2)\, F_{\varphi^*}^{t^1}(\gamma) = F_{\varphi^*}^{t^2}(\gamma). \tag{IITM}$$

That is to say:

$$\big[(\forall a^1, a^2, p^{f1}, p^{f2}, t^1, t^2)(\forall \gamma)\big(F_{\varphi^*}^{t^1 a^1 p^{f1}}(\gamma) = F_{\varphi^*}^{t^2 a^2 p^{f2}}(\gamma)\big)\big] \Rightarrow \mathbf{IITM}.$$

But this is the only valid implication among these four conceptions of EOp. Why, for example, does the conclusion of (2) not imply (IITM)?

In general this is the case because the distribution of $p^f$ will differ in types $t^1$ and $t^2$.

Thus, in the presence of $\mathbf{A}^*$, IITM is a necessary condition for EOp4, the most radical conception of equality of opportunity. In contrast, suppose we have: ($\mathbf{B}^*$) The joint distribution of $(a, p)$ is identical in all types. Denote that common probability measure by $\Psi$. Then, by definition, for any $t$: $F^t = \int F^{tap} \, d\Psi \, (a, p)$ and it follows that:

$$\mathbf{B}^* \cap \left[ (\forall a, p^f, t^1, t^2)(\forall \gamma)\left(F_{\varphi^*}^{t^1 a p^f}(\gamma) = F_{\varphi^*}^{t^2 a p^f}(\gamma)\right)\right] \Rightarrow \text{IITM, and}$$

$$\mathbf{B}^* \cap \left[ (\forall a^1, a^2, p^f, t^1, t^2)(\forall \gamma)\left(F_{\varphi^*}^{t^1 a^1 p^f}(\gamma) = F_{\varphi^*}^{t^2 a^2 p^f}(\gamma)\right)\right] \Rightarrow \text{IITM.}$$

But the assumption that the distribution of $(a, p)$ is independent of type is a poor one. So, assuming that we can identify these various distributions of agent characteristics, the only robust implication appears to be that IITM, in the presence of $\mathbf{A}^*$, is a necessary condition for EOp4.

## 3 Summary

In this chapter, I have made precise the meaning of "equality of opportunity" and suggest that it does not, except under rather extreme circumstances, imply complete intergenerational income mobility. The suggestion that equality of opportunity is reflected in a situation of no association at all between parent and child incomes is difficult to accept for the following reasons. First, complete intergenerational mobility, as reflected for example in an intergenerational income transition matrix with equal entries regardless of parental income, is a necessary condition for only the most radical conception of equality of opportunity, one that I have termed EOp4. This conception implies policy makers should level the playing field by eliminating the influence of not only social connections, family culture and investment, and the genetic transmission of ability, but also of the influence of family background on the formation of preferences and aspirations among children. In my view this is not a conception that most people currently endorse. Second, most analyses of intergenerational mobility are based on market incomes and market economies cannot be expected to equalize market incomes independent of ability. Consequently if policy makers adopt an interpretation of equality of opportunity as given by EOp4 as their social goal, then income after taxes and transfers must be used as the objective. Finally, parental education – rather than income – is

arguably a better proxy for the influences that impact upon the preferences and aspirations of children. The analytical basis for a discussion
of **EOp4** would have to move beyond intergenerational income mobility to parental education and status.

I should also reiterate a point about efficiency made in Section 1.
Equalizing distribution functions can be accomplished by starving
everyone: what societies really desire is to equalize distribution functions "at the highest possible levels." It is beyond the scope of this
chapter to show exactly how this is done: one wishes to "maximize
the minimum distribution function," but there are various procedures
for doing this, which I discuss in Roemer (2002). In simple cases,
this amounts to maximizing the average value of the objective for
the most disadvantaged type. Where an unambiguously most disadvantaged type does not exist, the policy maker maximizes the average value of the objective along the left-hand envelope of the distribution functions that are appropriate for the version of EOp in
question.

In conclusion, I wish to say that my critique should not be taken to
nullify our interest in estimates of intergenerational income mobility.
In many countries this is the best we can do in studying equality of
opportunity given the data that are available. Indeed, my co-authors
and I have recently published a multi-country study that takes statement **IITM** as the necessary condition of equal opportunity (Roemer
*et al.* 2003). Nevertheless, the availability of sophisticated data sets
should enable researchers to test for equality of opportunity according
to the **EOp2** and **EOp3** views that I have described – the elimination of
influences associated with social connections and family culture, and in
addition with the genetic transmission of ability – as such studies would
be more in tune with the current egalitarian sentiments of democratic
polities.

### References

Dworkin, R. (1981). "What is Equality? Part 2: Equality of Resources."
    *Philosophy & Public Affairs*. Vol. 10, pp. 283–345.
Roemer, John E. (1998). *Equality of Opportunity*. Cambridge, MA: Harvard
    University Press.
    (2002). "Equality of Opportunity: A Progress Report." *Social Choice and
    Welfare*. Vol. 19, pp. 455–71.

Roemer, J. E., R. Aaberge, U. Colombio, J. Fritzell, S. Jenkins, A. Lefranc, I. Marx, M. Page, E. Pommer, J. Ruiz-Castillo, M. J. San Segundo, T. Tranaes, A. Trannoy, G. Wagner, and I. Zubiri (2003). "To What Extent do Fiscal Regimes Equalize Opportunities for Income Acquisition among Citizens?" *Journal of Public Economics*. Vol. 87, pp. 539–65.

# 4 | *Intergenerational mobility for whom? The experience of high- and low-earning sons in international perspective*

NATHAN D. GRAWE

R ESEARCHERS have devoted considerable attention to understanding and overcoming a number of methodological concerns
needed to obtain an unbiased estimate of the degree of intergenerational mobility. Solon (1992) and Zimmerman (1992) highlight
measurement errors associated with the use of annual as opposed to
longer-term measures of earnings; Jenkins (1987), Reville (1995), and

I am indebted to several sources for the data used in this paper. The Panel
Study of Income Dynamics data are provided through the Survey Research
Center, Institute for Social Research, University of Michigan. The National
Longitudinal Survey data collection was funded by the US Department
of Labor, Bureau of Labor Statistics. My thanks to Miles Corak, Sophie
Lefebvre, and Statistics Canada for facilitating access to the Intergenerational Income Data from Canada. The German Socio-Economic Panel Study
data in this study are from the public use version. These data are provided by
the Deutsches Institut für Wirtschaftsforschung (DIW) in collaboration with
Cornell University. Material from the National Child Development Survey
is Crown Copyright and has been used by permission, having been made
available by the Office for National Statistics through the Data Archive.
Neither the Office for National Statistics nor the Data Archive bear any
responsibility for the analysis or interpretation of the data reported here.
The First and Second Malaysian Family Life Survey data were produced by
the RAND Corporation and distributed by the Inter-University Consortium
for Political and Social Science Research. The World Bank organized the
Living Standards Measurement Study data from Ecuador, Nepal, Pakistan,
and Peru. The source of the data from Ecuador is the Instituto Nacional
de Estadísticas y Censos del Ecuador (*INEC*). The source of the data from
Nepal is the Central Bureau of Statistics of Nepal. The source of the data
from Pakistan is the Federal Bureau of Statistics (FBS) of Pakistan. Finally,
the source of the data from Peru is the Instituto Nacional de Estadísticas e
Informática del Peru (INEI). In all cases, the responsibility for the analysis
and interpretation of the data reported here is the author's alone.

Grawe (2001b) point to related problems associated with the age at which parents and children are observed; and countless studies using multiple data sets have attempted to find "the number" that best estimates intergenerational mobility in earnings and income. But a new line of literature seeks to move beyond strict measurement in an effort to better understand the transmission of economic status. Even if estimates are biased, if the biases are similar across groups or across time, then the results may yet be useful. For instance, Couch and Lillard in Chapter 8 look for cross-country differences in regression non-linearities and the authors of Chapters 5 and 6 examine trends in mobility estimates over time. In fact, as Grawe and Mulligan (2002) discuss, an entire literature has developed to determine the extent to which credit constraints affect intergenerational correlations.

This chapter joins this endeavor, addressing several largely unexplored questions. The first is perhaps the most basic: what exactly is meant when an economy is said to be open or to exhibit equality of opportunity? Nearly all of the empirical economics literature has answered this question in terms of an average regression slope, though a number of studies also employ measures based on transition matrices. In this literature an equal opportunity economy is one, at least implicitly, in which the expected earnings of children are independent of parental earnings. While this definition sounds plausible at first, significant objections are easily raised and Chapter 3 has clarified some of these. Isn't it reasonable to expect market abilities (and therefore earnings) to be correlated across generations? Even if everyone shared the same level of market ability, isn't it reasonable to expect similarity in preferences for education and work among members of the same family? If this is so then it is hardly surprising that the average child born to low-earning parents earns less than the average child born to high-earning parents.

Roemer (1998) argues that a better conception of equal opportunity can be found in comparing children with similarly successful outcomes relative to other children born to similar families. That is, he compares the highest-, median-, or lowest-earning child born to low-earning parents to the highest-, median-, or lowest-earning child born to high-earning parents. In Roemer's view, proper social policy "levels the playing field" so that individuals are not held accountable for circumstances beyond their control (for instance, parental earnings). Individuals who exert the same degree of effort (where the degree of effort is measured relative to others facing the same exogenous circumstances) should attain the same level of welfare.

In the opening section of this chapter, I discuss this perspective further by offering a justification based upon the fact that observed earnings reflect a combination of available opportunities and individual preferences, and by offering – through quantile regressions – a practical measure of intergenerational mobility for "exceptional" children. There may be value in basing international comparisons on this alternative conception of mobility, and this is pursued in detail in the remainder of the chapter. Existing studies comparing the rate of intergenerational mobility for the average individual suggest that mobility in the United States is – at the least – no faster than in the rest of the world. Could these similarities and differences among average children coexist with important differences in the experiences of exceptional children? In order to facilitate comparison, I present intergenerational mobility estimates (using both the mean regression and exceptional mobility conceptions) employing careful sample selection rules to mitigate comparability concerns. I find that exceptional mobility appears to be faster in North America than in Europe. Finally, using Two-Sample Instrumental Variables techniques as well as a newly developed two-sample quantile regression procedure, I provide a first look at mobility in five developing nations: Malaysia, Ecuador, Nepal, Pakistan, and Peru. The differences among developed countries appear small when compared with the developed–developing gap; mobility is much slower in several developing countries using both mean and quantile measures. In fact, I cannot reject the hypothesis that incomes regress away from the mean in Ecuador.

## 1  The exceptional child: an alternative conception and measure of intergenerational earnings mobility

The discussion in Chapter 3 and in Roemer (1998) presumes that, even with identical opportunities, we expect to find higher average earnings among children from high-earning families since preferences for education and effort are likely correlated across generations. Despite the tendency for children's preferences to reflect those of their parents, deviations from this general rule can reasonably be expected. Consequently, if opportunities are truly identical for all individuals, the highest-earning child born to a low-earning family will not necessarily earn any less than a high-earning child born into some other earnings class. This is the sense in which I use the term "exceptional."

While this approach may appear novel, emphasizing the experience of exceptional cases is hardly new at all. For example, the typical study of wage discrimination explores the regression

$$w_i = \alpha + \beta_1 HK_i + \beta_2 J_i + \beta 3 D_i + \varepsilon_i \tag{4.1}$$

where $w_i$ is the wage (or log wage), $HK_i$ measures human capital (education, experience, etc.), $J_i$ represents characteristics of the individual's job (amenities or dis-amenities, occupation, industry), and $D_i$ is an indicator variable representing race or gender. Blau and Kahn (1994), Ginther and Hayes (1999), and Hoffman (1976) offer representative examples of such studies. Wage differences after controlling for human capital and job characteristics are construed as evidence of discrimination. Implicit in this approach is the recognition that earnings combine both opportunity and preferences. If a woman's preferences lead her to choose to work part time, or to work in a low-wage occupation, or to acquire less education, this will be reflected in lower wages even if opportunity is equal. Women and minorities who make unusual choices become the focus of study. The question explored by regression (4.1) is: given a woman has made the same choices as high-earning males, does she too receive high compensation? This is very similar to measuring intergenerational opportunity by focusing on the performance of exceptional children.

By allowing researchers to separate mobility among high-, medium-, and low-achieving children this alternative conception may also enhance understanding of the intergenerational transmission process. For instance, researchers wondering why earnings are persistent across the generations may gain insight by considering rates of mobility at different levels of child achievement. If children generally occupy the same position in the earnings distribution as their parents, is this largely because parents are able to pass advantages on to their most able children? Or does persistence in intergenerational earnings reflect parental provision of a safety net for the least able children born into high-earning families?

An example of the usefulness of this approach is found in Grawe (2001a). Exposure to credit constraints has often been implicitly equated with low family earnings. But as Corak and Heisz (1999) point out, low-earning families are unlikely candidates for credit constraints if low-earning parents also have children with relatively low market ability. The optimal parental investment, as described in Becker and Tomes (1979, 1986), may not require more education than freely provided secondary school. Parental earnings are simply a poor proxy for the presence of a credit constraint. Grawe (2001a) points out that conditional on the level of parental earnings, the more education required by the child, the more likely a family is to be constrained. Since children with more education are also children with higher earnings, this means that credit constraints will limit mobility among high-achievement children while not affecting the outcomes of low achievers. Grawe (2001a) applies this approach to data from Canada with no evidence of distortions in mobility due to binding credit constraints.

No doubt the tendency for analysts to study mobility among average children reflects the fact that it is relatively easy to derive estimates of mobility for the average individual, requiring only an application of Ordinary Least Squares regression. Without an analogous estimator, the alternative conception of exceptional mobility that I have outlined is of little practical significance. Fortunately, quantile regression captures precisely this notion of exceptional mobility.

For those less familiar with this method, first consider the task of finding the 80$^{\text{th}}$ centile son within the distribution of sons' earnings. Eighty percent of sons earn less than he and 20 percent earn more. In the context of this paper, quantile regression simply divides these sons into cells based on their fathers' earnings. Within each cell, the 80$^{\text{th}}$ centile son is found. Quantile regression essentially looks across cells and asks: by how much do the earnings of an 80$^{\text{th}}$ centile son (conditional on his father's earnings) increase as the earnings level of the father increases? For example, equation (4.2) is the main concern of the empirical analysis in this chapter:

$$y_{s,n} = \hat{\delta}_{1,n} + \hat{\delta}_{2,n} y_f. \tag{4.2}$$

In this equation $y_{s,n}$ refers to the expected adult earnings of a son at the $n^{th}$ quantile of the earnings distribution of all sons whose fathers earn $y_f$ (permanent) earnings.[1] (Annual earnings of both fathers and sons are

---

[1] Earnings are a poor measure of status for women because of fertility and labor force participation decisions. For this reason, my analysis

adjusted for age to create a measure of "permanent, lifetime" earnings.) Quantile regressions allow the estimation of separate intercept and slope coefficients – as represented respectively by $\hat{\delta}_{1,n}$ and $\hat{\delta}_{2,n}$ – for each separate quantile of the sons' earnings distribution (conditional on fathers' earnings). This is a direct analogy to Least Squares which offers these coefficients only at the (conditional) sample mean.[2] As an example, in Figure 4.1 the 95th quantile regression line with slope 0.185 has been superimposed on data from a simulated society. Consider two family types: a father in a family of type A earns the average earnings (for fathers) while a father in a family of type B earns 50 percent more. The 95th percentile son among type-B families is estimated to earn roughly $0.5 \times 18.5\% = 9.25\%$ more than the 95[th] percentile son among type-A families.

In Figure 4.1, the mean regression slope (0.280) exceeds the slope of the 95th quantile regression line, and the regression slope at the 5th centile is even steeper (0.448). One interpretation of these differences is that there is more exceptional mobility than average mobility, but from the perspective of a supporter of the exceptional conception of mobility this confounds the issue. The mean regression line simply does not contain information about what opportunities are available since it also reflects different preferences. Since readers are likely to differ in their interpretation of these two alternative conceptions of mobility, I report estimates of both in the analysis that follows. In

focuses only on men. The research with women that has been done in the United States indicates that mobility is similar to that found among men (Chadwick and Solon 2002). It should not be assumed this will also be true in other countries with different institutions and traditions. I leave to later work the international comparison of intergenerational mobility among women but Chapter 5 offers an interesting analysis over time for the United States.

[2] Koenker and Basset (1978) show that equation (4.2) can be estimated by

$$\hat{\delta} = \min_{\delta} \frac{1}{K} \sum_{i=1}^{K} [n - .5\mathrm{sgn}(y_i - x_i'\delta)](y_i - \delta x_i'\delta)$$

where $K$ is the sample size. Buchinsky (1998) offers a summary of developments in quantile regression estimation. Quantile regression is not entirely new to studies of intergenerational mobility. Eide and Showalter (1999) estimate several quantile regressions using data from the Panel Study of Income Dynamics (PSID); Minicozzi (1997) and Corak and Heisz (1999) present median regression as corroborating evidence of mean regression.

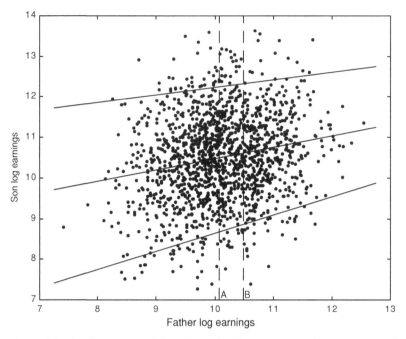

**Figure 4.1** An illustration of the relationship between quantile regression and equality of opportunity: regression in earned income at the 95th quantile compared with regression at the average and at the 5th quantile.

addition, since some readers may prefer to think of opportunity in terms of rank orders, I also report estimates of rank correlation when possible.

## 2 Data and methods

Approximately half of the data sources in this study come from the standard data sets employed in intergenerational mobility studies. In addition, by using Two-Sample Instrumental Variables (TSIV) methods, the investigation will include several countries for which only cross-section data is available. Table 4.1 lists the data sets used in the analysis of the next section. In this section, I will briefly outline the considerations used to determine sample selection rules. A fuller description of the data sets and the exact sample selection criteria is available in Grawe (2001b).

Table 4.1   *Data sources for the analysis of intergenerational earnings mobility*

| Source country | | Data set | Reference period |
|---|---|---|---|
| United States | PSID | Panel Study of Income Dynamics | 1968–93 |
| United States | NLS | National Longitudinal Survey | 1966–81 |
| Canada | IID | Intergenerational Income Data | 1978–98 |
| Germany | GSOEP | German Socio-economic Panel | 1984–98 |
| United Kingdom | NCDS | National Child Development Survey | 1974–91 |
| Malaysia | MFLS | Malaysian Family Life Survey | 1976–89 |
| Ecuador | | World Bank Living Standards Measurement Study* | 1994 |
| Nepal | | World Bank Living Standards Measurement Study* | 1995 |
| Pakistan | | World Bank Living Standards Measurement Study* | 1991 |
| Peru | | World Bank Living Standards Measurement Study* | 1985 |

*Note:* * denotes cross-section data sets.

When conducting cross-country comparisons, care must obviously be taken to ensure that differences caused by sample differences are not mistakenly interpreted as real economic differences. Given the nature of intergenerational data sets, one important sample characteristic is the age of the father and son at the point of measurement. Grawe (2001b) points out that estimates of earnings persistence based on data from mature fathers may naturally be lower than those based on young fathers since earnings variance grows over the life cycle and the importance of transitory earnings has increased in many of the observed countries over time. I will refer to this as a "life-cycle bias."

Figure 4.2, taken from Grawe (2001b), summarizes the magnitude of the problem. The figure plots published estimates of earnings persistence – the elasticity between a child's adult earnings and parental earnings as described, for example, in Chapter 1 – against the mean age of the fathers in each study. Most of the studies employ Least Squares (LS) using multi-year averages of fathers' earnings, but several use Instrumental Variables (IV). The two lines represent the relationship between fathers' average age and estimated earnings persistence according to

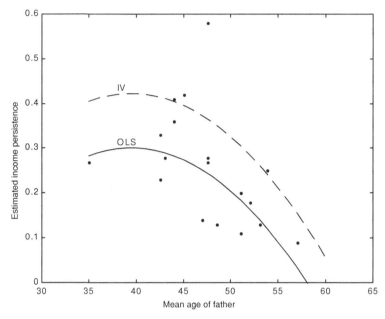

**Figure 4.2** Sensitivity of published estimates of intergenerational earnings elasticities to life-cycle bias.
*Note:* Collected by the author, based on 17 published estimates from 15 studies.

these two methods. As predicted, the estimates of the intergenerational earnings elasticities are negatively related to age. In fact, roughly one-half of the variation in earnings persistence estimates can be attributed to differences in fathers' ages and the method of estimation (IV versus LS). Figure 4.2 points out the dangers of meta-analysis in the comparison of earnings persistence across countries. If estimates are to be compared, the selection criteria must control for the age of the fathers in both data sets. In the following analysis I report only pair-wise comparisons between the United States and other countries since the available data sets do not permit the same age in every country to be chosen. In addition to controlling for the age of fathers and sons, I also control for the calendar year of observation in order to minimize the effects of business-cycle fluctuations.

A second obvious concern is that of measurement error. Since collection methods differ across data sources, it is likely that the magnitude of measurement error also differs. Proceeding with no correction and hoping that biases are similar across countries is insufficient. Following Solon (1992) and Zimmerman (1992), I use time averages of fathers' and sons' earnings when possible. Unfortunately, only one year of earnings observation is available in the United Kingdom's National Child Development Survey (NCDS) and the Malaysian Family Life Survey (MFLS). An alternative correction is required in these cases. IV corrections of mean regression for measurement error are well studied, and I use this approach to instrument fathers' earnings with fathers' education. But the problem of measurement error in quantile regression is, at this point in time, unsolved (Buchinsky 1998). I propose a maximum likelihood-based correction of quantile regressions, a detailed description of which is included in Grawe (2001b). The strategy I employ exploits the fact that quantile regression slopes differ from mean regression slopes only insofar as the data are heteroskedastic. I first estimate the mean regression coefficient, and then in a second stage estimate (using maximum likelihood) the variance about the regression line as a function of parent earnings:

$$\sigma(y_f) = a + by_f. \tag{4.3}$$

Finally, the mean regression coefficient and the variance coefficients are combined to form estimates of the quantile regression slopes. Standard errors are estimated with bootstrapping.

While quantile regression analysis of already explored data is an interesting contribution to the existing literature, perhaps even more interest lies in estimates of mobility from countries that have yet to be studied. The collection of intergenerational panel data is costly and time consuming. It is understandable that progress in expanding the number of countries researchers have examined is slow if the analysis requires direct observation of fathers' and sons' adult earnings over long periods of time. However, Björklund and Jäntti (1997) suggest a path around this problem: Two-Sample Instrumental Variables (TSIV) techniques. Intuitively, TSIV is identical to the more commonly used (single-sample) IV estimator. To examine the effect on $y$ of a marginal change in $x$, one might examine directly the relationship between the two variables. Alternatively, one might find a third variable $z$ which directly affects $x$, but does not directly affect $y$. Then a comparison of covariance$(y,z)$ and covariance$(x,z)$ yields the effect of $x$ on $y$. In this description of instrumental variables estimation there is no mention of whether $x$ and $y$ are taken from the same data set. While we often do observe both $x$ and $y$ together, covariance$(y,z)$ and covariance$(x,z)$ can be estimated in two different samples so long as $z$ is in both. For a fuller description, two-sample estimation is discussed in Angrist and Krueger (1992) and Arellano and Meghir (1992). Björklund and Jäntti (1997) apply TSIV to repeated cross-section data in Sweden and the US. This is a significant step forward since repeated cross-sections are far less expensive than panel data to collect. In many countries, however, only a single cross-section exists. I propose to divide single cross-sections into two samples based on the age of the respondent in order to form two cross-sectional data sets, one with "fathers" and one with "sons." After briefly describing the data, I will discuss several of the limitations of this approach and what biases will likely result.

The World Bank has initiated Living Standards Measurement Surveys in many developing countries. In four countries – Ecuador, Nepal, Pakistan, and Peru – the data include a report of fathers' education, the instrument I have chosen. These cross-sectional data sets were collected in 1994, 1995, 1991, and 1985 respectively. I create two samples for each country from the available data. In Sample I, the respondent's earnings, age, and the highest level of education attained by the respondent's father ($ed_f$) are recorded for respondents between the ages of twenty-four and forty. These are the "sons" in the analysis. In Sample II, observations of the respondent's earnings, age, and self-reported education are recorded for respondents between the ages of forty-five and sixty. Men of this age are of the same generation as the fathers of the Sample I men. To be clear, these are not the actual fathers, but rather representative members of the population belonging roughly to the same age cohorts as the actual fathers.

Consistent with all of the analysis in this chapter, log earnings in both samples are initially regressed on the respondent's age and age-squared to adjust for the mean-age effects. All subsequent analysis is performed on the residuals of these first-stage regressions. The first step of TSIV is to estimate the coefficients from a regression of log earnings on own education using the Sample II observations (those representing the fathers). With these estimates in hand, estimates of fathers' log earnings can be constructed in Sample I using $ed_f$ as a predictor, which I refer to as $\hat{y}_{fI}$. In Sample II, the predicted fathers' earnings, $\hat{y}_{fII}$, are also estimated. If the Sample I respondents' log earnings are denoted $y_s$, then

$$\hat{\beta}_{TSIV} = \frac{\operatorname{cov}(y_s, \hat{y}_{fI})}{\operatorname{var}(\hat{y}_{fII})}. \tag{4.4}$$

Several concerns about TSIV should be addressed. First, the life cycle bias identified above suggests estimates of intergenerational mobility from TSIV, as derived in these samples, will overstate the true rate of earnings mobility since the fathers are of necessity observed late and sons observed early in their life cycles. In other words, estimates of $\beta$ using the World Bank data probably contain a downward bias. A second concern is that over time the covariance of education and fathers' earnings may have changed due to technological change or other shifts in the economy. If the data had come from developed countries, countries in which the returns to skill have in some cases increased substantially, this problem would almost certainly be crippling. Its effect on the World Bank data is less clear. It should be noted, however, that increases in the returns to education among the fathers in the last twenty years would produce a downward bias in the TSIV estimate since the estimated covariance between fathers' education and own earnings would be larger than the true value. Once more, this suggests that my TSIV estimates should be viewed as lower bounds. Finally, the two-sample method requires a valid instrument. Results in Grawe (2001b) and Lillard and Kilburn (1995) are inconsistent with the assumption that fathers' education is exogenous and so IV estimates include a positive bias. This offsets some of the bias introduced by the previous two concerns. In total, it is not clear whether the bias will be positive or negative. However, the magnitudes of the life cycle and endogeneity biases found in Grawe (2001b) are roughly equal in the PSID data, suggesting that the results of the two-sample approach may be fairly close to the true slopes.

With the TSIV estimate of the persistence parameter in hand, it is possible to estimate the quantile regression slopes using the method described above. However, the fact that no OLS estimate of $\beta$ is available raises one additional complication: an estimate of (earnings) measurement error variance is no longer directly available since no signal-to-noise ratio can be estimated. The model is under-identified without this information. A simple solution is available since any consistent estimate of the variance of measurement error in the earnings variable can be used. I estimate the effect of log earnings on housing consumption using both LS and IV. The signal-to-noise ratio is then estimated from this set of regressions. All standard errors are estimated using bootstrapping.

## 3 Results

I begin the analysis by studying mobility in the United States. These initial results establish a base line using the "best" sample selection rules possible without regard for data limitations created when trying to match sample characteristics across countries. The remainder of this section reports comparisons of mobility between the United States and other countries with careful attention paid to holding sample selection criteria constant. Throughout, I report linear regression results; Grawe (2001b) explores non-linear regression.

### (a) The United States

The principal data used to estimate intergenerational earnings mobility in the United States have been the Panel Study of Income Dynamics (PSID) and the Original Cohort National Longitudinal Survey (NLS). The advantages of the PSID are both its breadth and its length. With observations in each year from 1968 to 1993, it is possible to compare the US to almost any other country, year for year, matching each selection rule. But the small sample size of the PSID suggests that including an analysis of the NLS data is profitable.

Table 4.2 reports estimates of earnings persistence in the PSID and NLS. A linear log-log relationship of the sort presented in equation (1.1) is assumed so that these estimates represent elasticities, the percentage change in a child's adult earnings for each percentage change in parental earnings. In this, and all subsequent tables, "average" refers to the least squares regression coefficient, "median" refers to median regression, and quantile regression results at various quantiles are referred to as the "$n^{th}$ quantile." In the PSID, fathers' real earnings are observed from 1967 to 1971, and an observation is included in the analysis if positive earnings are reported in at least three of these five years. Sons' real earnings are observed from 1990 to 1993, and positive earnings are required in three of the four years. In the NLS, fathers' real earnings are observed in 1965, 1966, 1968, and 1970 while the sons' are observed in 1978, 1980, and 1981. Once again, three years of positive earnings are required for inclusion in the sample. Finally the analysis also restricts the age of sons to those under the age of nineteen in 1966 in order to avoid over-sampling sons who live with parents after high school. Solon (1992) discusses the bias resulting from such over-sampling.

Table 4.2  *Estimates of the intergenerational earnings elasticity between fathers and sons: United States*

|  | National Longitudinal Survey | | Panel Study of Income Dynamics | |
|---|---|---|---|---|
|  | Coefficient estimate | Standard error | Coefficient estimate | Standard error |
| Average | 0.154 | 0.045 | 0.473 | 0.062 |
| 10th quantile | 0.275 | 0.130 | 0.355 | 0.169 |
| 25th quantile | 0.248 | 0.080 | 0.494 | 0.099 |
| Median | 0.261 | 0.030 | 0.535 | 0.068 |
| 75th quantile | 0.157 | 0.051 | 0.457 | 0.079 |
| 90th quantile | 0.005 | 0.052 | 0.396 | 0.219 |
| Rank correlation | 0.335 | 0.062 | 0.423 | 0.054 |
| Sample size | 233 | | 354 | |

*Note:* Average refers to Least Squares regression results. All other results are from quantile estimation. Standard errors are calculated using the method of Koenker and Bassett (1978). Rank correlation refers to the correlation between the rank of the father within the father earnings distribution and the rank of the son within the son earnings distribution.

The first notable result is that the NLS produces much lower estimates of earnings persistence than the PSID. This may be surprising to those familiar with the results of Solon (1992) and Zimmerman (1992). In both studies earnings persistence estimates hover near 0.45. My NLS estimates, and for that matter those of Altonji and Dunn (1991), are roughly half those of Zimmerman because he restricts his sample to fully employed fathers and sons, where full employment is defined as working thirty weeks per year, thirty hours per week. Consistent with many other studies, Zimmerman's restriction to highly attached workers increases the persistence estimate. Almost half of the difference between the two data sources can be attributed to differences in the age of the fathers within the samples since the average age of fathers in the PSID (40.2) and NLS (50.2) differ by a decade. (On average, the PSID sons are seven years older than NLS sons, but this is not likely to make a difference given the stability of persistence estimates at this point in the life cycle.) Nevertheless, life-cycle differences cannot explain the whole gap between the two samples; the PSID sample exhibits substantially less earnings mobility than the NLS sample.

The quantile regression results reveal a clear pattern in the NLS data. Earnings persistence is far weaker among exceptionally high-earning sons than among exceptionally low-earning sons. This is similar to the results found in Eide and Showalter (1999) who study the PSID; however, this is not confirmed in Table 4.2. In total, the results from the NLS and PSID conflict concerning both the rate and pattern of intergenerational mobility. Grawe (2001b) shows that differences in the pattern of quantile regression are reduced when non-linearities are allowed; in both samples lower quantiles are roughly linear while the upper quantiles are convex.

## (b) Canada

As many of the studies in Card and Freeman (1993) suggest, Canadian labor markets share much in common with those in the United States, but there are also important differences. In some respects social policy in Canada has more in common with many European countries than it does with the United States. Historically, Canada has provided unemployment benefits for longer durations with less stringent eligibility requirements. In addition, child benefits are distributed more widely and more generously than in the United States. Finally, while labor union participation has fallen in the United States, it has remained high in Canada. Card and Freeman (1993) offer a lengthy discussion of the social policy and labor market differences between the two countries during the time that the children who are the basis for my analysis were growing up. It may well be that these differences lead to different rates of intergenerational mobility in Canada and the United States.

The data from Canada are taken from the Intergenerational Income Data (IID) developed by Statistics Canada from Canadian income-tax files. A more detailed description of the nature and organization of these data is found in Corak and Heisz (1999). I average over five years the earnings of fathers and sons who are observed in 1978–82 and 1994–98 respectively. Table 4.3 presents regression estimates of the intergenerational earnings elasticity derived from the IID, NLS, and PSID data. While the NLS was collected almost a decade prior to the IID and PSID, the span between father and child observation is very similar across the three sources as is the age of the sons. The comparison to the NLS should be useful unless earnings mobility changed dramatically between the late 1960s and the late 1970s. Some of the results in Chapter 5 suggest that intergenerational earnings persistence decreased during the time period covered by the PSID, so the NLS estimates might be upward biased relative to the IID and PSID.

The results in Table 4.3 suggest that intergenerational earnings mobility is very swift in Canada, faster even than that implied by the summary 0.2 figure cited in the early mobility literature (Becker and Tomes 1986). In addition, the rate of regression among high-achieving sons is even faster. The share of parental advantage passed on to children at the 90th or 95th percentile is less than 10 percent. Like the NLS, the percentage difference in the child's adult earnings for each percentage change in parental earnings is higher among low-achieving sons.

The comparison between the United States and Canada is rather difficult to summarize since the patterns in the PSID and the NLS are entirely at odds. The NLS results are nearly equal to those from the IID, but the PSID results show the US to be far less mobile. In the NLS data the slowest mobility rates are found at the bottom of the joint distribution; the PSID data point to immobility in the highest quantiles. There is some concern about the accuracy of the PSID releases before they are finally cleaned (affecting 1993–96 data). If I exclude the preliminary release data the panel after 1978 is very short. I have repeated the analysis using only the 1993 incomes for sons and found results that were, by and large, very similar to those found using the 1994–96 data. But notably, like the IID and the NLS, the lower quantile regressions become steeper than the upper quantile regressions. In short, nothing conclusive can be offered by way of a comparison of linear intergenerational earnings mobility between these two countries without at the same time taking a stance on which data from the United States are the most appropriate.

## (c) Germany and the United Kingdom

The stereotypical view of the differences between Europe and North America suggests that years of monarchy in many European countries form the foundation of societies in which title and pedigree matter far beyond the impacts of natural ability. Rigid social classes restrict

**Table 4.3** *Estimates of the intergenerational earnings elasticity between fathers and sons: United States and Canada*

| | United States | | | | Canada | |
| --- | --- | --- | --- | --- | --- | --- |
| | National Longitudinal Survey | | Panel Study of Income Dynamics | | | |
| | Coefficient estimate | Standard error | Coefficient estimate | Standard error | Coefficient estimate | Standard error |
| Average | 0.196 | 0.046 | 0.381 | 0.090 | 0.152 | 0.004 |
| 10th quantile | 0.300 | 0.310 | 0.151 | 0.539 | 0.261 | 0.017 |
| 25th quantile | 0.324 | 0.149 | −0.021 | 0.236 | 0.256 | 0.011 |
| Median | 0.258 | 0.070 | 0.219 | 0.088 | 0.211 | 0.007 |
| 75th quantile | 0.264 | 0.036 | 0.409 | 0.107 | 0.157 | 0.004 |
| 90th quantile | 0.152 | 0.048 | 0.502 | 0.100 | 0.110 | 0.004 |
| Rank correlation | 0.031 | 0.092 | 0.363 | 0.199 | 0.086 | 0.005 |
| Sample size | 267 | | 161 | | 47,115 | |

*Note:* Average refers to Least Squares regression results. All other results are from quantile estimation. Standard errors are calculated using the method of Koenker and Bassett (1982). Rank correlation refers to the correlation between the rank of the father within the father earnings distribution and the rank of the son within the son earnings distribution.

Table 4.4 *Estimates of the intergenerational earnings elasticity between fathers and sons: United States and Germany*

| | United States | | | | Germany | |
| | National Longitudinal Survey | | Panel Study of Income Dynamics | | | |
| | Coefficient estimate | Standard error | Coefficient estimate | Standard error | Coefficient estimate | Standard error |
|---|---|---|---|---|---|---|
| Average | 0.188 | 0.048 | 0.140 | 0.080 | 0.095 | 0.101 |
| 10th quantile | 0.346 | 0.170 | 0.333 | 0.402 | −0.280 | 0.550 |
| 25th quantile | 0.198 | 0.070 | 0.238 | 0.112 | −0.042 | 0.086 |
| Median | 0.211 | 0.033 | 0.158 | 0.064 | 0.065 | 0.079 |
| 75th quantile | 0.165 | 0.043 | 0.223 | 0.121 | 0.171 | 0.094 |
| 90th quantile | 0.131 | 0.060 | 0.280 | 0.167 | 0.313 | 0.159 |
| Rank correlation | 0.335 | 0.062 | 0.249 | 0.070 | 0.105 | 0.084 |
| Sample size | 350 | | 177 | | 142 | |

*Note:* Germany refers to West Germany. Average refers to Least Squares regression results. All other results are from quantile estimation. Standard errors are calculated using the method of Koenker and Bassett (1982). Rank correlation refers to the correlation between the rank of the father within the father earnings distribution and the rank of the son within the son earnings distribution.

the educational choices of the younger generation, effectively passing status from one generation to the next. Reality is obviously more complicated than this view suggests, but, even so, comparisons between North America and Europe are certainly apt. The two European countries with readily available data are Germany and the United Kingdom, but high quality data have also been collected in the Nordic countries. The latter are examined in Chapter 9. Because data are available and because these countries offer contrasting models upon which to base a comparison with the United States, I focus on Germany and the United Kingdom. For instance, the United Kingdom holds firm to a symbolic monarchy. If the prejudice of class or status is maintained by any country, it might be suspected in a country that still recognizes transfer of title through birth. And in Germany, as discussed in Jenkins and Schlute (2002), a highly tracked educational system "locks" children into an educational path long before the end of high school. This may diminish the relationship between innate ability and educational attainment and increase the correlation in education across generations.

The analysis uses the German Socio-Economic Panel (GSOEP) Cross-National Equivalent File and the National Child Development Survey (NCDS). The GSOEP is modelled after the PSID and began in 1984 as a representative sample of the Federal Republic of Germany (West Germany). East Germans were added to the sample when Germany was united in 1990. My analysis uses only households in the original West German sample. I define fathers' earnings in the GSOEP as the average (positive) earnings reported from 1984 to 1988; sons' earnings are defined as the average (positive) earnings observed from 1995 to 1998. Unlike the other samples, I do not restrict the sons to be younger than age eighteen in the year they are matched to their fathers. Adding this restriction results in samples too small to be of practical use. Table 4.4 reports the coefficient estimates in the three samples. The results suggest a good deal of intergenerational mobility in the GSOEP data. This might simply reflect the fact that the GSOEP is a very short panel and requires the fathers to be relatively older (the average age is 47.5 years). The sample size is also relatively small, making precise estimation difficult. The estimates of intergenerational mobility at all quantiles cannot be statistically distinguished from zero. But the point estimates suggest less mobility among exceptional sons than among sons at or below the mean.

The rate of intergenerational mobility for the average appears similar in the GSOEP and the US data sets. This is consistent with the findings in Couch and Dunn (1997); the slight difference that does exist cannot be differentiated statistically. But this similarity masks differences in the regression pattern across quantiles. Once again, the NLS shows a neat pattern with more mobility among high-achieving sons – exactly the opposite pattern found in the GSOEP – while the PSID shows no difference across quantiles. Unfortunately, the small sample sizes make it difficult to distinguish between even large variations in point estimates.

The United Kingdom data are drawn from all children born during the second week of March, 1958. The NCDS includes five follow-up surveys of these children, including one during adolescence and two during adulthood. Since those captured by the NCDS are only twenty-three years old at the point of their first adult observation, I only use the second earnings observation in 1991 when they are thirty-three years old. When earnings at twenty-three years are averaged with those at thirty-three years the estimates of intergenerational mobility are much higher. This is almost certainly due to the fact that earnings at age twenty-three are a particularly poor measure of permanent status. For instance, Björklund (1993), finds that the correlation between annual and permanent earnings in Sweden is roughly 0.1 when individuals are studied in their early twenties, compared to around 0.8 after age thirty-five.

The data from the United States are again taken from the NLS and PSID, but it should be noted that it is not possible with the NLS (as it is with the PSID) to match year for year the observation years in the NCDS. I use 1965 (rather than 1969) to observe fathers and 1981 (rather than 1991) to observe sons. I have selected the samples such that the ages of fathers and sons are similar across samples. The results are presented in Table 4.5. Consistent with Dearden, Machin, and Reed (1997), intergenerational mobility appears to be very low in the United Kingdom when IV estimates are used (the IV estimate being more than double the LS estimate). In the United States, the IV results mirror those found in Altonji and Dunn (1991) and Solon (1992). By comparison, average mobility in the United States appears to be far greater than in the United Kingdom when the NLS is used, but little difference can be found if the PSID data are used. Despite this conflict between the two data sources at the mean, there is no difference in the results

Table 4.5 *Estimates of the intergenerational earnings elasticity between fathers and sons: United States and the United Kingdom*

|  | United States | | | | United Kingdom | |
|  | National Longitudinal Survey | | Panel Study of Income Dynamics | | | |
|  | Coefficient estimate | Standard error | Coefficient estimate | Standard error | Coefficient estimate | Standard error |
| --- | --- | --- | --- | --- | --- | --- |
| 10th quantile | 0.587 | 0.258 | 0.937 | 0.247 | 0.344 | 0.197 |
| 25th quantile | 0.428 | 0.181 | 0.753 | 0.199 | 0.455 | 0.125 |
| Median/average | 0.251 | 0.104 | 0.549 | 0.165 | 0.579 | 0.069 |
| 75th quantile | 0.075 | 0.076 | 0.344 | 0.165 | 0.703 | 0.099 |
| 90th quantile | −0.084 | 0.126 | 0.160 | 0.194 | 0.814 | 0.167 |
| Sample size | 350 | | 267 | | 1,945 | |

*Note:* All results are from Two-Sample Instrumental Variables quantile estimation. Standard errors are calculated by bootstrapping using 50 replications.

in the upper and lower quantile regressions. Opportunities to rise to the top in the United States are far more equal across earnings groups than in the United Kingdom in both the NLS and the PSID. In fact, there is more persistence in the United Kingdom at the top of the distribution than at the bottom. Depending upon the reader's point of view, this is either very disturbing or very encouraging for advocates of equal opportunity. It means that while the outcomes of exceptionally able children are not very dependent (if at all) on parental earnings in the United States, there is a very strong dependence in the United Kingdom. This seems to suggest an important limitation on the capacity of low-earning families to rise to the top. However, the faster rate of mobility in the United Kingdom among under-achieving children suggests a more agreeable picture. Those with low earnings benefit from a high social safety net so that their children fare little worse than low-earning children born to families with greater financial resources.

## (d) Malaysia

Longitudinal information for the analysis of intergenerational mobility is hard to come by, and to the best of my knowledge there is only one source available for an Asian country. The Malaysian Family Life Survey (MFLS) was collected by the RAND Corporation in 1976–77 and 1988–89, and includes earnings data for fathers and sons. Unfortunately, the sample of almost 1,300 households includes only one contemporaneous measure of fathers' earnings. The survey does ask the fathers to fill out a work history that includes a recall of past earnings, but it is unlikely that these data truly constitute independent earnings observations with independent measurement errors. Consequently, I choose to use only the contemporaneous earnings measure. As in the case of the United Kingdom, I will present estimates using IV corrections for the mean regression; quantiles are corrected following the method described in the previous section.

The NLS data are again unavailable in the particular years observed in the MFLS. I choose to observe fathers in 1965 and sons in 1978 to approximate the time gap between observations in the MFLS. Sample selection based on age mitigates life-cycle bias concerns. The results are presented in Table 4.6. Using the Malaysian sample selection rules, the NLS suggests complete intergenerational mobility in the United States. The results from the PSID at the mean are comparable to those

**Table 4.6** *Estimates of the intergenerational earnings elasticity between fathers and sons: United States and Malaysia*

| | United States | | | | Malaysia | |
| | National Longitudinal Survey | | Panel Study of Income Dynamics | | | |
| | Coefficient estimate | Standard error | Coefficient estimate | Standard error | Coefficient estimate | Standard error |
|---|---|---|---|---|---|---|
| 10th quantile | −0.055 | 0.291 | 0.439 | 0.171 | 0.791 | 0.356 |
| 25th quantile | −0.042 | 0.216 | 0.395 | 0.133 | 0.671 | 0.282 |
| Median/average | −0.028 | 0.141 | 0.345 | 0.098 | 0.537 | 0.215 |
| 75th quantile | −0.013 | 0.094 | 0.296 | 0.083 | 0.404 | 0.177 |
| 90th quantile | 0.000 | 0.112 | 0.212 | 0.094 | 0.283 | 0.187 |
| Sample size | 326 | | 198 | | 153 | |

*Note:* All results are from Two-Sample Instrumental Variables quantile estimation. Standard errors are calculated by bootstrapping using 50 replications.

previously reported and mobility is greater for exceptionally high-earning children. The Malaysian IV estimates exhibit substantially more persistence, but the standard errors are large. By comparison, the median/average slope coefficient of 0.537 reported in Table 4.6 is roughly twice that found by Lillard and Kilburn (1985), but it should be noted that their analysis is based on the retrospective earnings history and does not use the IV approach. The authors justify their choice not to employ IV methods by noting that fathers' education is likely an endogenous variable, but to prefer a method based on retrospective earnings reports requires an assumption that recall produces a less error-ridden measure of earnings than the available single-year measure. I am not convinced that this is the case since the retrospective data are likely to be influenced by current earnings. If the estimates reported by Lillard and Kilburn (1985) are correct, then the signal-to-noise ratio in the single-year earnings measure must be 0.75. By comparison, the results in Solon (1992) suggest a signal-to-noise ratio of 0.78 in the PSID. I am not sure I believe that data collected in a country with a substantial agrarian component could be so accurate, but acknowledge that the IV estimates probably overstate the degree of persistence in earnings. In sum, I believe that the IV estimates are more or less equally biased in Malaysia and the US.

In spite of the fact that the sample sizes in this exercise are small (and hence the standard errors large), several items are worth noting. When an instrumental variable is used to correct for measurement error correction, Malaysia appears to be less mobile than the United States. In addition, intergenerational mobility is especially slow in the lower quantile regressions. This pattern of greater mobility at the top of the joint distribution is qualitatively similar to the results reported between the United States and Canada.

## (e) First evidence from other countries

In this section, I use Two-Sample IV techniques to overcome data limitations and produce mobility estimates in Ecuador, Nepal, Pakistan, and Peru using World Bank Living Standards Measurement Study data. Not surprisingly, we lack ideal data sources for the study of intergenerational mobility in developing countries, and in the surveys that are available earned income is difficult to define. In particular, many workers are self-employed farmers or small-business owners. This raises the likelihood that labor and asset income will be combined. In the World Bank surveys of Ecuador and Peru all respondents are asked to identify total wage income, but in the surveys of Nepal and Pakistan small-business owners and farmers are not asked this question. In these surveys, profits from the family business or farm are calculated and added to earnings.

The estimated slopes for mean and quantile regressions in the four countries using the available income definitions are reported in Table 4.7. The first sample size indicated in the table refers to the number of observations in the sons' sample, the second to the number of observations in the fathers' sample. Earnings persistence in Ecuador and Peru are substantially higher than estimates from developed countries. The results from Nepal and Pakistan are not much different than those reported in North America and Europe, but it is important to keep in mind that life-cycle bias and skill-biased technical change both suggest the coefficients are lower-bound estimates. Across quantiles, the pattern in Nepal and Peru is similar to previous results with upper quantiles exhibiting faster intergenerational mobility. But in Ecuador and Pakistan, mobility is faster at the bottom of the joint distribution (though the standard errors are large).

One possible explanation for the generally higher estimates of persistence is that the inclusion of capital income in earnings reports artificially inflates intergenerational correlations. This explanation, however, does not fit the data. First, the questionnaire in the Ecuadorian and Peruvian surveys specifically requests only labor income, and these are the countries with the least mobility. Admittedly, respondents may not be able to easily distinguish labor and capital income in some cases. But in both Pakistan and Nepal, wage income and self-employment income are recorded separately. Table 4.8 shows that restricting the data set to only utilize wage income (excluding business and farm income) results in higher estimates of earnings persistence in both cases.

The construction of the IV estimator reminds us that high earnings persistence can result either from strong relationships between child earnings and parent characteristics or from low association between parent characteristics and parent earnings. In the case of my estimates, the relevant parent characteristic is the father's education. And among labor economists it is generally accepted that returns to education vary little across countries. Psacharopoulos (1985, Table 3) confirms this stylized fact, summarizing existing estimates of education returns as

Table 4.7 *Estimates of the intergenerational earnings elasticity between fathers and sons: selected developing countries*

| | Ecuador | | Nepal | | Pakistan | | Peru | |
|---|---|---|---|---|---|---|---|---|
| | Coefficient estimate | Standard error | Coefficient estimate | Standard error | Coefficient estimate | Standard error | Coefficient estimate | Standard error |
| 10th quantile | 1.062 | 0.270 | 0.653 | 0.527 | −0.204 | 0.447 | 0.923 | 0.226 |
| 25th quantile | 1.096 | 0.268 | 0.498 | 0.355 | 0.005 | 0.346 | 0.802 | 0.194 |
| Median/average | 1.134 | 0.294 | 0.324 | 0.197 | 0.236 | 0.301 | 0.667 | 0.172 |
| 75th quantile | 1.172 | 0.316 | 0.153 | 0.197 | 0.467 | 0.355 | 0.532 | 0.172 |
| 90th quantile | 1.207 | 0.355 | −0.003 | 0.336 | 0.675 | 0.461 | 0.411 | 0.191 |
| Sample size – sons | 1,461 | | 229 | | 171 | | 98 | |
| Sample size – fathers | 685 | | 239 | | 441 | | 166 | |

*Note:* All results are based on Two-Sample Instrumental Variables. Sample sizes for each stage of the analysis are indicated separately for sons and fathers. Quantile estimation is used throughout. Standard errors are calculated by bootstrapping using 50 replications.

Table 4.8  *Estimates of the intergenerational earnings elasticity between fathers and sons (excluding business and farm income): Nepal and Pakistan*

|  | Nepal | | Pakistan | |
|---|---|---|---|---|
|  | Coefficient estimate | Standard error | Coefficient estimate | Standard error |
| 10<sup>th</sup> quantile | 0.539 | 0.320 | 0.773 | 0.244 |
| 25<sup>th</sup> quantile | 0.490 | 0.252 | 0.626 | 0.172 |
| Median/ average | 0.436 | 0.193 | 0.463 | 0.121 |
| 75<sup>th</sup> quantile | 0.381 | 0.171 | 0.300 | 0.134 |
| 90<sup>th</sup> quantile | 0.333 | 0.194 | 0.153 | 0.195 |
| Sample size – sons | 116 | | 98 | |
| Sample size – fathers | 104 | | 199 | |

*Note:* All results are based on Two-Sample Instrumental Variables. Sample sizes for each stage of the analysis are indicated separately for sons and fathers. Quantile estimation is used throughout. Standard errors are calculated by bootstrapping using 50 replications.

Table 4.9  *Estimates of the return to education in the father generation*

|  | Ecuador | Nepal | Pakistan | Peru | NLS |
|---|---|---|---|---|---|
| Return to education | 0.123 (0.009) | 0.130 (0.018) | 0.129 (0.043) | 0.153 (0.026) | 0.089 (0.010) |
| Correlation | 0.432 | 0.417 | 0.261 | 0.413 | 0.516 |

*Note:* Sample sizes for each regression are the same as those in Sample II in previous tables. Standard errors are in parentheses.

just under 10 percent per year of education in advanced economies; estimates of the return to education in developing nations lie between 11 and 14 percent per year. So it is not surprising that, as Table 4.9 shows, the relationship between education and earnings among fathers in Ecuador, Nepal, Pakistan, and Peru is slightly greater than that in the United States (on the basis of the NLS). This, in turn, means that the exceptionally persistent nature of earnings in Ecuador and Peru is due to a strong correlation between a child's earnings and his father's education.

## 4 Interpretations and conclusions

As important as Least Squares regression is to the study of intergenerational mobility, there are at least two reasons to begin to study mobility at points other than the average: welfare economists like Roemer conceive of equal opportunity in a manner more consistent with a quantile regression and many economic models generate predictions that apply only to above- or below-average children. This paper operationalizes the idea of mobility among "exceptional" children in countries for which data are available by studying quantile regression in addition to average regression. The results both corroborate and expand upon the findings in the existing literature.

First, caution is needed in making comparisons of cross-country differences in the average degree of intergenerational mobility. There is a certain ambiguity to the findings even when careful attention is paid to sample selection rules and to measurement issues associated with life-cycle and transitory variations in income. These are the result of often conflicting estimates derived from the two sources of data used for the United States. To the extent that comparisons can be made, it looks as though Canada may on average be more mobile than the United Kingdom and Germany. Further, if the Panel Study of Income Dynamics data are representative, then Germany and Canada exhibit more mobility than the United States and the United Kingdom.

Second, the examination of exceptional mobility adds important insights to the discussion. The United States and Canada exhibit less earnings persistence in upper quantiles than in lower quantiles. This is notably not the case in Germany and the United Kingdom. So whatever the differences on average, above-average North American children (conditional on parent earnings) experience more mobility than their European counterparts while below-average North American children experience less mobility. However, once again it is difficult to draw firm conclusions due to the lack of consistency in the results from the two surveys used to analyse the United States.

Throughout, sample selection rules also prove to be critical determinants of intergenerational earnings mobility estimates, underscoring the need to carefully apply common criteria to each data set when making international comparisons. But the cost of this care is seen in the sample sizes. In the end, sample sizes are so small and the standard errors are so large in the data from the United States and Germany that it is impossible to reject multiple hypotheses. This problem cannot be directly solved without efforts like those in Canada and the Nordic countries, which produce administrative data for intergenerational analysis. Even if such large data sets were available for something like five or ten different countries, researchers would still be very limited in their ability to understand why one country is more mobile than another. With many possible explanations, five or ten data points are insufficient to draw any firm conclusions, even with a detailed understanding of the institutional setting .

In an effort to begin to address this problem, this chapter provides the first estimates of intergenerational earnings mobility for five developing nations. The results indicate that whatever the differences between developed countries, earnings regression in developing countries may be much slower. In Ecuador it is not even clear that earnings regress to the mean. Perhaps this distinction between the developed and the less developed world is by far more important, and since it is possible to pursue this question with cross-sectional data sets this is a promising area for future research.

Finally, with this information in hand, it is possible to offer some conjectures as to the cause of the lower rates of earnings mobility in developing economies. Clearly, it will be impossible to do much at this point to test these hypotheses since data exist for only a handful of countries, and these ideas represent starting points for future research. First, it may be that credit constraints affect these economies. While industrialized countries invest heavily in education in an effort to mitigate these constraints, constraints may yet exist in countries with less educational support. Alternatively, race or class discrimination may be important. For instance, discrimination against indigenous peoples in Ecuador and Peru is said to be widespread. Unfortunately, the World Bank surveys do not include information on ethnic origins. If future surveys do include this information then intergenerational earnings mobility could be estimated both within and across groups to test this hypothesis. Quantile regressions are important to differentiate the group-discrimination hypothesis from the credit-constraint hypothesis; while group discrimination reduces incomes of all children born to the group, credit market imperfections only affect the most able children since low-ability children do not require much education. Finally, it may be that economic development is itself part of the answer. In agrarian economies, economic status depends in large part on physical characteristics. Perhaps physical characteristics develop passively with little work on the part of the individual. To the extent that characteristics are inheritable, economic status would then tend to be rather persistent. In an industrialized economy, however, intellectual capacity is more dominant. Since thinking skills are largely learned, the intergenerational correlation of market abilities may be lower.

Obviously, it is impossible to make conclusive statements based on a cross-country analysis of nine countries. These results may be unique to this particular sample of economies. Future work expanding existing knowledge to even more countries will be required. Even if panel studies are deemed too costly and statistical agencies cannot make administrative information available, cross-section surveys like the World Bank Living Standards Measurement Studies are a possible source of additional estimates.

## References

Altonji, Joseph G., and Thomas A. Dunn (1991). "Family Incomes and Labor Market Outcomes of Relatives." In Ronald G. Ehrenberg (editor). *Research in Labor Economics*. Vol. 12, pp. 269–310. Greenwich, CT: JAI Press.

Angrist, Joshua D., and Alan B. Krueger (1992). "The Effect of Age at School Entry on Educational Attainment: An Application of Instrumental Variables with Moments from Two Samples." *Journal of the American Statistical Association*. Vol. 87, pp. 328–36.

Arellano, Manuel, and Costas Meghir (1992). "Female Labour Supply and On-the-Job Search: An Empirical Model Estimated Using Complementary Data Sets." *Review of Economic Studies*. Vol. 59, pp. 537–59.

Becker, Gary S., and Nigel Tomes (1979). "An Equilibrium Theory of the Distribution of Income and Intergenerational Mobility." *Journal of Political Economy*. Vol. 87, no. 6, pp. 1153–89.

(1986). "Human Capital and the Rise and Fall of Families." *Journal of Labor Economics*. Vol. 4, no. 3, pp. S1–S39.

Björklund, Anders (1993). "A Comparison between Actual Distributions of Annual and Lifetime Income: Sweden 1951–89." *Review of Income and Wealth*. Vol. 39, pp. 377–86.

Björklund, Anders, and Markus Jäntti (1997). "Intergenerational Income Mobility in Sweden Compared to the United States." *American Economic Review.* Vol. 87, pp. 1009–18.

Blau, Francine D., and Lawrence M. Kahn (1994). "Rising Wage Inequality and the US Gender Gap." *The American Economic Review.* Vol. 84, pp. 23–28.

Buchinsky, Moshe (1998). "Recent Advances in Quantile Regression Models: A Practical Guideline for Empirical Research." *Journal of Human Resources.* Vol. 33, pp. 88–126.

Card, David, and Richard B. Freeman, editors (1993). *Small Differences that Matter: Labor Markets and Income Maintenance in Canada and the United States.* Chicago: University of Chicago Press.

Chadwick, Laura, and Gary R. Solon (2002). "Intergenerational Income Mobility Among Daughters." *American Economic Review.* Vol. 92, pp. 335–44.

Corak, Miles, and Andrew Heisz (1999). "The Intergenerational Earnings and Income Mobility of Canadian Men: Evidence from Longitudinal Income Tax Data." *Journal of Human Resources.* Vol. 34, no. 3, pp. 504–33.

Couch, Kenneth A., and Thomas A. Dunn (1997). "Intergenerational Correlations in Labor Market Status: A Comparison of the United States and Germany." *Journal of Human Resources.* Vol. 32, no. 1, pp. 210–32.

Dearden, Lorraine, Stephen Machin, and Howard Reed (1997). "Intergenerational Mobility in Britain." *Economic Journal.* Vol. 107, no. 1, pp. 47–66.

Eide, Eric R., and Mark H. Showalter (1999). "Factors Affecting the Transmission of Earnings Across Generations: A Quantile Regression Approach." *Journal of Human Resources.* Vol. 34, no. 2, pp. 253–67.

Ginther, Donna K., and Kathy J. Hayes (1999). "Gender Differences in Salary and Promotion in the Humanities." *American Economic Review.* Vol. 89, pp. 397–402.

Grawe, Nathan D. (2001a). "In Search of Intergenerational Credit Constraints Among Canadian Men: Quantile Versus Mean Regression Tests for Binding Credit Constraints." Family and Labour Studies, Analytical Studies Branch Research Paper No. 158. Ottawa: Statistics Canada.

    (2001b). "Intergenerational Mobility in the US and Abroad." Ph.D. dissertation, University of Chicago.

Grawe, Nathan D., and Casey B. Mulligan (2002). "Economic Interpretations of Intergenerational Correlations." *Journal of Economic Perspectives.* Vol. 16, no. 3, pp. 45–58.

Hoffman, Emily P. (1976). "Faculty Salaries: Is There Discrimination by Sex, Race, and Discipline? Additional Evidence." *American Economic Review*. Vol. 66, pp. 196–98.

Jenkins, Stephen P. (1987). "Snapshots Versus Movies: 'Lifecycle Biases' and the Estimation of Intergenerational Earnings Inheritance." *European Economic Review*. Vol. 31, pp. 1149–58.

Jenkins, Stephen P., and Christian Schlute (2002). "The Effect of Family Income During Childhood on Later-Life Attainment: Evidence from Germany." Working Papers of the Institute for Social and Economic Research, paper 2002–20. Colchester: University of Essex.

Koenker, Roger, and Gilbert Bassett Jr. (1978). "Regression Quantiles." *Econometrica*. Vol. 46, pp. 33–50.

(1982). "Robust Tests for Heteroscedasticity Based on Regression Quantiles." *Econometrica*. Vol. 50, pp. 43–61.

Lillard, Lee A., and Rebecca M. Kilburn (1995). "Intergenerational Earnings Links: Sons and Daughters." RAND Working Paper Series, no. 95-17. Santa Monica, CA: RAND Corporation.

Minicozzi, Alexandra L. (1997). "Nonparametric Analysis of Intergenerational Income Mobility." Ph.D. dissertation, University of Wisconsin.

Psacharopoulos, George (1985). "Returns to Education: A Further International Update and Implications." *Journal of Human Resources*. Vol. 20, pp. 583–604.

Reville, Robert T. (1995). "Intertemporal and Life Cycle Variation in Measured Intergenerational Earnings Mobility." RAND Working Paper.

Roemer, John E. (1998). *Equality of Opportunity*. Cambridge, MA.: Harvard University Press.

Solon, Gary (1992). "Intergenerational Income Mobility in the United States." *American Economic Review*. Vol. 82, no. 3, pp. 393–408.

Zimmerman, David J. (1992). "Regression Toward Mediocrity in Economic Stature." *American Economic Review*. Vol. 82, no. 3, pp. 409–29.

# 5 | *What do trends in the intergenerational economic mobility of sons and daughters in the United States mean?*

SUSAN E. MAYER AND
LEONARD M. LOPOO

THE extent to which economic status is transmitted from one generation to the next has interested social scientists and policy makers because of the belief that the intergenerational transmission of economic status violates norms of equal opportunity. But, as this chapter shows, parents' and children's economic status can be correlated for many reasons, some of which may not violate norms of equal opportunity. In fact, some social changes that ostensibly promote equality of opportunity may raise the intergenerational correlation.

Economists usually estimate intergenerational economic mobility by estimating the percentage increase in a child's income for each percentage point increase in parents' income. Formally, the relationship between parents' economic status $(Y_p)$ and a child's $(Y_c)$ economic status (in adulthood) is estimated as:

$$ln Y_c = \alpha + \beta \, ln Y_p + \varepsilon_c. \tag{5.1}$$

In this equation, $\beta$ is the elasticity of children's income with respect to parents' income. As discussed in Chapter 2, the economic model underlying this estimate is a human capital model in which a child's economic status is a function of parental endowments and monetary investments. Endowments include characteristics, such as IQ and eye color, influenced by biology and genes. Monetary investments are goods and services that help children succeed, such as nutritious meals, schooling,

We wish to thank Miles Corak, Thomas DeLeire, Angela Fertig, Christopher Jencks, Helen Levy, and participants in seminars at the University of Chicago and Harvard University as well as participants at the workshop sponsored by Statistics Canada in Ottawa in February 2001 for helpful comments and suggestions.

and health care. According to this model, affluent parents can afford to invest more in their children. As a result, their children are more likely than children of low-income parents to become affluent once they are adults. Psychologists and sociologists usually emphasize a third mechanism to explain the relationship between parents' and children's economic status, namely non-monetary benefits such as good parenting, high expectations, and emotional support. Becker and Tomes (1979) allude to these factors when they make reference to "family culture." Poor parents might provide inferior non-monetary benefits to their children if low income increases stress or makes it harder to obtain information about the importance of non-monetary inputs. In this context it should also be noted that both the monetary and non-monetary investments parents make in their children and their pay-off may differ for sons and daughters because of traditional gender roles. If traditional gender roles have become less binding over time then the trends in the influence of parental income may also differ for sons and daughters.

Both the human capital and family culture models are central to the claim that the intergenerational correlation of income is an indicator of equality of opportunity since in both cases children's own earnings ability is at least partly the result of factors beyond their control, namely their parents' income. If rich parents can buy a better education for their children but rich and poor children benefit equally from better schooling, the fact that rich children get better schooling violates norms of equal opportunity. Similarly, many people would consider it unfair if poor parents are worse parents because of the stress of low income and if their children do worse because of it. A correlation between parents' and children's income could also violate norms of equal opportunity even if it has nothing to do with investment and everything to do with endowments. Endowments include characteristics such as height, attractiveness, IQ, skin color and perhaps temperament, all of which are affected by genes. Some of these factors affect skill levels, and differences in children's income based on such factors may sometimes be acceptable. But income differences based on endowments that are unrelated to skill or productivity may violate norms of equal opportunity. Chapter 3 and Jencks (1988) attempt to clarify the confusion over the definition of equal opportunity. The correlation between parents' and children's income could also be due to parents and children making the same choices. For example, if both parents and children choose to live in rural areas with low wages rather than urban areas with higher wages, their wages will be correlated but few would claim that this indicates unequal opportunity. Thus the causes of the correlation in parents' and children's income may derive from sources that do not imply injustice or unfairness.

This chapter focuses on changes over time in economic mobility. Economic mobility can change for many reasons, only some of which may reflect changes in opportunity. Given the human capital model, and assuming that over fairly short periods of time the genetic transmission of characteristics does not change, intergenerational mobility can change for at least three reasons: (1) changes in the relative investments in rich and poor children; (2) changes in the payoff to the investments; or (3) changes in the returns to genetic or biologically transmitted characteristics. When inequality increases as it has in most rich democracies over the last two decades, we might expect an increase in the inequality of investments that rich and poor parents can make in their children, and hence a decline in intergenerational mobility. However, parents are not the only source of investment in children. As Chapter 2 formally shows, if governments make significant investments in children, the correlation between parents' and children's income is likely to decline. Federal and state government expenditures on behalf of children have increased greatly over the past thirty years in the United States. Means-tested programs such as Medicaid, food stamps, the Special Supplemental Nutrition Program for Women, Infants, and Children (WIC), Head Start, and Pell Grants for college expenses were designed to increase investment in the health, nutrition, and knowledge of poor children. Between 1970 and 1992 real spending on Head Start doubled. Since it was implemented in 1977, the number of people served by the WIC has increased from 0.8 to 7.2 million and expenditures have increased from $668 million to $3.7 billion in constant 1996 dollars (United States House of Representatives 1996). The School Lunch and School Breakfast programs have experienced similar growth. In 1995 the federal government spent over $2,000 for every child under the age of eighteen in the United States, most of it targeted at low-income children (United States House of Representatives 1993, p. 1,567).

Universal government programs can also reduce the investment gap between rich and poor children under some circumstances. Most social scientists assume that a child's economic success increases at a diminishing rate as the level of investment in the child rises. Although the empirical evidence for this assumption is weak, some research suggests that the relationship between parental income and children's educational attainment and eventual wages is non-linear and concave downward (Duncan et al. 1998, Mayer 1997). This implies that the first dollar of investment creates the greatest increase in the economic well-being of the child. It also implies that when institutions outside the family invest equally in all children, poor children are likely to gain more than affluent children, because poor children's parents have not invested as much. Probably the most important government investment in children is public schools. Total per pupil spending on public education increased from $3,642 in 1972 to $5,576 in 1992 (in constant dollars) and it became more equal across school districts within states (Murray, Evans, and Schwab 1998). Reducing the investment gap between rich and poor children promotes equality of opportunity under most circumstances.

Changes in the returns to parental investments can also affect intergenerational mobility. Changes in returns do not change equality of opportunity *per se*, but they do change the social and economic costs of unequal opportunity. Returns to schooling have increased over the last twenty years. If parents continue to invest the same amount in their children's schooling and nothing else changes, an increase in the return to schooling would mean that inequality between affluent children (who are more likely to go to college) and poorer children (who are less likely to go to college) would increase. Put another way, if the effect of parental income on their children's schooling does not change, but the return to schooling increases, the effect of parental income on children's income will increase.

Changes in the returns to genetic traits passed from parents to children can also affect intergenerational mobility. Cognitive skills are partly genetically transmitted and parents with high cognitive skills have higher income than parents with low cognitive skills. When returns to cognitive test scores increase, as they seem to have done in the United States since 1980, and nothing else changes, the intergenerational correlation of economic status will increase. Historically, black parents averaged lower incomes than white parents and black children have averaged lower incomes than white children. If the cost of being black declines and nothing else changes, the intergenerational correlation of economic status could decrease.[1] The same argument can be made for the cost of being female.

The effect of parents' income can also change in ways that have nothing to do with changes in parental investments or endowments. In this chapter, we focus on the effect of two demographic trends that are arguably exogenous to parental income. These are the decline in marriage at age thirty and the increase in women's labor market work. The increase in women's labor market work is usually associated with more equality of opportunity for women. Many social scientists have also argued that the delay in marriage is also the result of an increase in opportunities for women. The decline in marriage at age thirty years could be due to people postponing marriage or to an increase in the number of people who will never marry. We use data from the United States, the Panel Study of Income Dynamics (PSID), to assess whether the effect of parental income on children's income at age thirty changed for cohorts born between 1949 and 1965. We find that the elasticity of children's income with respect to parental income declined for sons born after 1952; the elasticity increased for daughters born before 1961 and declined thereafter. Our evidence suggests that these trends are partly the result of the decline in marriage by age thirty. In summary, our results highlight patterns of change in intergenerational mobility, point toward some of the underlying causes, and caution against interpreting the elasticity solely as an indicator of equality of opportunity.

## 1 Previous research on intergenerational mobility

Solon (1999) reviews the many studies estimating the intergenerational transmission of economic status in the United States. Solon (2002) and Björklund and Jäntti (2000) review studies that compare economic mobility in the United States with economic mobility in other countries. When economic status is measured by income, wages, or earnings, the correlation between a measure of fathers' economic status in a

---

[1] Imagine that the following model accurately predicts child $c$'s income from parent $p$'s income and a dummy variable for being black, $I_c = \alpha + \beta_1 I_p + \beta_2 B_i + \varepsilon_i$. If at time 1 black parents have lower incomes than white parents, and $\beta_2$ is negative, then omitting $B_i$ from this model will produce an upwardly biased estimate of $\beta_1$. If then at time 2, $\beta_2$ is zero, $\beta_1$ will presumably decrease because it will no longer be upwardly biased.

randomly selected year and the same measure of sons' economic status in a randomly selected year is usually 0.20 or less (Becker and Tomes 1986, Behrman, Hrubec, Taubman, and Wales 1980, Behrman and Taubman 1990, Sewell and Hauser 1975). Averaging income over several years reduces the importance of transitory fluctuations in income, raising the estimated elasticity (Altonji and Dunn 1991, Solon 1992, Zimmerman 1992). Previous research also shows that estimates of the intergenerational transmission of economic status rise with the age at which children's outcomes are measured and are greater for wealth than for earnings, wages, or schooling (Bowles and Gintis 2000, Solon 1999).

Estimates of intergenerational mobility vary considerably across studies even when parental economic status is measured over several years and the same data are used for the same outcome. This is clear from the results in Chapter 4, and in Solon (1999). For example, Solon (1999, Table 3) reviews eighteen studies using PSID that average parental income over several years, and finds that the elasticity of sons' earnings with respect to fathers' earnings varies from 0.13 to 0.53. Of these estimates, three are less than 0.30, five are between 0.30 and 0.40, eight are between 0.40 and 0.50, and two are above 0.50. If we consider only the five studies that estimate the effect of fathers' earnings averaged over five years on sons' annual earnings measured in a specific year, the elasticities range from 0.32 to 0.53. Three of these five studies use data on sons born between 1951 and 1959. They yield elasticities of 0.39, 0.41, and 0.53. The other two studies include more recent cohorts and have lower estimates, 0.34 and 0.31. Much less is known about intergenerational mobility between parents and daughters. Chadwick and Solon (2002) report an elasticity of 0.43 between daughters' income and parental income, while Fertig (2001), also using the PSID, reports an elasticity of 0.46 between daughters' and fathers' earnings. Solon (1999), summarizing the mobility literature on daughters and parents, concludes that the magnitude of the intergenerational relationship seems to be similar for sons and daughters.

Only a few studies have tried to determine whether economic mobility has changed over time. Recent research finds that the relationship between fathers' and sons' occupational status has not increased and probably has decreased in the last thirty years (Biblarz, Bengslan, and Bucur 1996, Gottschalk, McLanahan, and Sandefur 1994, Grusky and DiPrete 1990, Hout 1988). Other work suggests a long-term gradual decrease in intergenerational occupational mobility. For example, Featherman and Hauser (1978) find that the effects of family background are lower in the 1973 than in the 1962 Occupational Changes in a Generation Survey. Occupational status and income are related, but they do not measure the same thing and the correlation is typically less than 0.50 in the United States (Duncan, Featherman, and Duncan 1972). Thus trends in the association between parents' and children's occupational status need not follow the same trend as the association between parents' and children's economic status.

Fertig (2001) finds a statistically significant increase in intergenerational earnings mobility between fathers and sons using PSID data, but no change in the relationship between fathers and daughters, mothers and sons, or mothers and daughters. She uses data for a relatively short period of time: cohorts of parents are sampled in every year from 1968 through 1976 and their children's earnings are measured seventeen years later in 1985 through 1993. A few studies estimate the trend in the effect of family income on sons' income using data from the United States. Corcoran (2001), using the PSID, finds that the effect of parental income on sons' labor market income, hourly wages, and family income is lower for sons who turned twenty in the 1980s than for sons who turned twenty in the 1970s. Levine (1999) uses data from the National Longitudinal Surveys of Labor Market Experience (young men and youth cohorts) to estimate changes in the effect of family background between sons born in 1942–52 and sons' born in 1957–65. He argues that the effect of parental income rose between the two periods. He obtains similar results using information on respondents to the General Social Survey (GSS) who were twenty-four to thirty-two years old in 1972–80 or in 1985–93.[2] Levine also argues that the effect of parental education on sons' income has declined. Because parental income and education are poorly measured and correlated, the effect of education may partly proxy the effect of permanent income.

Hauser (1998) uses GSS data and assigns each sampled father and son the mean income of his occupation. Using this income measure, Hauser finds no clear trend between 1972 and 1996 in the correlation

---

[2] Levine does not test the statistical significance of the change in the effect of income in either data set, nor does he discuss how income top-coding or other potential changes in coding are handled.

between fathers' and sons' income. His estimates of the intergenerational elasticity range from 0.365 to 0.277. Hauser uses the same technique to impute fathers' income and to estimate the trend in the relationship between fathers' and sons' income using the 1962 and 1973 Occupational Change in a Generation (OCG) surveys and 1986–88 Survey of Income and Program Participation. Again he finds no clear trend in the elasticity. Hauser's technique has the advantage of trying to capture the permanent component of income while Levine's (1999) measure may rely more on the transitory component. Hauser's estimate could provide biased trend estimates if the link between occupation and income weakened over time and this appears to have been the case. Inequality grew both within and between occupations over the late 1980s and early 1990s. Levine's estimates could be biased if the quality of sons' reports of parental income changed over time.

Harding, Jencks, Lopoo, and Mayer (forthcoming), using PSID data and pooling sons and daughters, find no discernable trend in the income elasticity. Mayer and Lopoo (2001), using the same data, show that the elasticity between parents' income and sons' income declined for sons born after 1952. The decline is statistically significant. Together, these studies suggest that the trend may differ for sons and daughters.

Thus two studies, both using PSID data, find that the effect of parental income on sons' income has declined. Using very different income measures, Levine (1999) finds opposite trends and Hauser (1998) finds no change.

## 2 Measuring intergenerational mobility

Most research on intergenerational mobility predicts children's economic status from a measure of parents' economic status. Usually, both measures are expressed as logarithms so that the result provides an elasticity. We estimate the trend in this elasticity. Generally, models of intergenerational mobility estimate the effect of a measure of parental economic status on the same measure for the child, say fathers' wage on sons' wage or fathers' earnings on sons' earnings. Such models are in the tradition of Galton (1886) and others who try to estimate the "heritability" of traits. In this framework it makes sense to estimate the effect of a parental characteristic on the same characteristic among children just as one would estimate the effect of parental eye color on child's eye color but not on child's IQ. In addition, the variance of the same outcome for parents and children is likely to be about equal, so that $\beta$ can be interpreted as the intergenerational correlation when models predict children's economic status from the same measure of parents' economic status. (Chapter 1 and the appendix to this chapter offer a discussion of the relationship between the elasticity and the correlation.)

Because we adopt the logic of the human capital model, we take family income as an indicator of parent's potential monetary investment in children. By family income we mean cash income from all sources including labor income, government transfers, child support, alimony, and any other source of cash income. Therefore we estimate the effect of family income on children's own eventual family income. Children's family income is a function of both their own income and the income of their spouse if they are married. Thus the elasticity between parents' income and children's income is the result of the effect of parents' income on their child's success in both the labor market and the marriage market.

## 3 Data

The PSID is a longitudinal data set initiated with a core sample of approximately 4,800 families in the United States in 1968. When children in the original sample establish their own households, they and all members of their new households are included in the data set, increasing the sample size over time. Our PSID sample includes all children born between 1949 and 1965 whose parents were respondents to the survey and who had positive income when they were thirty years old.[3] The structure of the PSID implies that when the respondents in our sample were thirty-one years old they were either heads of household or the spouse of the head. The appendix describes the data in more detail. We average parental income over the years when a child was aged nineteen to twenty-five. Family income when children are nineteen to twenty-five is strongly correlated with their family income when

---

[3] We use all available years of PSID data. In January of 2001, the Survey Research Center, Institute for Social Research, at the University of Michigan released an early version of family income data. We have incorporated the early release income data, which provides information on children born through 1965.

Table 5.1 *Sample characteristics for sons and daughters*

|  |  | Sample size | |
|---|---|---|---|
| *Birth year* | *Year turned 30* | *Sons* | *Daughters* |
| 1949–52 | 1979–82 | 346 | 383 |
| 1953–56 | 1983–86 | 422 | 514 |
| 1957–59 | 1987–89 | 291 | 337 |
| 1960–62 | 1990–92 | 282 | 329 |
| 1963–65 | 1993–95 | 226 | 294 |

*Source*: Authors' calculations from Panel Study of Income Dynamics data described in the text.

they were younger. This is formally tested in the Appendix. Parents with less than three years of income data were excluded from the analysis in order to minimize error in the measurement of their permanent income.

Although the PSID is one of the few data sets available with sufficient information on both parents and children to estimate intergenerational mobility, it is not ideal. The number of children who turned thirty in each year is small, and the cohorts span a fairly short historical period. Table 5.1 describes the sample of sons and daughters separately by three- or four-year birth cohorts. Although the cohorts span only seventeen years, they include a period in which important changes were taking place. Over the years when these children turned thirty years old (1979–95), marriage rates declined and the labor-force participation of women, especially married women, increased. These children also reached age thirty during years when economic inequality was growing, in part because of an increase in returns to skills. The means and standard deviations for the logarithm of parental income and the logarithm of children's income for three- or four-year cohorts are presented in Table 5.2. We express income in constant 1995 dollars so changes in principle reflect changes in purchasing power.[4] Sons' and daughters' income hardly changed while parental income increased over this time period. The standard deviation of income for sons, daughters, and the

---

[4] All income values are inflated using the CPI-U-X1. This should have no effect on trends in the relationship between parents' and children's income. We adjust the dollars for the purpose of presenting means.

Table 5.2  *Descriptive statistics for parents' income and child's income by three- or four-year cohorts*

|  | log *(Parents' family income)* | | log *(Child's family income)* | | Ratio of parent to child standard deviations |
|---|---|---|---|---|---|
|  | *Mean* | *Standard deviation* | *Mean* | *Standard deviation* |  |
| 1. Daughters |  |  |  |  |  |
| 1949–52 | 10.63 | 0.712 | 10.48 | 0.726 | 0.98 |
| 1953–56 | 10.73 | 0.686 | 10.41 | 0.786 | 0.87 |
| 1957–59 | 10.79 | 0.693 | 10.53 | 0.686 | 1.01 |
| 1960–62 | 10.74 | 0.733 | 10.54 | 0.787 | 0.93 |
| 1963–65 | 10.93 | 0.708 | 10.39 | 0.752 | 0.94 |
| Change 1965–49 | +0.30 | −0.004 | −0.09 | 0.026 |  |
| 2. Sons |  |  |  |  |  |
| 1949–52 | 10.73 | 0.620 | 10.59 | 0.593 | 1.05 |
| 1953–56 | 10.86 | 0.591 | 10.51 | 0.711 | 0.83 |
| 1957–59 | 10.89 | 0.676 | 10.49 | 0.705 | 0.96 |
| 1960–62 | 10.84 | 0.643 | 10.51 | 0.768 | 0.84 |
| 1963–65 | 10.89 | 0.720 | 10.52 | 0.723 | 0.99 |
| Change 1965–49 | +0.16 | +0.10 | −0.07 | 0.105 |  |

*Source:* Authors' calculations from Panel Study of Income Dynamics data described in the text.

parents of sons all increased over time, reflecting the rise in economic inequality. The standard deviation of parental income hardly changed in the daughter sample.

## 4 Results

Least Squares estimation of equation (5.1) shows that the elasticity of the income of 30-year-old sons born between 1949 and 1965 with respect to their parents' income is 0.344. Thus a 10 percent increase in parents' income on average increases sons' income by 3.4 percent. The elasticity for 30-year-old daughters born in the same years is 0.363. Both estimates are lower than the elasticity estimated by Solon (1992) and Chadwick and Solon (2002). For example, Solon finds that the elasticity between parental income measured in only one year and sons' family income is 0.483, and Chadwick and Solon find that the elasticity of daughter's income with respect to parents' income is 0.429. Our estimates are in the lower range of estimates for sons from other studies that use the PSID and average parental income over several years.

We selected observations from the PSID somewhat differently than Solon and his collaborators partly because our emphasis is on the trend in intergenerational mobility rather than its level. In particular, we include children whose fathers are not present in the home. When Solon (1992) includes such children in his sample the estimated elasticity decreases from 0.48 to 0.44. He also limits the analytical sample to children born between 1951 and 1959. When we limit our sample to sons born in these years, the estimated elasticity rises from 0.344 to 0.387.[5] We drop sons and daughters whose income is in the top or bottom 1 percent of the income distribution to avoid the influence of outliers. These observations may contain a lot of error. We do not, however, truncate the distribution of parental income in this way because errors in parental income have already been minimized by averaging over multiple years. Solon (1992) reports that the elasticity is reduced when fathers and sons with annual earnings less than $1,000 (in 1967 dollars) are excluded from the analysis. While these differences affect the estimated level of intergenerational mobility, they are less likely to affect the estimated trend.

The trend in the elasticity estimated separately for sons and daughters is depicted in Figure 5.1. We divide the sample into fourteen overlapping or "rolling" groups to smooth the trend. Children born

---

[5] There are other differences between our procedures and Solon (1992) that could conceivably lead to differences in results. Solon omits respondents who are part of the Survey of Economic Opportunity, a survey component that over-represented families with low-income in 1967. He reports that including these respondents increases $\beta$. We include these respondents. Solon measures fathers' economic status in 1967 to 1971, but in our data fathers' economic status is measured anytime between 1968 and 1990. Consequently, parents could be older when income is measured in our sample. Finally, Solon's sample includes sons between twenty-five and thirty-three years but the mean age of sons is 29.6 years. In our analysis sons' economic status is measured at age thirty.

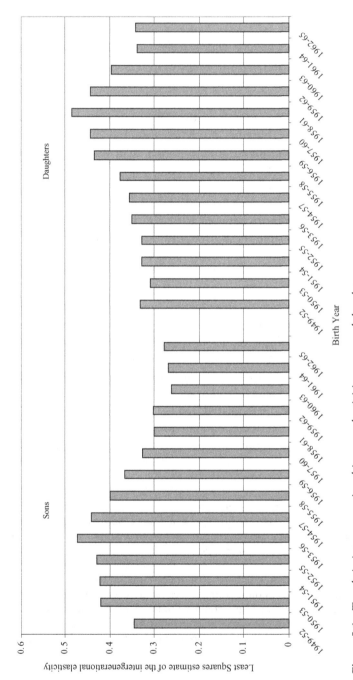

**Figure 5.1**  Trends in intergenerational income elasticities, sons and daughters.

between 1949 and 1952 are group one, those born between 1950 and 1953 are group two, and so on through children born in 1965. The estimated effect of parental income is thus a four-year moving average in which most individuals appear four times. The elasticity of sons' income with respect to parent's income rises for sons born between 1949–52 and 1953–56 and then declines. The elasticity rises for daughters born before 1958–61 and then declines. Both trends are curvilinear, but they peak in different years. As a result, the elasticity is lower for daughters than for sons during the first ten years and greater afterwards. Appendix Table 5A.1 shows the elasticity estimated separately for the rolling cohorts and Appendix Table 5A.2 shows the elasticity for each year.

To test whether these trends are statistically significant, we include a variable for the child's year of birth and the interaction between year of birth and parental income in our model, and estimate the following equation:

$$ln\ Y_c = \alpha + \delta\ birthyear_c + \beta\ ln\ Y_p + \gamma(ln\ Y_p \times birthyear_c) + \varepsilon_c. \quad (5.2)$$

The variable $birthyear_c$ is a continuous variable ranging in value from 0 for those children born in 1949 to 16 for children born in 1965. The coefficient $\delta$ indicates if children's average income is changing over time, while the coefficient $\gamma$ on the interaction term indicates if the effect of parental income on children's economic status changes over time. The t-statistic associated with $\gamma$ indicates whether the trend is statistically significant. The first column of Table 5.3 shows that the linear trend in the elasticity of parents' income and sons' income is negative but statistically insignificant, while it is positive and insignificant for daughters. Note that this finding is consistent with Page's estimates in Chapter 10 of the trend in the intergenerational correlation of parents' and daughters' income. However Figure 5.1 suggests that neither the trend for daughters nor the trend for sons is linear. The trend increases for sons born before 1952 but then declines. Column 3 in Table 5.3 shows that the trend for sons born after 1952 is negative and statistically significant at the 0.05 level. The trend for daughters increases before 1961 and declines thereafter. The last column in Table 5.3 shows that the trend for daughters born before 1961 is positive and statistically significant at the same level.

Table 5.3   *Test of linear trend in the elasticity of parental income and sons' and daughters' income*

|  | Entire sample | | Born after 1952 | Born before 1961 |
|---|---|---|---|---|
|  | Sons | Daughters | Sons | Daughters |
| Log parental | 0.412* | 0.325* | 0.578* | 0.250* |
| income | (0.060) | (0.061) | (0.107) | (0.072) |
| Log parental | −0.008 | 0.005 | −0.022* | 0.022* |
| income × | (0.007) | (0.007) | (0.010) | (0.010) |
| year |  |  |  |  |
| Year | 0.077 | −0.065 | 0.245* | −0.236* |
|  | (0.071) | (0.072) | (0.110) | (0.114) |
| Sample size | 1,567 | 1,857 | 1,221 | 1,354 |

* p-value < 0.05

*Source:* Estimations by the authors using Least Squares on Panel Study of Income Dynamics data described in the text. Standard errors in parentheses.

These results raise several questions. Why do the trends differ for sons and daughters? Why is the trend upward for sons born in 1949–53 and then downward? Why is the trend upward for daughters born before 1961 and then downward? One possible answer for all these questions is random error. The overall trend is not significant and even the parts of the trend line selected because they are the most likely to be significant are only marginally so. The extent to which one should take the trend seriously therefore depends on whether there is a plausible explanation. The intergenerational income elasticity reflects not only the effect of parental income on children's economic success, but also the effect of all its correlates. While there are numerous avenues through which this relationship can arise – including parents' cognitive skill, parenting skills, and educational attainment – no strong theoretical model explaining the intergenerational correlation of income currently exists. Like other studies of intergenerational mobility, we will not try to decompose the elasticity into its causal components. Instead, we use an accounting approach to investigate the extent to which two of the most important recent demographic trends in the United States affect the trend in the elasticity of children's income with respect to parents' income, namely the labor market work of women and the decline in marriage at age thirty.

The human capital model holds that parental income affects children's human capital, which in turn affects the human capital of the potential spouses available to them. The human capital of a child's potential partners then affects whether a child marries and the income of the spouse if the child does marry. The child's family income is the sum of the child's own income and the income of the spouse. Thus changes in the effect of parental income on a child's human capital and wage can change the effect of parental income on whether a child marries and how much the child's spouse is likely to earn. The intergenerational elasticity of income reflects all these influences. These trends are arguably exogenous with respect to parental income. Although parental advantages affect whether daughters work and whether a child marries, changes in parental advantages are unlikely to account for much of the trend in women's employment or in the proportion of sons or daughters who are married at age thirty.

Table 5.4 shows that the proportion of daughters working at least 500 hours during the year when they were thirty years of age increased for the oldest three cohorts. This trend corresponds with the trend from United States Census estimates. Labor force participation for all women increased from 51.5 percent in 1980 to 57.5 in 1990 and to 58.9 in 1995. The trend is similar for women twenty-five to thirty-four years of age (US Bureau of the Census 2000, Tables 644 and 645).

It is not obvious a priori that the effect of parental income should depend on whether daughters work. Parental income affects earnings among daughters who do work, while it affects the amount of public and private transfers among those who do not work, as reviewed in Chapter 10 in the context of the intergenerational transmission of welfare receipt. Table 5.5 shows elasticities for sons and daughters in our PSID sample by whether they work and whether they are married.[6] It shows that the elasticity is 0.289 for working daughters and 0.469 for daughters who do not work. This difference, which is statistically significant at the 0.05 level, suggests that the elasticity for daughters should decline as more daughters work as long as any change in the elasticity over time is the same for daughters who do and do not work.

---

[6] Marital status at age thirty is missing for fifty-one sons and seventy-eight daughters.

Table 5.4  *Employment and marital status
of children*

| Birth year | Percent who work | Percent married |
|---|---|---|
| 1. Daughters | | |
| 1949–52 | 66.2 | 63.0 |
| 1953–56 | 68.1 | 58.9 |
| 1957–59 | 71.4 | 56.6 |
| 1960–62 | 71.0 | 59.1 |
| 1963–65 | 71.8 | 45.7 |
| 2. Sons | | |
| 1949–52 | 95.0 | 77.5 |
| 1953–56 | 90.6 | 63.0 |
| 1957–59 | 93.5 | 63.4 |
| 1960–62 | 94.1 | 60.8 |
| 1963–65 | 94.8 | 57.3 |

*Source:* Tabulations by authors using Panel Study of
Income Dynamics data described in the text. Only respondents working more than 500 hours in the year are considered as employed.

Table 5.5  *Elasticity of sons' and daughters' income with respect to
parents' income by work and marital status*

| | Sons | | | Daughters | | |
|---|---|---|---|---|---|---|
| | Married | Not married | All | Married | Not married | All |
| Working | 0.285 | 0.308 | 0.302 | 0.186 | 0.346 | 0.289 |
| | (0.030) | (0.057) | (0.028) | (0.030) | (0.048) | (0.033) |
| Not working | 0.265 | 0.425 | 0.521 | 0.250 | 0.305 | 0.469 |
| | (0.231) | (0.180) | (0.170) | (0.050) | (0.134) | (0.065) |
| All | 0.288 | 0.407 | 0.343 | 0.210 | 0.437 | 0.363 |
| | (0.032) | (0.064) | (0.032) | (0.027) | (0.048) | (0.030) |

*Source:* Least Squares estimations by the authors using Panel Study of Income
Dynamics data described in the text. Standard errors indicated in parentheses.

When we estimate the trend in the elasticity separately for working and non-working daughters we find no statistically significant change over time for either group.[7]

To estimate the degree to which changes in women's labor market work contribute to the trend in the elasticity of family income for daughters, we predict an elasticity for each cohort by multiplying the proportion of women who work by the elasticity for women who work, and by multiplying the proportion of women who do not work by the elasticity for daughters who do not work, and then summing the two products. In other words the predicted elasticity for each cohort is derived as $\hat{\beta} = \varphi W_c \beta_w + \varphi L_c \beta_L$, where $\varphi W$ is the proportion of daughters who work, $\varphi L$ is the proportion of daughters who do not work, $\beta$ is the elasticity. Because the change in the elasticity is not statistically significant for either daughters who work or daughters who do not work, we treat it as invariant over time within each group. Thus we estimate the change in the elasticity due to the change in women's labor market work (and its correlates). As can be seen in Table 5.6, the observed elasticity for daughters increased over the first three cohorts – up to those born in 1957–59 – but because more women worked the elasticity predicted from changes in the labor market work of daughters declined. The observed elasticity declined from the third to the fifth cohorts but the predicted elasticity hardly changed. Thus, the change in the elasticity due to increases in female labor market work is opposite to the observed pattern. The increase in women who work probably affects economic mobility of daughters, but its effect is outweighed by other factors.

---

[7] These results are as follows for working daughters (with a sample size of 1,235, and standard errors indicated in parentheses):

$$\ln Y_c = 7.274 + 0.012 \; birthyear_c + 0.309 \; \ln Y_p$$
$$\quad (.730) \quad (.074) \qquad\qquad (.067)$$
$$- 0.002 \; \ln Y_p \times birthyear_c.$$
$$\quad (.007)$$

The results for daughters who do not work (with a sample size of 561) are:

$$\ln Y_c = 6.967 - 0.226 \; birthyear_c + 0.314 \; \ln Y_p$$
$$\quad (1.36) \quad (0.15) \qquad\qquad (0.13)$$
$$- 0.020 \; \ln Y_p \times birthyear_c.$$
$$\quad (0.014)$$

**Table 5.6** ***Observed and predicted trends in the elasticity of children's income with respect to parents' income due to changes in women's labor market work and marriage rates***

| | | | *Predicted elasticity* | | |
|---|---|---|---|---|---|
| *Birth year (sample size)* | *Sample Size* | *Observed elasticity* | *Due to women's labor market work* | *Due to marriage* | *Due to marriage and work* |
| 1. Daughters[a] | | | | | |
| 1949–52 | 376 | 0.340 | 0.350 | 0.285 | 0.257 |
| 1953–56 | 499 | 0.350 | 0.346 | 0.297 | 0.260 |
| 1957–59 | 318 | 0.423 | 0.341 | 0.303 | 0.263 |
| 1960–62 | 303 | 0.380 | 0.341 | 0.296 | 0.257 |
| 1963–65 | 284 | 0.341 | 0.340 | 0.334 | 0.278 |
| 2. Sons[b] | | | | | |
| 1949–52 | 338 | 0.345 | NA | 0.396 | NA |
| 1953–56 | 414 | 0.478 | NA | 0.422 | NA |
| 1957–59 | 276 | 0.367 | NA | 0.378 | NA |
| 1960–62 | 273 | 0.313 | NA | 0.348 | NA |
| 1963–65 | 213 | 0.225 | NA | 0.322 | NA |

[a] Assumes a constant elasticity over time.
[b] Takes into account the change in the elasticity shown in Table 5.8.
NA refers to not available. As explained in the text, we do not calculate predicted elasticities for men since so few did not work.
*Source:* Authors' calculations from PSID data described in the text. Includes only women and men with no missing values for marital status and employment. Observed elasticity is the elasticity predicted from equation (5.1). The predicted elasticity is based on changes in work or marriage described in the text.

Daughters' labor market work could in principle also affect the elasticity of sons' income with respect to parents' income if it affects how much sons work. However, the proportion of sons who work hardly changes after 1970 and the elasticity for neither working nor nonworking sons changes. Thus, changes in women's labor market work are unlikely to have affected the trend in the elasticity of sons' income with respect to parents' income.

Table 5.4 also shows that the percentage of daughters married at age thirty declined over time, with the exception of the cohort born in 1960–62.[8] (Countrywide statistics do not suggest an increase in the proportion of 25- to 34-year-old women who are married between 1987–89 and 1990–92.) The percentage of sons who are married at age thirty also declined. To see how changes in marriage can affect the elasticity for children, imagine that all sons and daughters are married, there is no assortative mating, and no wives work. In this scenario, family income equals husband's income. The elasticity for sons would be approximately the observed elasticity for sons who are married to a wife who does not work, namely 0.330. The elasticity for daughters would be zero because there is no assortative mating. Now imagine that some sons and daughters are not married. For unmarried sons and daughters, income equals their own earnings. If parental income predicts a child's own earnings better than it predicts his or her spouse's earnings, the elasticity will be greater for unmarried than for married children. As shown in Table 5.5, the elasticity of children's income with respect to parents' income is much greater for unmarried than for married daughters (0.437 versus 0.210, with a p-value of 0.01). It is also greater for unmarried than for married sons (0.407 versus 0.288, p-value of 0.110). This suggests that, all else being equal, a decline in marriage would raise the elasticity for both sons and daughters.

Differential changes in the elasticity for married and unmarried children can also affect the trend in the elasticity of sons and daughters income with respect to parental income. Table 5.7 shows that the trend in the elasticity for married and unmarried daughters as well as that for married sons is very small and statistically insignificant. However, the trend for unmarried sons is downward and statistically significant. In fact the decline in the elasticity for unmarried sons is large and statistically significant over all cohorts, whereas the decline for all sons is only significant (and half as large) for cohorts born after 1952 (see Figure 5.1).

[8] Table 5.4 shows that the percentage of married sons always exceeds the percentage of married daughters. The difference is large for the oldest cohort, over 14 percentage points. Overall in the United States the ratio of 30-year-old men to women of the same age is 0.97 (US Bureau of the Census 2000, table 12). In our sample, however, it is only 0.85 (1,516 sons and 1,779 daughters), suggesting the PSID is less representative of men than of women. Unmarried men may be harder to locate than unmarried women because the latter often have children, which increases their residential stability.

Table 5.7   *Least Squares estimates of the trend in the*
*intergenerational income elasticity by marital status for sons*
*and daughters*

|  | Sons | | Daughters | |
| --- | --- | --- | --- | --- |
|  | *Married* | *not Married* | *Married* | *not Married* |
| Log parental | 0.292* | 0.754* | 0.181* | 0.462* |
| income | (0.055) | (0.120) | (0.052) | (0.093) |
| Log parental | −0.000 | −0.042* | 0.004 | −0.004 |
| income×year | (0.007) | (0.013) | (0.006) | (0.009) |
| Year | 0.000 | 0.445* | −0.049 | 0.044 |
|  | (0.007) | (0.137) | (0.065) | (0.098) |
| Sample size | 987 | 529 | 1,020 | 759 |

* p-value < 0.05
*Source:* Estimations by the authors using Least Squares on Panel Study of Income
Dynamics data described in the text. Standard errors in parentheses.

It is plausible that, as marriage rates fall, the elasticity for sons initially increases because the elasticity was initially greater for unmarried sons. It then declines, reflecting the decline in the elasticity for unmarried men and the increase in the proportion of men who are unmarried. Table 5.6 shows that elasticities predicted from the change in sons' chances of being married and the decline in the elasticity among unmarried sons produces the observed elasticity, namely an initial increase followed by a decline.[9] However, the observed decline in the elasticity from the second to the fifth cohort $(0.478 - 0.225 = 0.253)$ is over half the cohort 2 elasticity, while the decline predicted from changes in marriage at age thirty $(0.422 - 0.322 = 0.100)$ is only about 23.7 percent of the predicted cohort 2 elasticity.

If we assume that the elasticity did not change over time for either married or unmarried daughters, the elasticity predicted from changes in marriage rates increased over the first three cohorts, as did the observed elasticity. But the predicted elasticity increased 0.018 or 6.3 percent of the elasticity for the first cohort, while the observed elasticity increased 0.083 or 24 percent of the cohort 1 elasticity. The

[9] Since the decline in the elasticity is statistically significant for unmarried sons, we take it into account when predicting the elasticity for each cohort.

predicted elasticity increases from the fourth to the fifth cohort while the observed elasticity declined. The trend in marriage accounts for some of the trend in the elasticity for sons. It also accounts for some of the rise but none of the decline in the elasticity for daughters.

For women, marriage and labor market work are related, so parental income could affect the income of unmarried and married daughters differently depending on whether they work (perhaps because of strong assortative mating). The results in Table 5.5 show that the difference in the elasticity for working and non-working daughters is greater among married daughters than among unmarried daughters. The difference in the elasticity for married and unmarried men is large among sons who do not work but the number of sons who do not work is very small so this difference is not statistically significant at the 0.05 level. The last column in Table 5.6 shows the combined effects of the increase in labor market work and the decline in marriage for daughters. Like the observed elasticity, this predicted elasticity rises over the first three cohorts but the increase is small, only 0.006 or 2.3 percent of the elasticity for the first cohort. We do not calculate the combined effect of changes in marriage and work for men because few men did not work and there is no trend in the probability of men working.

Changes in marriage at thirty years of age account for some of the trend in the elasticity for daughters, and changes in marriage combined with a downward trend in the effect of parental income on the income of unmarried sons accounts for some of the trend in the elasticity for sons. The fact that the elasticity declines for unmarried sons but not unmarried daughters may account for at least part of the difference in the trends for sons and daughters. But if these findings reflect reality it raises the question of why the elasticity declined for unmarried sons but not unmarried daughters. Because most men and women eventually marry, this trend could be an artefact of estimating the elasticity at age thirty. However, when we estimate the same models for 35-year-old sons, the trend in the elasticity is qualitatively the same as the trend for 30-year-old sons. The sample, however, is smaller for 35-year-olds so that trend is not statistically significant.

It is important to keep several limitations of our data and models in mind, and in what follows we examine the sensitivity of our findings to a number of different specifications. First, attrition over time is a major issue in the PSID. The information in Table 5.8 shows that the

Table 5.8  *Proportion of PSID sample lost to attrition, by gender*

| Year turned 30 years | Percent of Women who left the sample | Percent of Men who left the sample |
|---|---|---|
| 1979 | 12.0 | 16.3 |
| 1980 | 9.6 | 11.9 |
| 1981 | 7.8 | 10.3 |
| 1982 | 10.9 | 14.3 |
| 1983 | 11.5 | 9.9 |
| 1984 | 13.9 | 15.7 |
| 1985 | 11.4 | 17.3 |
| 1986 | 18.0 | 12.7 |
| 1987 | 26.1 | 20.1 |
| 1988 | 21.8 | 22.2 |
| 1989 | 13.8 | 26.3 |
| 1990 | 20.9 | 28.9 |
| 1991 | 26.1 | 30.8 |
| 1992 | 17.4 | 30.3 |
| 1993 | 24.7 | 36.4 |
| 1994 | 27.2 | 29.6 |
| 1995 | 22.2 | 30.6 |
| 1996 | 28.5 | 32.9 |

*Note:* Percentages indicate PSID respondents born into the PSID sample who left the sample before the survey year of their 30th birthday.
*Source:* Authors' calculations using complete PSID sample.

proportion of 30-year-olds who left the PSID sample increases over time. For instance, 12 percent of the women who were born in 1949 were no longer in the sample in 1979. Of those women who were born in 1966, 28.5 percent were no longer in the sample in 1996. Although attrition is usually higher for men than women, the trend is about the same across gender so it cannot account for the difference in the trend for sons and daughters.

Fitzgerald, Gottschalk, and Moffitt (1998) show that attrition is greater among poor respondents than among higher-income respondents. If the elasticity between parents' and children's income differs by family income, the increase in attrition could lead to error in the estimated trend in the elasticity. Fitzgerald, Gottschalk, and Moffitt (1998) estimate the importance of attrition bias in intergenerational earnings mobility between fathers and their sons who were aged twenty-six. They find no statistically significant difference in the elasticity of sons' income with respect to parents' income between a sample that includes both respondents who eventually left the survey and respondents who never left, and a sample that includes only those who had left the survey. Their findings apply to attrition between 1977 and 1989 and suggest that our estimates of the trend before 1990, at least among men, should not suffer from attrition bias.

Two other data issues deserve attention: top-coding and the use of early release data. The top-codes in the PSID change over time. Initially set at $99,999 in 1968, they eventually were reset to $999,999 in 1979 (for 1978 incomes) and then to $9,999,999 in 1980. Changes in top-codes can change the variance of income upon which the elasticity between parents' and children's income partly depends. Fortunately, no children in our sample ever have top-coded income. But in twenty-six cases average parental income was top-coded. Our analysis does not use these observations. Another approach is to adjust top-coded values to maintain a consistent upper tail in the distribution across years. In the 1978 sample, 0.24 percent of the income observations were top-coded. This year contained the highest proportion of top-codes for any year in our analysis. To maintain consistency across all survey years, we replace all values in the income distribution above the 99.76[th] percentile in each year with the value at the 99.76[th] percentile. Using this method the decline in the elasticity of parents' and sons' income among sons born after 1952 is −0.21 versus −0.22 when the top-coded cases are excluded. Thus our treatment of top-coded cases probably does not appreciably affect the trend.[10]

Finally, at the time we undertook our research the PSID had not made a final release of data after 1993. As explained above, we use three years of early release data. If these data have an unusual amount of measurement error then our estimates of the elasticity would be too small for children in the youngest cohort. When we re-estimate

[10] As explained earlier, several children in our sample are missing values for their marital status at age thirty. This missing value may signal a group of individuals with unreliable income measures. When we omit cases with missing values for the marital status of the children the results are nearly identical.

the trend omitting early release data the trend is about the same (a decline of −0.025 for sons born after 1952 and an increase of 0.021 for daughters born before 1961). Thus, as far as we can tell, using the early release data does not substantially alter our conclusions.

## 5 Conclusions

The elasticity of sons' income with respect to parents' income is roughly the same as the elasticity of daughters' income with respect to parents' income when the elasticity is examined for all children born between 1949 and 1965. In addition the trend in the elasticity is statistically insignificant when sons and daughters are pooled (Harding, Jencks, Lopoo, and Mayer forthcoming). However the income elasticity falls for sons born after 1952; it increases for daughters born before 1961; and it declines for both sons and daughters born after 1961. We cannot definitively explain the trends in intergenerational mobility. However, the decline in marriage at age thirty accounts for some of the increase in the elasticity for daughters born before 1961 and both the increase in the elasticity for sons born before 1956 and the decline for sons born after that year. The importance of this finding is not the effect of marriage *per se* on intergenerational mobility. Its importance is to demonstrate the ambiguity in the meaning of a change in measures of intergenerational mobility and hence the meaning of the level of intergenerational mobility. This ambiguity in turns highlights the need for revisions to the theory of intergenerational mobility. The elasticity between parents' income and children's income is often thought of as an indicator of equality of opportunity; the lower the effect of parental income on children's own economic fortunes the more equal is economic opportunity. However, the extent to which the elasticity indicates equality of opportunity depends on why we observe a correlation between parents and their children in the first place.

Several other results are notable. First, parental income has a greater effect on unmarried than on married children. This is presumably because sons and daughters do not marry spouses whose earnings are identical to their own so spouses introduce random variation in children's income. It is hard to argue that the difference in the elasticity for married and unmarried children is due to differences in opportunity. Second, the effect of parental income is lower for sons and daughters who work than for sons and daughters who do not work. Third, the decline in the effect of parental income on the income of unmarried sons is large. We do not have good explanations for the last two results.

The trend in income mobility for sons is consistent with the trend in occupational mobility and earnings for sons, lending credibility to the conclusion that intergenerational economic mobility has increased for sons. Nonetheless, these results are fragile. The sample sizes are small and the time period over which we estimate the trend in mobility is short. Unfortunately, because the changes in the direction of the trend occur at the beginning and end of our time series, we cannot tell if they were sustained beyond our time frame, and we have little data to determine their cause. Because the linear trend over all cohorts is not statistically significant for either sons or daughters, the extent to which one is persuaded that the trends that we document are real depends on what one thinks about the anomalous parts of the trend line. Only when we have additional data over a longer period of time will we be able to estimate the trend in intergenerational economic mobility with confidence.

## DATA APPENDIX

Using the Individual File from the Panel Study of Income Dynamics, we select all individuals who were born between 1949 and 1965, who had parents we could identify, who had positive income when they were thirty years old, and who were still in the survey in 1995. These individuals are assigned their 1995 core weight. We also include thirty-year-olds who left the sample at any point between 1983 and 1995. For these "attriters" we use the core weight assigned in the last year they were in the PSID (Hill 1992). To link all individuals to their parents, we use the Parent Identification File.

## 1 Measuring the elasticity

Research on intergenerational mobility often refers to $\beta$ as the intergenerational elasticity of economic status, defined as:

$$\beta = r_{lnYc,lnYp}(s_{lnYc}/s_{lnYp}) \qquad (5.3)$$

where $r_{lnYc,lnYp}$ is the sample correlation between the log of the parents' and the log of children's economic status and $s_{lnYc}$ and $s_{lnYp}$ are

Appendix Table 5A.1  *Unstandardized and standardized LS regression coefficients for the effect of the logarithm of parental income on the logarithm of child's income for three-year rolling cohorts*

|  | Sons | | | Daughters | | |
|---|---|---|---|---|---|---|
|  | Intergenerational income elasticity ($\beta$) | | Intergenerational income correlation (r) | Intergenerational income elasticity ($\beta$) | | Intergenerational income correlation (r) |
|  | Estimate | t-statistic | | Estimate | t-statistic | |
| 1949–52 | 0.346 | 5.59 | 0.361 | 0.333 | 5.03 | 0.326 |
| 1950–53 | 0.421 | 6.92 | 0.397 | 0.309 | 4.89 | 0.294 |
| 1951–54 | 0.423 | 6.88 | 0.377 | 0.328 | 5.13 | 0.303 |
| 1952–55 | 0.429 | 6.27 | 0.371 | 0.329 | 5.40 | 0.311 |
| 1953–56 | 0.473 | 6.50 | 0.393 | 0.352 | 5.91 | 0.307 |
| 1954–57 | 0.441 | 6.46 | 0.390 | 0.356 | 5.93 | 0.318 |
| 1955–58 | 0.400 | 5.91 | 0.368 | 0.377 | 6.14 | 0.351 |
| 1956–59 | 0.367 | 6.57 | 0.341 | 0.434 | 7.51 | 0.414 |
| 1957–60 | 0.327 | 6.08 | 0.304 | 0.443 | 7.44 | 0.427 |
| 1958–61 | 0.301 | 5.00 | 0.257 | 0.485 | 8.48 | 0.476 |
| 1959–62 | 0.302 | 5.07 | 0.257 | 0.444 | 7.42 | 0.421 |
| 1960–63 | 0.263 | 4.11 | 0.237 | 0.397 | 5.56 | 0.374 |
| 1961–64 | 0.270 | 3.88 | 0.240 | 0.339 | 4.74 | 0.325 |
| 1962–65 | 0.279 | 4.22 | 0.273 | 0.343 | 4.73 | 0.317 |

*Note:* Derivations by the authors using Panel Study of Income Dynamics data as described in the text and appendix. See Appendix equation (5.3) for the definition of the relationship between $\beta$ and $r$.

respectively the standard deviations of the logarithm of children's and the parents' economic status. If the variance of the measure of parents' economic status is equal to the variance of the children's economic status, then $\beta$ is equivalent to the correlation between the logarithm of the parents' and the logarithm of the child's economic status. The degree of intergenerational mobility is then $1-\beta$. However, when inequality is growing, estimating the intergenerational correlation using $\beta$ could be misleading. Unless the growth in inequality is the same for both generations, the ratio of the variance of parents' and children's economic status will change over time, and $\beta$ will be an increasingly inaccurate estimate of the intergenerational correlation of economic status. One can correct for the differences in the change of the variance by estimating the standardized regression coefficient using equation (5.3). Appendix Table 5A.2 shows that the trend in the standardized and unstandardized regression coefficients are about the same so we refer only to the elasticity in the body of this chapter.

## 2 Variable definitions

Parental Income is the average of the sum of mother and father incomes when the child is nineteen to twenty-five years old. In principle we wish to measure parental income over a child's entire childhood. However, averaging income over such a long period would reduce the sample size to an unworkably small number. We assume that family income when children are nineteen to twenty-five is strongly correlated with family income when they were younger. For the youngest cohorts, we estimate similar models measuring parental income when children are twelve to fourteen years old and obtain substantively similar results. We also select a subset of respondents for whom we had family income data both during early adolescence and during early adulthood. We then use a Chow test to determine if the coefficients in the sample with income measured at a young age are the same as the coefficients for the sample with income measured later. We fail to reject the null hypothesis that these coefficients were the same.

The child's income is total family income for sons who head their own household and for daughters who are either heads or wives measured in 1995 dollars using the CPI-U-X1. We trim the top and bottom one percent of the children's income distribution. Due to the data structure of the PSID, children who did not live at home in 1968 are excluded from the sample entirely. If the mean age at which children move out of home changes over time, our first cohort may be different from later cohorts. We estimate models selecting only those teenagers who lived at home at age nineteen. Using this selection criterion did not affect the trend estimates.

Working is an indicator variable equal to one if the child worked at least 500 hours during the year that he was age thirty, and Child's Marital Status is an indicator variable equal to one if the child was married at age thirty.

*Susan E. Mayer and Leonard M. Lopoo*

Appendix Table 5A.2   *Unstandardized and standardized LS regression coefficients for the effect of parental income on child's income by year*

| | Sons | | | Daughters | | |
|------|------|------|------|------|------|------|
| | Intergenerational income elasticity $(\beta)$ | | Intergenerational income correlation (r) | Intergenerational income elasticity $(\beta)$ | | Intergenerational income correlation (r) |
| | Estimate | t-statistic | | Estimate | t-statistic | |
| 1949 | 0.260 | 2.31 | 0.318 | 0.333 | 2.15 | 0.351 |
| 1950 | 0.555 | 4.25 | 0.559 | 0.233 | 1.86 | 0.230 |
| 1951 | 0.366 | 3.21 | 0.377 | 0.398 | 2.62 | 0.314 |
| 1952 | 0.256 | 2.16 | 0.246 | 0.357 | 3.06 | 0.394 |
| 1953 | 0.529 | 4.55 | 0.442 | 0.227 | 1.90 | 0.206 |
| 1954 | 0.622 | 4.54 | 0.497 | 0.365 | 3.15 | 0.310 |
| 1955 | 0.387 | 2.46 | 0.332 | 0.368 | 3.10 | 0.331 |
| 1956 | 0.411 | 2.69 | 0.344 | 0.462 | 4.09 | 0.391 |
| 1957 | 0.404 | 4.15 | 0.421 | 0.185 | 1.51 | 0.201 |
| 1958 | 0.392 | 3.77 | 0.392 | 0.444 | 3.43 | 0.435 |
| 1959 | 0.285 | 2.99 | 0.252 | 0.579 | 7.44 | 0.576 |
| 1960 | 0.247 | 2.07 | 0.214 | 0.511 | 4.06 | 0.436 |
| 1961 | 0.340 | 2.27 | 0.238 | 0.422 | 4.10 | 0.472 |
| 1962 | 0.367 | 3.35 | 0.343 | 0.267 | 1.73 | 0.229 |
| 1963 | 0.145 | 1.21 | 0.166 | 0.464 | 3.09 | 0.470 |
| 1964 | 0.281 | 1.72 | 0.227 | 0.227 | 1.96 | 0.198 |
| 1965 | 0.355 | 2.62 | 0.411 | 0.403 | 3.81 | 0.391 |

*Note:* Derivations by the authors using Panel Study of Income Dynamics data as described in the text and appendix. See Appendix Equation (5.3) for the definition of the relationship between $\beta$ and $r$. Sample sizes vary from a low of 67 in 1950 for sons, to a high of 138 in 1956 for daughters.

### References

Altonji, Joseph G. and Thomas A. Dunn (1991). "Relationships among the Family Incomes and Labor Market Outcomes of Relatives." Cambridge, MA: National Bureau of Economic Research, Working Paper No. 3724.

Becker, Gary S., and Nigel Tomes (1979). "An Equilibrium Theory of the Distribution of Income and Intergenerational Mobility." *Journal of Political Economy*. Vol. 87, no. 6, pp. 1153–89.

(1986). "Human Capital and the Rise and Fall of Families." *Journal of Labor Economics*. Vol. 4, no. 3, pp. S1–S39.

Behrman, Jere, Zdenek Hrubec, Paul Taubman, and T. Wales (1980). "Socioeconomic Success: A Study of the Effects of Genetic Endowments." *Family Environment, and Schooling*. New York: North-Holland.

Behrman, Jere R. and Paul Taubman (1990). "The Intergenerational Correlation Between Children's Adult Earnings and Their Parent's Income: Results from the Michigan Panel Study of Income Dynamics." *Review of Income and Wealth*. Vol. 36, no. 2, pp. 115–27.

Biblarz, T. J., V. L. Bengslan, and A. Bucur (1996). "Social Mobility Across Three Generations." *Journal of Marriage and the Family*. Vol. 58, pp. 188–200.

Björklund, Anders, and Markus Jäntti (2000). "Intergenerational Mobility of Economic Status in Comparative Perspective." *Nordic Journal of Political Economy*. Vol. 26, no. 1, pp. 3–32.

Bowles, Samuel, and Herbert Gintis (2000). "The Inheritance of Economic Status: Education, Class and Genetics." University of Massachusetts: unpublished.

Chadwick, Laura, and Gary Solon (2002). "Intergenerational Income Mobility Among Daughters." *American Economic Review*. Vol. 92, pp. 335–44.

Corcoran, Mary (2001). "Mobility, Persistence, and the Consequences of Poverty for Children: Child and Adult Outcomes." University of Michigan: unpublished.

Duncan, Greg, W. Yeung, J. Brooks-Gunn, and J. Smith (1998). "How Much Does Childhood Poverty Affect the Life Chances of Children." *American Sociological Review*. Vol. 63, pp. 406–23.

Duncan, Otis Dudley, David Featherman, and Beverly Duncan (1972). *Socioeconomic Background and Achievement*. New York: Seminar Press.

Featherman, D. L., and R. M. Hauser (1978). *Opportunity and Change*. New York: Academic Press.

Fertig, Angela R. (2001). "Trends in Intergenerational Earnings Mobility." Princeton, NJ: Center for Research on Child Wellbeing, Princeton University, Working Paper No. 2001-23.

Fitzgerald, John, Peter Gottschalk, and Robert Moffitt (1998). "An Analysis of the Impact of Sample Attrition on the Second Generation of Respondents in the Michigan Panel Study of Income Dynamics." *Journal of Human Resources*. Vol. 33, pp. 300–44.

Galton, Francis (1886). "Regression Towards Mediocrity in Hereditary Stature." *Journal of the Anthropological Institute of Great Britain and Ireland*. Vol. 15, pp. 246–63.

Gottschalk, Peter, Sara McLanahan, and Gary D. Sandefur (1994). "The Dynamics of Intergenerational Transmission of Poverty and Welfare Participation." In Sheldon Danziger, Gary D. Sandefur, and Daniel H. Weinberg (editors). *Confronting Poverty: Prescriptions for Change.* Cambridge, MA: Harvard University Press and Russell Sage.

Grusky, David, and Thomas DiPrete (1990). "Recent Trends in the Process of Stratification." *Demography.* Vol. 27, no. 4, pp. 617–36.

Harding, David J., Christopher Jencks, Leonard M. Lopoo, and Susan E. Mayer (forthcoming). "The Changing Effect of Family Background on the Incomes of American Youths." In Samuel Bowles, Herbert Gintis, and Melissa Osborne (editors). *Unequal Chances: Family Background and Economic Success.* New York: Russell Sage.

Hauser, Robert M. (1998). "Intergenerational Economic Mobility in the United States: Measures, Differentials and Trends." University of Wisconsin: unpublished.

Hill, Martha S. (1992). *The Panel Study of Income Dynamics: A User's Guide.* Newbury Park, CA: Sage Publications.

Jencks, Christopher (1988). "Whom Must We Treat Equally for Educational Opportunity to Be Equal?" *Ethics.* Vol. 98, pp. 518–33.

Kremer, Michael (1997). "How Much Does Sorting Increase Inequality?" *Quarterly Journal of Economics.* Vol. 112, no. 1, pp. 115–39.

Levine, David I. (1999). "Choosing the Right Parents: Changes in the Intergenerational Transmission of Inequality between the 1970s and the Early 1990s." Institute for Industrial Relations, University of California, Berkeley, Working Paper No. 72.

Mayer, Susan E. (1997). *What Money Can't Buy: Family Income and Children's Life Chances.* Cambridge, MA: Harvard University Press.

Mayer, Susan E., and Leonard M. Lopoo (2001). "Has the Intergenerational Transmission of Economic Status Changed?" Joint Center for Poverty Research, Working Paper No. 227.

Murray, Shelia, William Evans, and Robert Schwab (1998). "Education-Finance Reform and the Distribution of Education Resources." *American Economic Review.* Vol. 88, no. 4, pp. 789–812.

Sewell, William, and Robert M. Hauser (1975). *Education, Occupation and Earnings: Achievement in the Early Career.* New York: Academic Press.

Solon, Gary (1992). "Intergenerational Income Mobility in the United States." *American Economic Review.* Vol. 82, no. 3, pp. 393–408.

(1999). "Intergenerational Mobility in the Labor Market." In Orley C. Ashenfelter and David Card (editors). *Handbook of Labor Economics, Volume 3A.* Amsterdam: North-Holland.

(2002). "Cross-Country Differences in Intergenerational Earnings Mobility." *Journal of Economic Perspectives*. Vol. 16, pp. 59–66.

United States Bureau of the Census (2000). *Statistical Abstract of the United States, 2000*. (120th edition). Washington, DC: Government Printing Office.

(2000). *Statistical Abstract*. Web Version: http://www.census.gov/prod/www/statistical-abstract-us.html.

Zimmerman, David J. (1992). "Regression Towards Mediocrity in Economic Stature." *American Economic Review*. Vol. 82, no. 3, pp. 409–29.

# 6 Changes in intergenerational mobility in Britain

JO BLANDEN, ALISSA GOODMAN,
PAUL GREGG, AND STEPHEN MACHIN

THE extent to which children's economic or social success is shaped by the economic or social position of their parents is a contentious and hotly debated issue, both within academic circles and in a wider policy context. There is a large body of academic work, carried out predominantly by sociologists, on social mobility – where social class of individuals is related to parental social class – and a smaller body of work which considers mobility in terms of economic status (usually measured by labor market earnings of children and parents). An example of the former is the survey undertaken in the Performance and Innovation Unit (2001) paper on social mobility, while Solon (1999) offers an overview of the latter. Further, the issue of intergenerational inequalities crops up in the political arena time and time again, and one increasingly sees discussion of the issue in the political press.

The experiences of the last twenty years or so probably make such issues even more relevant than ever. In the United Kingdom income inequality increased very rapidly since the late 1970s (Goodman, Johnson, and Webb 1997). Much of this has been due to changing rewards from paid work as earnings gaps between the highest- and lowest-paid workers widened out by a considerable amount (Machin 1996, 1998, 1999). One consequence of this has been a massive rise in the proportion of children growing up in poverty. In 1979, 13 percent of children lived in households where income was less than half of the average income. By 1996, this had risen to 33 percent (Gregg, Harkness and Machin, 1999). The UK Prime Minister pledged in his Beveridge

We would like to thank Miles Corak and other participants in a workshop on Intergenerational Mobility held at Statistics Canada in February 2001, the follow-up Berlin meeting of June 2001, the conference for the opening of the LSE research laboratory and the Research Council of Norway's Labour Market and Wage Formation conference in Oslo for a number of helpful comments.

Lecture given in March of 1999 to "end child poverty in a generation." Behind this lies the explicit belief that "childhood experience lays the foundations for later life. Children growing up in low-income households are more likely than others to have poor health, to do badly at school, become teenage mothers or come into early contact with the police, to be unemployed as adults or to earn lower wages."[1]

From a theoretical perspective there are a number of ways in which growing inequality and child poverty can influence intergenerational mobility. These are discussed in Grawe and Mulligan (2002). For example, the classic model of Becker and Tomes (1986) shows that that the presence of credit constraints can lead to persistence of economic status across generations. If increased income inequality leads to a rise in the frequency or severity of credit constraints then this will lead to a fall in mobility (see also Cameron and Heckman 1998, 2001). This may operate through stronger links between education and family income generated by increased credit market imperfections (Blanden, Gregg, and Machin 2003). They may also be reinforced through increased labor market inequality generated by changing wage returns to education.

Previous empirical work has identified the importance of educational attainment as a transmission mechanism between background and later outcomes (Gregg and Machin 1999). Another important development for Britain in the past twenty years or so is the very rapid educational upgrading that has taken place among the young. In 1980, 13 percent of young people entered higher education.[2] This rose sharply to 19 percent by 1990 and 31 percent by the year 2000. In addition, the numbers of young people having no qualifications has fallen dramatically. The major objective of this chapter is to examine the implications of these changes for intergenerational mobility. The extent to which improved educational attainment is spread equally or unequally among the population has clear implications for how intergenerational mobility may have altered through time. We consider

---

[1] "Tackling Child Poverty: Giving Every Child the Best Possible Start in Life," HM Treasury, December 2001, p. v.

[2] These numbers are the higher education age participation index for young people, taken from the Department for Education and Skills Labour Market Information Database (Skillsbase). The exact definition used by DfES is the number of young (under twenty-one) home initial entrants expressed as a percentage of the averaged 18- to 19-year-old population. Initial entrants are those entering a course of full-time higher education for the first time.

this explicitly in our model and empirical work by comparing and contrasting estimates of the extent of intergenerational income mobility over time in Britain.

We look at these questions using data on two birth cohorts (one born in 1958, the other in 1970). The chapter begins, in the next section by considering how existing work relates to our questions of interest and by describing the empirical methods we use. Section 2 describes the data. Section 3 presents our empirical results, where we report evidence showing that intergenerational immobility increases between the two cohorts we study. In other words, intergenerational mobility appears to have fallen for people who grew up in the 1960s and 1970s (the 1958 birth cohort) as compared to a cohort who grew up in the 1970s and 1980s (the 1970 birth cohort). This occurs for both the regression and transition matrix approaches to studying intergenerational mobility. We also find that differing educational attainment accounts for part of the change in the association between parental income and children's earnings. We discuss the implications of these findings in the concluding section of the paper. In particular, our findings support theoretical notions that the widening wage and income distribution that occurred from the late 1970s onwards, together with the fact that the rapid expansion of education supply over this period was concentrated among people from higher-income backgrounds, acted to slow down the extent of mobility up or down the distribution across generations.

## 1 Related work and modelling questions

Recent years have seen significant developments in the literature dealing with parent–child correlations of economic and social status, in large part because of the increasing availability of good quality longitudinal data. Even so, the majority of this growing literature has yet to address issues dealing with changes in the extent of intergenerational mobility in any detail. The usual approach taken is to estimate log-linear regressions of children's economic status on that of their parents. The typical formulation for children and parents in family $i$ is:

$$ln\ Y_i^{child} = \alpha + \beta\ ln\ Y_i^{parents} + \varepsilon_i \qquad (6.1)$$

where $Y$ is economic status of an individual in family $i$ (usually labor-market earnings), and $\varepsilon$ is an error term. The coefficient $\beta$ is the intergenerational elasticity and reflects how strongly children's status is associated with parental economic stature. The literature usually proceeds to say a value for $\beta$ of zero (where child and parental $Y$ are uncorrelated) corresponds to complete intergenerational mobility, while a value of unity (the child's $Y$ is fully determined by parental $Y$) corresponds to complete immobility. The empirical question of interest then concerns estimating the magnitude of $\beta$, paying careful attention to problems of measurement of $Y$ and associated econometric difficulties. The other commonly adopted approach is to look at transition matrices between generations. All of what we discuss in this section could be framed in terms of the transition matrix approach and we do present results based on both it and regression analysis. However, for the time being we focus on the regression approach for reasons of clarity. This, of course, goes back a long way in time, even to the analysis of child–parent height correlations by Galton (1886).

The more recent work using regression analysis very clearly points out the potential pitfalls associated with estimating $\beta$ from data on children and their parents. An older literature surveyed in Becker and Tomes (1986) concluded that, for correlations based on labor market earnings, $\beta$ was around 0.2. This led Becker and Tomes to conclude that "aside from families victimized by discrimination, regression to the mean in earnings in the United States and other rich countries appears to be rapid" (Becker and Tomes 1986, p. S32). However, the methodological problems associated with the data used in the majority of this work mean that this estimate was biased downwards. Solon (1989) shows that the use of homogeneous samples and measurement errors in $Y_i^{parents}$ both induce an attenuation bias, meaning that the $\beta$ coefficients from the earlier work tended to be too low. More recent work using better quality data and appropriate econometric methods concludes that the intergenerational elasticity for labor market earnings is in fact quite a lot higher, and more likely to be around 0.4 (Solon 1999). Some studies, for example Mazumder (2000), report even higher estimates (this is due to reducing attenuation bias as a result of time averaging parental earnings over a reasonably large number of years).

These findings have potentially important implications for social welfare. Various authors have demonstrated a link between inequality and the extent of intergenerational mobility, with less mobility (higher $\beta$) implying greater inequality. Atkinson (1981), for example, writes down a simple model where this occurs. This link is important, especially if lack of mobility constrains higher-ability children from lower-income families. That is, if a higher $\beta$ results in such children having less access to resources while growing up or facing credit constraints that cut short their education by stopping them from attending university. The study of how the intergenerational elasticity may change through time becomes very important when placed in the context of this discussion. As already noted, income inequality has risen in recent years, especially in the United Kingdom and the United States, and there have been big increases in the numbers of children growing up in relatively poor families. Yet we know little of how this relates to possible changes in the intergenerational mobility of economic status. Part of this lack of knowledge is due to the strong data requirements that are likely to hinder researchers who would like to address this question. With the exception of research reported in Chapter 5, we know of only three studies that have attempted to consider this. Fortin and Lefebvre (1998) use Canadian data from the General Social Surveys of 1986 and 1994. These surveys give the occupation, employment status, education, and industry of fathers when the respondent was fifteen and matching this with earnings data from the Canadian Census allows the authors to construct father's income. Comparing individuals in the same age groups across the two surveys fails to show any clear trend in Canadian intergenerational income mobility over time. Mayer and Lopoo (2001, and Chapter 5 of this book) and Fertig (2001) use the Panel Survey of Income Dynamics from the United States to consider how intergenerational transmissions have changed in that country. Both studies find an increase in intergenerational earnings mobility (that is, a falling $\beta$) over time, despite there being a widening of inequality over the period considered. Mayer and Lopoo (2001) argue that this is a consequence of the increased investments made in children by the state that have counteracted the differences in the investments parents are able to make and in Chapter 5 also relate these developments to changes in marital and work patterns. However, in the Mayer and Lopoo studies and in that by Fertig (2001) the sample sizes used are small and some reported results are very much on the borders of statistical significance.

What mechanisms are likely to underpin changes in the extent of intergenerational mobility? Mayer and Lopoo discuss three possibilities: (a) the relative investments in children made by rich and poor parents might change; (b) the payoff to these investments might change; (c) the returns to genetic or biologically transmitted characteristics might change. In Chapter 2, Solon formalizes the first two of these factors in an intuitively appealing economic model. Suppose we are interested in intergenerational earnings mobility. In generation $t$ labor market earnings $W$ are a function of human capital $H$ so that $W_t = \emptyset_t H_t + u_t$, where $u_t$ is a random error term. If we then believe that children's human capital is related to parental income through differences in investments made by rich and poor parents we can write (with $v_t$ being an error term) $H_t = \psi W_{t-1} + v_t$. One can combine these equations to generate an intergenerational mobility function, $W_t = \emptyset_t \psi W_{t-1} + \varepsilon_t$ where $\varepsilon_t = \emptyset_t v_t + u_t$. According to this formulation, intergenerational mobility will be higher if: (a) there are lower returns to human capital for children ($\emptyset_t$ is lower); or (b) if children's human capital is less sensitive to parental earnings ($\psi$ is lower). On the former, there is plenty of evidence that educational wage differentials have been rising in the United States and the United Kingdom in recent years.[3] This would imply reduced mobility. We know less about links between education and parental income, but Acemoglu and Pischke (2001) identify strong links between the two across regions in the United States over time. We do know that educational attainment has been rising very sharply. In the United Kingdom in 1975, 5.6 percent of men had a degree; by 2000 this had risen to 17.9 percent (Machin, Harkness, and McIntosh 2001). For women the rise is even faster, from 2.3 to 15.3 percent over the same time period. If this increased educational attainment differentially benefited more children from lower-income families (lower $\psi$) then this would raise mobility. On the other hand, if children from richer families were more likely to reach higher-educational qualifications (higher $\psi$) this will result in reduced mobility. For these reasons we also consider the role played by changing educational attainment in the empirical work we present below.

One of the motivating influences for our interest in changing intergenerational mobility is the fact that income inequality has been

[3] The evidence on this is very clear in the United States where wage gaps between the more and less educated have been rising since the late 1970s (Card 1999). The picture is less clear in the United Kingdom. Educational wage differentials rose sharply in the 1980s. Since then there has been less upward movement. However, the supply of educated workers has risen very sharply which one would normally think should depress educational wage differentials. This certainly has not happened: the 1990s pattern most likely displays a small rise, even in the face of increased supply (Machin 2003).

rising over time. This has important implications for the measurement of the intergenerational elasticity. Grawe (2003, Chapter 4 of this book) demonstrates the implications of changing variances in parent and child earnings for the measurement of intergenerational mobility. His interest is in terms of the bias induced by measuring the parameter at different stages in the generations' lifecycles. Frequently in the literature the earnings measure for parents is taken later in life than the one for children. As the variance of earnings increases with age this can lead to biased estimates compared to when both measures are taken at the same point of the lifecycle. The bias in the estimated coefficient will be downward, and can be corrected for by using the sample correlation between parental and child $Y$ measures:

$$r_{lnY^{parents},lnY^{child}} = \beta \times (\sigma_{lnY^{parents}}/\sigma_{lnY^{child}}). \tag{6.2}$$

In this equation, $r_{lnY^{parents},lnY^{child}}$ is the sample correlation between the generations' $lnY$ and $\sigma$ denotes a standard deviation. In the light of this discussion, it becomes clear that when comparing intergenerational mobility over a period when inequality is changing it is particularly important to correct for changes in the inequality of $Y$. Therefore all our estimates report both the estimated regression coefficient $\beta$ and the sample correlation, which we term "$\beta$ adjusted for changes in inequality."

## 2 The data

We look at changing intergenerational mobility using data from two very rich British birth cohorts. These are the National Child Development Study (NCDS), a survey of all children born in the United Kingdom between 3 and 9 March 1958, and the British Cohort Survey (BCS), a survey of all children born between 5 and 11 April 1970. The NCDS is a very rich data set that has been used for previous work on intergenerational mobility, for example by Dearden, Machin, and Reed (1997), and consists of the birth population with follow-up samples at ages 7, 11, 16, 23, 33, and 42. The NCDS data have also been used to look at the transmission mechanisms that may underpin intergenerational mobility, Gregg and Machin (1999, 2000), Hobcraft (1998), or Kiernan (1995). The BCS is very similar in style, with data collected at ages 5, 10, 16, 26, and 30. As well as being similar in spirit the questions asked in the two cohorts are frequently identical, although there are some difficulties inherent in using them in a comparative study over time.

Ideally one would like to have measures of the same permanent economic status (be it wages or income) for both generations from both cohort studies. Unfortunately, due to different survey designs, this is not possible. The NCDS parental-income data comes from separate measures of fathers' earnings, mothers' earnings and other income (all defined after taxes). Because of this breakdown, earlier work on the NCDS was able to compare sons' and fathers' earnings. However, the BCS only has data on parents' combined income.[4] We are therefore forced to base our estimates on the relationship between the cohort member's earnings or income and parental income and are not able to look at changes in the pattern of intergenerational correlations of earnings.

As already mentioned, previous work in this area stresses the need to look at parents and children at the same stage of the lifecycle. This is because one does not want to contaminate estimates with measurement error due to the transitory components of earnings or income. We are able to get fairly close to this in our work, using income and earnings data on children at age thirty-three in the NCDS and thirty in the BCS. In case parents are of different ages across the studies we also control for the average age of parents. Controlling for average age rather than age of mother and father separately avoids limiting the sample to families with two parents. The issue of whether the children are with their natural parents may be a cause of concern and is explicitly considered in Dearden, Machin, and Reed (1997). We have re-run our estimates excluding children without both natural parents but find it does little to change our results. However our sample does exclude children with no traditional "parent" figure such as those living solely with grandparents or in an institutional setting.

Our estimation samples are restricted to those in employment at the time the age 30–33 data was collected. This is, of course, a necessary restriction in order for us to have wage data but is a non-trivial selection rule, particularly for women and is an issue that we hope to return to in future work. Table 6.1 offers some descriptive statistics associated with these samples. The first thing to notice is confirmation of the rising

---

[4] In the NCDS income data, parents are asked to include child benefit income, in the BCS they are asked to exclude it. We therefore impute child benefit data for the BCS based on family composition.

Table 6.1  *Descriptive statistics for two cohorts of men and women in the United Kingdom*

|  | Men | | Women | |
|---|---|---|---|---|
|  | *1958 birth cohort* | *1970 birth cohort* | *1958 birth cohort* | *1970 birth cohort* |
| Weekly wage | 311.58 | 331.80 | 161.75 | 222.49 |
|  | (169.80) | (231.15) | (114.37) | (170.68) |
| Family income | 384.09 | 436.98 | 380.07 | 429.76 |
|  | (202.39) | (323.35) | (223.10) | (300.56) |
| Parental income at age 16 | 321.91 | 337.87 | 321.35 | 337.14 |
|  | (114.86) | (165.59) | (125.72) | (163.61) |
| Proportion below poverty line at age 16 | 0.07 | 0.11 | 0.08 | 0.09 |
| Proportion with degree | 0.17 | 0.26 | 0.12 | 0.26 |
| Sample size | 2,246 | 2,053 | 1,908 | 2,017 |

*Notes:*
1. 1958 birth cohort data are from the National Child Development Study, 1970 birth cohort data are from the British Cohort Study.
2. Standard deviations in parentheses for wage and income measures.
3. Wage and income in UK pounds and in January 2001 prices, measured at age 33 for the 1958 cohorts and age 30 for the 1970 cohorts. The proportion with a degree is measured at the same ages.
4. The indicated sample sizes are for all variables except for family income. In this case they are: (a) 2,110 for the 1958 cohort of men and 2,015 for the 1970 cohort; (b) 2,156 for the 1958 cohort of women and 2,285 for the 1970 cohort.

inequality of earnings between the cohorts, as shown by the higher standard deviations (in parentheses) for the 1970 cohort in the top row. There is also a rise in the inequality of cohort member's family incomes and in the inequality of parental incomes measured at age sixteen (in 1974 for the NCDS and in 1986 for the BCS). The table also shows the fraction of cohort members who were in poor families at age sixteen – defined as having income below a poverty line of half mean equivalised national income[5] – to be higher for the 1970 cohort,

[5] This poverty line is from income data in the appropriate years from the Family Expenditure Survey, a representative household survey carried out annually in Britain.

which is in line with the national trends in child poverty reported in Gregg, Harkness and Machin (1999). Finally, substantial educational upgrading occurs. Many more BCS cohort members have a degree by their early thirties as compared to the older cohort.

## 3 Estimates of changes in intergenerational mobility

Table 6.2 reports a set of baseline results, showing estimates of intergenerational mobility from both cohorts, for male and female cohort members separately. Three sets of results are reported for each. The first, in panel 1 of the table, is a regression of the log of cohort members' earnings on log parental income. The second, in panel 2 and referred to as the augmented earnings regression, adds a large set of pre-labor market entry controls to the first specification. These variables (listed in the notes to the table) are a set of child-specific and family factors. They are included in an attempt to identify the effect of changes in family income for otherwise identical individuals.[6] The final set of results uses cohort members' family income as the dependent variable.

Our main interest concerns changes in the extent of mobility over time. The results in Table 6.2 paint a strong and consistent pattern, with the intergenerational persistence rising over time. For men, the changes are sizeable with the inequality-adjusted estimates rising by 0.095 to 0.260. Similar rises are seen in the augmented and family income regressions. All of the increases for men are strongly significant, showing a steep rise across cohorts that resulted in substantial falls in the extent of intergenerational mobility. For women, the results are more muted with the top panel showing an inequality-adjusted rise of 0.059 with a standard error of 0.031, placing the change on the margins of statistical significance. To fully understand the differences in the results for men and women one would need to take account of changes

---

[6] One way of thinking about the inclusion of these characteristics is that they in some sense 'level the playing field' between cohort members by controlling for detailed observables and as such proxy child/family fixed effects. Or at least that they show how the coefficients would alter if one moved more towards a fixed effects specification that would wash out child and family characteristics not previously controlled. The cohort studies are particularly suited to this estimation strategy as they contain much richer childhood data than other similar surveys (like the National Longitudinal Survey of Youth in the United States).

Table 6.2  *Least Squares estimates of the changes in intergenerational income mobility*

| | Regression β | | β Adjusted for changes in inequality | | | Sample size | |
|---|---|---|---|---|---|---|---|
| | 1958 birth cohort | 1970 birth cohort | 1958 birth cohort | 1970 birth cohort | Change in adjusted β | 1958 birth cohort | 1970 birth cohort |
| 1. Earnings regressions | | | | | | | |
| Sons | 0.175 | 0.250 | 0.166 | 0.260 | 0.095 | 2,246 | 2,053 |
| | (0.021) | (0.021) | (0.020) | (0.024) | (0.031) | | |
| Daughters | 0.310 | 0.317 | 0.168 | 0.227 | 0.059 | 1,908 | 2,017 |
| | (0.041) | (0.030) | (0.022) | (0.022) | (0.031) | | |
| 2. Augmented earnings regressions | | | | | | | |
| Sons | 0.109 | 0.186 | 0.103 | 0.194 | 0.091 | 2,246 | 2,053 |
| | (0.023) | (0.026) | (0.022) | (0.027) | (0.035) | | |
| Daughters | 0.183 | 0.215 | 0.099 | 0.154 | 0.054 | 1,908 | 2,017 |
| | (0.047) | (0.037) | (0.026) | (0.026) | (0.0370) | | |
| 3. Family income regressions | | | | | | | |
| Sons | 0.159 | 0.300 | 0.123 | 0.261 | 0.139 | 2,110 | 2,015 |
| | (0.028) | (0.026) | (0.022) | (0.022) | (0.031) | | |
| Daughters | 0.219 | 0.307 | 0.137 | 0.221 | 0.085 | 2,156 | 2,285 |
| | (0.033) | (0.029) | (0.021) | (0.021) | (0.029) | | |

Notes:
1. 1958 birth cohort data are from the National Child Development Study, 1970 birth cohort data are from the British Cohort Study.
2. Standard errors in parentheses.
3. All regressions control for parents' age and age-squared.
4. Augmented regressions include controls for ethnicity, parental education, family structure, whether father was unemployed during childhood, and maths and reading test score quintiles at age 10/11.
5. In the family income regressions the dependent variable is the sum of cohort members' earnings plus those of any partner.

in participation effects. We do not attempt to do this here but rather place it on the agenda for future research. Despite the differences in the size of the changes for men and women we nonetheless find falls in intergenerational mobility for both sexes, particularly in the third panel when we consider the family incomes. This is the main empirical result of this chapter. Links between child and parent economic status appear to have strengthened considerably in this cross-cohort comparison. We next go on to consider the robustness of this finding.

Our estimates enable us to calculate the difference in the earnings of young people in the top and bottom quintiles of the family income distribution in the two different years. In the NCDS, families in the top income quintile had an average income 2.78 times that of families from the bottom quintile. Our estimate of intergenerational mobility there-fore suggests that the sons of the richest parents earned 120 percent more than the poorest sons.[7] The same calculation for the BCS, where the parental income distribution is wider, shows that sons from the richest quintile earned 140 percent more than sons from the poorest family income quintile.[8]

It is important to consider the robustness of these findings. Readers familiar with earlier work in this field may worry that the NCDS esti-mates of the intergenerational mobility coefficient for the NCDS are lower than the 0.4 "consensus estimate" mentioned earlier and also the estimates found for the same data in Dearden, Machin, and Reed (1997). In what follows we aim to allay these fears. We begin by repeat-ing the basic analysis of Dearden, Machin, and Reed (1997) on our NCDS sample. We obtain a Least Squares coefficient (and associated standard error) from a regression of sons on fathers' earnings of 0.248 (0.026) for 2,048 observations. This compares with 0.240 (0.027) for the more limited sample of 1,565 observations in the original work.

Further analysis implies that it is the use of family income rather than fathers' earnings as the independent variable of interest that results in

---

[7] Corak (2001) shows that by taking the antilog of $\ln Y_i^{\text{Child}} = \alpha + \beta \ln Y_i^{\text{Parents}} + \varepsilon_i$ then (ignoring $\varepsilon_i$) it is possible to show that the ratio of the earnings of children from high parental income backgrounds (H) to those from low parental income backgrounds (L) is just the ratio of their parents' income raised to the power $\beta$, namely $Y_{H,t}/Y_{L,t} = (Y_{H,t-1}/Y_{L,t-1})^{\beta}$.

[8] In the BCS, the top quintile of parents had an average income 3.84 times that of the bottom quintile.

different magnitudes in the estimated intergenerational elasticities. One plausible hypothesis that then emerges is that it may be differences in the influence of mothers' earnings that underpin the rise in $\beta$ between the cohorts. If true this would imply that if we looked at family income where fathers' earnings were the only component then the estimates of $\beta$ would not change. To test this we repeat the baseline estimations for families in which only the father works. With these samples the gap in the adjusted $\beta$ falls for both sexes, from 0.095 in the full sample to 0.086 in the restricted sample for sons and from 0.059 to 0.031 for daughters. Therefore there is some (moderate) evidence that the changing influence of mothers may be driving some of the observed change.[9] Once more, this signals the importance of gender differences and dynamics within families and provides further inspiration for considering these issues more fully in subsequent work. Great care has been taken in recent work in this area to try to ensure that results are not contaminated by measurement errors that can cause attenuation bias in estimates of intergenerational elasticities. This involves attempts to eliminate or at least minimize measurement errors in the variables entered on the right-hand side of intergenerational mobility regressions. Two main approaches are followed. First, one can try and time average multiple observations on parental income to eliminate transitory components of income thereby getting closer to a measure of permanent economic status. Second, one can use Instrumental Variables techniques to get rid of measurement error. We have some difficulties with implementing both of these approaches. Time averaging is not possible because the NCDS data has only one parental income measure. Similarly, we do not believe that we have any credible instruments for parental income.[10] Because of this we choose to follow a different route. We first take a look at the likely extent of measurement error in the BCS by time averaging over the age ten and sixteen income observations, then move to the cross-cohort comparison and

[9] One should note that, due to increased labor force participation by women, the sample size is reduced by much more by placing this restriction on the BCS data than on the NCDS data.

[10] This is despite the use of parental education and social class as instruments in Dearden, Machin, and Reed (1997). Some limited experimentation here revealed that their use, especially in the cross-cohort context, seemed rather dubious, both on the basis of Sargan tests and on the sensitivity of IV estimates to choice of instruments.

Table 6.3  *Assessing measurement error in the British Cohort Study, the impact of time-averaging parental income on the intergenerational income elasticity*

| | Regression β | BCS Sample size |
|---|---|---|
| 1. Sons | | |
| Income at age 16 | 0.240 | 1,580 |
| | (0.027) | |
| Income at age 10 | 0.230 | 1,580 |
| | (0.031) | |
| Time-averaged (age 10 and age 16) | 0.301 | 1,580 |
| income | (0.033) | |
| 2. Daughters | | |
| Income at age 16 | 0.342 | 1,528 |
| | (0.037) | |
| Income at age 10 | 0.285 | 1,528 |
| | (0.041) | |
| Time-averaged (age 10 and age 16) | 0.400 | 1,528 |
| income | (0.044) | |

Standard errors indicated in parentheses.

discuss theoretically what potential biases could overturn the result that intergenerational mobility is falling. We discuss how plausible or implausible these might be, considering our own estimates of measurement error and those found in the literature.

Table 6.3 reports a set of $\beta$ estimates based on the age ten and age sixteen income data contained in the BCS data. The reported estimates are the age sixteen estimates from Table 6.2, plus estimates based on age ten data and then upon the time averaged age ten and sixteen income data. The first thing to notice is that the estimates based on age ten and sixteen data are almost identical for sons. There is a little more variation for daughters, with the age ten estimate somewhat lower than the one measured using income at age sixteen. Furthermore, when one looks at the time averaged estimates of $\beta$ they show the expected pattern: the estimated $\beta$ rises for both sons and daughters, revealing some evidence of attenuation bias from measurement errors, and the estimates rise by around 0.06 for sons and somewhere between 0.06 and 0.11 for daughters.

Moving on to the cross-cohort implications of measurement error, the starting point is clearly the observation that one would require more attenuation bias in the NCDS sample as compared to the BCS sample to start to question our findings. It is not obvious from the outset why there should be any reason to think this to be the case, but there are several relevant points to be made. In the past, analysts have worried that the timing of the UK "Three-Day Week" might have led to measurement error in the NCDS age sixteen family income data. This question has been considered in Dearden, Machin, and Reed (1997) and in Grawe (2000a). By comparing income measures taken during and after the policy, Grawe finds that 5 percent of the whole NCDS sample is likely to have reported three-day income variables rather than standard ones, meaning that, overall, the attenuation bias from this possible source of measurement error is unlikely to be large.

Table 6.4 shows a calibration exercise on how much bigger the measurement error would be required to be in the NCDS for us to conclude that there is no statistically significant rise in the adjusted $\beta$ for sons across the cohorts, for various assumptions on measurement error in the BCS. For example, the first row of the table shows that if we assume complete accuracy in the BCS one would require measurement error in the NCDS to be 17 percent for sons. As we relax the assumptions on the accuracy of the BCS data it is clear that the measurement error required in the NCDS to get rid of the rise also increases and is often substantial. For example, if measurement error in the BCS is as high as Mazumder (2000) suggests, the NCDS measurement error would need to be 71 percent for the rise we observe to be rendered statistically insignificant. The table shows under various assumptions that one would need substantially higher measurement error in the NCDS data to eliminate the pattern of rising intergenerational mobility across the two cohorts.

As mentioned, transitory income is usually thought of as the main source of measurement error in parental earnings or income mentioned in the literature. In order to get a handle on the effect this may have on our cohort estimates we have also investigated changes in the permanent versus transitory component of labor income in a large British data source, the New Earnings Survey panel. The New Earnings Survey is a one percent employer-reported database covering all British employees carried out in April of each year. It contains very accurate wages data from employer records and enables one to follow people

Table 6.4 Sensitivity analysis of the extent of possible measurement error across birth cohorts for sons

| Assumptions on British Cohort Survey error | Regression β from British Cohort Survey | BCS β adjusted for changes inequality | Implied adjusted β for NCDS if there were no statistically significant change across cohort | Implied NCDS regression β | Implied NCDS error |
|---|---|---|---|---|---|
| No error | 0.250 | 0.260 | 0.199 | 0.210 | 17% |
| 10% | 0.278 | 0.289 | 0.228 | 0.240 | 27% |
| Solon – 14.5% | 0.292 | 0.304 | 0.243 | 0.256 | 32% |
| Mazumder – 58% | 0.595 | 0.619 | 0.558 | 0.588 | 71% |
| New Earnings Survey – 21% | 0.316 | 0.329 | 0.268 | 0.282 | 38% |

Notes:
1. For sons, no significant rise would require a difference in the adjusted coefficients of 0.061 or less.
2. Empirical estimates of the permanent component of earnings in the New Earnings Survey panel indicate that in our worst case the transitory component of labor income can have only risen to 32% in the NCDS, well within the bounds in the table (see text of main body of paper).

through time. One can use such data to work out the permanent and transitory components of earnings and compare them with the NCDS and BCS data.[11]

If the relative importance of the transitory component of income has decreased through time then this provides some independent evidence from another data source for the possibility of higher attenuation bias in the NCDS. It seems that the data are partly in line with this. Estimating a fixed effect earnings equation over five years of data for a cohort equivalent to the BCS fathers shows that transitory fluctuations in income account for 21 percent of the total variance. A comparable figure for NCDS fathers is slightly higher at 32 percent. However the last row of Table 6.4 shows the variance contribution of transitory income would need to be higher than this, at 38 percent, to result in no statistically significant fall in mobility. In summary then, Table 6.4 shows that measurement error in the NCDS would need to be quite substantial to even reduce our observed rise to statistically insignificant levels, let alone to account for it entirely.

All this gives us confidence that we are picking up a genuine rise in the child–parent correlations across the NCDS and BCS cohorts. We next therefore consider how much of the observed increase can be explained by the substantial educational upgrading we see across the cohorts. As noted, changes in intergenerational correlations could come about if the correlations between earnings, education, and parental income alter through time. To explore this we add variables measuring the education levels of cohort members to the intergenerational mobility regressions. The results are reported in Table 6.5. They show education to have an important impact on the magnitude of the estimated $\beta$ for both cohorts, with a bigger (moderating) impact on the size of the BCS mobility parameter. As such, the increased educational attainment of children and parents of the BCS cohort *vis-à-vis* the NCDS cohort can explain part of the fall in intergenerational mobility.

The magnitude of this differs for sons and daughters. For sons the increase in the inequality adjusted $\beta$ is 0.095 unconditional on education. This falls to 0.078 once we control for sons' education. For daughters the fall is bigger, going from an unconditional rise of 0.059

---

[11] Dickens (2000) undertakes a detailed study of how much of the rise in earnings inequality seen in Britain is due to a rise in the permanent versus the transitory components of earnings. He finds about half of the rise in the variance of hourly earnings between 1975 and 1995 to be permanent.

Table 6.5   *Changes in intergenerational mobility and educational upgrading*

| | Regression β | | β adjusted for changes in inequality | | Gap in adjusted β | Sample size |
|---|---|---|---|---|---|---|
| | NCDS | BCS | NCDS | BCS | | |
| **1. Sons** | | | | | | |
| Table 6.2, | 0.175 | 0.250 | 0.166 | 0.260 | 0.095 | NCDS: 2,246 |
| panel 1 | (0.021) | (0.021) | (0.020) | (0.024) | (0.031) | BCS: 2,053 |
| Plus sons' | 0.105 | 0.170 | 0.099 | 0.177 | 0.078 | NCDS: 2,246 |
| education | (0.020) | (0.023) | (0.019) | (0.024) | (0.031) | BCS: 2,053 |
| **2. Daughters** | | | | | | |
| Table 6.2, | 0.310 | 0.317 | 0.168 | 0.227 | 0.059 | NCDS: 1,908 |
| panel 1 | (0.041) | (0.030) | (.022) | (0.022) | (0.031) | BCS: 2,017 |
| Plus | 0.154 | 0.167 | 0.084 | 0.119 | 0.036 | NCDS: 1,908 |
| daughters' | (0.037) | (0.030) | (0.020) | (0.021) | (0.029) | BCS: 2,017 |
| education | | | | | | |

*Notes:*
1. Standard errors in parentheses.
2. All regressions control for parents' age and age-squared. They suggest that changes in traditional gender roles may lead the influence the role of parental income to differ between sons and daughters.
3. Educational attainment is modelled via educational qualification dummies (less than O level; O level or equivalent; greater than O level but less than degree; degree or higher).

to a rise of 0.036 conditional on daughters' education. Measured education accounts, therefore, for 18 percent of the fall in mobility for sons and 40 percent for daughters. According to the simple economic model outlined earlier, this result is in line with the fact that, particularly for females, the expansion in educational achievement between the cohorts has been concentrated on those from higher-income backgrounds. This inequality in increased education supply has been acknowledged by the British Department for Education and Employment (DfEE) who say, "The increase in participation in the 1990s amongst socio-economic groups A to C has been double that among groups D and E".[12] Figures from the DfEE show an increase in the participation rate of those

[12] From David Blunkett's foreword to "Higher Education for the 21st Century: Change in Higher Education" (1998), London, HMSO. The Department for Education and Employment has become the Department for Education and Skills since the 2001 General Election.

from socio-economic groups D–E of 5 percentage points (from 11 to 16 percent) and an increase of 10 percentage points for those from groups A–C from (from 26 to 36 percent).[13] This question is the focus of the (related) paper by Blanden and Machin (2004) who report evidence that the education–parental income relationship strengthened significantly across the two cohorts studied here, thereby confirming that the education expansion heavily favored children from higher-income backgrounds.

All of our analysis so far has concentrated on regression estimates of the extent of intergenerational mobility and how it has changed through time. The beauty of this approach lies in its simplicity and ease of interpretation but, of course, because of its focus on the single number average $\beta$ it is unclear about the way in which the nature of the mobility process is altering. One can explore this in more detail by looking at transition matrices, which show where child–parent pairs are moving across the distribution of economic status. Tables 6.6a and 6.6b report a set of transition matrices for NCDS and BCS sons and daughters. They show the proportion in each parental income quartile that move into each quartile of the sons' or daughters' earnings distribution. The extent of immobility can be summarised by an immobility index that computes the sum of the leading diagonal and its adjacent cells. These are reported at the top of the tables. These numbers can be interpreted relative to the immobility index in the case of perfect mobility. If all individuals had an equal chance of experiencing an adult income in each quartile all cells would contain 0.25 and the immobility index would be 2.5. As we might expect, given what we learned from the regression analysis, all the immobility indices we observe in the tables are above this number.

It is clear that transition analysis confirms the regression finding that mobility has fallen between the cohorts. In almost every case, a higher proportion remain in the same quartile as their parents in the later cohort and there are less extreme movements between generations. In the NCDS, 17 percent of sons and daughters with parents in the bottom quartile rise to the top; in the BCS this falls to 14 percent for sons and 13 percent for daughters. Moving in the other direction the growth

---

[13] Broadly, groups A–C are those with parents in skilled occupations, including professionals, managers, and skilled manual workers and groups D and E are those with parents in partly or unskilled jobs such as chefs and construction workers.

Table 6.6a   *Quartile transition matrices for sons*
*Immobility Index: NCDS 2.78 BCS 2.95*

| Parental income quartile | Sons' earnings quartile | | | |
| --- | --- | --- | --- | --- |
| | Bottom | $2^{nd}$ | $3^{rd}$ | Top |
| NCDS | | | | |
| Bottom | 0.31 | 0.29 | 0.23 | 0.17 |
| $2^{nd}$ | 0.30 | 0.24 | 0.23 | 0.23 |
| $3^{rd}$ | 0.23 | 0.26 | 0.26 | 0.26 |
| Top | 0.17 | 0.20 | 0.29 | 0.34 |
| BCS | | | | |
| Bottom | 0.39 | 0.25 | 0.22 | 0.14 |
| $2^{nd}$ | 0.28 | 0.29 | 0.24 | 0.19 |
| $3^{rd}$ | 0.20 | 0.28 | 0.27 | 0.25 |
| Top | 0.13 | 0.17 | 0.28 | 0.42 |

Table 6.6b   *Quartile transition matrices for daughters*
*Immobility Index: NCDS 2.69 BCS 2.86*

| Parental income quartile | Daughters' earnings quartile | | | |
| --- | --- | --- | --- | --- |
| | Bottom | $2^{nd}$ | $3^{rd}$ | Top |
| NCDS | | | | |
| Bottom | 0.27 | 0.31 | 0.25 | 0.17 |
| $2^{nd}$ | 0.30 | 0.24 | 0.22 | 0.24 |
| $3^{rd}$ | 0.25 | 0.24 | 0.26 | 0.24 |
| Top | 0.19 | 0.20 | 0.27 | 0.34 |
| BCS | | | | |
| Bottom | 0.33 | 0.31 | 0.23 | 0.13 |
| $2^{nd}$ | 0.28 | 0.28 | 0.25 | 0.19 |
| $3^{rd}$ | 0.24 | 0.22 | 0.28 | 0.26 |
| Top | 0.16 | 0.19 | 0.26 | 0.39 |

*Note:* The immobility index is the sum of the leading diagonal and adjacent cells.

Table 6.7a   *Quartile transition matrices for sons conditional on education*
*Immobility Index: NCDS 2.66 BCS 2.76*

| Parental income quartile | Sons' earnings quartile | | | |
|---|---|---|---|---|
| | Bottom | $2^{nd}$ | $3^{rd}$ | Top |
| **NCDS** | | | | |
| Bottom | 0.30 | 0.26 | 0.25 | 0.19 |
| $2^{nd}$ | 0.28 | 0.25 | 0.24 | 0.23 |
| $3^{rd}$ | 0.22 | 0.27 | 0.25 | 0.26 |
| Top | 0.20 | 0.25 | 0.24 | 0.31 |
| **BCS** | | | | |
| Bottom | 0.33 | 0.26 | 0.22 | 0.19 |
| $2^{nd}$ | 0.27 | 0.27 | 0.25 | 0.21 |
| $3^{rd}$ | 0.23 | 0.24 | 0.27 | 0.26 |
| Top | 0.17 | 0.22 | 0.26 | 0.35 |

Table 6.7b   *Quartile transition matrices for daughters conditional on education*
*Immobility Index: NCDS 2.62 BCS 2.65*

| Parental income quartile | Daughters' earnings quartile | | | |
|---|---|---|---|---|
| | Bottom | $2^{nd}$ | $3^{rd}$ | Top |
| **NCDS** | | | | |
| Bottom | 0.27 | 0.29 | 0.23 | 0.21 |
| $2^{nd}$ | 0.27 | 0.24 | 0.25 | 0.23 |
| $3^{rd}$ | 0.25 | 0.23 | 0.25 | 0.27 |
| Top | 0.21 | 0.24 | 0.26 | 0.29 |
| **BCS** | | | | |
| Bottom | 0.30 | 0.26 | 0.24 | 0.19 |
| $2^{nd}$ | 0.27 | 0.24 | 0.25 | 0.24 |
| $3^{rd}$ | 0.23 | 0.25 | 0.24 | 0.28 |
| Top | 0.20 | 0.24 | 0.26 | 0.30 |

*Note:* The immobility index is the sum of the leading diagonal and adjacent cells.

in immobility is similar with almost one-fifth (17 percent for sons and 19 percent for daughters) of those who start life in the top quartile falling to the bottom in the NCDS while in the BCS the corresponding percentages are 13 for sons and 16 for daughters. The overall pattern of reduced mobility is very much confirmed by the pattern of results in the transition matrices.

We further investigate the role of education as an explanatory factor in accounting for the fall in mobility in the transition matrices presented in Tables 6.7a and 6.7b that control for education. For both sons and daughters, an important portion of the observed fall in mobility is accounted for by the education variables. For sons, the immobility index rises by 0.10 conditional on education compared with 0.17 in the unconditional matrices in Table 6.6a. For daughters, the conditional rise is 0.03 compared with 0.17 unconditionally. Thus the non-linearities allowed for in the transition matrix approach do seem to imply a bigger education effect for both sons and daughters as compared to the average regression approach considered earlier (the immobility index is reduced by 41 percent for sons and by 80 percent for daughters). As such, the increased educational attainment of the younger birth cohort seems to matter in interpreting the fall in intergenerational mobility observed across cohorts.

## 4 Conclusions

In this chapter, we have considered how the extent of intergenerational mobility has changed across two British birth cohorts, the first born in March 1958 and the second in April 1970. Even though these cohorts are only twelve years apart, we see sharp falls in cross-generation mobility of economic status between the cohorts. The economic status of the 1970 cohort is much more strongly connected to parental economic status than the 1958 cohort, with the earnings premium associated with being from the top, rather than the bottom, parental income quintile being 20 percent for NCDS sons and 40 percent for BCS sons. We find evidence that this fall in mobility can partly be accounted for by the fact that a greater share of the rapid educational upgrading of the British population has been focused on people with richer parents. This unequal increase in educational attainment is thus one factor that has acted to reinforce more strongly the link between earnings and income of children and their parents. This seems to be an unintended consequence of the expansion of the university system that occurred in the late 1980s and early 1990s and an issue that needs to be borne in mind when considering future educational reforms.

## References

Acemoglu, D., and S. Pischke (2001). "Changes in the Wage Structure, Family Income, and Children's Education." *European Economic Review*. Vol. 45, pp. 890–904.

Atkinson, A. B. (1981). "On Intergenerational Income Mobility in Britain." *Journal of Post Keynesian Economics*. Vol. 3, no. 2, pp. 194–218.

Becker, Gary R. and Nigel Tomes (1986). "Human Capital and the Rise and Fall of Families." *Journal of Labor Economics*. Vol. 4, no. 3, pp. S1–S39.

Blanden, J., and S. Machin (2004). "Educational Inequality and the expansion of UK Higher Education." *Scottish Journal of Political Economy*, Vol. 51, pp. 230–50.

Cameron, S., and J. Heckman (1998). "Life Cycle Schooling and Dynamic Selection Bias: Models and Evidence for Five Cohorts of American Males." *Journal of Political Economy*. Vol. 106, pp. 262–333.

——— (2001). "The Dynamics of Educational Attainment For Black, Hispanic and White Males." *Journal of Political Economy*. Vol. 109, pp. 455–99.

Card, David (1999). "The Causal Effect of Education on Earnings." In Orley C. Ashenfelter and David Card (editors). *Handbook of Labor Economics, Volume 3A*. Amsterdam: North-Holland.

Corak, Miles (2001). "Are the Kids All Right? Intergenerational Mobility and Child Well-Being in Canada." In Keith Banting, Andrew Sharpe, and France St. Hilaire (editors). *The Review of Economic Performance and Social Progress*. Montreal and Ottawa: Center for the Study of Living Standards and Institute for Research on Public Policy.

Department for Education and Employment (1998). "Higher Education for the 21st Century: Change in Higher Education." HMSO: London.

Dearden, Lorraine, Stephen Machin, and Howard Reed (1997). "Intergenerational Mobility in Britain." *Economic Journal*. Vol. 107, no. 1, pp. 47–64.

Dickens, R. (2000). "The Evolution of Individual Male Earnings in Great Britain: 1975–95." *Economic Journal*. Vol. 110, pp. 27–49.

Fertig, Angela R. (2001). "Trends in Intergenerational Earnings Mobility." Princeton, NJ: Center for Research on Child Wellbeing, Princeton University Working Paper No. 2001–23.

Fortin, N., and S. Lefebvre (1998). "Intergenerational Income Mobility in Canada." In Miles Corak (editor). *Labour Markets, Social Institutions and the Future of Canada's Children*. Ottawa: Statistics Canada.

Galton, Francis (1886). "Regression Towards Mediocrity in Hereditary Stature." *Journal of the Anthropological Institute of Great Britain and Ireland*. Vol. 15, pp. 246–63.

Goodman, A., P. Johnson, and S. Webb (1997). *Inequality in the UK*. London: Institute for Fiscal Studies.

Grawe, Nathan D. (2000a). "The Three-Day Week of 1974 and Measurement Error in the NCDS and FES Data Sets." Unpublished mimeo.

(2003). "Lifecycle Bias in the Estimation of Intergenerational Income Persistence." Statistics Canada Analytical Studies Branch Research Paper No. 207.

(2001). "In Search of Intergenerational Credit Constraints Among Canadian Men: Quantile Versus Mean Regression Tests for Binding Credit Constraints." Family and Labour Studies, Analytical Studies Branch Research Paper No. 158. Ottawa: Statistics Canada.

Grawe, Nathan D., and Casey B. Mulligan (2002). "Economic Interpretations of Intergenerational Correlations." *Journal of Economic Perspectives*. Vol. 16, no. 3, pp. 45–58.

Gregg, P., S. Harkness, and S. Machin (1999). "Poor Kids: Child Poverty in Britain, 1966–96." *Fiscal Studies*. Vol. 20, pp. 163–87.

Gregg, P., and S. Machin (1999). "Childhood Disadvantage and Success or Failure in the Labour Market." In D. Blanchflower and R. Freeman (editors). *Youth Employment and Joblessness in Advanced Countries*. Cambridge, MA: National Bureau of Economic Research.

(2000). "The Relationship Between Childhood Experiences, Subsequent Educational Attainment and Adult Labour Market Performance." In Koen Vleminckx and Timothy Smeeding (editors). *Child Well Being in Modern Nations: What do We Know?* London: Policy Press.

Hobcraft, J. (1998). "Intergenerational and Life-Course Transmission of Social Exclusion: Influences and Childhood Poverty, Family Disruption and Contact with the Police." CASE Paper 15, Centre for Analysis of Social Exclusion, London School of Economics.

Kiernan, K. (1995). "Transition to Parenthood: Young Mothers, Young Fathers – Associated Factors and Later Life Experiences." STICERD, LSE, Welfare State Programme Discussion Paper No. WSP/113.

Machin, S. (1996). "Wage Inequality in the UK." *Oxford Review of Economic Policy*. Vol. 7, pp. 47–64.

(1998). "Recent Shifts in Wage Inequality and the Wage Returns to Education in Britain." *National Institute Economic Review*. Vol. 166, pp. 87–98.

(1999). "Wage Inequality in the 1970s, 1980s and 1990s." In P. Gregg and J. Wadsworth (editors). *The State of Working Britain*. Manchester: Manchester University Press.

(2003). "Wage inequality since 1975." In R. Dickens, P. Gregg and J. Wadsworth (editors). *The Labour Market Under New Labour.* Palgrave, MacMillan.

Machin, S., S. Harkness, and S. McIntosh (2001). "Changes in Educational Wage Differentials in Britain: Supply Changes and the Evolution of Wage Differentials by Sex and Subject of Study." Unpublished mimeo.

Mayer, Susan E., and Leonard M. Lopoo (2001). "Has the Intergenerational Transmission of Economic Status Changed?" Joint Center for Poverty Research Working Paper No. 227.

Mazumder, Bhashkar (2000). "Earnings Mobility in the US: A New Look at Intergenerational Mobility." Unpublished mimeo.

Performance and Innovation Unit (2001). "Social Mobility: a Discussion Paper." Available at http://www.cabinet-office.gov.uk/innovation/site/ site.html.

Solon, Gary R. (1989). "Biases in the Estimation of Intergenerational Earnings Correlations." *Review of Economics and Statistics.* Vol. 71, pp. 172–74.

(1999). "Intergenerational Mobility in the Labor Market." In Orley C. Ashenfelter and David Card (editors). *Handbook of Labor Economics, Volume 3A.* Amsterdam: North-Holland.

# 7 | Intergenerational mobility in Britain: new evidence from the British Household Panel Survey

## JOHN ERMISCH AND MARCO FRANCESCONI

I N this chapter, we analyse the degree of intergenerational mobility in Britain using a data source that has never been used before for this purpose: the British Household Panel Survey (BHPS) for the period 1991–99. Examination of this issue is, at present, limited by the short life of the survey – indeed, the first wave of data of the BHPS was collected in 1991. Nonetheless, such data allow us to make two distinct contributions. The first is substantive and refers to a better understanding (and measurement) of social mobility in Britain for a large sample of individuals from several cohorts and different backgrounds. This can be achieved by employing a measure of socio-economic position that is commonly used in sociology, the Hope–Goldthorpe score of occupational prestige. The results from this analysis are interesting in their own right, and may help integrate the findings that have emerged from sociology and economics in the recent past. The second contribution is methodological, and suggestive of the potentials that the BHPS offers for future research in this and related areas. This goal is achieved by matching parents to their young adult children who are in the labor market, and allows us to examine mobility using measures of economic position that are more conventional for economists, such as earnings and income. Although the estimates are far from conclusive, they are suggestive of avenues for future research.

The two contributions have consequences both for the academic and policy debate on the extent of social mobility in Britain and for

We thank Miles Corak, Nathan Grawe, Christopher Jenks, an anonymous referee, and the participants in the workshop on Intergenerational Mobility sponsored by Statistics Canada, February 2001, for helpful comments. We are grateful to the Economic and Social Research Council for financial support for this study.

future methodological developments and data gathering on this topic. However, more emphasis is given to the first substantive contribution, as it is based on reliable estimates and is suited for straightforward comparisons with existing studies. One important comparison is with the work on Britain in Chapter 6.

Our chapter proceeds as follows. In the next section, we provide background against which our contributions can be seen, while in Section 2 we describe the data source, the samples, and the measures of socio-economic status used. In Section 1 we also discuss the econometric issues and the methodology used to estimate intergenerational mobility in our samples. The main results using the Hope–Goldthorpe score of occupational prestige are presented in Section 3. We pay special attention to issues of measurement error, non-linear effects, and differences by cohort. Results using the earnings and income data are offered in Section 4. Although these results are more speculative, the underlying analysis is relevant for laying down a methodological strategy which can be used in similar future studies. Section 5 summarizes our main findings and concludes.

In summary, we find that the estimates obtained from a sample of all adults who provide information on their parents' occupation when they were aged fourteen point to an intergenerational elasticity – measured in terms of Hope–Goldthorpe scores of occupational prestige – of the order of 0.15 to 0.30. After adjusting for possible measurement error, the estimated intergenerational correlations range from 0.45 to 0.75 for father–child pairs and from 0.30 to 0.50 for mother–child pairs. In addition, we find strong non-linear effects (typically, the intergenerational elasticity increases with parental status), and a substantial decline in cross-generation correlations in occupational prestige over time. The analysis of the young adults we match to one or both of their biological or adoptive parents interviewed in at least one of the nine years of the panel survey is far from conclusive. With monthly earnings and annual income as measures of economic status, Least Squares (LS) estimates of the intergenerational correlation are at most around 0.05, while Instrumental Variables (IV) estimates are at most around 0.20. The implied high economic mobility for this sample is arguably due to life-cycle considerations. This is an area that deserves additional research attention as more data become available.

## 1 Background and related literature

The relationship between people's economic status and their family background is believed to be an important indicator of equality of opportunity and the inclusiveness of a society. One important reason for this belief is the judgment that "equal opportunity" (rather than equal outcomes) is a desirable characteristic of a prosperous society. The meaning of this term is discussed in much more detail in previous chapters. In our context, it means that children from different families but with equal abilities have equal options in terms of investments in their human capital, occupational careers, and expected income (Behrman and Taubman 1990, Stokey 1996).

Several models have been developed to explain why parents' and children's status (income, earnings, or social class) are correlated, many of which show that a limited access to capital markets or other means of financing human capital decrease the degree of intergenerational mobility (Behrman 1997, Mulligan 1997). Similarly, ever since the studies of Becker (1981), Becker and Tomes (1979, 1986) and Loury (1981), a growing body of empirical research has estimated a relationship between the log of a son's or daughter's socio-economic status and the log of the same (or other) measure of economic status for his or her parent or parents. Solon (1999) offers a survey of the empirical literature. He reviews about fifty intergenerational mobility studies using data from the United States, and ten that use data from other countries (including Sweden, Canada, Germany, and Finland). For Britain, only two economic studies are mentioned as well as two contributions from sociology. Indeed, the empirical evidence on intergenerational mobility in Britain is scarce. Table 7.1 lists all the existing studies at the time we undertook our research. In contrast, there is a large body of sociological research. Early research on occupational mobility across generations has been done by Ginsberg (1929) and Glass (1954). More recently, reference should be made to the studies of Halsey, Heath, and Ridge (1980), Goldthorpe (1980), and Erickson and Goldthorpe (1992). Björklund and Jäntti (2000) present a critical overview of the existing sociological literature, which typically measures mobility in class and status, and its links to the economic literature, which typically measures mobility in earnings and income.

**Table 7.1** *Studies of intergenerational income and earnings mobility in Britain*

| Author | Data | Estimation method | Estimate of the intergenerational elasticity |
|---|---|---|---|
| Atkinson (1981) | Rowntree follow-up study; 307 father–son pairs interviewed in 1950 in the city of York to their children subsequently interviewed over the period 1975–78 | LS (weekly earnings; raw data) LS (life-cycle adjusted) | 0.358 0.415 |
| Atkinson, Maynard, and Trinder (1983) | Same data source as in Atkinson (1981); 373 father–son pairs | LS (earnings) LS (earnings; adjusted for measurement error) | 0.436 0.441–0.525 |
| Dearden, Machin, and Reed (1997) | National Child Development Survey (NCDS); 1,565 father–son pairs and 747 father–daughter pairs | LS (net income; adjusted for measurement error) LS (observed wages for 1,565 fathers–sons) LS (observed wages for 747 fathers–daughters) IV (instruments = father's education dummies) | 0.148 (unadjusted) 0.221 (adjusted) 0.240 0.351 0.581 (sons) 0.627 (daughters) |
| Blanden et al. (Chapter 6, this volume) | NCDS and 1970 British Cohort Survey (BCS); matched to their parents, there are 2,751 males and 2,931 females from NCDS and 2,062 and 2,026 females from BCS | LS (earnings); NCDS sons LS; BCS sons LS; NCDS daughters LS; BCS daughters | 0.126 0.250 0.116 0.231 |
| Ermisch and Francesconi (2002) | British Household Panel Survey (BHPS); 2,151 and 2,382 males matched with fathers or parents; 2,046 and 2,266 females matched with fathers or parents | SURE (Goldthorpe–Hope measure of occupational prestige): Parents–sons Parents–daughters Parents–child (adjusted for measurement error) | 0.208 0.234 0.439 (sons) 0.494 (daughters) |

*Note:* LS = ordinary least squares; IV = instrumental variables; SURE = seemingly unrelated regression equations.

Perhaps one of the reasons why so little is known about intergenerational income mobility in Britain is the limited availability of appropriate data. Data requirements to estimate the extent of intergenerational mobility are in fact rather stringent. Dearden, Machin, and Reed (1997) underline five major problems that intergenerational mobility studies typically face: (1) homogeneity of sample; (2) small sample sizes; (3) lack of other control variables; (4) retrospective questioning to obtain data on parents; and (5) having only one observation on income or earnings for parents. This paper focuses on specific ways to avoid or minimize the impact of these five problems on new estimates of intergenerational mobility for Britain.

The studies by Atkinson (1981) and Atkinson, Maynard, and Trinder (1983) use samples of father–son pairs with fathers interviewed in the 1950 Rowntree survey in the city of York and sons subsequently traced between 1975 and 1978. By stressing issues of measurement error, looking at earnings and net income mobility, and performing both regression and quantile transition matrix analyses, these studies are still a classic reference in this literature. However, they suffer from all of the problems above, with the exception of the fourth.

Dearden, Machin, and Reed (1997) use longitudinal data from the National Child Development Survey (NCDS), which follows all individuals born in Britain in a week in March 1958. The NCDS is a rich longitudinal survey with a relatively long time-series component and provides a substantial improvement to our understanding of social mobility in Britain. Even so, there is only a single measure of parents' earnings from the third sweep collected in 1974 when the children were aged 16. Another potential problem is the homogeneity of the sample in terms of age. Indeed, the fact that all individuals were born at one specific point in time means that they all faced the same school and legal systems, the same macroeconomic conditions, and the same cultural climate towards abortion, birth control, cohabitation, and the like. This can be desirable in some respects, but limiting in others and possibly in the study of intergenerational links. The analysis in Chapter 6 extends the literature in one important dimension by looking at changes in intergenerational mobility over time. To do so, the authors compare the NCDS cohort to another cohort of individuals drawn from the British Cohort Survey (BCS), a longitudinal survey of all children born in a week in April 1970. The comparison across cohorts is likely to avoid the problem of sample homogeneity in age. But the BCS also contains only one observation on parental income (collected in 1986 when the children were aged sixteen). In addition, the BCS only has data on parents' combined income, rather than on separate measures of fathers' earnings, mothers' earnings and other income. As discussed in Chapter 6, and as the different estimates from the NCDS samples reported in Table 7.1 suggest, care is needed in interpreting the results.

By using data from the British Household Panel Survey (BHPS), Ermisch and Francesconi (2002) fill a gap in the previous research. This chapter continues in this vein. The BHPS has a few advantages. First, the data are more recent and provide a better reflection of contemporary family life. The households tracked by the BHPS have been interviewed annually since 1991, and some of the samples under analysis are composed of individuals born between 1970 and 1983. Mothers' employment and lone parenthood (to mention two salient changes) are much more common among BHPS families than when the 1958 NCDS cohort was growing up. Second, although the NCDS and the BCS have large sample sizes and include more measures of non-economic background factors, the BHPS yields more detailed information on parents' earnings and income patterns. Third, both children and parents come from more (and thus more heterogeneous) cohorts than children and perhaps parents from the cohort studies. This will reduce the bias arising from sample homogeneity described in Solon (1989) and Dearden, Machin, and Reed (1997). In sum, analyses of the BHPS data are relevant because they complement and possibly extend our understanding of intergenerational mobility issues beyond what we already know from analyses of the cohort studies.

## 2 Data and methods

Our analysis uses longitudinal data drawn from the first nine waves of the British Household Panel Survey (BHPS), 1991–99. In autumn 1991, the BHPS interviewed a representative sample of 5,500 households, containing about 10,000 people. The same individuals have been re-interviewed each successive year. If they leave their original household to form new households, then all the adult members (those aged sixteen or more) of the new households are also interviewed as part of the survey. Children in the original households are also interviewed once they reach the age of sixteen. Some 88 percent of the original BHPS sample was re-interviewed for the second wave (1992) and the response rates from the third wave onwards have been consistently higher than 95 percent. The BHPS data, therefore, do not suffer from serious attrition bias. This means that the samples used in our analyses remain broadly representative of the population of Britain as it changed through the 1990s.[1] At present, a clear limitation of the BHPS is that it is too short a panel to allow us to follow children from birth to adulthood and have earnings (or income) information about them and their parents at comparable points of the life cycle.

Bearing this limitation in mind, there are two directions of research that can be pursued in analysing socio-economic mobility across generations using the BHPS. As explained, we pursue both of them. The first direction points to the analysis of all individuals who report information on their parents' occupations when they (the children) were aged fourteen. This yields what we call the "General Sample," in which the Hope-Goldthorpe index of occupational prestige for both parents and children is taken as the measure of socio-economic status. The second direction is to analyse a sample of young adults (aged sixteen or above) who could be matched to one or both of their biological or adoptive parents interviewed in at least one of the available waves of the BHPS. This gives us what we call the "Matched Sample," in which contemporaneous (gross monthly) earnings and annual incomes of parents and children are our measure of socio-economic status. Because neither of these samples has ever been used before to study intergenerational mobility issues, we describe them in more detail. We also describe the sample-specific techniques that will be employed in the econometric analysis.

## 2.1 The General Sample

The BHPS does not contain any retrospective information on parents' income or earnings. It does, however, ask respondents to give information on their parents' occupations when they were aged fourteen. This information has been collected in waves 1, 8, and 9 (that is, 1991, 1998, and 1999). Such information is then used to compute an index of occupational prestige according to the technique proposed by Goldthorpe and Hope (1974) and is available in the official releases of the BHPS.

[1] More information about the BHPS can be found at http://www. iser.essex.ac.uk/bhps/index.php.

This index is based on the rankings of occupations made by a random sample of individuals interviewed throughout England and Wales in 1972.[2] Using this parental occupation information provided by each adult (aged sixteen to sixty-eight, that is, all people born after 1930) in the survey allows us to obtain a very heterogeneous and large sample, with several control variables which refer to the children. The General Sample consists of 3,105 father–son pairs, 2,744 father–daughter pairs, 1,785 mother–son pairs, and 1,764 mother–daughter pairs. We analyse each parent–child pair separately.

Apart from avoiding the problems listed in Section 2, this sample has a few other advantages by employing the Hope–Goldthorpe (HG) index of occupational prestige as a measure of socio-economic status. First, the HG index is highly correlated with earnings (Phelps Brown 1977, Nickell 1982). Using the first nine waves of the BHPS, we find a correlation between the log of gross monthly earnings and the HG index of 0.70 for men and 0.75 for women. This evidence suggests that the HG measure of occupational prestige and the more traditional measures of economic status (earnings and income) may provide similar pictures of intergenerational mobility. Second, the position of individuals in the occupational hierarchy is relatively stable over time: for example, the occupational position of workers at the time they enter the labor force is the best single predictor of their occupational position when they are at the peak or at the end of their working career (Nickell 1982, Ermisch and Francesconi 2002). Therefore, the HG scale is also likely to be a good measure of people's permanent socio-economic status.

By using this measure, however, the General Sample faces three limitations. First, we have only one HG score observation for parents. As shown by Solon (1992) and Zimmerman (1992), this may produce downward-biased estimates of the intergenerational elasticity, thus misleadingly inflating social mobility across generations. Second,

[2] Goldthorpe and Hope (1974) suggest that the scale resulting from their occupational prestige grading exercise should not be viewed as a grading of social status, in the sense of unpacking some underlying structure of social relations of "deference, acceptance and derogation" (p. 10). Instead, it should be viewed as "a judgement which is indicative of what might be called the 'general goodness' or . . . the 'general desirability' of occupations" (pp. 11–12).

the data on parental occupation are obtained from adult children (and not from the parents themselves) and refer to the parents' occupation when the child was aged fourteen. This retrospective questionin is likely to be affected by recall error, whose severity may depend on the child's age at interview. The third limitation is introduced by the shifting structure of occupations over generations (Atkinson 1981), in particular when a new occupation is observed for the children's generation and an old occupation (relevant to the parents' generation) disappears. Clearly, this generates a misclassification error. Both recall and misclassification errors are again likely to bias the intergenerational elasticity downward.

Little can be done to eliminate the problems induced by such errors, all of which produce an errors-in-variables bias. To minimize at least part of this bias, we exploit the fact that the General Sample contains repeated observations on the HG score of adult children, and that it is arguably subject to less measurement error than the parents' scores. Specifically, we switch from the relationship that is typically estimated, that is,

$$Y_i = \beta X_i + \varepsilon_i \qquad (7.1)$$

to:

$$X_i = \gamma Y_i + u_i \qquad (7.2)$$

where $Y_i$ is the long-run socio-economic status (the "permanent" component of the log of HG score) for a child in family $i$, $X_i$ is the same variable for the child's father or mother, and $\varepsilon_i$ and $u_i$ are white-noise error terms. Because of measurement error in $X_i$, $\varepsilon_i$ is correlated with $X_i$, but $u_i$ is possibly not correlated with $Y_i$. The intergenerational elasticity $\beta$ is the parameter of interest here. By estimating (7.2) rather than (7.1), we can recover $\beta$ from $\gamma$, simply by computing $\gamma \dfrac{\sigma_Y^2}{\sigma_X^2} = \beta$, where $\sigma_w^2$ is the population variance of $w = Y, X$. If the population variance in socio-economic status is the same across generations, then $\beta = \gamma$. These variances, however, may differ across generations in general. Furthermore, we only have information on their sample counterparts, $\tilde{\sigma}_Y^2$ and $\tilde{\sigma}_X^2$, and the variance in the socio-economic status of parents, $\tilde{\sigma}_X^2$, is likely to be biased because we only have one single observation on parents' occupational prestige. Notice also that because we can only measure current (rather than permanent) status for children, $Y_{it}$, and the parents' HG score when the child was aged fourteen, $X_{i0}$, the relationship that we end up estimating is of the form:

$$X_{i0} = \gamma Y_{it} + \varphi R_{it} + u_{it} \tag{7.3}$$

where $R_{it}$ is a vector of child characteristics (information on fathers in the General Sample is limited), and $u_{it}$ is assumed to be a white-noise disturbance. After having estimated (7.3), we then calculate

$$\hat{\beta} = \hat{\gamma} \frac{\tilde{\sigma}_Y^2}{\tilde{\sigma}_X^2}. \tag{7.4}$$

In an attempt to reduce further the errors-in-variables bias embedded in the measurement of child status, we estimate (7.3) using five different measures of $Y_{it}$ (log of HG score). The first, labelled *observed single-year*, uses the HG index observed in the last available year for each individual (child) in the panel. The second measure is called *observed* and refers to the child's occupational prestige that is observed in all available years of the panel. The third measure is the average of child status over all available years (*average*). As shown in Solon (1992), Zimmerman (1992), and Mazumder (2001), averaging across years still produces downward inconsistent estimates of $\gamma$, but the magnitude of the inconsistency should be reduced (and thus the resulting estimates of $\gamma$ should be higher) because both the measurement error and the transitory fluctuations in $Y_{it}$ are averaged away. The fourth measure, labelled *predicted*, uses the HG score obtained from prediction equations which contain a large set of variables meant to approximate the permanent status for children (see Dearden, Machin, and Reed 1997).[3] The variables included in such least squares regressions are both time-varying and time-invariant, and include age, ethnic origin, education, region of residence, house tenure, number of children by age group, marital status, occupation, industry, and employing sector. The

---

[3] As argued in Dearden, Machin, and Reed (1997), the LS estimates based on the predicted measures may over- or underestimate the true value of the intergenerational transmission parameter $\gamma$. This crucially depends on how the unobserved permanent status $\alpha_i$ in equation (7.5) is transmitted across generations within the same family line.

last measure, called *permanent*, differs from the previous one in that we estimate fixed-effects prediction equations of the child's occupational prestige, that is:

$$Y_{it} = \delta Z_{it} + \alpha_i + v_{it}, \tag{7.5}$$

where $Z_{it}$ is a vector of time-varying child characteristics that are assumed to influence child status (age, marital status, employing sector, and industry), $\alpha_i$ is the child-specific fixed effect that picks up unobserved aspects of permanent status, and $v_{it}$ is a transitory white noise. Exploiting the longitudinal nature of the General Sample, we estimate $\delta$ in equation (7.5) with standard fixed-effects methods and use

$$\hat{\alpha} = \overline{Y} - \hat{\delta}\overline{Z} \tag{7.6}$$

as our measure of permanent child status (with the overbar denoting child-specific means of the variables $Y_{it}$ and $Z_{it}$). In the empirical analysis below, we separately employ two sets of $Z$ variables, which differ in terms of their potential endogeneity with $Y_{it}$. Most of the discussion in Section 4 will focus on the "permanent" estimates of $\gamma$ (and $\beta$) obtained with Z-variables that are arguably exogenous to child status, age, and (broadly defined) regions of residence.

## 2.2 The Matched Sample

As mentioned, this sample matches young adults (aged sixteen or above) to one or both of their biological or adoptive parents interviewed in at least one of the nine years of the panel survey. We then use the information that parents provide on their earnings and incomes and the information that each child provides on the same variables to determine the extent of intergenerational mobility in earnings and incomes. In addition, we use the information that parents had provided about their family and employment backgrounds to determine the patterns of family structure and parental work experience that applied when their children were growing up (from birth to age sixteen).[4]

---

[4] Ermisch and Francesconi (2001a) describe how family and employment histories from the BHPS can be used to construct measures of family

This sampling strategy yields a sample of 948 men and 839 women (a total of 1,787 individuals) who: (a) are aged sixteen or over and were born between 1970 and 1983; (b) do not have any serious health problems or disabilities; (c) were living with their biological, adoptive, or step-parent(s) for at least one year during the first nine waves of the panel study (1991–99); and (d) have mothers from whom complete employment histories have been gathered covering their entire childhood (from birth to their sixteenth birthday) as well as information on other potentially relevant control variables. In the BHPS, a few adults live with their elderly (retired) parents. For such parents, there is no information on earnings and only some limited information on incomes. We impose condition (a) in order to have a group of young adults who went through a relatively similar educational system, yet allowing for a sufficiently large number of different birth cohorts. Condition (b) is introduced to reduce the problem of parents choosing their employment patterns (thus earnings and incomes) during their child's childhood based on health considerations of the child. This selection rule is commonly used in similar studies, as for example in Blau and Grossberg (1992) and the references they offer. Condition (c) allows us to recover a precise measure of family structure, which a huge body of research has demonstrated to be extremely important for youth outcomes (McLanahan and Sandefur 1994, Haveman and Wolfe 1995, Ermisch and Francesconi 2001b). Finally, we impose condition (d) so that, by construction, we would have full information on the variables that are crucial to construct parental employment during childhood, and other variables which are relevant for this sample of young people.[5]

---

structure and parents' employment patterns over the entire childhood of each young adult that can be matched with his/her parents.

[5] Because condition (c) creates the potential for sample selection bias if there are unobserved factors affecting young adults' earnings or incomes that also affect the chances that children would be living with their parents, we have also performed our analysis on a restricted sample, consisting of individuals from the main Matched Sample who were living with at least one parent when aged 16–17. The justification for doing this is that, over the 1990s, 95 percent of all young people aged 16–17 live at home with their parents (Ermisch 1999). The results from this sample are quite similar to those reported below, and thus, for convenience, are not shown. They can be obtained from the authors upon request.

The analysis is on (almost) contemporaneous (and possibly repeated) measures of child's and parents' earnings or income, that is:[6]

$$Y_{it} = \beta X_{it} + \psi V_{it} + \varepsilon_i \qquad (7.7)$$

where $\varepsilon_i$ is a white noise disturbance and $V_{it}$ is a vector of child's characteristics at time $t$ (age, education, and their interactions). These should be included in the analysis because parents and children not only are at different points of their working cycles, but also because the Matched Sample consists of relatively young children whose selection into paid work is likely to be non-random (Griliches 1976, Ermisch and Francesconi 2000). Indeed, in the analysis of earnings mobility, the effective sample size is of 421 father–son, 382 father–daughter, 616 mother–son, and 553 mother–daughter pairs. (These figures apply for the analysis of earnings mobility, and are slightly different in the case of income mobility.) The smaller sample size in part reflects missing information on parental earnings or income (this involves roughly 17 percent in the father–child pairs and 8 percent in the mother–child pairs), and largely reflects the fact that the children in these samples are still out of the labor force (about 45 percent). Apart from the small sample size issue, however, the Matched Sample is likely to avoid the other problems listed in Section 2. Furthermore, as more waves of BHPS data are accumulated, this sample is bound to become increasingly important for the analysis of intergenerational links.

Parents' economic status, $X_{it}$ in equation (7.7), is likely to be measured with error and picks up transitory fluctuations, which are likely to exacerbate the downward bias that characterizes the LS estimates of (7.7). For this reason, besides the LS (level) estimates of $\beta$ in equation (7.7), we shall use other methods that have been suggested to reduce/eliminate this bias. One common approach uses an

---

[6] We ought to stress that the measures of child's and parents' earnings or income are "almost" contemporaneous. That is, parents and child may be employed and report earnings and income either in the same BHPS year or in different survey years. In our empirical analysis, we will use as many child–parent pairs as possible and control for the different timing of the earnings/income report by deflating the earnings/income figures with the 1999 Retail Price Index.

average of parents' economic status, which increases the ratio of signal to total variance and thus reduces the extent of error-in-variables bias.[7] Another option is to apply Instrumental Variables (IV) estimation to equation (7.7) using a measure of parents' status which is correlated with earnings or income, but uncorrelated with the error term $\varepsilon_{it}$. Instruments used in the literature include indices of father's socioeconomic status, social class, and father's education (Solon 1992, Zimmerman 1992, Dearden, Machin, and Reed 1997). However, Solon (1992) has shown that if the instruments are themselves direct determinants of the child's status attainment, then, under some plausible assumptions, the IV estimates are biased upward.[8] If this is the case, these estimates provide an upper bound on the estimates of the intergenerational elasticity, and, therefore, combining the IV estimates with the downward-biased LS estimates should provide bounds for the true value of $\beta$ in (7.7). In the empirical analysis below, our instruments will be parents' HG scores and parents' education, in line with previous research. In addition, we will use two other parental variables – the local unemployment rate and childhood family structure – that are negatively correlated with parental earnings or income.[9] Again, these new estimates are likely to be biased upward so that the probability limits of the LS estimates and the new IV estimates bracket the true value of the intergenerational elasticity, and thus provide an upper bound of $\beta$

[7] Mazumder (2001) shows that, despite averaging parents' earnings over a few years, there still might be considerable attenuation bias due to persistence (that is, serial correlation) in transitory earnings/income. With at most nine repeated observations on parents' economic status, our averaged estimates are likely to face this problem. This should be kept in mind when interpreting the results in Section 4.

[8] In the case of father's education or socio-economic status, the assumptions needed to get an upward-biased estimate of $\beta$ are: (a) that father's education (or status) positively and directly affects child's earnings or income; and (b) that father's education (or status) is positively correlated with father's earnings/income (Solon 1992, Zimmerman 1992). Indeed, both conditions are borne out by the data. Of course, because condition (a) is satisfied, then father's education is not a valid instrument (see also the discussion in Solon 1992, p. 400).

[9] The local unemployment rate is the ratio of the number unemployed to the total labor force in the local labor market, defined by 303 travel-to-work areas. (The source of these data is the National On-line Manpower Information Service.) Parents' childhood family structure is obtained directly from individual responses to the sixth wave (1996) of the BHPS.

under the same (but of opposite sign) plausible assumptions introduced for parental education and social status.[10]

## 2.3 Descriptive statistics

Table 7.2 presents summary statistics of some of the variables in the two samples. In the General Sample, described in the first panel of the table, the average age of sons and daughters who have information on their fathers is thirty-eight years. For those who report information on their mothers it is thirty-six years. It should be noted that the age range is fairly broad, with the youngest individuals being sixteen years old in the next-to-the-last interview (those born in 1982) and the oldest being sixty-eight in 1999 (those born in 1931), for a total of fifty-two birth cohorts. The lowest age cut-off (aged at least sixteen in 1998) is because we need at least two years of data to estimate equation (7.3) using the "average," "predicted," and "permanent" methods described earlier. The top age cut-off (aged, at most, sixty-eight in 1999) is because individuals who have passed retirement age may have a labor market involvement that systematically differs from their involvement at earlier stages in the work cycle, and also because the information on parents' occupation is more likely to be contaminated with recall error as individuals become older. The mean HG score for children is systematically higher than the corresponding mean HG score for parents, except in the case of father–daughter pairs. Notice also that the standard deviations are larger in the HG score distributions of sons and daughters than in the parents' distributions. This reflects, in part, a mean displacement in the distribution of occupational prestige that has occurred across generations. Figure 7.1 documents this point. The HG score kernel density distributions for fathers, mothers, and children by child gender is plotted. Notice that daughters' and mothers' distributions share similar features, while the sons' distribution is closer to their fathers'. The child distributions are bimodal, but more clearly so in the case of daughters (this is also the case for mothers). The spike on the left (which corresponds to lower occupational prestige) is also more

---

[10] In this case, the assumptions needed for the IV estimates to be upwardly inconsistent are: (a) that local unemployment rate (or childhood family structure) of the parents reduces child's earnings; and (b) that parents' local unemployment rate (or parents' childhood family structure) and parents' economic status are negatively correlated. Both conditions are borne out by the data.

Table 7.2　*Descriptive statistics of selected variables of interest by sample: means and standard deviations*

|  | Son | | Daughter | |
|---|---|---|---|---|
| *Sample and variable* | *Father* | *Mother* | *Father* | *Mother* |
| 1. General Sample | | | | |
| Age (child) | 38.4 | 35.9 | 38.3 | 36.4 |
|  | (11.3) | (10.7) | (11.1) | (10.6) |
| HG score: | | | | |
|   Child | 49.7 | 49.4 | 45.4 | 45.6 |
|  | (15.9) | (15.7) | (15.8) | (15.6) |
|   Parent[a] | 46.7 | 39.3 | 46.8 | 39.7 |
|  | (14.9) | (14.7) | (14.9) | (14.8) |
| Number of child–parent pairs | 3,105 | 1,785 | 2,744 | 1,764 |
| Number of child-year observations | 20,611 | 11,514 | 19,119 | 11,987 |
| 2. Matched Sample | | | | |
| Age of: | | | | |
|   Child | 23.1 | 22.8 | 22.5 | 22.3 |
|  | (4.8) | (4.8) | (4.3) | (4.4) |
|   Parent | 51.1 | 48.5 | 51.2 | 48.8 |
|  | (6.6) | (6.2) | (6.2) | (6.2) |
| Monthly earnings of: | | | | |
|   Child | 847 | 787 | 636 | 628 |
|  | (587) | (517) | (449) | (567) |
|   Parent | 1,577 | 669 | 1,635 | 730 |
|  | (963) | (536) | (947) | (557) |
| Total annual income of: | | | | |
|   Child | 5,922 | 6,408 | 4,711 | 5,143 |
|  | (6,578) | (6,861) | (4,753) | (5,311) |
|   Parent | 16,069 | 7,782 | 17,037 | 7,710 |
|  | (12,066) | (7,693) | (11,349) | (6,768) |
| Number of child–parent pairs | 421 | 616 | 382 | 553 |
| Number of child-year observations | 2,316 | 3,221 | 2,036 | 2,800 |

*Note:* ( ) indicates standard deviation

[a] Measured at age 14 of the child. Statistics are computed on the last available wave for each child.

Sons

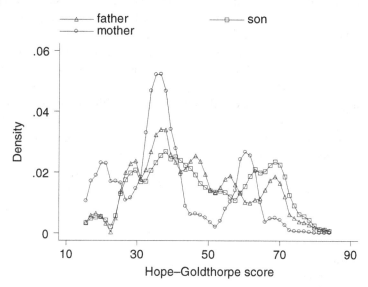

Daughters

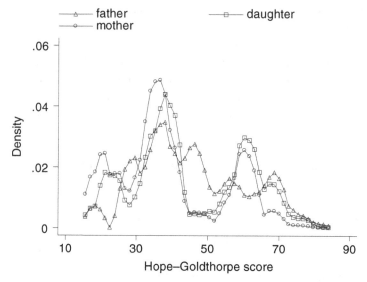

**Figure 7.1** Kernel density estimates of the father's, mother's, and child's HG score distribution by child gender.

pronounced for women (mothers and daughters), possibly reflecting the fact that women are more concentrated in low-prestige occupations and can be found in fewer occupations than men (Heath and Payne 2000). More importantly, the figure reveals that the HG score distribution is not stable across generations, with low-prestige occupations – which characterized the parents' distribution – having increasingly disappeared in the child's distribution. This may partly be taken as evidence of the misclassification problem mentioned in subsection 2.1. Little can be done to avoid this problem, but in the empirical analysis below we shall be as careful as possible to point out where these issues can be problematic and work out solutions to test the robustness of our findings.

The information in Table 7.2 also shows the gap in the average occupational prestige between sons and fathers to be in the order of three HG points (about one-fifth of a standard deviation), while that between sons and mothers is significantly larger and around 10 HG points (two-thirds of a standard deviation). This may capture the lower prestige of mothers' occupations in the General Sample. The smaller four-point difference between men (sons) and women (daughters) witnesses the advancement in occupational prestige that daughters in the General Sample experience as compared to their mothers.

In the Matched Sample, children are about twenty-two to twenty-three years old, fathers are on average fifty-one, and mothers are nearly forty-nine. Unsurprisingly, children earn much less than their fathers (approximately only half as much). This is clearly due to the substantially different points in the life cycle at which we observe parents and children. Nonetheless, sons report higher earnings than their mothers do (£787 versus £669). In addition, fathers have the highest annual income, in the range of £16,000 and £17,000. Mothers report a substantially lower gross annual income – around £7,700 – but still higher than their children's, which ranges between £4,700 for daughters (when matched with their fathers) and £6,400 for sons (when matched with their mothers).

## 3 Main results from the General Sample

### 3.1 Benchmark estimates

Table 7.2 presents the permanent fixed-effects estimates of $\gamma$, the sample values of, $\sigma_Y^2/\sigma_X^2$, and the implied intergenerational elasticity

Table 7.3 *Estimates of intergenerational mobility in occupational status: permanent fixed-effects estimates using the general sample*[a]

|  | $\gamma$ | $\sigma_Y^2/\sigma_X^2$ | $\beta$ | *Sample size* |
|---|---|---|---|---|
| Fathers–sons | 0.299 | 0.826 | 0.247 | 3,105 |
|  | (0.019) |  |  |  |
| Fathers–daughters | 0.263 | 1.091 | 0.287 | 2,744 |
|  | (0.017) |  |  |  |
| Mothers–sons | 0.256 | 0.647 | 0.166 | 1,785 |
|  | (0.029) |  |  |  |
| Mothers–daughters | 0.258 | 0.786 | 0.203 | 1,764 |
|  | (0.026) |  |  |  |

*Note:* The first column reports the estimates of $\gamma$ obtained from equation (7.3); the second columns shows the ratio in the sample values of the variance of the Hope–Goldthorpe scores for children and parents; while the third column reports the intergenerational elasticity computed using equation (7.4). The sample size (last column) refers to the number of parent–child pairs. Asymptotic standard errors are in parentheses.

[a] The term "permanent" refers to child's predicted Hope–Goldthorpe score obtained from fixed-effects regressions with age (in quartic polynomial) and region of residence dummies (16) as regressors (see equations (7.5) and (7.6) in the text).

$\beta$, along with the number of parent–child pairs. In the Appendix Table 7A.1 we report the other estimates obtained using the alternative methods described in subsection 3.1, namely, observed single-year, observed, average, predicted, and another permanent fixed-effects (which uses a fuller set of regressors). The observed single-year OLS estimates of $\gamma$ in Table 7A.2 are 0.205 and 0.208 for father–son and father–daughter pairs, and 0.208 and 0.198 for mother–son and mother–daughter pairs respectively. The observed OLS estimates are slightly higher in the case for father–son and mother–daughter pairs, and smaller in the other two groups of parent–child pairs. But there are clearly bias-related problems associated with these estimates. As expected, averaging over HG scores yields substantially higher estimates. The average estimates of $\gamma$ are in fact 0.281 and 0.239 in the case of son–father and son–mother pairs, respectively. For daughters, the corresponding estimates are 0.259 and 0.247. Further increases in the estimated values of $\gamma$ are obtained from the prediction methods described earlier. Table 7.3 shows that the permanent (fixed-effect) estimates of $\gamma$ are 0.299 and 0.263 for father–son and father–daughter, and 0.256 and 0.258 for mother–son and mother–daughter, respectively. However, the implied values of the intergenerational elasticity, $\beta$, are smaller than $\gamma$ (except in the case of father–daughter pairs), because the value of $\sigma_Y^2/\sigma_X^2$ is less than unity. In particular, the lowest value of $\beta$ emerges for mother–son pairs, 0.166, partly reflecting sample selection of mothers into employment and possibly a genuinely larger intergenerational mobility between mothers and sons. The highest value of $\beta$ occurs in the case of father-daughter pairs, 0.287. This is in part due to the value of $\sigma_Y^2/\sigma_X^2$ which magnifies the estimated $\gamma$, but it may also reflect a lower intergenerational mobility in occupational prestige between fathers and daughters (despite the steep rise in labor-force participation of women during the late 1970s and early 1980s, when, on average, most women in our sample entered the labor market).

With estimates ranging between 0.17 and 0.29, our intergenerational elasticities are small in comparison to what Atkinson et al. (1983) suggest as a benchmark: Galton's regression of fathers' height on sons' height that produced an intergenerational transmission coefficient of 0.5 (Galton 1886). But is the impact of our estimates actually small? To obtain suggestive results, we follow the approach suggested by Solon (1992) and assume that long-run status (the permanent component of log HG score) is normally distributed across generations. We then calculate the probability that a child's social position lies in different intervals of the status distribution as a function of the percentile of the father's (or mother's) status. The results of this exercise suggest that, conditional on father's position, the extent of occupational mobility is relatively small even if $\beta = 0.3$. For example, an individual whose father's status is at the 25th percentile has a 0.32 chance of remaining in the bottom quartile, a 0.42 chance of rising above the median and only a 0.07 chance of reaching the top decile. The child of an even poorer father, whose status is at the tenth percentile, will have a 0.39 chance of being in the bottom quartile, a 0.35 chance of rising above the median, and only less than 0.05 chance of reaching the top decile. For an individual whose father is at the 95th percentile of the prestige distribution, these three probabilities are 0.12, 0.69, and 0.22, respectively.[11] Naturally, if $\beta = 0.15$, the degree of mobility is higher.

---

[11] The occupations at the bottom quartile of the fathers' distribution are clearly very different from the occupations in the top decile. In the bottom

An individual whose father's status is at the 25$^{th}$ percentile has a 0.28 chance of staying in the bottom quartile, a 0.46 chance of rising above the median, and a 0.08 chance of reaching the top decile. Higher values of $\beta$, say $\beta = 0.5$ (Galton's benchmark), imply a dramatically less mobile society. Indeed, in this case, an individual whose father's status is at the 25$^{th}$ percentile has a 0.37 chance of remaining in the bottom quartile, another 0.37 probability of rising above the median, and a mere 0.05 chance of reaching the top decile.

## 3.2 Adjusting the estimates for measurement error

Not only are our intergenerational elasticities below Galton's benchmark, but they are also smaller than those presented in earlier British studies of intergenerational mobility, notably Atkinson (1981) and Dearden, Machin, and Reed (1997). Our estimates are instead about the same as (or possibly higher than) those shown in Atkinson, Maynard, and Trinder (1983), when they use living standards rather than earnings as their variable of interest. They are also similar to the estimates found in Chapter 6 from regressions of the log of children's earnings on the log of total parental income. In the General Sample, socio-economic status is proxied by the HG score of occupational prestige, not by individual earnings, so the comparison with previous results may not be appropriate.

Our estimates of $\beta$ are nonetheless below their true values, because $Y_{it}$ in equation (7.3) is likely to be measured with error. Unfortunately, we cannot apply any standard method to eliminate or reduce the resulting bias, for example, averaging parental HG scores over time (because

quartile, more than 40 percent of fathers are involved in such occupations as truck drivers, coal-mining laborers and workers, farm laborers, and security guards; whereas 70 percent of the fathers in the top decile of the distribution are managers (marketing, sales, bank, service industries, and transport) and professionals (engineers, architects, university professors, medical doctors, solicitors, and chartered accountants). Using the earnings data on children (there is no information on parents' earnings in the G-sample), those occupational differences are also reflected in substantial pay differentials. For example, the 1999 average monthly earnings is £1,069 for men and women in the lower-level (bottom quartile) occupations, while men and women at the top-level occupations (top decile) earn £1,497, approximately 40 percent more.

we only have information on parents' HG score when the child was aged fourteen) or using instrumental variables techniques (because we do not have information on parents' education or other family background variables that are uncorrelated with the child's social position). However, we can think of two sources of measurement error affecting the estimates of $\beta$ in (7.4). The first reduces the true effect of $\gamma$ directly, because we estimate (7.3) using a mismeasured proxy of the true long-run status, $Y_i$. The second source operates through the term $\sigma_Y^2/\sigma_X^2$, and underestimates the dispersion in child status relative to the dispersion in father's (or mother's) status.[12] Joining those two sources of measurement error, the error-corrected estimate of $\beta$ will be $\hat{\gamma}(1 + \mu_1)\dfrac{\tilde{\sigma}_Y^2}{\tilde{\sigma}_X^2}(1 + \mu_2)$, where $\mu_1$ and $\mu_2$ represent the amounts by which the estimated $\gamma$ and $\sigma_Y^2/\sigma_X^2$ ought to be adjusted to account for measurement error. Table 7.4 reports the results from this adjustment for four values of $\mu_1$ (0, 0.2, 0.5, and 1.0) and four values of $\mu_2$ (0.1, 0.2, 0.3, and 0.5).

Even in the absence of any adjustment in the dispersion of the status distribution across generations ($\mu_2 = 0$), a value of $\mu_1$ equal to 1 means that the value of $\beta$ is twice as large as the estimated $\gamma$. Given the results reported in a number of previous studies which used Instrumental Variables estimators to correct for the measurement error problem of raw earnings/income LS estimates, a value of 1 for $\mu_1$ is probably an upward bound to adjust the estimates of $\gamma$ (Solon 1992, Zimmerman 1992, Dearden, Machin, and Reed 1997, Mazumder 2001). A value of 0.5 for $\mu_2$ means that the variance of the child's HG score is 50 percent higher than the variance of the parents' HG score. It is possible that in periods of growing inequality, such as in the late 1980s to mid 1990s, the variance of children's income (and occupational prestige) grows faster than the variance of parents' income, but in other periods, the opposite could have been true. Therefore, we hold no priors on the size of $\mu_2$, and $\mu_2$ can in principle be either positive or negative. But if we do not assume $\mu_2$ to be positive, the resulting values of $\beta$ would be smaller (and not greater) than the values of $\gamma$, implying no attenuation bias. With $\mu_2 = 0.5$, the ratio $\sigma_Y^2/\sigma_X^2$ is always greater than unity (and

[12] Clearly, if there is overestimation of $\sigma_Y^2/\sigma_X^2$, then the two sources of measurement error would cancel each other out. Although the final impact on $\gamma$ would be unknown, the extent of the bias in this case would be less problematic. See also below.

**Table 7.4** *An assessment of the influence of measurement error on intergenerational mobility in occupational status*

| Values of $\mu_1$ | Values of $\mu_2$ | | | |
|---|---|---|---|---|
| | 0.1 | 0.2 | 0.3 | 0.5 |
| $\mu_1 = 0$ (as in Table7.3) | | | | |
| Fathers–sons | 0.272 | 0.296 | 0.321 | 0.370 |
| Fathers–daughters | 0.315 | 0.344 | 0.373 | 0.430 |
| Mothers–sons | 0.182 | 0.199 | 0.215 | 0.248 |
| Mothers–daughters | 0.223 | 0.243 | 0.263 | 0.304 |
| $\mu_1 = 0.2$ | | | | |
| Fathers–sons | 0.326 | 0.356 | 0.385 | 0.445 |
| Fathers–daughters | 0.379 | 0.413 | 0.448 | 0.516 |
| Mothers–sons | 0.219 | 0.239 | 0.258 | 0.298 |
| Mothers–daughters | 0.268 | 0.292 | 0.316 | 0.365 |
| $\mu_1 = 0.5$ | | | | |
| Fathers–sons | 0.408 | 0.445 | 0.482 | 0.556 |
| Fathers–daughters | 0.473 | 0.516 | 0.560 | 0.646 |
| Mothers–sons | 0.273 | 0.298 | 0.323 | 0.373 |
| Mothers–daughters | 0.335 | 0.365 | 0.395 | 0.456 |
| $\mu_1 = 1.0$ | | | | |
| Fathers–sons | 0.543 | 0.593 | 0.642 | 0.741 |
| Fathers–daughters | 0.631 | 0.689 | 0.746 | 0.861 |
| Mothers–sons | 0.364 | 0.398 | 0.431 | 0.497 |
| Mothers–daughters | 0.446 | 0.487 | 0.527 | 0.608 |

*Note:* Original values of $\gamma$ and $\sigma_Y^2/\sigma_X^2$ come from estimates presented in Table 7.3 (see the note to that table for definitions). The terms $\mu_1$ and $\mu_2$ represent the amounts by which the estimated $\gamma$ and $\sigma_Y^2/\sigma_X^2$ are adjusted to account for measurement error.

approximately 1.64 for father–daughter pairs), except in the case of mother–son pairs, for which it is just below one, at 0.97. Notice that even in the data used by Mayer and Lopoo (2001, Table 1) for sons drawn from the Panel Survey of Income Dynamics and born between 1949 and 1965, the value of $\sigma_Y^2/\sigma_X^2$ is greater than one only for three birth cohorts out of nine. So, our guess is that $\mu_2 = 0.5$ is likely to yield an upper limit for the adjustment of $\sigma_Y^2/\sigma_X^2$.

After having set $\mu_1$ and $\mu_2$ judiciously (say $\mu_1$ between 0.5 and 1, and $\mu_2$ between 0.2 and 0.3), Table 7.4 shows that $\beta$ ranges from

0.445 and 0.642 for father-son pairs and between 0.516 and 0.746 for father–daughter pairs. The intergenerational elasticity is slightly lower for mother–child pairs, between 0.30 and 0.43 in the case of sons, and between 0.37 and 0.53 in the case of daughters. In all cases, our new estimates become comparable to those reported in previous studies, and more importantly, we obtain a picture of a dramatically less mobile society.

## 3.3 Non-linearities and differences by cohort

The discussion so far has focused on intergeneration mobility in terms of a single parameter for the entire HG score distribution. As pointed out in Solon (1999), the implicit assumption of a constant-elasticity relationship between child's and parent's socio-economic status, however, is not supported by a number of studies for different countries (Atkinson, Maynard, and Trinder 1983, Behrman and Taubman 1990, Solon 1992, Zimmerman 1992, Dearden, Machin, and Reed 1997, Corak and Heisz 1999, Grawe in Chapter 3). Most of these studies find that the intergenerational regression to the mean is stronger from the bottom than from the top of earnings or income distributions. We test whether this is also true in the case of the HG score distribution.

For this purpose, we estimate equation (7.3) by quantile regressions at five quantiles of the HG score of the parent (either father or mother), that is, the $10^{th}$, $25^{th}$, $50^{th}$ (or median), $75^{th}$, and $90^{th}$ quantile. The equation is estimated using the five methods previously described at each quantile. Table 7.5 presents the estimates of $\gamma$ (rather than $\beta$) and their standard errors obtained from the permanent fixed-effect procedure,[13] with the variables included in $Z$ in equation (7.5) containing a quartic polynomial in age and sixteen dummy variables for region of residence. The results from the other methods (and those obtained with number of children by age group, and dummies for marital status, house tenure, industry, and sector as $Z$-variables in equation (7.5)) are

---

[13] To the extent that $\sigma_Y^2/\sigma_X^2$ is smaller than one, the values of $\beta$ would be below those shown in Table 7.5. Naturally, these (and the unreported $\beta$'s) are underestimates because of the presence of measurement error. But since here we are concerned with the differences of $\gamma$'s by quantile rather than their overall levels, we do not attempt to correct for the measurement error bias.

Table 7.5  *Permanent fixed-effects estimates of intergenerational mobility by percentile of parents' Hope–Goldthorpe score: quantile regressions estimates using the General Sample*

| | Percentile of parent's Hope–Goldthorpe score | | | | |
|---|---|---|---|---|---|
| | 0.1 | 0.25 | 0.5 | 0.75 | 0.90 |
| Father–son | 0.143 | 0.281 | 0.356 | 0.368 | 0.163 |
| | (0.018) | (0.024) | (0.033) | (0.021) | (0.013) |
| Father–daughter | 0.089 | 0.225 | 0.316 | 0.334 | 0.141 |
| | (0.017) | (0.021) | (0.026) | (0.021) | (0.014) |
| Mother–son | 0.322 | 0.442 | 0.121 | 0.432 | 0.084 |
| | (0.042) | (0.041) | (0.022) | (0.065) | (0.034) |
| Mother–daughter | 0.209 | 0.339 | 0.180 | 0.444 | 0.110 |
| | (0.048) | (0.046) | (0.018) | (0.031) | (0.027) |

*Note:* Figures are estimates of $\gamma$ from equation (7.3), and obtained from quantile regressions of log permanent child Hope–Goldthorpe score on log father Hope–Goldthorpe score. "Permanent" refers to child's predicted Hope–Goldthorpe score obtained from fixed-effects regressions with age (in quartic polynomial) and region of residence dummies (16) as regressors. Asymptotic standard errors are in parentheses.

not presented for brevity, but are broadly consistent with those shown in Table 7.5.

For both father–son and father–daughter pairs, the highest value of $\gamma$ emerges at the 75th percentile, the second highest is at the median, and the lowest is at the bottom decile. As long as such a relationship is preserved when we move to the $\beta$ parameters (that is, $\sigma_Y^2/\sigma_X^2$ is not higher at the bottom than at the top of the distribution), this reveals a higher degree of upward mobility from the bottom than downward mobility from the top, which is consistent with most of the previous literature. Non-linearities are even clearer in the case of mother–child pairs, where two peaks emerge at the 25th and 75th percentiles, with the lowest estimates being at the top decile. Interestingly, these findings are not consistent with Becker and Tomes's (1986) conjecture, according to which the intergenerational elasticity is lower as parental income (occupational prestige, in our case) increases.[14]

---

[14]  A legitimate concern is that this finding may be the result of the misclassification errors that contaminate the HG score distribution. In particular,

Another important issue is related to the possibility that the degree of intergenerational mobility changes through time. Both in the British and other advanced economies, the recent rise in income/earnings inequality has been accompanied by a growing number of children growing up in relatively poor families. The individuals in our General Sample have also faced a number of different policy initiatives and macroeconomic cycles during their childhood and adulthood. For example, important legislation on schooling was introduced in the 1944 Education Act, with the provision for raising the minimum school-leaving age from fourteen to fifteen occurring in 1947. A further increase from fifteen to sixteen subsequently occurred in 1973 (see Micklewright, Pearson, and Smith 1989). Similarly, individuals in the mid-to-late 1980s faced house prices that were up to 50 percent higher than those faced by individuals twenty-five years earlier (Banks, Blundell, and Smith 2001), and unemployment rates that were three times as large (Layard, Nickell, and Jackman 1991). As pointed out in Chapters 2, 4, and 5, it is important to see whether or not such inequality, policy, and macroeconomic shifts are also associated with changes in the intergenerational transmission of socio-economic status.

To address this issue at least partially, we stratify the General Sample by year of birth of the child in eight groups ("child birth cohort"). The oldest group consists of people born between 1931 and 1940, the youngest group consists of individuals born after 1970 (and up to 1983), and the remaining six groups are made up of individuals born in equally spaced five-year intervals between 1941 and 1970. Tables 7A.2 and 7A.3 contain the estimates of $\gamma$ and $\beta$ and the sample sizes for each cohort for father–child and mother–child pairs, respectively. Looking

individuals whose parents were at the bottom of the HG score distribution may have moved up simply because low-prestige occupations have disappeared. If this is the case, we would expect to observe high upward mobility from the bottom only because, in the child's generation, there are no longer low-prestige occupations and not because there is a genuine improvement in the social position of people coming from the bottom of the distribution. Ermisch and Francesconi (2002) show that mean-displacement shifts in the HG score distribution are inconsequential. They also show that explanations of these findings based on life-cycle effects and differential measurement errors do not receive support in the data. Convincing support is instead found by an alternative explanation based on the notion of intergenerational transmission of social and intellectual capital.

at Table 7A.3 first, both the correlation $\gamma$ and the elasticity $\beta$ point at the same phenomenon across cohorts: the intergenerational transmission linking mother's occupational prestige to her son's or daughter's prestige seems to have weakened over time, implying an increase of social mobility. (The one exception is the case of mother–son pairs for the 1956–60 cohort.) Of course, the cohort pattern of $\beta$ is not monotonic but varies over time, and sometimes quite substantially. This may be due to the small size of some of our subsamples.

In contrast, and particularly for father–son pairs, the cohort patterns of $\gamma$ differ from the cohort patterns of $\beta$ (see Table 7A.2). This occurs for the three cohorts between 1951 and 1965 in the case of sons, and for the 1956–60 cohort in the case of daughters. Such differences are driven by differences in the dispersion (variance) of economic status across generations. For example, looking at father–son pairs, the increase in $\gamma$ from 0.274 for cohort 1956–60 to 0.327 for cohort 1960–65 is reflected in a *decline* in $\beta$ from 0.288 to 0.266. This is because the variance of sons' prestige grew faster than the variance of fathers' prestige for the 1956–60 cohort ($\sigma_Y^2/\sigma_X^2 = 1.051$), whereas the opposite happened for the 1961–65 cohort ($\sigma_Y^2/\sigma_X^2 = 0.813$). Despite these discrepancies, however, we again observe a clear decline in $\beta$ over time. In the case of father–son pairs, the intergenerational elasticity for the oldest cohort is almost twice as large as that for the youngest. Comparing the 1941–45 cohort to the 1966–70 cohort, we find that $\beta$ has declined by about 30 percent in the case of father–son pairs and by 40 percent in the case of father–daughter pairs.

These findings are not in line with the evidence for Britain reported in the previous chapter. Clearly, the measure of socio-economic status used in Chapter 6 is parental income rather than the HG scores of occupational prestige for fathers and mothers. Furthermore, the authors compare only two cohorts of individuals born twelve years apart (in 1958 and 1970), while we have a greater number of birth cohorts covering a long period of time going from the early 1930s to the early 1980s. So, comparing the two sets of results may not be straightforward. Additional analysis of the patterns of socio-economic mobility across generations seems to be necessary.[15]

---

[15] In comparing data from the 1958 NCDS and the 1970 BCS, Breen and Goldthorpe (2001) find that the pattern of intergenerational correlations in social class has remained largely unchanged over this time period. It

Finally, the two issues outlined in this subsection (non-linearity in the estimated $\gamma$'s or $\beta$'s, and different degrees of mobility across cohorts) may be jointly at work. We analyse this hypothesis by estimating equation (7.3) using, again, quantile regressions with the permanent fixed-effects method described above (the variables included in $Z$ in (7.5) contain a quartic in age and region of residence). Similar results emerge when equation (7.3) is estimated using any of the other methods presented in subsection 3.1, or when the vector $Z$ in (7.5) contains the number of children by age group, and dummy variables for marital status, house tenure, industry, and sector. The estimated $\gamma$ parameters for father–child and mother–child pairs are presented in Figures 7.2 and 7.3. As pointed out earlier, in the case of father–son and father–daughter pairs, the relationship between the intergenerational correlation in occupational prestige and father's status is inversely U-shaped, with the highest values of $\gamma$ occurring around the third quartile (50th to 75th quantiles). Figure 7.2 shows that, at these quantiles, there is not a monotonic relationship across cohorts. The 1961–65 cohort displays the largest correlation (at about 0.40), while earlier cohorts have, in general, the lowest correlation (between 0.20 and 0.30), but in the case of daughters at the $75^{th}$ percentile, the lowest value of $\gamma$ is for the youngest cohort (with $\gamma$ being approximately equal to 0.15). Figure 7.3 reveals that the patterns of $\gamma$ by cohort and mother's percentile are possibly even more complex. The peaks at the $25^{th}$ and

should be stressed, however, that the empirical method followed in Breen and Goldthope's (2001) study (and a number of other sociological studies cited therein) is different from the method used here and in Chapter 6. Breen and Goldthorpe estimate relative rates of class mobility using a two-stage strategy: the first stage is to fit a parsimonious log-linear model to mobility tables, and the second stage is to re-estimate the log-linear model for grouped data as a multinomial logit model for individual-level data. It would be interesting to check whether our results are robust to this alternative method and vice versa. Interestingly, the results in Tables 7A.2 and 7A.3 are consistent with those reported in Chapter 5 and Mayer and Lopoo (2001) for the United States. Mayer and Lopoo (2001) find that the reduction in intergenerational correlations is mainly due to a reduction in the effect of parental income on children's educational attainment. They argue that this may be due to an increase in investments made in children by the state, which compensated for the difference in investments made by parents. This is certainly a possibility for Britain too. But it is not within the scope of this paper to test this hypothesis.

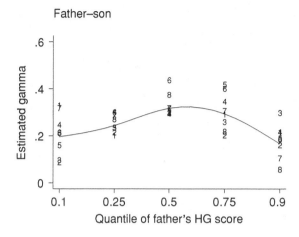

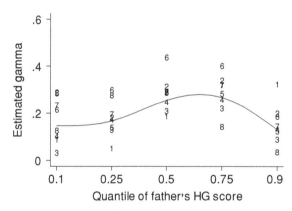

**Figure 7.2** Estimated $\gamma$ for father–child pairs by cohort and percentile of the father's Hope–Goldthorpe score – quantile regressions.

*Note:* 1 = born before 1941; 2 = 1941–45; 3 = 1946–50; 4 = 1951–55; 5 = 1956–60; 6 = 1961–65; 7 = 1966–70; 8 = born after 1970. Solid line is weighted average of all estimates over cohorts (weights are the proportions of the sample size in each cohort-percentile cell). The terms "Estimated gamma" refer to the estimates of $\gamma$ in equation (7.3), which are obtained from quantile regressions using permanent fixed-effects derived from regressions with a quartic polynomial and region of residence dummies (16) as regressors.

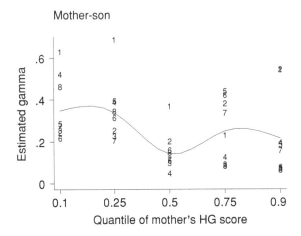

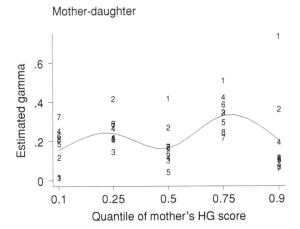

**Figure 7.3** Estimated $\gamma$ for mother–child pairs by cohort and percentile of the mother's Hope–Goldthorpe score – quantile regressions.

*Note:* 1 = born before 1941; 2 = 1941–45; 3 = 1946–50; 4 = 1951–55; 5 = 1956–60; 6 = 1961–65; 7 = 1966–70; 8 = born after 1970. Solid line is weighted average of all estimates over cohorts (weights are the proportions of the sample size in each cohort-percentile cell). The terms "Estimated gamma" refer to the estimates of $\gamma$ in equation (7.3), which are obtained from quantile regressions using permanent fixed-effects derived from regressions with a quartic polynomial and region of residence dummies (16) as regressors.

$75^{\text{th}}$ quantiles are driven by the 1956–60 cohort in the case of sons and by the early cohorts (born before 1946) in the case of daughters. The values of $\gamma$ at these percentiles range from 0.40 to 0.50. The lowest values, which arise at the median (for both sons and daughters) and at the 10th quantile (for daughters only), are not associated with one specific group but with different cohorts, from the oldest to the 1961–65 cohort, and range from 0 to 0.05 (but are never statistically different from zero).

Two observations on all the estimates by cohort are in order. First, inferring time patterns using differences across cohorts may be problematic. Ideally, one would like to have a long panel of information on parents and children from several cohorts. In this case, the length of the longitudinal component would allow us to identify the temporal evolution of the within-cohort intergenerational transmission, whereas the presence of many cohorts would permit us to see whether this relationship has changed for different people at different points in time. As it stands, however, our current analysis is a comparison of intergenerational elasticities for different cohorts of individuals at different points in their life cycles. Second, if misclassification of the HG score is worse in the later cohorts (because the measures of occupation are further away in time from the early 1970s when the HG score was constructed), this alone can account for the reduction in the estimates of $\beta$ as we move through the cohorts. This point can be simply illustrated as follows. Suppose the observed $X_i$ accurately measures the social status of parents. But the observed $Y_i$ only captures a fraction of the true social status of children, $Y_i = bY_i^*$, where $Y_i^*$ is the true social status of children, and $0 < b < 1$ captures the "degree of precision" with which the true social status is observed (the higher $b$, the higher the precision with which we measure $Y_i$; clearly, if $b$ is close to unity, the true social status is nearly perfectly observed). Under this assumption, it is easy to verify that the estimation of equation (7.3) will yield an overestimate of $\gamma$ and conversely, an underestimate of $\beta$ (that is, $\hat{\gamma} = \gamma/b$, and $\hat{\beta} = b\beta$). If misclassification of the HG score across cohorts were a serious problem, we would expect to observe divergent patterns of the estimates of $\gamma$ and $\beta$ by cohort. Inspection of Tables 7A.2 and 7A.3, however, shows that this is not the case, suggesting that the estimated temporal patterns of the intergenerational transmission of occupational prestige are probably not a statistical artefact generated by increasing imprecision in reporting parental occupation as we move across birth cohorts further back in time.

## 4 Results from the Matched Sample

### 4.1 Earnings mobility

The LS, average, and IV estimates of $\beta$ from the estimation of equation (7.7), where $Y_{it}$ is the natural logarithm of the child's (either son or daughter) annual earnings and $X_{it}$ is the natural logarithm of the parent's (either father or mother) annual earnings in year $t$, $t = 1991 \ldots$ 1999, are displayed in the first panel of Table 7.6. Results are reported for all the available years for child–parent pairs pooled, except in the case of the "average" estimates, in which we take the average for each child/parent pair over all the available years. The OLS estimates of $\beta$ are 0.048 for son–father and 0.067 for daughter–father pairs. Both estimates are statistically significant but are not statistically different from each other. The corresponding estimates for child–mother pairs are even smaller, and statistically not different from zero in the case of sons. As mentioned earlier (see subsection 2.2), there are clear bias-related problems associated with these estimates. Averaging parent's earnings should improve the ratio of signal to total variance, thus reducing the extent of the error-in-variables bias. As compared to the uncorrected OLS, the average estimates indeed show an increase in the estimated intergenerational elasticity for all four child–parent pairs. In general, however, the increase is not substantial, so the extent of intergenerational mobility appears to be always very high.

The Instrumental Variable (IV) estimates, which correct the error-in-variables bias in the LS case, are shown in the remaining four columns of Table 7.6 (top panel). The estimates in each column are obtained from a different instrument for $X_{it}$. Namely, in column (1), the instrument is parent's education (this is the instrument used by Solon 1992, and Dearden, Machin, and Reed 1997); in column (2), the instrument is parent's Hope–Goldthorpe score (this is, in many respects, equivalent to the instrument used by Zimmerman 1992); in column (3), the instrument is the parent's childhood family structure (whether the parent has ever lived in a non-intact family between birth and his/her sixteenth birthday); while in column (4), the instrument is the parent's

Table 7.6   *Estimates of intergenerational mobility in earnings and income: LS, LS average, and IV based upon the Matched Sample*

|  | LS | Average | Instrumental variables (IV) | | | |
|---|---|---|---|---|---|---|
|  |  |  | (1) | (2) | (3) | (4) |
| **1. Log monthly earnings** | | | | | | |
| Father–son | 0.048 | 0.059 | 0.118 | 0.108 | 0.221 | 0.200 |
|  | (0.024) | (0.023) | (0.036) | (0.069) | (0.076) | (0.051) |
| Father–daughter | 0.067 | 0.070 | 0.105 | 0.178 | 0.216 | 0.213 |
|  | (0.028) | (0.032) | (0.056) | (0.085) | (0.092) | (0.042) |
| Mother–son | 0.019 | 0.042 | 0.025 | 0.030 | 0.035 | 0.057 |
|  | (0.014) | (0.013) | (0.034) | (0.029) | (0.028) | (0.018) |
| Mother–daughter | 0.037 | 0.042 | 0.048 | 0.052 | 0.063 | 0.067 |
|  | (0.017) | (0.014) | (0.041) | (0.038) | (0.047) | (0.022) |
| **2. Log annual income** | | | | | | |
| Father–son | 0.026 | 0.047 | 0.129 | 0.086 | 0.182 | 0.205 |
|  | (0.015) | (0.021) | (0.035) | (0.072) | (0.093) | (0.090) |
| Father–daughter | 0.019 | 0.029 | 0.138 | 0.094 | 0.175 | 0.192 |
|  | (0.011) | (0.014) | (0.038) | (0.041) | (0.091) | (0.082) |
| Mother–son | 0.018 | 0.031 | 0.051 | 0.078 | 0.137 | 0.128 |
|  | (0.012) | (0.012) | (0.027) | (0.033) | (0.191) | (0.109) |
| Mother–daughter | 0.016 | 0.029 | 0.030 | 0.041 | 0.104 | 0.062 |
|  | (0.019) | (0.014) | (0.017) | (0.034) | (0.136) | (0.028) |

*Note:* Table entries are estimates of $\beta$ in equation (7.7) of the text. Robust standard errors are in parentheses. The instrumental variable used in the IV estimates is: parent's education in specification (1); parent's Hope–Goldthorpe score in specification (2); parent's childhood family structure (whether ever lived in a non-intact family between birth and age 16) in specification (3); and parent's local (travel-to-work area) unemployment rate in specification (4).

local unemployment rate. We expect that the estimates generated by instrumenting for parent's status with any of these four instruments would yield upward-biased estimates of $\beta$, with the magnitude of the bias depending on the separate effect of each instrument on status and on the degree of correlation between the instrument itself and the parent's long-run status. It may be seen that the IV estimates are typically much higher than the corresponding LS estimates, but their standard errors are generally larger. In the case of father–son pairs, the estimates range from 0.108 (when the instrument is the father's HG score) to 0.221 (when the instrument is the father's childhood family structure). In the case of father–daughter pairs, the increase is between 57 percent (when the instrument is father's education, column (1)) and 222 percent (column (3)). In the cases of mother–son and mother–daughter pairs, the increase in the point estimates is always sizeable but less substantial. In sum, the IV estimates are higher than the LS or LS-average estimates, but the extent of intergenerational mobility that we can infer from them is substantially higher than previous British studies have suggested.

Our conjecture is that this is the case because the children in our Matched Sample are, on average, much younger. The NCDS children analysed in Dearden, Machin, and Reed (1997) are aged thirty-three at the time their earnings are measured during 1991. In the Rowntree Follow-up Survey used in Atkinson (1981) and Atkinson, Maynard, and Trinder (1983), 70 percent of sons and 74 percent of daughters are aged thirty-five or more, with a substantial 15 percent of sons and 12 percent of daughters being over sixty-five. In contrast, most of the children in our Matched Sample have just left full-time education and can be observed only at the beginning of their working careers. Therefore, any life-cycle consideration across generations cannot be appropriately addressed with our data. Since the work of Mincer (1962), Becker (1964), and Schultz (1967), it is widely accepted that, besides formal education, workers can influence their labor market income through various investment activities, which, however, in the case of the children in the Matched Sample, have not had enough time to take place or come to (even partial) maturity. Indeed, one of the major stylised facts that the life-cycle theory explains is the existence of a life-cycle earnings profile that is increasing at early ages and declining towards the end of the working period (Weiss 1986). The observed life-cycle earnings profiles of the children under study (but not their parents) would only imperfectly reflect individual economic choices and other technological or biological processes, and consequently they are likely to be only weakly correlated with their parents. On these grounds, therefore, these (and the next) sets of estimates should be considered for their contribution to the methodological use of BHPS data in the analysis of intergenerational mobility issues rather than for the immediate policy implications that can be derived from them.

## 4.2 Income mobility

To supplement the results on intergenerational earnings correlations, the bottom panel of Table 7.6 presents the results in which economic status is measured in terms of log gross annual income. The first column of the table reports the (uncorrected) LS estimates $\beta$, based on all available child–parent pairs. These estimates are even smaller than the corresponding earnings estimates: the highest elasticity is 0.026 and is found for father–son pairs. None of these estimates is significantly different from zero. As expected, the OLS-average elasticities are higher and more precisely measured, but never exceed 0.050.

The IV estimates, which are reported in the last four columns, are obtained using the same instruments as before. As in the case of earnings mobility, the IV estimates are larger than the LS estimates and the LS-average estimates. However, they are never greater then the corresponding IV estimates shown in the top panel. For instance, in the case of father–son pairs, they range from a lowest of 0.086 (when father's education is the instrument, column (2)) to a highest of 0.205 (when the father's local unemployment rate is the instrument, column (4)). For father–daughter pairs, the highest elasticity is also found when father's local unemployment rate is used as instrument for $X_{it}$ ($\beta = 0.192$). The mother–child estimates are slightly lower, going from 0.030 (daughters, column (1)) to 0.137 (sons, column (3)). It should be noticed that, without exceptions, the standard errors associated with all the IV estimates are larger than the corresponding standard errors of the LS estimates, and in a number of cases˙the estimated elasticity is not statistically different from zero.

## 5 Conclusion

In this chapter we provide the first full account of intergenerational mobility in Britain using the British Household Panel Survey (BHPS) for the period 1991–99. The BHPS is the British equivalent of the widely used Panel Study of Income Dynamics for the United States and the German Socio-Economic Panel. Having started in 1991 (rather than 1968 or 1984), it is clearly a younger panel. In years to come, we therefore expect to see a host of intergenerational studies for Britain using the BHPS. Our primary contribution is to estimate intergenerational correlations for father–child and mother–child pairs using a number of methods to account for measurement errors. For this goal, we use information on the occupational status of children and parents for a large sample of individuals from more than fifty birth cohorts. With the same data, we also chart the trends of the intergenerational transmission estimates across cohorts and test for the presence of non-linearities at different points of the distribution of parental status. A huge sociological literature has long dealt with social mobility in Britain employing measures of occupational prestige (Erikson and Goldthorpe 1992, Heath and Payne 2000, and the references therein). But the value added of our work is to embed the findings into an economic interpretation. Further, in many respects, the analyses on non-linearities and time trends are new.

Our estimates point to an intergenerational elasticity – measured in terms of Hope–Goldthorpe scores of occupational prestige – of the order of 0.15 to 0.30. This is considerably smaller than the values found in previous British studies, namely Atkinson (1981), Atkinson, Maynard, and Trinder (1983) and Dearden, Machin, and Reed (1997). All these studies, however, use different measures of status, such as earnings or income. Instead, our estimates are similar to those reported in Heath (1981), who also correlates occupational prestige scores across generations. Somewhat more surprising is the fact that they are also comparable to the estimates reported in Atkinson, Maynard, and Trinder (1983) when net income is their measure of interest, or to the estimates reported in Chapter 6 where child's weekly wages or family income are regressed on parental income. In any case, because of the different nature of the measures of status used in most of these studies, a comparison of results is not straightforward.

There are good reasons to believe that our estimates are contaminated by various sources of measurement errors. If we take care of the bias induced by measurement errors in the variables entered on the right-hand side of our mobility regressions, we find much higher values for the intergenerational transmission coefficient and, thus, much less social mobility. In particular, the estimated intergenerational correlations range from 0.45 to 0.75 for father–child pairs and from 0.30 to 0.50 for mother–child pairs, after being adjusted for possible measurement error. These are closer to (and possibly even greater than) the "consensus" estimates found for Britain and the United States. Of course, the social welfare considerations implied by a coefficient of 0.6 are radically different from those implied by a coefficient of, say, 0.2. In the latter case, an individual whose father is at the 25th percentile of the occupational prestige in his generation would have a 29 percent chance of falling in the bottom quartile, a 24 chance of moving to the third quartile (that is between the median and the 75th percentile), and another 8 percent chance of rising to the top decile. But if the intergenerational elasticity is equal to 0.6, these three chances for the same individual are 39 percent, 20 percent, and only 4.5 percent, respectively. In this instance, we unarguably get a picture of a much less mobile society.

We also detect strong non-linear effects. That is, the intergenerational elasticity tends to increase with parental status, producing an asymmetry such that upward mobility from the bottom is more likely than downward mobility from the top of the occupational prestige distribution. While this finding is in line with several previous studies for Britain and other countries, it does not support the assumption introduced in most economic models of intergenerational mobility, according to which the intergenerational elasticity declines with parents' income or status (Loury 1981, Becker and Tomes 1986, Behrman, Pollak, and Taubman 1989). The reason is that low-income parents transfer assets to their children largely as human resource investments because in equilibrium, for small human resource investments, the marginal rate of return on such investments tends to be above the marginal rate of return on investments in financial assets. Wealthier parents, however, tend to invest much more in their children. As a result, their children tend to achieve an educational level at which the marginal rate of return to schooling equals the rate of return to financial assets, with additional resources transferred to children taking the form of monetary assets. The finding that there is a greater upward mobility from the bottom than downward mobility from the top suggests a reformulation of the basic framework.

We observe a substantial decline in cross-generation correlations in occupational prestige over time. With cohorts that are up to fifty years different in age, the social position of later cohorts appears to be less strongly connected to parental status than that of earlier cohorts. By comparing the 1970 to the 1958 birth cohorts in Britain, the authors of Chapter 6 find instead an increase in the intergenerational transmission parameters. The different result may be driven not only by the different time span of the two studies, but also by the different measures of socio-economic status. The argument – used by Mayer and Lopoo (2001) to explain the trend of higher intergenerational economic mobility in the US, which is based on increased investments in children made by the state to offset the differences in child investments made by rich and poor families, may also be valid for Britain, particularly when the time frame is half a century (as in our case) rather than twelve years.

Our analysis of measures of economic status (monthly earnings and annual income) for both children and parents can only be performed on the special sample of children who co-reside with at least one of their parents. We view our results here as suggestive, offering a loose benchmark to future studies that use BHPS data. If the LS estimates of the intergenerational correlation, which are at most around 0.05, are biased downward, the IV estimates, which are at most around 0.20, are likely to be an upper bound of the true elasticity. Either way, they are clearly lower than the estimates found in earlier British studies, and lower than our own estimates using occupational status. We conjecture that the very high economic mobility for this sample is due to life-cycle considerations. This is clearly an area that deserves more attention and more longitudinal data, and is left for future research.

At the broadest level, our findings suggest two avenues for future research. A unified framework of analysis that incorporates both sociological and economic perspectives would probably enhance our understanding of intergenerational mobility and may represent an important goal for subsequent work. Second, our analysis of the sample in which young adults are matched to their parents is totally new, but the contribution is mainly methodological and the estimates are far from conclusive. Adopting this approach as the number of BHPS waves grows and young children, who currently live with their parents, become older and enter the labor market, possibly represents the most promising avenue of research in the years to come.

**Table 7A.1** *Estimates of intergenerational mobility in occupational status: alternative measures of child's Hope–Goldthorpe score using the General Sample*

| Measure of child Hope–Goldthorpe score | Fathers | | Mothers | |
|---|---|---|---|---|
| | Sons [N = 3,105; 20,611] | Daughters [N = 2,744; 19,119] | Sons [N = 1,785; 11,514] | Daughters [N = 1,764; 11,987] |
| **Observed single-year** | | | | |
| $\gamma$ | 0.205 (0.017) | 0.208 (0.016) | 0.208 (0.025) | 0.198 (0.024) |
| $\beta$ | 0.223 | 0.265 | 0.177 | 0.191 |
| **Observed** | | | | |
| $\gamma$ | 0.233 (0.015) | 0.206 (0.014) | 0.167 (0.023) | 0.199 (0.021) |
| $\beta$ | 0.251 | 0.257 | 0.146 | 0.189 |
| **Average** | | | | |
| $\gamma$ | 0.281 (0.019) | 0.259 (0.018) | 0.239 (0.028) | 0.247 (0.027) |
| $\beta$ | 0.259 | 0.256 | 0.176 | 0.188 |
| **Predicted** | | | | |
| $\gamma$ | 0.324 (0.019) | 0.277 (0.018) | 0.261 (0.028) | 0.275 (0.026) |
| $\beta$ | 0.229 | 0.238 | 0.145 | 0.181 |
| **Permanent** | | | | |
| $\gamma$ | 0.310 (0.020) | 0.269 (0.018) | 0.267 (0.030) | 0.264 (0.027) |
| $\beta$ | 0.241 | 0.271 | 0.162 | 0.192 |

*Note:* "Observed single-year" refers to the (log) child's actual Hope–Goldthorpe (HG) score measured in the last available year in the panel. "Observed" refers to the (log) child's actual Hope–Goldthorpe score measured in all available years. "Average" is the mean child's Hope–Goldthorpe score over all the available years. "Predicted" refers to the child's predicted Hope–Goldthorpe score obtained from LS regressions with age (in quartic polynomial), region of residence dummies (16), number of children by age group (5 age groups: 0–2, 3–4, 5–11, 12–15, 16–18) and dummies for marital status (3), house tenure (3), industry (9), employing sector (4), highest educational qualification (5), occupation (8), and ethnic origin (4) as regressors. "Permanent" refers to child's predicted permanent Hope–Goldthorpe score obtained from fixed-effects regressions with age (in quartic polynomial), region of residence dummies (16), number of children by age group (5 age groups: 0–2, 3–4, 5–11, 12–15, 16–18) and dummies for marital status (3), house tenure (3), industry (9), and employing sector (4) as regressors. $N$ is number of parent–child pairs in the "observed single-year", "average", and "permanent" regressions; $N$ is number of child-wave observations in the other regressions. In square brackets, the first figure refers to the number of parent–child pairs, whereas the second figure refers to the number of child-wave observations. In the case of the "Observed" and "Predicted" regressions, robust standard errors are used. Standard errors ( ) are in parentheses.

**Table 7A.2** *Permanent occupational prestige by cohort:*
*father–child pairs from the General Sample*

| Child birth cohort | Fathers and sons | | | Fathers and daughters | | |
|---|---|---|---|---|---|---|
| | $\gamma$ | $\beta$ | N | $\gamma$ | $\beta$ | N |
| Before 1941 | 0.293 | 0.330 | 238 | 0.174 | 0.276 | 172 |
| | (0.058) | | | (0.059) | | |
| 1941–45 | 0.211 | 0.288 | 282 | 0.264 | 0.342 | 233 |
| | (0.050) | | | (0.055) | | |
| 1946–50 | 0.244 | 0.308 | 359 | 0.138 | 0.168 | 376 |
| | (0.045) | | | (0.046) | | |
| 1951–55 | 0.289 | 0.284 | 351 | 0.173 | 0.283 | 329 |
| | (0.052) | | | (0.042) | | |
| 1956–60 | 0.274 | 0.288 | 474 | 0.194 | 0.232 | 384 |
| | (0.043) | | | (0.046) | | |
| 1961–65 | 0.327 | 0.266 | 464 | 0.269 | 0.294 | 421 |
| | (0.049) | | | (0.045) | | |
| 1966–70 | 0.258 | 0.220 | 449 | 0.237 | 0.243 | 394 |
| | (0.050) | | | (0.048) | | |
| After 1970 | 0.224 | 0.176 | 488 | 0.222 | 0.176 | 435 |
| | (0.050) | | | (0.053) | | |

*Note:* Obtained from "permanent fixed-effects" regressions with age (in quartic polynomial) and region of residence dummies (16) as regressors. Asymptotic standard errors are in parentheses. N is number of child-year observations.

**Table 7A.3** *Permanent occupational prestige by cohort:*
*mother–child pairs from the General Sample*

| Child birth cohort | Mothers and sons | | | Mothers and daughters | | |
|---|---|---|---|---|---|---|
| | $\gamma$ | $\beta$ | N | $\gamma$ | $\beta$ | N |
| Before 1941 | 0.414 | 0.352 | 80 | 0.315 | 0.284 | 66 |
| | (0.113) | | | (0.126) | | |
| 1941–45 | 0.241 | 0.205 | 133 | 0.330 | 0.344 | 116 |
| | (0.092) | | | (0.086) | | |
| 1946–50 | 0.142 | 0.141 | 158 | 0.106 | 0.109 | 204 |
| | (0.079) | | | (0.069) | | |
| 1951–55 | 0.230 | 0.238 | 187 | 0.230 | 0.289 | 184 |
| | (0.070) | | | (0.064) | | |
| 1956–60 | 0.244 | 0.204 | 279 | 0.119 | 0.090 | 249 |
| | (0.064) | | | (0.070) | | |
| 1961–65 | 0.197 | 0.156 | 289 | 0.157 | 0.138 | 303 |
| | (0.065) | | | (0.061) | | |
| 1966–70 | 0.182 | 0.129 | 313 | 0.246 | 0.196 | 291 |
| | (0.067) | | | (0.064) | | |
| After 1970 | 0.172 | 0.103 | 346 | 0.192 | 0.117 | 351 |
| | (0.069) | | | (0.068) | | |

*Note:* Obtained from "permanent fixed-effects" regressions with age (in quartic polynomial) and region of residence dummies (16) as regressors. Asymptotic standard errors are in parentheses. N is number of child-year observations.

## References

Atkinson, A. B. (1981). "On Intergenerational Mobility in Britain." *Journal of Post Keynesian Economics*. Vol. 3, no. 2, pp. 194–218.

Atkinson, A. B., A. K. Maynard, and C. G. Trinder (1983). *Parents and Children: Incomes in Two Generations*. London: Heinemann.

Banks, J., R. Blundell, and J. P. Smith (2001). "Wealth Portfolios in the UK and the US." Mimeo, University College London, August.

Becker, Gary S. (1964). *Human Capital: A Theoretical and Empirical Analysis*. New York: Columbia University Press.

(1981). *A Treatise on the Family*. Cambridge, MA: Cambridge University Press.

Becker, Gary S., and Nigel Tomes (1979). "An Equilibrium Theory of the Distribution of Income and Intergenerational Mobility." *Journal of Political Economy*. Vol. 87, no. 6, pp. 1153–89.

(1986). "Human Capital and the Rise and Fall of Families." *Journal of Labor Economics*. Vol. 4, no. 3, pp. S1–S39.

Behrman, Jere R. (1997). "Intrahousehold Distribution and the Family." In M. R. Rosenzweig and O. Stark (editors). *Handbook of Population and Family Economics*. Amsterdam: North-Holland.

Behrman, Jere R., R. A. Pollak, and Paul Taubman (1989). "Family Resources, Family Size, and Access to Financing for College Education." *Journal of Political Economy*. Vol. 97, no. 2, pp. 398–419.

Behrman, Jere R., and Paul Taubman (1990). "The Intergenerational Correlation Between Children's Adult Earnings and Their Parents' Income: Results from the Michigan Panel Survey of Income Dynamics." *Review of Income and Wealth*. Vol. 36, no. 2, pp. 115–27.

Björklund, Anders, and Markus Jäntti (2000). "Intergenerational Mobility of Economic Status in Comparative Perspective." *Nordic Journal of Political Economy*. Vol. 26, no.1, pp. 3–33.

Blau, Francine D., and A. J. Grossberg (1992). "Maternal Labour Supply and Children's Cognitive Development." *Review of Economics and Statistics*. Vol. 74, pp. 474–81.

Breen, R., and John H. Goldthorpe (2001). "Class, Mobility and Merit: the Experience of Two British Birth Cohorts." *European Sociological Review*. Vol. 17, no. 2, pp. 81–101.

Corak, Miles, and Andrew Heisz (1999). "The Intergenerational Earnings and Income Mobility of Canadian Men: Evidence from Longitudinal Income Tax Data." *Journal of Human Resources*. Vol. 34, no. 3, pp. 504–33.

Dearden, Lorraine, Stephen Machin, and Howard Reed (1997). "Intergenerational Mobility in Britain." *Economic Journal*. Vol. 107, no. 1, pp. 47–64.

Erickson, Robert, and John H. Goldthorpe (1992). *The Constant Flux: A Study of Class Mobility in Industrial Societies.* Oxford: Clarendon Press.

Ermisch, J. (1999). "Prices, Parents and Young People's Household Formation." *Journal of Urban Economics.* Vol. 45, no. 1, pp. 47–71.

Ermisch, J., and M. Francesconi (2000). "Educational Choice, Families and Young People's Earnings." *Journal of Human Resources.* Vol. 35, no. 1, pp. 143–76.

(2001a). *The Effects of Parents' Employment on Children's Lives.* London: Family Policy Study Centre for the Joseph Rowntree Foundation.

(2001b). "Family Structure and Children's Achievements." *Journal of Population Economics.* Vol. 14, no. 2, pp. 249–70.

(2002). "Intergenerational Social Mobility and Assortative Mating in Britain." ISER Working Paper No. 2002-06. University of Essex, March.

Galton, Francis (1886). "Regression Towards Mediocrity in Hereditary Stature." *Journal of the Anthropological Institute of Great Britain and Ireland.* Vol. 15, pp. 246–63.

Ginsberg, M. (1929). "Interchange between Social Classes." *Economic Journal.* Vol. 29, pp. 555–65.

Glass, D. V., editor (1954). *Social Mobility in Britain.* London: Routledge.

Goldthorpe, John H. (1980). *Social Mobility and Class Structure in Modern Britain.* Oxford: Oxford University Press.

Goldthorpe, John H., and K. Hope (1974). *The Social Grading of Occupations: A New Approach and Scale.* Oxford: Clarendon Press.

Griliches, Zvi (1976). "Wages of Very Young Men." *Journal of Political Economy.* Vol 84, no. 4, pt. 2, pp. S69–S85.

Halsey, A. H., A. F. Heath, and J. M. Ridge (1980). *Origins and Destinations.* Oxford: Oxford University Press.

Haveman, R., and B. Wolfe (1995). "The Determinants of Children's Attainments: A Review of Methods and Findings." *Journal of Economic Literature.* Vol. 33, no. 4, pp. 1829–78.

Heath, A. (1981). *Social Mobility.* London: Fontana Paperbacks.

Heath, A., and C. Payne (2000). "Social Mobility." In A. H. Halsey and J. Webb (editors). *Twentieth-Century British Social Trends.* London: Macmillan.

Layard, Richard, Stephen Nickell, and Richard Jackman (1991). *Unemployment: Macroeconomic Performance and the Labour Market.* Oxford: Oxford University Press.

Loury, G. C. (1981). "Intergenerational Transfers and the Distribution of Earnings." *Econometrica.* Vol. 49, no. 4, pp. 843–67.

Mayer, Susan E., and Leonard M. Lopoo (2001). "Has the Intergenerational Transmission of Economic Status Changed?" Harris School Working Paper No. 01-16. University of Chicago.

Mazumder, Bhashkar (2001). "Earnings Mobility in the US: A New Look at Intergenerational Inequality." University of California, Berkeley, Center for Labor Economics, Working Paper No. 34.

McLanahan, Sara S., and G. Sandefur (1994). *Growing Up with a Single Parent: What Hurts, What Helps?* Cambridge, MA: Harvard University Press.

Micklewright, J., M. Pearson, and S. Smith (1989). "Has Britain an Early School Leaving Problem?" *Fiscal Studies*. Vol. 10, no. 1, pp. 1–16.

Mincer, J. (1962). "On the Job Training Costs Returns and Some Implications." *Journal of Political Economy*. Vol. 70 (supplement), pp. S50–S79.

Mulligan, Casey B. (1997). *Parental Priorities and Economic Inequality.* Chicago: University of Chicago Press.

Nickell, Stephen (1982). "The Determinants of Occupational Success in Britain." *Review of Economic Studies*. Vol. 49, pp. 43–53.

Phelps Brown, H. (1977). *The Inequality of Pay.* Oxford: Oxford University Press.

Schultz, T. W. (1967). *The Economic Value of Education.* New York: Columbia University Press.

Solon, Gary R. (1989). "Biases in the Estimation of Intergenerational Earnings Correlations." *Review of Economics and Statistics*. Vol. 71, pp. 172–74.

 (1992). "Intergenerational Income Mobility in the United States." *American Economic Review*. Vol. 82, no. 3, pp. 393–408.

 (1999). "Intergenerational Mobility in the Labor Market." In Orley C. Ashenfelter and David Card (editors). *Handbook of Labor Economics, Volume 3A.* Amsterdam: North-Holland.

Stokey. N. L. (1996). "Shirtsleeves to Shirtsleeves: The Economics of Social Mobility." Nancy L. Schwartz Lecture. Evanston, IL: Northwestern University.

Weiss, Y. (1986). "The Determinants of Life Cycle Earnings: A Survey." In O. Ashenfelter and R. Layard (editors). *Handbook of Labor Economics.* Vol. 1. Amsterdam: North-Holland.

Zimmerman, David J. (1992). "Regression Toward Mediocrity in Economic Stature." *American Economic Review*. Vol. 82, no. 3, pp. 409–29.

# 8 | Non-linear patterns of intergenerational mobility in Germany and the United States

KENNETH A. COUCH AND
DEAN R. LILLARD

NTIL recently, the literature examining economic mobility
across generations has focused almost exclusively on the average association between earnings of parents and their children
(Altonji and Dunn 1991, Becker and Tomes 1986, Solon 1992, and
Zimmerman 1992). This viewpoint has largely been maintained in
studies of individual countries as well as in the few existing direct international comparisons (Björklund and Jäntti 2000, Couch and Dunn
1997, and Dearden, Machin, and Reed 1997). A more recent literature, appealing to policy concerns as well as theoretical predictions,
has begun using non-linear estimation techniques to examine intergenerational mobility at different points in the distribution of earnings.
This chapter extends prior research by examining whether patterns
of mobility in Germany and the United States are similar across the
distribution of earnings.

The motivations for this type of study primarily originate from concerns regarding economic opportunity. The economic position of the
family into which a person is born is a matter of chance. If people, based on their family of origin, face fundamentally different life
prospects, many feel that public policy should attempt to equalize those
life chances. One measure of whether an individual born into a particular type of family faces different prospects than others is whether
his earnings as an adult are closely related to those of his parents. If
earnings are closely related across generations, so that the poor remain
poor and the rich remain rich, this might be seen as evidence that we
should seek to understand the underlying reasons and adopt policies
to assist upward mobility. If a society is characterized by high mobility
throughout the distribution, then policy intervention is typically not
viewed as necessary.

The theoretical motivations are similar. Well-known models of the
linkage between education, earnings, and family wealth predict that

for two students of equal ability in a system that requires some private financing of education, the student from the economically disadvantaged family will be able to finance less education, achieve fewer years of completed schooling, and have lower earnings as a result (Becker and Tomes 1986). Thus, in the presence of financing constraints, theory predicts a stronger relationship between the earnings of children and their parents at the bottom of the parental earnings distribution. Similarly, educational policies that provide free education but limit access based on measures of ability would be expected to reduce the strength of the relationship between the economic status of a family and the relative economic success of their children. Thus, there are predictions from economic theory that would lead us to expect that the strength of the association between earnings of parents and their children would vary systematically. Moreover, one might expect those associations to vary systematically across countries that pursue different policies with respect to educational finance and admission.

Germany and the United States are examples of countries with different policies toward both the financing of education and admissions. Germany has far fewer students as a percentage of the population attending post-secondary institutions but the government pays for education within a system where access is limited and competitive. The United States has a much larger proportion of students who attend post-secondary education and while entry certainly has a competitive nature, non-governmental financing plays a much larger role than in Germany. Similar observations can also be drawn at the secondary level. Students in Germany are streamed into education aimed at college attendance based on academic performance. The majority of high-school-level students in Germany are involved in an active program of education in courses that support apprenticeships in the industry where they expect to find employment. In the United States, course selections are more often based on student interest in attending college; education providing direct work experience and streaming into a specific profession is seldom found at the high-school level.

While there are certainly other major factors that could reasonably influence the degree of association in earnings across the two countries, it might be expected that German education policy would lead to relatively more mobility in earnings. However, one advantage of the US system is a greater opportunity for upward mobility since a larger proportion of students attend post-secondary institutions. It is difficult to make a clear prediction about differences in the degree of intergenerational mobility between the two countries. Our analysis is motivated by these concerns and in what follows we provide a more detailed review of the recent literature on intergenerational earnings focusing on research that has either investigated the non-linear nature of the relationship of the earnings of parents and their children or made international comparisons. We then describe the data from Germany and the United States and discuss the estimation techniques. After presenting our results, we discuss our findings.

In summary, our objective is to examine the similarity in the association between earnings of sons and fathers in Germany and the United States. We estimate elasticities between the earnings of fathers and sons using the German Socio-Economic Panel and the National Longitudinal Surveys and a variety of estimation models. The average association between earnings of fathers and sons across the two countries looks similar. We also find that in both countries the earnings of sons are more like their fathers when the father is a relatively high earner.

## 1 Literature review

The literature related to intergenerational economic mobility has largely proceeded on methodological grounds relating to the proper way to measure permanent rather than transitory earnings. Early studies in this area, as summarized in Becker and Tomes (1986), often used a single cross-section of data to estimate the correlation in permanent economic status between a parent and child. Generally, daughters are not incorporated into the analysis, the focus being restricted to pairs of employed fathers and sons in order to abstract from the difficulties of modeling labor force participation. Becker and Tomes (1986) conclude that at the time of their writing the consensus estimate of the intergenerational correlation in earnings was 0.20 or lower.

An important methodological development in this literature was the recognition that earnings measured in a single year were noisy and were imperfect measures of permanent economic status. Among others Altonji and Dunn (1991), Peters (1992), Solon (1992), and Zimmerman (1992) have studied this issue. In this view, averaging earnings over many years provides a better measure of permanent economic status because it is less contaminated by measurement error than measures of earnings from a single year. A common finding among researchers is that, as earnings are averaged over more years, the estimated intergenerational correlation rises, presumably due to the reduction of measurement error. Many studies that employ this method for the United States report intergenerational correlations in earnings exceeding 0.40, roughly double the consensus estimate using a single year of data. There is some evidence that this finding flows partly from the sample selection criteria commonly employed in these studies (Behrman and Taubman 1990, Couch and Lillard 1998, Peters 1992, as well as Chapter 4).

The emphasis in this literature has largely been on a single point estimate of an average elasticity or correlation of earnings between fathers and sons. This contrasts with the approach taken by sociologists in the status attainment literature where transition matrices examining movements across broad categories are the normative frame of analysis. The economics literature evolved in this way partly because theoretical models (taken at face value) suggest there is a common parameter relating earnings of parents to children, and partly because the interest in a continuous variable (earnings) does not naturally lend itself to gradations of economic status. A natural extension of the literature has been to examine how the relationship between the economic status of parents and children varies across the distribution of earnings. Some studies have presented transition matrices across deciles of the earnings distribution (Corak and Heisz 1999, Couch and Lillard 1998, and Peters 1992). Each of these papers has concluded that the strength of the intergenerational relationship varies with the earnings of the father. Given evidence of this variation in the intergenerational earnings relationship, others have used kernel density and quantile regression techniques. Some excellent examples of this type of work include the examination of earnings mobility across generations in Canada by Corak and Heisz (1999) using kernel density techniques, in the United States by Eide and Showalter (1999) using quantile regressions and in the United States and Germany by Lillard (2001) using both quantile and OLS estimations. In these papers, the authors demonstrate that intergenerational mobility varies widely across the distribution of earnings.

The evolution of the literature towards direct international comparisons of the degree of intergenerational mobility has been fairly recent. The data requirements to undertake analyses that have become standard are fairly stringent. Earnings data on both fathers and sons from the same families are needed over several years. Studies comparing Germany, Sweden, and the United Kingdom to the United States have been undertaken (Björklund and Jäntti 1997, Couch and Dunn 1997, Dearden, Machin and Reed 1997, and Lillard 2001). Sweden appears to be a more mobile society than the United States, Great Britain appears to be less mobile, and Germany is about the same. Of these studies, only Lillard (2001) examines whether there are comparable patterns of mobility that vary with the position of the son in the distribution of earnings, and finds evidence that mobility varies across the distribution of earnings.

Within this group of comparative papers, the two most important for our research are those by Couch and Dunn (1997) and Lillard (2001). Couch and Dunn (1997) examine the degree of association between the earnings of fathers and sons in Germany and the United States using panel data from the Panel Study of Income Dynamics (PSID) and the German Socio-Economic Panel (GSOEP). They make use of data from similar years and pay close attention to handling the two data sets in an identical manner. Using a standard model of the average intergenerational correlation in earnings, they conclude that the relationship is very similar in Germany and the United States. Couch and Dunn (2000) extend the horizon to include more years of data from both countries, and find that the average intergenerational earnings elasticities are very similar. Lillard (2001) directly examines whether the association in earnings in Germany and the United States varies across the earnings distribution. Although he finds it does, the results are based on a sample that is younger on average than usually employed in this literature. Our analysis uses the approach of Lillard (2001) to reexamine Couch and Dunn's (1997) finding. We first replicate the analysis of Couch and Dunn (1997), which focused on the average relationship between earnings of fathers and sons. We then investigate whether intergenerational earnings elasticities vary with the economic status of the father.

## 2 Data

The empirical analysis is based on data from the National Longitudinal Surveys (NLS) for the United States and from the German Socio-Economic Panel (GSOEP) for Germany. There is an issue in our choice of the NLS over the Panel Study of Income Dynamics. Couch and Dunn

(1997, 2000) use the latter in their comparison with the GSOEP. We felt that using the NLS data would allow us to assess the robustness of the results to the choice of data. Grawe in Chapter 4 raises this as a possible concern. For the NLS, data are taken from the Older Men, Older Women, and Young Men cohorts. Nationally representative samples of 5,020 men aged 45–59 and 5,225 younger men aged 14–24 were collected in 1966 (NLS 1987); 5,083 older women aged 30–44 were first surveyed in 1967 (US Department of Labor Statistics 1997). Data from sons and fathers are linked in both of the Older Cohorts. Of 3,219 matched father–son pairs, 1,694 pairs had non-missing data needed to estimate the earnings models. In the GSOEP, a nationally representative sample of just under 6,000 households and approximately 16,000 individuals was first surveyed in 1984. All members of the original households and all members of the households subsequently formed have been resurveyed in each subsequent year. Data from 1985 through the most recent survey year (1998) are included in our analysis. Of 1,170 matched father–son pairs, 657 pairs had non-missing data needed to estimate the earnings models. As in the NLS data, German sons are matched to fathers. Unlike the NLS, however, no distinction is made between biologically related or unrelated fathers and sons.

We select our analytical samples by age and labor force status. Men are admitted to the initial sample if they report earnings between the ages of eighteen and sixty-five in the NLS, and between the ages of eighteen and sixty in the GSOEP. We construct a second sample in which the lower age threshold is set to twenty-five in each country. Earnings are not counted for men who were in school, retired, or not in the labor force. In the NLS, to have earnings counted, men must have worked at least forty weeks in one of the years for which earnings were measured. Since weeks of work are not available in the GSOEP, we count men's earnings if they worked at least 850 hours in one of the years for which earnings were measured. Many studies in the existing literature only include earnings of men who are age twenty-five or older. Estimated elasticities tend to be larger when one excludes earnings of younger men. When panel data are used, age restrictions may introduce attrition bias because young men who drop out of school also tend to exit earlier from panel survey data. Some authors have argued in favor of this exclusion (Behrman and Taubman 1990), noting that the coefficient of variation for earnings is much higher among younger men. The potential for bias based on this sort of exclusion can be seen in the following calculations based on our NLS sample. Of 1,694 sons in the NLS sample, 292 left the sample before they turned twenty-five years of age. Those who left are less well educated, have parents who are less well educated, and fathers with lower average earnings than the men who remain in the sample past age twenty-five. Of those who left, 23.3 percent completed eleven or fewer grades versus 11.5 percent who survived in the twenty-five or older sample. Of the parents who left, 68.8 percent of the fathers and 89.9 percent of the mothers completed fewer than twelve years of schooling versus 51.8 percent and 84.4 percent of fathers and mothers respectively in the sample who survived. Further, fathers of men who left earned an average of $18,298 versus $21,173 among the survivors (measured in 1984 constant dollars). In our empirical work, we will provide estimates for a sample that includes those aged eighteen and older and a supplementary sample that includes only those aged twenty-five and older.

The earnings of sons and fathers are calculated as the mean reported wage and salary income over all years for which data are available and in which they met the additional selection rules mentioned. Earnings are averaged over one to eighteen years for fathers and one to twelve years for sons in the NLS data, and over one to fourteen years for fathers and sons in the GSOEP data. In the NLS data, if earnings are missing or reported to be zero in any given year, two steps are taken. First, if business income is reported, then the business income is used and a dummy variable coded to denote the substitution. If no business income is reported, the earnings are included as a zero in the average only if it could be established that the respondent was unemployed for all weeks in that year. An observation was dropped if earnings were zero in all observed years. Earnings data in the GSOEP are imputed in a very few cases, and these data are used in the analysis. Each model has the same basic set of control variables. These include the number of years used to calculate average earnings for both fathers and sons and, in the NLS data, dummy variables indicating if business income proxied for earnings. In addition, the age and age-squared of both father and son are included to account for differences that arise because sons and fathers are being compared in different life-cycle stages. Table 8.1 presents descriptive sample statistics for the samples including sons aged eighteen and older and sons aged twenty-five and older.

Table 8.1 *Descriptive statistics for analytical samples: United States and Germany*

| | Germany | | | | United States | | | |
|---|---|---|---|---|---|---|---|---|
| | Sons 18 years and older | | Sons 25 years and older | | Sons 18 years and older | | Sons 25 years and older | |
| | Mean | Standard deviation | Mean | Standard deviation | Mean | Standard deviation | Mean | Standard deviation |
| Earnings for sons | 44,241 | (29,788) | 54,415 | (30,312) | 14,795 | (8,132) | 20,417 | (11,814) |
| Number of years in average, sons | 7.81 | (5.01) | 6.48 | (4.08) | 6.18 | (2.68) | 3.30 | (1.45) |
| Earnings for fathers | 63,982 | (29,592) | 66,315 | (30,721) | 21,208 | (15,140) | 21,615 | (15,522) |
| Number of years in average, fathers | 11.21 | (5.49) | 11.46 | (5.07) | 6.62 | (3.80) | 6.80 | (3.81) |
| Average age – sons | 26.34 | (3.73) | 29.22 | (2.62) | 24.02 | (2.34) | 28.61 | (1.45) |
| Average age – fathers | 49.91 | (5.54) | 51.35 | (4.46) | 52.07 | (5.05) | 52.18 | (4.89) |
| Sample size | 657 | | 549 | | 1,694 | | 1,398 | |
| Number of households | 457 | | 375 | | 1,349 | | 1,146 | |

*Notes:* US dollar values are reported in constant 1997 dollars. German marks are constant 1997 deutschmarks. Data for the United States are based upon authors' calculations from the National Longitudinal Survey–Original Cohorts, those for Germany are from authors' calculations using the German Socio-Economic Panel.

## 3 Estimation methods

We first estimate a standard linear equation to obtain the earnings elasticity between the earnings of sons and fathers in the United States and
Germany as a way of benchmarking our estimates against the findings
in the existing literature. After averaging the earnings information for
the sons and fathers, the following equation is estimated using ordinary
least squares:

$$\overline{Y}_s = \alpha + \beta \overline{Y}_F + \lambda X_{FS} + \varepsilon. \tag{8.1}$$

The subscripts refer to whether the information is obtained from the
sons $(S)$ or fathers $(F)$ for the averaged earnings $(Y)$. Other regressors $(X)$ are the age and age-squared of the father and son. While
it is important to replicate prior studies, the larger purpose of this
paper is to examine potential nonlinearities in the relationship between
the earnings of fathers and sons. To provide some initial evidence of
whether relaxing the functional form affects the estimated relationship, we include higher order terms in the father's earnings in equation (8.1). Higher order terms statistically different from zero indicate that the relationship between the earnings of sons and fathers is
likely to vary across the distribution of the fathers' earnings. The equations relating the earnings of sons to fathers cannot be directly interpreted as elasticities in all of the equations we estimate. Consequently,
we use the regression coefficients from the estimations and calculate
the elasticity between sons' earnings and fathers' earnings at each quintile of the fathers' earnings distribution. We also provide standard
errors for these elasticity estimates.

## 4 Results

The results from estimating equation (8.1) for both Germany and the
United States and for the two analytical samples we use are offered in
Tables 8.2 and 8.3. In each table, the columns numbered (1) through
(3) contain estimates obtained when the natural logarithm of earnings
is used in the calculations. Columns (4) through (6) offer estimates
obtained when the level of earnings is used in the estimates. The results
in Table 8.2 are for the sample including all sons aged eighteen and
older, those in Table 8.3 are for the sample of those aged twenty-five

**Table 8.2** *Least Squares regression estimates of intergenerational earnings mobility in the United States and Germany: sons 18 years and older*

| | Germany | | | | | | United States | | | | | |
|---|---|---|---|---|---|---|---|---|---|---|---|---|
| | (1) | (2) | (3) | (4) | (5) | (6) | (1) | (2) | (3) | (4) | (5) | (6) |
| Log (father earnings) | 0.129 | 0.144 | 6.151 | | | | 0.070 | −0.071 | −2.609 | | | |
| | (0.072) | (0.836) | (7.730) | | | | (0.025) | (0.175) | (0.871) | | | |
| Log (father earnings)$^2$/10 | | −0.007 | −6.103 | | | | | 0.079 | 3.213 | | | |
| | | (0.389) | (7.598) | | | | | (0.103) | (1.126) | | | |
| Log (father earnings)$^3$/100 | | | 2.030 | | | | | | −1.249 | | | |
| | | | (2.466) | | | | | | (0.468) | | | |
| Father earnings/1,000 | | | | 0.093 | 0.212 | 0.047 | | | | 0.074 | 0.161 | 0.270 |
| | | | | (0.047) | (0.065) | (0.140) | | | | (0.018) | (0.029) | (0.058) |
| Father earnings$^2$/100,000 | | | | | −0.040 | 0.100 | | | | | −0.099 | −0.385 |
| | | | | | (0.014) | (0.115) | | | | | (0.032) | (0.152) |
| Father earnings$^3$/10$^7$ | | | | | | −0.025 | | | | | | 0.159 |
| | | | | | | (0.020) | | | | | | (0.079) |
| Intercept | 3.56 | 3.48 | −15.8 | −96.9 | −100.0 | −95.5 | −0.505 | 0.195 | 6.86 | −5.05 | −5.08 | −4.99 |
| | (1.57) | (4.82) | (25.9) | (50.5) | (50.90) | (51.0) | (2.07) | (2.32) | (2.81) | (1.97) | (1.99) | (2.01) |
| R$^2$ | 0.288 | 0.288 | 0.292 | 0.253 | 0.263 | 0.267 | 0.135 | 0.135 | 0.138 | 0.176 | 0.183 | 0.186 |
| p-value on F-test (joint) | 0.073 | 0.047 | 0.098 | 0.050 | 0.005 | 0.004 | 0.005 | 0.016 | 0.001 | 0.000 | 0.000 | 0.000 |
| Sample size | 657 sons in 375 households | | | | | | 1,694 sons in 1349 households | | | | | |

*Notes:* Huber–White standard errors in parentheses are corrected for observations of multiple sons from the same household. All models include linear and quadratic terms for the average age of sons and fathers in the years for which earnings are observed and the number of years over which earnings are averaged. Models for Germany estimated with waves B-O of the GSOEP using robust regression estimation. Models for the United States estimated with data from the NLS Older-Cohort Databases 1966–91. The p-value in the F-Statistic row corresponds to the test of the hypothesis that the coefficients on the father's earnings variables are jointly equal to zero.

Table 8.3  *Least Squares regression estimates of intergenerational earnings mobility in the United States and Germany: sons 25 years and older*

| | Germany | | | | | | United States | | | | | |
|---|---|---|---|---|---|---|---|---|---|---|---|---|
| | (1) | (2) | (3) | (4) | (5) | (6) | (1) | (2) | (3) | (4) | (5) | (6) |
| Log (father earnings) | 0.168 | −0.541 | −2.772 | | | | 0.156 | −0.569 | −3.26 | | | |
| | (0.064) | (0.583) | (5.04) | | | | (0.032) | (0.187) | (1.00) | | | |
| Log (father earnings)$^2$/10 | | 0.344 | 2.59 | | | | | 0.406 | 3.74 | | | |
| | | (0.270) | (5.11) | | | | | (0.109) | (1.29) | | | |
| Log (father earnings)$^3$/100 | | | −0.744 | | | | | | −1.33 | | | |
| | | | (1.69) | | | | | | (0.532) | | | |
| Father earnings/1,000 | | | | 0.132 | 0.312 | 0.195 | | | | 0.153 | 0.319 | 0.408 |
| | | | | (0.057) | (0.077) | (0.171) | | | | (0.030) | (0.046) | (0.089) |
| Father earnings$^2$/100,000 | | | | | −0.058 | 0.039 | | | | | −0.183 | −0.415 |
| | | | | | (0.017) | (0.123) | | | | | (0.042) | (0.218) |
| Father earnings$^3$/10$^7$ | | | | | | −0.017 | | | | | | 0.127 |
| | | | | | | (0.021) | | | | | | (0.111) |
| Intercept | 5.20 | 9.07 | 16.2 | −194 | −211 | −204 | 14.9 | 17.1 | 25.1 | 8.92 | 9.24 | 10.1 |
| | (2.87) | (4.19) | (16.5) | (144) | (146) | (146) | (5.71) | (5.70) | (6.21) | (9.73) | (10.0) | (10.2) |
| R$^2$ | 0.009 | 0.001 | 0.001 | 0.021 | 0.000 | 0.000 | 0.000 | 0.000 | 0.000 | 0.000 | 0.000 | 0.000 |
| p-value on F-test (joint) | 0.096 | 0.102 | 0.103 | 0.109 | 0.131 | 0.133 | 0.036 | 0.043 | 0.047 | 0.065 | 0.079 | 0.080 |
| Sample size | 549 sons in 375 households | | | | | | 1,398 sons in 1,146 households | | | | | |

*Notes:* Huber–White standard errors in parentheses are corrected for observations of multiple sons from the same household. All models include linear and quadratic terms for the average age of sons and fathers in the years for which earnings are observed and the number of years over which earnings are averaged. Models for Germany estimated with waves B-O of the GSOEP using robust regression estimation. Models for the United States estimated with data from the NLS Older-Cohort Databases 1966–91. The p-value in the F-Statistic row corresponds to the test of the hypothesis that the coefficients on the father's earnings variables are jointly equal to zero.

and older. Both tables contain a rough replication of Couch and Dunn (1997). In column (1) of each table, we report results of a regression of the log of average earnings of sons on the log of average earnings of fathers. The only major difference between our analysis and Couch and Dunn (1997) is that we use NLS data for the United States rather than the Panel Study of Income Dynamics. In both samples, the elasticities of earnings across generations are of a similar magnitude. In the sample of sons aged eighteen and older in Table 8.2, the estimate from column (1) for Germany is 0.129 versus 0.070 for the United States. The sample of older sons in Table 8.3 leads to an estimate for Germany from column (1) of 0.168 versus 0.156 for the United States. Like Couch and Dunn (1997), we would conclude that based on the standard model estimated in this literature, there does not appear to be a great deal of difference across the two countries in the association of the earnings of sons with those of their fathers.

For each country, we also estimate models including higher order terms in earnings of the father. The inclusion of these terms allows the estimates to take a curvilinear form. For the United States, whether the earnings data are expressed in logs or levels, all of the higher order terms are statistically significant at the 0.05 level. Also, the results of F-tests for the inclusion of the higher order terms reported in the tables, indicate that jointly, the parameters are significantly different from zero in all cases. For the German data, in the log specification, none of the individual parameter estimates for the higher order terms are significantly different than zero at the 0.05 level. In the level specifications, the parameters for the squared term in column 5 is significantly different from zero. None of the terms in the cubic specification in column 6 are significantly different from zero. Since the inclusion of higher order earnings terms is suggested by theory, we can also examine whether the coefficient estimates on the earnings coefficients are jointly different from zero when the higher order terms are added. F-tests reported for the inclusion of the higher order terms indicate that they are jointly significantly different from zero at conventional levels in all but two cases.

Tables 8.4 and 8.5 contain calculations of elasticities and standard errors based on the estimates contained in Tables 8.2 and 8.3. An average elasticity is presented at the base of each column. For example, for the sample of sons aged eighteen and older in the bottom panel of Table 8.4, the average elasticity in column (3) is 0.098 for German

Table 8.4 *Estimated intergenerational earnings elasticities by father's earnings quintile, Germany and the United States: sons 18 years and older*

| Father's earnings quintile | Germany | | | | | | United States | | | | | |
|---|---|---|---|---|---|---|---|---|---|---|---|---|
| | (1) | (2) | (3) | (4) | (5) | (6) | (1) | (2) | (3) | (4) | (5) | (6) |
| Bottom | 0.129 (0.072) | 0.129 (0.065) | 0.039 (0.103) | 0.077 (0.039) | 0.154 (0.047) | 0.086 (0.065) | 0.079 (0.023) | 0.070 (0.021) | 0.150 (0.041) | 0.036 (0.017) | 0.075 (0.014) | 0.114 (0.022) |
| Second | 0.129 (.072) | 0.128 (0.052) | 0.072 (0.083) | 0.113 (0.057) | 0.210 (0.064) | 0.154 (0.068) | 0.079 (0.023) | 0.092 (0.029) | 0.124 (0.029) | 0.068 (0.018) | 0.126 (0.022) | 0.164 (0.025) |
| Third | 0.129 (0.072) | 0.128 (0.054) | 0.086 (0.075) | 0.120 (0.061) | 0.216 (0.065) | 0.175 (0.064) | 0.079 (0.023) | 0.100 (0.034) | 0.096 (0.035) | 0.089 (0.019) | 0.150 (0.025) | 0.170 (0.024) |
| Fourth | 0.129 (0.072) | 0.128 (0.060) | 0.109 (0.065) | 0.136 (0.069) | 0.232 (0.070) | 0.217 (0.064) | 0.079 (0.023) | 0.105 (0.038) | 0.072 (0.044) | 0.108 (0.019) | 0.166 (0.028) | 0.160 (0.029) |
| Top | 0.129 (0.072) | 0.127 (0.083) | 0.181 (0.084) | 0.200 (0.102) | 0.267 (0.082) | 0.384 (0.137) | 0.079 (0.023) | 0.115 (0.046) | 0.011 (0.071) | 0.189 (0.020) | 0.193 (0.043) | 0.064 (0.097) |
| Average | 0.129 | 0.128 | 0.098 | 0.129 | 0.216 | 0.203 | 0.079 | 0.096 | 0.091 | 0.098 | 0.142 | 0.134 |
| Sample size | 657 sons in 457 households | | | | | | 1,694 sons in 1,349 households | | | | | |

*Notes:* Standard errors in parentheses. Slopes, elasticities, and standard errors calculated using coefficient estimates and variance–covariance matrix from regressions in Table 8.2.

Table 8.5 *Estimated intergenerational earnings elasticities by father's earnings quintile, Germany and the United States: sons 25 years and older*

| Father's earnings quintile | Germany | | | | | | United States | | | | | |
|---|---|---|---|---|---|---|---|---|---|---|---|---|
| | (1) | (2) | (3) | (4) | (5) | (6) | (1) | (2) | (3) | (4) | (5) | (6) |
| Bottom | 0.168 | 0.177 | 0.208 | 0.099 | 0.204 | 0.163 | 0.158 | 0.124 | 0.219 | 0.060 | 0.129 | 0.140 |
| | (0.064) | (0.057) | (0.107) | (0.043) | (0.050) | (0.074) | (0.032) | (0.027) | (0.052) | (0.012) | (0.016) | (0.024) |
| Second | 0.168 | 0.202 | 0.224 | 0.138 | 0.267 | 0.230 | 0.158 | 0.205 | 0.243 | 0.108 | 0.231 | 0.216 |
| | (0.064) | (0.054) | (0.087) | (0.059) | (0.064) | (0.080) | (0.032) | (0.034) | (0.037) | (0.022) | (0.025) | (0.029) |
| Third | 0.168 | 0.211 | 0.229 | 0.133 | 0.250 | 0.223 | 0.158 | 0.234 | 0.230 | 0.142 | 0.303 | 0.247 |
| | (0.064) | (0.055) | (0.079) | (0.057) | (0.060) | (0.069) | (0.032) | (0.040) | (0.039) | (0.029) | (0.029) | (0.029) |
| Fourth | 0.168 | 0.224 | 0.234 | 0.173 | 0.308 | 0.294 | 0.158 | 0.254 | 0.215 | 0.166 | 0.352 | 0.252 |
| | (0.064) | (0.057) | (0.068) | (0.074) | (0.073) | (0.074) | (0.032) | (0.044) | (0.046) | (0.034) | (0.031) | (0.032) |
| Top | 0.168 | 0.255 | 0.239 | 0.204 | 0.292 | 0.340 | 0.158 | 0.292 | 0.171 | 0.273 | 0.565 | 0.229 |
| | (0.064) | (0.069) | (0.070) | (0.088) | (0.067) | (0.086) | (0.032) | (0.053) | (0.073) | (0.056) | (0.041) | (0.086) |
| Average | 0.168 | 0.214 | 0.227 | 0.149 | 0.264 | 0.250 | 0.158 | 0.222 | 0.215 | 0.150 | 0.316 | 0.217 |
| Sample size | 549 sons in 375 households | | | | | | 1,398 sons in 1,146 households | | | | | |

*Notes:* Standard errors in parentheses. Slopes, elasticities, and standard errors calculated using coefficient estimates and variance–covariance matrix from regressions in Table 8.3.

youth versus 0.091 for youth in the United States. The same comparison for the older sample of sons in Table 8.5 shows an average elasticity of 0.227 for Germany versus 0.215 in the United States. It would be difficult to conclude that either the United States or Germany is more mobile across generations on the basis of a comparison of all the average elasticities shown in the tables.

Tables 8.4 and 8.5 also contain estimates of the elasticity of the sons' earnings conditional on the earnings quintile of the father. For the sample of younger sons, the elasticity estimates in Table 8.4 are generally imprecise for the log-log models estimated with the German data as can be seen by comparing the standard errors to the estimates. The log-log specification that includes a quadratic term for the German sample with younger sons fits the data well. For all other specifications in both countries, the elasticity estimates are precisely estimated for all but three cases (quintiles 4 and 5 in column (3), and quintile 5 in column (6) for the United States). In general, earnings of sons appear more related to those of their fathers when the father is a relatively high earner. This pattern is much more obvious in the estimates using the sample of older sons in Table 8.5. In every model allowing for non-linearities, the earnings of sons are more like their fathers when the father is a relatively high earner. This pattern is evident in both countries. All of the elasticities presented in Table 8.5 are statistically significant at the 0.05 level.

## 5 Conclusion

This chapter provides estimates of the average elasticity between the earnings of sons and fathers in Germany and the United States. In standard models, we find – as others have reported – that the average association in earnings is similar in the two countries. Following Lillard (2001) we investigate whether extending the standard model to allow for a curvilinear relationship between the earnings of sons and fathers is supported by the data. We also extend the analysis to include a sample of sons who are on average older. When we include higher order terms in the estimations they are typically statistically significant. This finding indicates that the intergenerational elasticity of earnings likely varies across the fathers' earnings distribution. Our results also confirm that the elasticity of earnings is higher when one restricts the sample to sons at older ages. We extend the examination of this issue to the estimation of the intergenerational elasticity of earnings in the two countries conditional on the quintile of the father's earnings, and find that in each country the intergenerational relationship varies across the distribution. For both the United States and Germany, earnings of sons appear more related to those of fathers who are relatively high earners.

The analysis presented in this paper indicates that, on average, the earnings of sons in Germany and the United States are influenced to a similar degree by their fathers' earnings. Both countries also show a tendency for sons with higher-earning fathers to have a stronger relationship than those with fathers who earned less. The similarity in these relationships, both on average and across the distribution of the fathers' earnings is surprising given the differences in the educational systems and labor markets of the two countries. While we might speculate on how the influences of social institutions in each country have led to the outcomes we have observed, instead we offer a final observation. Germany and the United States are each advanced industrial nations with genuine concerns about opportunity and equity for their citizens. Although their institutions differ, each would argue that their policy choices have been intended to enhance mobility for their peoples. While they certainly have arrived there by different paths, the association between the earnings of fathers and sons in the two countries is similar.

# References

Altonji, Joseph G., and Thomas A. Dunn (1991). "Family Incomes and Labor Market Outcomes of Relatives." In Ronald G. Ehrenberg (editor). *Research in Labor Economics*. Vol. 12, pp. 269–310. Greenwich, CT: JAI Press.

Becker, Gary S., and Nigel Tomes (1986). "Human Capital and the Rise and Fall of Families." *Journal of Labor Economics*. Vol. 4, no. 3, pp. S1–S39.

Behrman, Jere R., and Paul Taubman (1990). "The Intergenerational Correlation Between Children's Adult Earnings and Their Parents' Income: Results from the Michigan Panel Survey of Income Dynamics." *Review of Income and Wealth*. Vol. 36, no. 2, pp. 115–27.

Björklund, Anders, and Markus Jäntti (1997). "Intergenerational Income Mobility in Sweden Compared to the United States." *American Economic Review*. Vol. 87, pp. 1009–18.

Corak, Miles, and Andrew Heisz (1999). "The Intergenerational Earnings and Income Mobility of Canadian Men: Evidence from Longitudinal

Income Tax Data." *Journal of Human Resources.* Vol. 34, no. 3, pp. 504–33.

Couch, Kenneth A., and Thomas Dunn (1997). "Intergenerational Correlations in Labor Market Status." *Journal of Human Resources.* Vol. 32, no. 1, pp. 210–32.

——— (2000). "Intergenerational Correlations in Earnings in Three Countries: The United Kingdom, Germany, and the United States." *Vierteljahrshefte zur Wirtschaftsforschung.* Vol. 68, no. 2, pp. 290–96.

Couch, Kenneth A., and Dean R. Lillard (1997). "Divorce, Educational Attainment, and the Earnings Mobility of Sons." *Journal of Family and Economic Issues.* Vol. 18, no. 3, pp. 231–45.

——— (1998). "Sample Selection Rules and the Intergenerational Correlation of Earnings." *Labour Economics.* Vol. 5, pp. 313–29.

Dearden, Lorraine, Stephen Machin, and Howard Reed (1997). "Intergenerational Mobility in Britain." *Economic Journal.* Vol. 107, no. 1, pp. 47–66.

Eide, Eric R., and Mark H. Showalter (1999). "Factors Affecting the Transmission of Earnings Across Generations: A Quantile Regression Approach." *Journal of Human Resources.* Vol. 34, no. 2, pp. 253–67.

Lillard, Dean R. (2001). "Cross-National Estimates of the Intergenerational Mobility in Earnings." *Vierteljahrshefte zur Wirtschaftsforschung.* Vol. 70, no. 1, pp. 51–58.

National Longitudinal Survey (1987). Surveys of Young Men 14–24 Codebook Supplement Appendix 9 Public Release Version 1966–1981. Center for Human Resource Research, The Ohio State University.

Peters, H. Elizabeth (1992). "Patterns of Intergenerational Mobility in Income and Earnings." *Review of Economics and Statistics.* Vol. 74, no. 3, pp. 456–66.

Solon, Gary R. (1992). "Intergenerational Income Mobility in the United States." *American Economic Review.* Vol. 82, no. 3, pp. 393–408.

US Department of Labor Statistics (1997). NLS Handbook. Bureau of Labor Statistics, Washington, DC.

Zimmerman, David J. (1992). "Regression Toward Mediocrity in Economic Stature." *American Economic Review.* Vol. 82, no. 3, pp. 409–29.

# 9 Family structure and labor market success: the influence of siblings and birth order on the earnings of young adults in Norway, Finland, and Sweden

ANDERS BJÖRKLUND,
TOR ERIKSSON, MARKUS JÄNTTI,
ODDBJØRN RAAUM, AND
EVA ÖSTERBACKA

THE last ten years have seen an upsurge in research on intergenerational earnings and income mobility. A good deal has been learned about this topic, as witnessed in the survey by Solon (1999), the collection of papers published in the 2002 volume of the *Journal of Economic Perspectives*, as well as the chapters of this book. On the methodological side, empirical researchers are now much better equipped with data and techniques to avoid various biases that plagued earlier attempts to estimate parent–offspring and siblings correlations in long-run earnings. Further, the order of magnitude of father–son elasticities and brother correlations has been established with some degree of confidence in a number of countries. Nonetheless, it is almost an understatement to claim that much more needs to be learnt before analysts can claim to have uncovered the mechanisms that generate these relationships and how various policies could affect them.

There are different opinions about how research on intergenerational mobility should best proceed. A theorist could complain about the lack of a theoretical underpinning in much empirical research published

The authors gratefully acknowledge financial support from the Nordic Social Science Research Councils (NOS-S). They also thank Erik Ø. Sørensen for providing the STATA program for the correlation estimator. Further, Jäntti's and Österbacka's collection of Finnish data was possible thanks to a grant from the Yrjö Jahnsson Foundation, and Björklund's collection of Swedish data from the Swedish Social Science Research Council. Österbacka's work for this project was also supported by the Academy of Finland. Tom Erik Aabø provided competent assistance with the Norwegian data analysis.

since the early 1990s. A more empirically oriented researcher could argue that natural experiments generating useful exogenous information should be identified and used so that truly causal mechanisms can be identified. Most likely there is much room for both these approaches. The goal of the research reported in this chapter, however, is different and in a sense quite modest. Both theoretical and empirical research has much to benefit from more detailed stylized facts about the empirical patterns of family background–earnings relationships, and therefore the focus here is on three dimensions of family structure: (1) the number of children in the family; (2) birth order; and (3) the gender composition of siblings.

Research using data from the United States has found a strong negative relationship between the number of children and outcomes like educational attainment and earnings during adult life.[1] In an often cited book, Blake (1989) reports schooling differences of more than one year between individuals who grew up in families with two children and those from families with four or more children. Further, the former group of individuals had almost two more years of schooling than those from families with seven or more children. Among others Hanushek (1992) and Becker (1992) have interpreted such results as the outcome of parental investment decisions reflecting a quantity–quality tradeoff. These significant differences in education levels (and by extension earnings) raise concerns about whether summary measures of intergenerational dynamics like parent–offspring and sibling correlations are affected by family size.

Birth order has also been a much discussed concern. For example, Sulloway (1997) claims that firstborns are different in that they are more authoritative than their younger siblings. There is less of a consensus as to whether the level of earnings or schooling is associated with birth order. Behrman and Taubman (1986) suggest birth order could be related to earnings and schooling. Their analysis, however, is not based on representative data, and the robustness of their findings has as a result been questioned by Griliches (1986). Nonetheless, it is reasonable to suggest that intergenerational effects may vary by birth

---

[1] There is also a literature on family structure and health. See Modin (2002) for recent research and references to this literature. Needless to say, the impact of family structure on earnings and education could be mediated by health.

order. It is certainly the case that primogeniture was prevalent in some traditional societies, and it would be useful to know if there are direct financial implications associated with being the oldest son in advanced societies. If the practice of passing on financial and other assets directly to the first born still resonates it would very likely generate a distinctly higher correlation in long-run labor market outcomes between fathers and first-born sons than between fathers and other sons. More subtly, however, it is also possible that first-borns receive a disproportionate amount of non-monetary investments of parental time and attention in the first years of life in the manner partly described by Sulloway (1997), but also discussed in the early childhood development literature. These types of investments may also have important implications for longer-term labor market success and would therefore distinguish first-borns from their siblings.

Another example of non-monetary investments within the family that might be important for longer-term outcomes is related to the gender composition of siblings. Butcher and Case (1994) argue that the gender composition of the children in a family may matter for educational attainment and labor market outcomes. They suggest that women who had brothers end up getting more education than those without brothers. The explanation offered is based on the idea that sons act as role models for the educational choices made by daughters. Butcher and Case (1994) use the gender composition of sibling relationships in an instrumental–variable estimation of the returns to schooling. Subsequent research using larger data sets has questioned these findings. Hauser and Kuo (1998) do not find similar impacts of gender composition. In spite of this controversy over the causal role of the gender composition of siblings, the results do suggest that summary measures of the influence of family background might be systematically related to siblings' gender composition.

A major reason why these issues have not been addressed in the rapidly growing intergenerational income-mobility literature is that research in many countries is based on longitudinal surveys with limited sample sizes. Although survey data provide detailed information about family background and outcomes during adulthood for representative samples, the sample sizes are often not large enough to allow separate analysis of smaller subgroups. Administrative data are an important alternative source and their availability in the Nordic countries offers an opportunity to examine these issues using samples that are orders of magnitude larger. In this chapter, we make use of such register-based data sets from Finland, Norway, and Sweden to take a close look at the association between family background and earnings in these countries. The analysis starts by analyzing how the level of earnings is related to family structure as defined by family size, birth order, and gender composition. Sibling correlations in long-run earnings by the number of children in the family and the gender composition of siblings are then estimated. This part of the chapter follows research summarized in Björklund, Eriksson, Jäntti, Raaum, and Österbacka (2002). The analysis also involves separate estimations for men and women (brothers and sisters) in both the level and the correlation analyses.

We find substantially higher earnings among individuals who grew up in small families compared to those who grew up in larger ones. Despite these gaps in earnings levels by family background, the sibling correlations are strikingly similar by family background. Both of these results show up in all three countries.

## 1 An overview of the data

The analysis is based on data drawn specifically for our intergenerational research from registers held by the public statistical agencies in each country. A major advantage of this information is that sample sizes are very large. The disadvantage is that detailed information on a host of individual characteristics that are often routinely collected in surveys is not available.

Table 9.1 offers a brief overview of the structure of the data for each country and the sample sizes involved. The Finnish data are based on a sample of families drawn from the 1970 census. Since the number of children is an important variable in the analysis, younger siblings born after 1970 who lived in the same household are taken into account when defining family structure. Tax-register-based measures of annual earnings from 1990 and 1995 are used. Earnings are defined to include wages, salaries, and income from self-employment. There is no information on whether the children are biological siblings, and in what follows they are simply referred to as social siblings. Such sibling relationships depend on household composition in 1970, (1975, and 1980 if there are newborns to the mother). Siblings may either be full biological siblings, half-siblings, or children of two separate parents who are living together as a married couple or who are cohabiting. Half-siblings may also be included in two-parent families.

**Table 9.1**  *An overview of the data used in the earnings analysis: Finland, Norway, and Sweden*

|                      | Finland | Norway  | Sweden               |
|----------------------|---------|---------|----------------------|
| Years of birth       | 1955–65 | 1953–69 | 1951–68              |
| Years in which       | 1990    | 1992    | 1987                 |
| earnings are         | 1995    | 1993    | 1990                 |
| observed             |         | 1994    | 1993                 |
|                      |         | 1995    | 1996                 |
| Number of individuals| 18,883  | 583,318 | 219,888 and 210,402  |

*Note:* Children used to define family structure can be born in other years. The first sample size for Sweden refers to biological siblings and the second to social siblings, as discussed in the text.
*Source:* Administrative data as provided to authors.

The Norwegian data are constructed from a complete register of all residents in Norway on 1 January 1993. Statistics Norway administers this data base. Our sample, however, is restricted to individuals with parents alive and living in Norway in 1993. The biological mother and father are identified for each individual. These familial links enable a definition of various biological sibling relationships, and the data used in the analysis consist of siblings with the same parents. Annual earnings in 1992 through to 1995 are collected from the registers of Statistics Norway. These administrative data are based on reports from employers, various public offices, and tax declarations. Earnings are defined to include wages and salaries, income from self-employment, and some sick-leave payments.

The Swedish data are randomly selected from a sample of 100,000 individuals born in Sweden and living in the country in 1992. Björklund, Eriksson, Jäntti, Raaum, and Österbacka (2002) offer more details on these data. The siblings of these persons are identified in two different ways. First, a population register is used to locate biological (and adopted) full siblings and half-siblings. Second, social siblings are identified from the 1960, 1965, 1970, 1975, and 1980 censuses. Individuals are considered to be social siblings if they lived with a randomly selected person in any of these censuses and were between zero and seventeen years of age at the time of the census. Of course, most of these siblings are also full siblings, but other sibling types are also included. Two different samples from this general data set are used.

One is based on biological full siblings, and in this way mimics the Norwegian sample. The other is based on social siblings in the 1970 census similar to the Finnish sample. In this way, the robustness of the results to differences in the sibling definition can be examined. The main concern is with the technical issue of whether the choice of one of the two feasible family definitions leads to different conclusions. The exact definition of a sibling is not always explicitly spelled out in the existing literature on family structure and socio-economic outcomes. The choice between biological and social (or adoptive) family relationships is also related to the classic issue of "nature versus nurture" in intergenerational transmittance of economic status. Directly addressing this issue, however, would require an analytical approach other than the one followed here and is left to future analysis. For example, Björklund, Jäntti, and Solon (forthcoming) address the nature versus nurture issue using this Swedish data set as well as data on identical and fraternal twins from the Swedish Twin Registry. Annual earnings data for 1987, 1990, 1993, and 1996 are available for both the random sample of register individuals and their siblings. This information is based on employers' compulsory reports to tax authorities. And as in the Finnish and Norwegian data, self-employment earnings and taxable sickness and parental leave benefits are also included in the definition of earnings.

There are many subtle decisions to be made in developing the data sets used in the estimation of the results. In the first instance, the analysis is restricted to individuals between the ages of twenty-five and forty for whom earnings are observed. Further, only persons with at least two earnings observations are included since most intergenerational mobility studies focus on long-run earnings. This is done to address the long-standing concern in this literature suggesting that transitory earnings fluctuations will lead to an underestimation of the degree of intergenerational earnings mobility. As a result, the average of all earnings observations, for those with at least two observations, is used in the analysis. This argument does not apply to our earnings levels estimation since a transitory error in the dependent variable does not create biased regression coefficients. Nonetheless, we use long-run earnings as the dependent variable in these estimations in order to have comparable samples in the analysis of earnings levels and earnings correlations.

Family structure is defined according to the actual number of children even if earnings information for some children might be missing due to lack of valid data during the observation window. The analysis is based on the natural logarithm of earnings and therefore the results might be sensitive to low-earnings observations. In the raw data the lower observable limit for earnings varies among the countries and a common cut-off in the equivalent of $100 (measured in 1995 constant dollars) is used. Björklund, Eriksson, Jäntti, Raaum, and Österbacka (2002) examine the sensitivity of the results to choices of this sort.

## 2 Family structure and the level of earnings

The analysis in this section addresses several straightforward issues. The average relative earnings differentials are examined between groups of people who differ in the number of their siblings, birth order, and in the gender composition among their siblings. The tool of analysis is a log earnings equation with controls for age and indicators for family structure.[2] Education and work experience are not controlled for although any impact of family background is most likely mediated through these variables. Further, separate analyses for men and women are undertaken.

Although these questions are quite simple, they could be complicated by so called interaction effects among the three dimensions of family structure. An example would be the case in which the difference between a first-born and a second-born child depends upon the total number of siblings. Large data sets offer an opportunity to investigate interactions of this kind, but a complete analysis of all possible combinations of family size, birth order, and gender composition would quickly become complicated and too burdensome to present in a clear way. The compromise is to group some of this information and use broader categories in the analysis. For this reason the number of children in the family is defined as either 1, 2, 3, 4, and 5 or more, and these are used as measures of family size; birth order is based simply on whether an individual is first-born, middle-born, or last-born; and gender composition is indicated by three groups (only brothers, only

---

[2] Note that the estimations are done slightly differently than described in order to have the same approach in the level and correlation analysis. In a first step, log earnings are regressed on age, $age^2$, $age^3$, and time dummies. In a second step, the residuals from this equation are regressed on the variables used in the equations reported in Table 9.3.

sisters, and both brothers and sisters). The analysis is based on models allowing for interaction effects between the dimensions of family structure defined in these three ways. The results (not shown) suggest, however, that the interaction effects are insignificant and only complicate the presentation. Therefore the focus in what follows is on results from a simpler model with only main effects of family size, birth order, and gender composition.

Table 9.2 reports descriptive statistics for the samples used in the analysis of earnings levels. As noted, the sample sizes for Norway and Sweden are very large, with over 300,000 men and 276,000 women for Norway and slightly more than 100,000 men and women for Sweden. The Finnish sample is smaller, yet still high by most standards. Further, there are some differences in family structure across the countries. The fraction of only children is higher among biological Swedish siblings than among the Norwegian biological siblings (12.8% versus 6.4% for men). There are also more only-children among Swedish social siblings than among Finnish social siblings. Otherwise, the broad patterns are quite similar across the countries.

The Least Squares regression results are reported in Table 9.3. A number of common patterns for the three countries emerge. First, family size matters a great deal. The largest earnings differential by family size is between two children and five or more. For men in Finland this differential is estimated at 17.5 percent, in Norway 9.4 percent, and in Sweden 14.3 and 14.2 percent for biological and social siblings respectively. (The log point differentials are interpreted as relative differentials, although this approximation understates the true relative differential at higher values.) For women the differential is 12.7 percent in Finland, 17.5 percent in Norway, and 12.4 percent in Sweden (13.6 percent for social siblings). These magnitudes can be considered to be quite large. Year-of-schooling coefficients in standard log-earnings equations in these countries are close to 0.05, suggesting that the estimated differentials between families of two and of five or more children represents two to three years of extra schooling (Asplund and Pereira 1999, Harmon, Walker, and Westergard-Nielsen 2001). Second, the pattern in the family-size coefficients is neither linear nor monotonous. For all countries and both genders, the coefficient for two children is positive and significantly different from the reference level (the only-child group). But the estimated coefficient falls as larger families are considered. Third, both birth-order

Table 9.2  *Descriptive overview of family structure by gender*

|  | Finland | Norway | Sweden | |
| --- | --- | --- | --- | --- |
|  | Social siblings | Biological siblings | Biological siblings | Social siblings |
| | (proportion of total) | | | |
| **1. Men** | | | | |
| One child | 0.088 | 0.064 | 0.128 | 0.200 |
| Two children | 0.267 | 0.312 | 0.350 | 0.344 |
| Three children | 0.290 | 0.340 | 0.282 | 0.261 |
| Four children | 0.183 | 0.174 | 0.135 | 0.120 |
| Five or more children | 0.172 | 0.109 | 0.105 | 0.074 |
| First-born | 0.290 | 0.399 | 0.323 | 0.307 |
| Middle-born | 0.355 | 0.292 | 0.231 | 0.197 |
| Last-born | 0.266 | 0.245 | 0.318 | 0.296 |
| Only brothers | 0.255 | 0.273 | 0.281 | 0.265 |
| Only sisters | 0.223 | 0.266 | 0.259 | 0.250 |
| Brothers and sisters | 0.434 | 0.397 | 0.332 | 0.284 |
| Number of individuals | 10,240 | 306,625 | 113,066 | 108,002 |
| **2. Women** | | | | |
| One child | 0.086 | 0.064 | 0.131 | 0.201 |
| Two children | 0.269 | 0.313 | 0.351 | 0.345 |
| Three children | 0.289 | 0.338 | 0.279 | 0.262 |
| Four children | 0.186 | 0.177 | 0.133 | 0.116 |
| Five or more children | 0.170 | 0.108 | 0.105 | 0.075 |
| First-born | 0.289 | 0.400 | 0.320 | 0.303 |
| Middle-born | 0.358 | 0.290 | 0.229 | 0.196 |
| Last-born | 0.267 | 0.246 | 0.319 | 0.300 |
| Only brothers | 0.255 | 0.287 | 0.281 | 0.270 |
| Only sisters | 0.218 | 0.251 | 0.258 | 0.246 |
| Brothers and sisters | 0.442 | 0.398 | 0.330 | 0.283 |
| Number of individuals | 8,643 | 276,693 | 106,822 | 102,400 |

*Note:* Table entries are proportions of the total sample size for each gender with indicated characteristic. First- born and last-born indicate the fraction that is both first- or last-born and belongs to families with two or more children. Middle-born refers to the fraction that is both middle-born and belongs to a family with three or more children.

*Source:* Calculations by authors from administrative data.

**Table 9.3** *The influence of family background on earnings: least squares regression results*

| | Finland | Norway | Sweden | |
|---|---|---|---|---|
| | Social siblings | Biological siblings | Biological siblings | Social siblings |
| **1. Men** | | | | |
| Two children | 0.061 (0.025) | 0.096 (0.007) | 0.056 (0.007) | 0.042 (0.006) |
| Three children | 0.011 (0.027) | 0.089 (0.007) | 0.024 (0.008) | 0.010 (0.008) |
| Four children | −0.026 (0.030) | 0.063 (0.008) | −0.017 (0.009) | −0.029 (0.009) |
| Five or more children | −0.114 (0.032) | 0.002 (0.009) | −0.087 (0.010) | −0.100 (0.001) |
| Middle-born | −0.008 (0.017) | 0.001 (0.004) | −0.026 (0.006) | −0.015 (0.006) |
| Last-born | −0.009 (0.016) | 0.001 (0.004) | −0.014 (0.005) | −0.006 (0.005) |
| Only sisters | −0.015 (0.017) | −0.008 (0.004) | −0.004 (0.005) | −0.002 (0.005) |
| Brothers and sisters | 0.001 (0.018) | −0.003 (0.004) | −0.003 (0.006) | −0.002 (0.007) |
| F-test, family size | 13.1 (0.00) | 120.7 (0.000) | 79.9 (0.000) | 58.3 (0.000) |
| F-test, birth order | 0.21 (0.81) | 2.85 (0.060) | 11.3 (0.000) | 3.05 (0.050) |
| F-test, gender composition | 0.47 (0.63) | 1.97 (0.14) | 0.38 (0.068) | 0.11 (0.900) |
| $R^2$ | 0.0092 | 0.0018 | 0.0059 | 0.0042 |
| **2. Women** | | | | |
| Two children | 0.033 (0.027) | 0.092 (0.008) | 0.041 (0.007) | 0.040 (0.006) |
| Three children | 0.014 (0.029) | 0.052 (0.008) | 0.024 (0.008) | 0.019 (0.008) |
| Four children | −0.013 (0.032) | −0.005 (0.009) | −0.016 (0.009) | −0.031 (0.009) |
| Five or more children | −0.094 (0.034) | −0.083 (0.010) | −0.083 (0.010) | −0.096 (0.011) |
| Middle-born | −0.018 (0.017) | −0.023 (0.005) | −0.021 (0.006) | −0.014 (0.006) |
| Last-born | −0.020 (0.016) | −0.012 (0.004) | −0.012 (0.005) | −0.002 (0.005) |
| Only brothers | 0.000 (0.018) | −0.016 (0.005) | −0.015 (0.005) | −0.013 (0.005) |
| Brothers and sisters | 0.001 (0.020) | −0.014 (0.005) | −0.014 (0.006) | −0.005 (0.007) |
| F-test, family size | 7.86 (0.000) | 159.2 (0.000) | 65.8 (0.000) | 62.7 (0.000) |
| F-test, birth order | 0.91 (0.400) | 12.8 (0.000) | 7.27 (0.000) | 2.64 (0.000) |
| F-test, gender composition | 0.00 (1.000) | 6.57 (0.000) | 5.28 (0.010) | 3.33 (0.040) |
| $R^2$ | 0.0065 | 0.0044 | 0.0051 | 0.0043 |

*Note:* The dependent variable is defined as the average age and period-adjusted log annual earnings as discussed in the text. At least two observations are used to compute the average. The estimating equation also includes a constant. The reference case is an only child, first-born, only brothers (for men) or only sisters (women). Rows labeled F-test offer F statistics for separate tests of the null hypotheses that all blocks of coefficients associated with family size, with birth order, and with the gender composition are equal to zero. ( ) indicates standard errors and p-values in the case of F-statistics.

and gender-composition differentials are small compared to those for family size. It is the case that the null hypothesis that the birth-order coefficients are jointly equal to zero can be rejected for Norway and Sweden. But due to the large samples, the estimated standard errors are small, so the focus should instead be on the size of the coefficients. The general pattern is that the birth-order coefficients for middle born and last born are negative compared to the reference level of first-borns. The most important coefficients are $-0.026$ (Swedish men, biological siblings) and $-0.023$ (Norwegian women) for middle born. At most, these differentials represent around half a year of schooling. It should be noted that due to the simplified definitions of the co-variates, the estimated coefficients for middle-born children could be capturing the impact of having many siblings. The probability of being middle-born is higher in families with many children, and it is likely that those belonging to large families have lower earnings. Fourth, the magnitude of the gender-composition differentials is smaller than those for birth order. The only cases when the null hypothesis that these two coefficients are jointly equal to zero can be rejected are in the equations for Norwegian and Swedish women. Women who have only brothers or both brothers and sisters average around 1.5 percent lower earnings than those women who only have sisters. Finally, all these results are basically the same for the two sibling definitions used for Sweden.

## 3 Family structure and sibling correlations

A sibling correlation in an outcome like earnings is an appealing measure of the overall importance of childhood conditions. Intuition suggests that the more factors influencing adult earnings that siblings share during their childhood, the higher the correlation in their respective outcomes. Siblings who have grown up together share not only the same family background but also the same neighborhood conditions. Thus, the correlation captures many more factors than just parental economic resources and can be considered an omnibus measure of the impact of childhood conditions. Recent estimates of neighborhood correlations using data from the United States and Norway suggest, however, that family factors are more important. See Solon, Page, and Duncan (2000) and Raaum, Salvanes, and Sørensen (2003).

The sibling correlation, however, has one limitation. By definition, it cannot be applied to those who have no siblings. So if the intergenerational transmission mechanism is much different for only children, the sibling correlation would be a misleading measure. Indeed, this concern is one reason for an interest in sibling correlations by family size. If there are economically significant differences across families of different sizes then it is reasonable to suggest that only-children are affected by family background in a different way from those who have siblings. Some care must be taken in using the sibling correlation as an indicator of the impact of childhood conditions.

The now standard practice of using long-run measures of earnings in order to approximate permanent income is adopted in what follows. This implies that the analysis is based on individuals who have at least two valid earnings observations between twenty-five and forty years of age. Family structure is defined without imposing any age restrictions. Once again, the estimation technique is implemented in two steps. First, using Least Squares the logarithm of annual earnings is estimated as a function of age, $age^2$, $age^3$, and time dummies. Then the residuals from this equation are used to estimate the sibling correlation. The estimator for the sibling correlation, including the weights attached to families with different numbers of siblings, is reported in the Appendix. Sample sizes for the sibling correlation estimates are reported in Table 9.4 for both men and women. Both the number of individuals and the number of family units used are presented. The sample sizes are smaller than in the earnings-level analysis in the previous section since those who are only children cannot be included and at least two brothers (or two sisters) must be observed twice between twenty-five and forty years. Nonetheless, the samples remain large by most standards in this field of research. Note also that birth order is not a useful concept in sibling correlation analysis. So other subgroups are used in this part of the analysis.

The estimated correlations are presented in Table 9.5. In the first instance, the results suggest that the magnitude of the brother correlations for all brothers range from 0.14 in the case of Norway to 0.20 for Swedish biological siblings, and to 0.24 for Finland. The estimates are quite close to those reported by Björklund, Eriksson, Jäntti, Raaum, and Österbacka (2002), but they are not identical as somewhat different sample criteria and estimation techniques are used. Second, the estimated sister correlations are lower than the brother correlations.

Table 9.4 Sample sizes for the estimation of sibling correlations: numbers of individuals and families

| | Finland | | Norway | | Sweden | | | |
| | Social siblings | | Biological siblings | | Biological siblings | | Social siblings | |
| | (1) | (2) | (1) | (2) | (1) | (2) | (1) | (2) |
|---|---|---|---|---|---|---|---|---|
| **1. Men** | | | | | | | | |
| All brothers | 5,123 | 2,265 | 167,631 | 73,658 | 66,914 | 28,732 | 57,402 | 25,019 |
| Two brothers, no sisters | 888 | 444 | 33,768 | 16,884 | 18,946 | 9,473 | 17,728 | 8,864 |
| Three brothers, no sisters | 712 | 304 | 24,924 | 9,859 | 8,940 | 3,128 | 7,704 | 2,684 |
| Two brothers, one sister | 882 | 441 | 38,970 | 19,485 | 14,684 | 7,342 | 13,132 | 6,566 |
| Four brothers, no sisters | 248 | 88 | 7,384 | 2,354 | 2,232 | 594 | 1,930 | 511 |
| Three brothers, one sister | 601 | 258 | 18,911 | 7,422 | 6,025 | 2,120 | 5,115 | 1,781 |
| Two brothers, two sisters | 358 | 179 | 14,518 | 7,259 | 4,922 | 2,461 | 4,238 | 2,119 |
| Two brothers or more, five or more children | 1,434 | 551 | 29,156 | 10,395 | 3,403 | 916 | 2,147 | 591 |
| **2. Women** | | | | | | | | |
| All sisters | 3,930 | 1,789 | 141,696 | 62,942 | 60,599 | 26,296 | 52,509 | 23,095 |
| Two sisters, no brothers | 620 | 310 | 27,442 | 13,721 | 17,040 | 8,520 | 16,020 | 8,010 |
| Three sisters, no brothers | 440 | 194 | 19,593 | 7,929 | 7,241 | 2,556 | 6,528 | 2,268 |
| Two sisters, one brother | 738 | 369 | 33,844 | 16,922 | 13,930 | 6,965 | 12,772 | 6,386 |
| Four sisters, no brothers | 143 | 54 | 6,084 | 1,995 | 1,898 | 511 | 1,530 | 405 |
| Three sisters, one brother | 523 | 230 | 16,343 | 6,492 | 5,019 | 1,778 | 4,192 | 1,471 |
| Two sisters, two brothers | 346 | 173 | 13,148 | 6,574 | 4,962 | 2,481 | 4,252 | 2,126 |
| Two sisters or more, five or more children | 1,119 | 458 | 25,242 | 9,309 | 3,152 | 900 | 1,912 | 553 |

Notes: Columns labeled (1) indicate the number of individuals, those labeled (2) indicate the number of families. All sample sizes are based on individuals used in the estimations, those with at least two valid observations for earnings between the ages of 25 and 40 years. Family structure is defined without reference to sample-selection rules.

**Table 9.5** *Estimated sibling correlations by family structure*

| | Finland | Norway | Sweden | |
| --- | --- | --- | --- | --- |
| | Social siblings | Biological siblings | Biological siblings | Social siblings |
| **1. Men** | | | | |
| All brothers | 0.242 (0.032) | 0.142 (0.004) | 0.203 (0.003) | 0.189 (0.006) |
| Two brothers, no sisters | 0.133 (0.047) | 0.152 (0.009) | 0.216 (0.014) | 0.206 (0.012) |
| Three brothers, no sisters | 0.214 (0.051) | 0.139 (0.009) | 0.191 (0.010) | 0.171 (0.014) |
| Two brothers, one sister | 0.191 (0.068) | 0.139 (0.009) | 0.203 (0.009) | 0.182 (0.013) |
| Four brothers, no sisters | 0.247 (0.133) | 0.133 (0.016) | 0.187 (0.018) | 0.161 (0.026) |
| Three brothers, one sister | 0.147 (0.048) | 0.129 (0.009) | 0.176 (0.015) | 0.153 (0.016) |
| Two brothers, two sisters | 0.212 (0.066) | 0.107 (0.014) | 0.191 (0.026) | 0.172 (0.026) |
| Two brothers or more, five or more children | 0.313 (0.070) | 0.149 (0.009) | 0.201 (0.032) | 0.194 (0.025) |
| **2. Women** | | | | |
| All sisters | 0.114 (0.020) | 0.122 (0.004) | 0.150 (0.006) | 0.146 (0.006) |
| Two sisters, no brothers | 0.115 (0.057) | 0.122 (0.009) | 0.167 (0.012) | 0.155 (0.012) |
| Three sisters, no brothers | 0.140 (0.054) | 0.104 (0.009) | 0.160 (0.015) | 0.166 (0.015) |
| Two sisters, one brother | 0.100 (0.047) | 0.121 (0.008) | 0.142 (0.012) | 0.140 (0.013) |
| Four sisters, no brothers | 0.091 (0.063) | 0.103 (0.014) | 0.146 (0.026) | 0.130 (0.028) |
| Three sisters, one brother | 0.096 (0.055) | 0.118 (0.010) | 0.120 (0.018) | 0.097 (0.020) |
| Two sisters, two brothers | 0.175 (0.079) | 0.102 (0.013) | 0.081 (0.021) | 0.101 (0.023) |
| Two sisters or more, five or more children | 0.077 (0.033) | 0.120 (0.007) | 0.113 (0.018) | 0.105 (0.021) |

*Note:* Calculations by authors as described in the text and Appendix. ( ) indicates standard errors.

Gender differences of this sort are also found in many recent intergenerational earnings studies (Chadwick and Solon 2002 (United States), Österbacka 2001 (Finland), and Österberg 2000 (Sweden)). Needless to say, this is an interesting finding and future research should examine the reasons in more detail. It cannot be ruled out, however, that the explanation has less to do with the underlying intergenerational mechanisms than with measurement issues related to a larger transitory component in female earnings.[3]

The basic issue regarding the results in Table 9.5, however, is whether the sibling correlations are systematically related to family structure. The estimates for Finland are quite imprecise by subgroup, due to small sample sizes. The results for both men and women using the Norwegian data suggest that there is no relationship in the sibling correlations across family structure. The same holds for men in Sweden, but for Swedish women there is a slight tendency for the estimates to be lower for large families than for small ones. The magnitudes of the differences are not large and the null hypothesis that they are equal cannot be rejected at a high level of statistical significance. Overall, it makes sense to emphasize the similarity of sibling correlations by family type rather than the differences. Finally, the distinction between biological and social siblings in the Swedish data does not matter very much.

## 4 Conclusions

The analysis in this chapter uses large administrative-based data sets from Finland, Norway, and Sweden to investigate the relationship between family background and earnings. The relationship between three dimensions of family structure – number of children, birth order, and the gender composition of siblings – and adult long-run earnings is examined. A large earnings differential by number of siblings is found for all three countries. Although the relationship is non-linear in all cases, the average earnings differential between those who belong to a family of two children and those who belong to a family of five

---

[3] This explanation is a less likely applicable to the results in Chadwick and Solon (2002). They use household income for both generations and there is no reason to believe that such an income concept differs by gender in terms of the transitory variance component.

or more exceeds 10 percent, and amounts to two to three years of extra schooling. These differentials are in line with a large literature that finds similar patterns between socio-economic outcomes like earnings and schooling on the one hand, and number of siblings on the other.

The analysis also addresses whether there are any earnings differentials by birth order and gender composition among the siblings once family size is controlled. Most previous studies addressing this issue have been limited by small sample sizes or non-representative data sets. The analysis in this chapter is not subject to these limitations and finds that such differentials are small compared to those related to the number of siblings. Estimated birth-order differentials are significantly different from zero in Norway (women only) and Sweden, and first-born children earn 2 to 2.5 percent more than middle and last-born children. The differentials by gender composition are even smaller. If anything, the results imply that for women it is advantageous to have only sisters, contradicting the controversial finding by Butcher and Case (1994).

Finally, the analysis addresses whether an overall measure of the impact of childhood conditions – the correlation in long-run adult earnings between siblings – is systematically related to family structure. Many economists have argued that the systematic relationship between family size and outcomes like earnings and schooling reflects parental investment behavior. If this is the case, it could be hypothesized that intergenerational patterns also are related to family size. In smaller families the children embody more parental investment, making them more like their parents and making siblings more similar to each other. In large families there may be a large variation in parental investment across the children and consequently a larger variation in outcomes. The results suggest no systematic relationship between family structure and sibling correlations; the estimated sibling correlations in long-run earnings are of the same magnitude in small and large families, and in families with different gender composition. This implies that the systematic earnings differentials by number of siblings have no counterpart in differences of sibling correlations. This finding is corroborated with Lindahl (2002) for Sweden, who finds that intergenerational father–son and father–daughter elasticities are not systematically related to family size. This is an important stylized fact to consider in future research on the intergenerational transmission mechanism.

In interpreting our two main findings – the combination of huge earnings differentials and similar sibling correlations by family size – one should also keep in mind that, by means of taxes, transfers, and public expenditures, the Nordic welfare states help equalize labor market outcomes so that disposable equivalent income differentials by family structure are not as big as in other countries. For this reason, we find it unlikely that the earnings-level differentials by family structure are causally driven by parents' financial resources.

In conclusion, it is also important to note that other dimensions of family structure could be systematically related to intergenerational earnings inheritance. It is likely that more closely spaced siblings share more family and community background factors and thus get more equal outcomes than more widely spaced ones. This issue is more complicated to study since it requires a longer observation window than available in the data used here. Further, it could be that birth order matters for the intergenerational earnings transmission. By focusing on sibling correlations rather than parent–child associations, this chapter does not address this issue. Lindahl (2002) offers some evidence suggesting later-born children's earnings are more weakly associated with father's earnings than early-born children. It would be useful to examine if such a pattern also exists for other countries.

## APPENDIX

### Estimator of the correlation in sibling earnings

The sibling correlation is defined as the ratio between the covariance and the variance. The co-variance estimator $\hat{\eta}$ is taken from Solon, Page, and Duncan (2000)

$$\hat{\eta} = \frac{\sum\limits_{f=1}^{F} W_f \sum\limits_{s \neq s'} \dfrac{y_{sf} y_{s'f}}{S_f(S_f - 1)/2}}{\sum\limits_{f=1}^{F} W_f} \tag{9.1}$$

where the earnings variable $y$ is age-adjusted and standardized such that $E(y) = 0$, $W_f$ measures the weight given to family $f$. When $W_f$, is equal to the number of distinct sibling pairs in the sample (that is, brothers or sisters), the covariance estimator collapses to

$$\hat{\eta} = \frac{\sum_{f=1}^{F} \sum_{s \neq s'} y_{sf} y_{s'f}}{\sum_{f=1}^{F} S_f(S_f - 1)/2}. \tag{9.2}$$

The estimated covariance is simply divided by the estimated variance to provide the sibling correlation. The covariance estimates are not very sensitive to the choice of weighting scheme (Solon, Page, and Duncan 2000, Raaum, Salvanes and Sørensen 2003). As a result the focus is on one natural alternative. When $W_f = S_f (S_f - 1)/2$, all sibling pairs are given equal weight, regardless of whether they come from large or small families. As there is no analytical expression for the variance of this estimator, regular bootstrapping based on 200 replications (drawing families as clusters) is used to derive estimated standard errors.

### References

Asplund Rita, and Pedro Telhado Pereira, editors (1999). *Returns to Human Capital in Europe: A Literature Survey*. Helsinki: ETLA.

Becker, Gary S. (1992). "Fertility and the Economy." *Journal of Population Economics*. Vol. 5, pp. 185–201.

Behrman, Jere R., and Paul Taubman (1986). "Birth Order, Schooling and Earnings." *Journal of Labor Economics*. Vol. 4, pt. 2, pp. S121–S145.

Björklund Anders, Tor Eriksson, Markus Jäntti, Oddbjørn Raaum, and Eva Österbacka (2002). "Brother Correlations in Earnings in Denmark, Finland, Norway and Sweden Compared to the United States." *Journal of Population Economics*. Vol. 4, pp. 757–72.

Björklund Anders, Markus Jäntti, and Gary Solon (forthcoming). "Influences of Nature and Nurture on Earnings Variation: A Report from a Study of Various Sibling Types in Sweden." In S. Bowles, H. Gintis, and M. Osborne (editors). *Unequal Chances: Family Background and Economic Success*. New York: Russell Sage.

Blake, Judith (1989). *Family Size and Achievement*. Berkeley: University of California Press.

Butcher, Kristin, and Anne Case (1994). "The Effect of Sibling Sex Composition on Women's Education and Earnings." *Quarterly Journal of Economics*. Vol. 109, pp. 531–63.

Chadwick, Laura, and Gary Solon (2002). "Intergenerational Income Mobility among Daughters." *American Economic Review*. Vol. 92, pp. 335–44.

Griliches, Zvi (1986). "Comment on Behrman and Taubman." *Journal of Labor Economics*. Vol. 4, pt. 2, pp. S146–S150.

Hanushek, Eric A. (1992). "The Trade-off between Child Quantity and Quality." *Journal of Political Economy*. Vol. 100, pp. 84–117.

Harmon Colm, Ian Walker, and Niels Westergaard-Nielsen, editors (2001). *Education and Earnings in Europe*. Cheltenham, UK: Edward Elgar.

Hauser, Robert M, and Hsiang-Hui Daphne Kuo (1998). "Does the Gender Composition of Sibships Affect Women's Educational Attainment?" *Journal of Human Resources*. Vol. 33, pp. 644–57.

Lindahl, Lena (2002). "Do Birth Order and Family Size Matter for Intergenerational Income Mobility? Evidence from Sweden." Swedish Institute for Social Research, Stockholm University, Working Paper 5/2002.

Modin, Bitte (2002). "Setting the Scene for Life." Health Equity Studies No 1, Centre for Health Equity Studies, Stockholm University/ Karolinska Institutet.

Österbacka, Eva (2001). "Family Background and Economic Status in Finland." *Scandinavian Journal of Economics*. Vol. 103, pp. 467–84.

Österberg, Torun (2000). "Intergenerational Income Mobility in Sweden: What do Tax-Data Show?" *Review of Income and Wealth*. Vol. 46, no. 4, pp. 421–36.

Raaum, Oddbjørn, Kjell G. Salvanes, and Erik Ø. Sørensen (2003). "The Neighbourhood is Not What it Used to Be. IZA Discussion Paper no. 952.

Solon, Gary R. (1999). "Intergenerational Mobility in the Labor Market." In Orley C. Ashenfelter and David Card (editors). *Handbook of Labor Economics, Volume 3A*. Amsterdam: North-Holland.

   (2002). "Cross-Country Differences in Intergenerational Income Mobility." *Journal of Economic Perspectives*. Vol. 16, pp. 59–66.

Solon, Gary, Marianne Page, and Greg, J. Duncan (2000). "Correlations between Neighboring Children in their Subsequent Educational Attainment." *Review of Economics and Statistics*. Vol. 82, pp. 383–92.

Sulloway, F. J. (1997). *Born to Rebel: Birth Order, Family Dynamics and Creative Lives*. New York: Vintage Books.

# 10

## New evidence on the intergenerational correlation in welfare participation

MARIANNE E. PAGE

I T is widely believed that welfare participation in one generation encourages welfare participation in the next generation. This perception helped motivate the 1996 overhaul of the welfare system in the United States: it was hoped that the combination of time limits and work requirements that were imposed as part of the Personal Responsibility and Work Opportunity Reconciliation Act would reduce mothers' participation in (and children's exposure to) welfare programs. Limiting the length of time that children experience welfare is expected to reduce the likelihood that they participate as adults.

There are at least three different reasons why welfare receipt might promote dependence among future generations. The most frequently discussed idea is that parents' participation may lower children's distaste for welfare. While Moffitt (1983) and others have suggested that stigma may act as an important participation deterrent for many families, children who grow up on welfare may learn to think of it as the default means of support. Another reason is that such children may face lower participation costs as adults since they will already have had first-hand experience with how the system works. A third story is that parents' participation reduces their offspring's informal access to job opportunities. Welfare parents are less connected to the labor market, so their children may be less likely to learn about jobs that are available, useful job search strategies, or proper work etiquette.

These scenarios all spell out a causal link between parents' welfare participation and that of their children, but the connection across generations could reflect other factors. For example, since welfare can only be received if income is sufficiently low, the observed correlation

I would like to thank Sami Kitmitto for his exemplary research assistance, and participants at the Statistics Canada and DIW workshops on Intergenerational Mobility for their helpful comments. This project was largely conducted while I was a Visiting Scholar at the Joint Center for Poverty Research.

226

may be nothing more than evidence of an intergenerational correlation in income. Likewise, it is well known that children growing up in single-parent families are more likely to form single-parent families when they grow up, and in the United States family structure has traditionally helped determine welfare eligibility. More generally, the transmission of welfare participation across generations may reflect other characteristics of welfare parents that are passed down to their children. The policy implications of these types of linkages are unclear because policies reducing parents' participation would not be expected to alter the transmission of other characteristics.

Putting these debates aside, evidence on the intergenerational transmission of welfare dependency is limited to only a handful of studies (Rainwater 1987, Duncan, Hill, and Hoffman 1988, McLanahan 1988, Solon, Corcoran, Gordon, and Laren 1988, Antel 1992, Gottschalk 1990, 1992, 1996, An, Haveman, and Wolfe 1993, Levine and Zimmerman 1996, and Borjas and Sueyoshi 1997). Many of these analyses are based on small samples, outdated data and/or measures of welfare participation that could result in biased estimates. The purpose of this chapter is to provide new evidence on the magnitude of the intergenerational correlation in welfare participation by making use of more recent waves of the Panel Study of Income Dynamics (PSID). The time period covered by the PSID (1968–93) is now long enough to justify another study: additional cohorts have come of age, significantly increasing sample size over those used in previous analyses and allowing for correlation estimates that are more relevant for the current generation of young women. It also provides an opportunity to investigate whether the importance of family and community background has changed over time. In Chapter 5, Mayer and Lopoo find that for sons born between 1949 and 1965 there has been a weakening of the relationship between their own income and that of their parents. In contrast, the intergenerational income correlation has increased for daughters born prior to 1961. Among daughters born after 1961 the correlation has declined. Since a primary determinant of welfare eligibility is family income, changes in the intergenerational income correlation may translate into changes in the intergenerational welfare correlation.

In the process of providing an updated estimate of welfare correlation I also investigate whether previous estimates have been biased by their reliance on short observation windows. Most correlation estimates are based on measures of welfare receipt derived from an observation period of three years or less. It is well known that estimates of income and earnings correlations based on a single year of data are severely downward biased and Wolfe, Haveman, and An (1996) find that estimates of the effect of family background characteristics on the probabilities of high-school graduation and teenage childbearing are also influenced by the number of years over which family background information is available. An analogous problem may affect estimates of intergenerational welfare correlations (Gottschalk 1992, 1996). Many women use public assistance for brief periods, and these periods may not overlap with the observation window. As a result, measures of welfare participation derived from only a few years of data may be noisy proxies for whether the individual ever received welfare, and therefore lead to underestimates of the true correlation. On the other hand, since short observation windows will disproportionately identify long-term recipients, an upward bias on the population correlation may occur if the effect of growing up in a family using public assistance for a long period of time is larger than the effect of growing up in a family that only briefly participates in a welfare program. This chapter will explore whether and to what extent this shortcoming of the data has influenced existing estimates.

Using the more recent PSID data, I estimate the intergenerational correlation in welfare participation to be 0.302. This is higher than what is reported in earlier studies. I also demonstrate that previous estimates may be biased downward because they are typically based on only a few years of observations for young women. I find no evidence that the intergenerational correlation in welfare participation is declining over time.

## 1  Estimating intergenerational correlations in welfare participation

My first objective is to provide updated estimates of the intergenerational correlation in welfare participation. It can be shown that the intergenerational welfare correlation is $P_1 - P_0$, where $P_1$ is the conditional probability a woman has participated given that her parent was a welfare recipient and $P_0$ is the conditional probability a woman has participated given that her parent was not a recipient. Estimates of these quantities can be derived in the following way: $\hat{P}_1$ is estimated by counting the number of participants in the sample whose parents participated and dividing by the total number of women whose parents were welfare recipients. Likewise, $\hat{P}_0$ is estimated by counting the number of women in the sample whose parents did not participate and then calculating the fraction of that group that did participate. Formally, the estimators $\hat{P}_1$ and $\hat{P}_0$ are:

$$\hat{P}_1 = \frac{n_{11}}{n_{01} + n_{11}} \qquad (10.1)$$

and

$$\hat{P}_0 = \frac{n_{10}}{n_{00} + n_{10}} \qquad (10.2)$$

where $n_{00}$ represents the number of daughters in the sample who neither grew up in a household receiving public assistance nor became welfare recipients themselves, $n_{01}$ represents the number of women whose parents received welfare but who did not themselves participate, $n_{10}$ the number who participated in a welfare program but whose parents did not participate, and $n_{11}$ the number whose parents received public assistance and who later went on to become welfare recipients themselves.

Since the PSID systematically oversamples the low-income population, I weight the counts of observations $n_{00}$, $n_{01}$, $n_{10}$, $n_{11}$, used in the estimators by the inverse of the daughters' probabilities of selection into the sample. These individual weights are provided by the PSID for each individual and each year. I use the PSID weight provided at age twenty-seven. Standard error estimates for the parameters are calculated using a balanced half-sample replication procedure. This procedure, a cousin to the jackknife and bootstrap procedures, is explained in Wolter (1985) and has been applied previously in sibling and neighbor correlation studies (Solon, Corcoran, Gordon, and Laren 1988, 1991, and Solon, Page, and Duncan 2000).

The parameter estimates are based on a sample of 1,899 women in the PSID who were between the ages of twenty-seven and forty-two at the time of the 1993 interview and had become heads of their own households or wives of heads by that time. A woman is identified as having participated in a welfare program if the family in which she was a head or wife ever reported receiving Aid to Families with Dependent Children (AFDC), General Assistance, Food Stamps, or Supplemental

Security Income between the time that she became a head or wife and age twenty-seven. Parents are identified as having participated in a public assistance program if they report receiving welfare (as defined above) sometime between 1968 and the year in which the daughter left home.

The first panel of Table 10.1 shows the results for the intergenerational correlations in welfare participation obtained by using the estimators described in equations (10.1) and (10.2). The unconditional probability of participating in a welfare program is 0.275, and is consistent with previous estimates of the probability of ever participating in a welfare program (Duncan, Hill, and Hoffman, 1988). The probability of participating given that one's parents participated is 0.468, suggesting that the majority of women who experience a period of welfare receipt during childhood do not become dependent adults. The probability of participating given one's parents did not participate is 0.166. This suggests that factors other than childhood exposure to welfare influence participation among a significant fraction of women. Nevertheless, $\hat{P}_1$ is almost three times higher than $\hat{P}_0$. Taken together, $\hat{P}_1 - \hat{P}_0$ yields an estimate of the intergenerational correlation of 0.302, which is a little higher than previous estimates. As can be seen from Table 10.2, the estimates produced by previous studies center around 0.24, though ranging from a high of 0.280 (Duncan, Hill, and Hoffman,1988) to a low of 0.170 (Levine and Zimmerman, 1996).[1] Unlike most studies, I have estimated a standard error on the welfare correlation estimate, and the resulting 95 percent confidence interval does not include 0.240.

## 2 Potential biases

Estimates of the intergenerational correlation in welfare participation are frequently based on only a few years of data. Researchers have noted that short observation windows may lead to biased estimates of

---

[1] Some of the estimates in Table10.2 are calculated from other statistics found in the papers. Intergenerational welfare relationships estimated net of other individual characteristics are not included because they are not directly comparable to estimates of simple intergenerational welfare correlations. An, Haveman, and Wolfe (1993), Antel (1992), and McLanahan (1988) have all produced such estimates and they are of similar magnitude to those in Table 10.2. They are also typically based on short observation windows for either parents or daughters.

Table 10.1 *Estimated probabilities of welfare participation using different observation windows*

| | Sample size | Probability of welfare receipt | | | Mother–daughter correlation of welfare receipt $(\hat{P}_1 - \hat{P}_0)$ | Relative probability of welfare receipt $(\hat{P}_1 / \hat{P}_0)$ |
| --- | --- | --- | --- | --- | --- | --- |
| | | Unconditional $(\hat{P})$ | Mother received welfare $(\hat{P}_1)$ | Mother did not receive welfare $(\hat{P}_0)$ | | |
| 1. Full sample | 1,899 | 0.275 (0.019) | 0.468 (0.024) | 0.166 (0.018) | 0.302 (0.029) | 2.81 (0.328) |
| 2. Parent observed until daughter leaves home | | | | | | |
| a. Daughter observed until age 27 | 1,618 | 0.265 (0.017) | 0.440 (0.023) | 0.163 (0.018) | 0.277 (0.028) | 2.70 (0.328) |
| b. Daughter observed between 25 and 27 | 1,618 | 0.184 (0.013) | 0.334 (0.022) | 0.097 (0.014) | 0.237 (0.027) | 3.46 (0.576) |
| c. Daughter observed at age 27 only | 1,618 | 0.118 (0.012) | 0.258 (0.024) | 0.062 (0.012) | 0.197 (0.029) | 4.18 (0.963) |
| 3. Parent observed when daughter is 14 to 16 years old | | | | | | |
| a. Daughter observed until age 27 | 1,618 | 0.265 (0.017) | 0.513 (0.034) | 0.210 (0.018) | 0.303 (0.039) | 2.45 (0.263) |
| b. Daughter observed between 25 and 27 | 1,618 | 0.184 (0.013) | 0.410 (0.035) | 0.134 (0.013) | 0.277 (0.039) | 3.07 (0.403) |
| c. Daughter observed at age 27 only | 1,618 | 0.118 (0.012) | 0.331 (0.041) | 0.091 (0.012) | 0.240 (0.046) | 3.65 (0.746) |
| 4. Parent observed when daughter is 14 years old | | | | | | |
| a. Daughter observed until age 27 | 1,618 | 0.265 (0.017) | 0.520 (0.034) | 0.227 (0.017) | 0.293 (0.037) | 2.29 (0.222) |
| b. Daughter observed between 25 and 27 | 1,618 | 0.184 (0.013) | 0.419 (0.041) | 0.150 (0.013) | 0.269 (0.044) | 2.80 (0.365) |
| c. Daughter observed at age 27 only | 1,618 | 0.118 (0.012) | 0.345 (0.050) | 0.103 (0.012) | 0.242 (0.055) | 3.34 (0.691) |

*Notes:* Calculations by author using data from the Panel Study on Income Dynamics. ( ) indicates standard error calculated using the balanced half-sample replication procedure described in the text.

Table 10.2  *Published estimates of the intergenerational correlation of welfare receipt in the United States*

| | Data source and sample | Observation window | | Intergenerational correlation |
|---|---|---|---|---|
| | | Parent | Child | |
| Borjas and Sueyoshi (1997) | NLSY individuals 14 to 22 in 1979 | 1978 | through 1989 | 0.250 |
| Duncan, Hill, and Hoffman (1988) | PSID women 21 to 23 | when child was 13 to 15 | 21 to 23 | 0.280 |
| Gottschalk (1990, 1992) | NLSY women 14 to 19 in 1979 | years child at home | until first birth | 0.220 |
| Gottschalk (1996) | PSID women 14 to 23 in 1983 | when child was 14 to 23 | from 14 to first birth or age 23 | whites: 0.277 blacks: 0.544 |
| Levine and Zimmerman (1996) | NLSY women 14 to 22 in 1979, NLS women 29 to 39 in 1983 | 1979 1968 to 1971 | 1989 1983 | 0.170 |
| Solon, Corcoran, Gordon, and Laren (1988) | PSID 137 sister pairs 27 to 32 in 1983 | until child leaves home | through age 27 | 0.214 |

NLSY – National Longitudinal Survey of Youth
PSID – Panel Study of Income Dynamics
NLS – National Longitudinal Survey
*Source:* Compiled by the author.

family background effects (Gottschalk 1992, 1996, Wolfe, Haveman, and An 1996), but no one has investigated empirically the extent to which welfare correlation estimates are affected by limited observation periods. The estimate in the first row of Table 10.1 may be larger than in the existing literature because daughters and their parents are observed over a longer time period. The time period covered by the PSID is now long enough to allow an investigation of this issue.

There are two relevant observations windows: one for daughters and one for parents. Both have been constrained in previous studies.[2]

[2] Observation windows for daughters and their parents are not always constrained simultaneously. For example, Gottschalk (1996) uses observations

One of the most frequently used longitudinal surveys is the National Longitudinal Survey of Youth (NLSY), which began with a sample of individuals aged fourteen to twenty-two. Because the youngest survey respondent's initial age is fourteen, researchers using the NLSY are limited to observing parental welfare receipt during adolescence. While the PSID provides information about parental welfare receipt over a longer time period, most PSID studies have followed daughters' outcomes only through their very early twenties. Reliance on short observation windows for either group could lead to estimates of intergenerational welfare correlations that are biased in either direction. On the one hand, if data from only a few years are used to estimate parental welfare receipt then some parents who have participated in the past (or who will participate in the future) will be miscoded as non-participants. This will lead to an upward-biased estimate of $P_0$ and a downward-biased estimate of $P_1 - P_0$. On the other hand, participants identified during a short observation window are disproportionately likely to be in the midst of a long welfare spell. If the effect of growing up in a household that participates in a welfare program for a long period of time is larger than the effect of growing up in a family that only briefly participates in welfare, then estimates of $P_1$ based on short observation windows will be higher than the average $P_1$ over the whole population. Upward-biased estimates of the intergenerational correlation will result. When daughters' participation is observed over a short period then estimates of $P_1$ and $P_0$ will both be downward biased, and $\hat{P}_1 - \hat{P}_0$ may be biased in either direction. The extent to which the "window problem" biases estimates of the intergenerational correlation is, therefore, an empirical question.

The remaining panels of Table 10.1 show what happens to the estimated intergenerational correlation when shorter observation windows are used to identify welfare receipt. The estimates are based on cohorts born between 1953 and 1966. This restriction allows a comparison of estimates based on all of the available parental information (panel 2) to estimates based on data collected over the three year period when the daughter was aged fourteen to sixteen (panel 3), and to estimates based on parental data collected when the daughter was age fourteen (panel 4). Data on parents' welfare receipt during the time

on parents from 1968 to 1985 (a long window) but only observes daughters until age twenty-three or until their first birth (whichever is earlier).

the daughter was fourteen to sixteen years of age are not available for cohorts born prior to 1953 as these cohorts were older than fourteen at the time of the 1968 survey.

Panel 2 shows how estimates of the intergenerational correlation are affected when daughters' observation windows are shortened, but parental welfare receipt continues to be observed over a long interval. It is readily apparent that short observation windows for daughters lead to substantially smaller correlation estimates. As expected, both $\hat{P}_1$ and $\hat{P}_0$ are lower when daughters' welfare receipt is measured between the ages of twenty-five and twenty-seven than when daughters' potential welfare receipt is observed through age twenty-seven. This results in an estimated intergenerational correlation (0.237) that is 14 percent lower than the estimate based on all the available data, though the two estimates are not statistically different from each other. The estimated correlation is further reduced when the daughters' observation window is restricted to age twenty-seven, and is now outside the 95 percent confidence interval around the 0.277 estimate derived when all of the daughters' information is used.

This pattern suggests that previous estimates have been biased downward because they have been based on only a few years of data. A related question is whether the age at which the daughters are observed makes a difference. In order to investigate this question I have replicated Table 10.1 using information on daughters' welfare receipt up to age twenty-three, between ages twenty and twenty-two and at age twenty-two only. The resulting intergenerational correlation estimates are on average 24 percent lower than those based on observations at older ages (in other words, compared to the estimates in column 5 of Table 10.1). The intergenerational correlation based on whether a woman has participated in a welfare program at any time before age twenty-three is 0.238, or 21 percent lower than the 0.302 reported in panel 1 of Table 10.1. One explanation for the substantive difference is that 37 percent of women who become welfare recipients before age twenty-seven do so for the first time after age twenty-three. Calculations based on very young women, therefore, miss a substantial fraction of women who will eventually participate.

The next two panels repeat the analysis in panel 2, using progressively shorter observation windows for the parents. As expected, fewer years of parental data lead to higher estimates of $P_1$: this suggests that daughters of long-term welfare recipients are more likely to become welfare recipients themselves than are daughters of short-term recipients. $P_0$ is also overestimated when only a few years of parental data are used because some parents who participate outside the observation window are misclassified as non-participants. In absolute terms, the upward bias in $\hat{P}_1$ is a little larger than the upward bias in $\hat{P}_0$ so that the intergenerational correlation estimates tend to become slightly larger as parents' observation windows are shortened, but the magnitude of the bias appears to be small.

One might be tempted to conclude that the length of parents' observation windows is irrelevant to obtaining accurate estimates of the intergenerational welfare correlation but the fact that short windows yield biased estimates of both $\hat{P}_1$ and $\hat{P}_0$ suggests that estimates of the intergenerational transmission of welfare status that are based on only a few years of parental data should be viewed cautiously. Another measure of the intergenerational transmission of welfare receipt is $P_1/P_0$. This ratio is simply the probability that a daughter participates given that her parents received welfare divided by the probability she participates given that her parents did not receive welfare. The estimate of this ratio for the full sample is 2.81, indicating that women whose parents were welfare recipients are almost three times as likely to become recipients themselves. Comparing this ratio across the different rows of the table suggests that downward-biased estimates result when the observation window on parents is restricted; although $\hat{P}_1$ declines by more than $\hat{P}_0$ in absolute terms, $\hat{P}_1$ declines by less than $\hat{P}_0$ in percentage terms. As in the case of the intergenerational correlation, however, the magnitude of the estimates is more strongly influenced by the length of time over which the daughters' potential participation is observed. In contrast to the correlation estimates, shorter observation windows for daughters make this measure of the intergenerational transmission of welfare participation larger.

Taken together, the estimates in Table 10.1 suggest that the intergenerational correlation in welfare participation is slightly larger than previously thought, and that the smaller estimates produced in previous research may result in part from their tendency to focus on short observation windows for very young women. Researchers' inability to observe parental welfare receipt over long intervals apparently has a smaller affect on the accuracy of the parameter estimates.

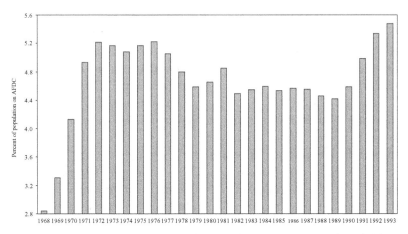

**Figure 10.1**   Number of recipients of aid for families with dependent children as a proportion of the total US population.

## 3  Changes in the intergenerational correlation over time

The long period covered by the PSID provides an opportunity to investigate whether the intergenerational transmission of welfare receipt has changed over time. Chapters 2, 5, and 6 all elaborate on why generational economic mobility may change over time, and Chapter 5 documents a decline in the estimated correlation between parental income and children's economic status in the United States. Since a primary determinant of welfare eligibility in the United States is family income, this suggests that declines in the intergenerational income correlation may have translated into declines in the intergenerational welfare correlation. Other changes over time, such as increases in the fraction of children living in single-parent families, or changes in welfare-program rules may also strengthen or weaken the importance of family and community background in determining whether a daughter eventually receives welfare.

Figure 10.1 shows that during the time period covered in the PSID annual welfare receipt essentially doubled, from about 2.8 percent of the population to more than 5 percent in the mid 1970s, before declining to about 4.5 percent during the 1980s. As is well known, during the early 1990s there was a marked increase in the fraction of individuals participating in welfare programs. The patterns suggest that compared to the oldest cohorts in my sample, the younger cohorts are less likely

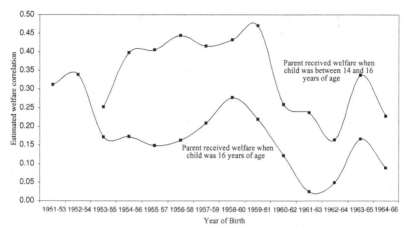

**Figure 10.2** Intergenerational welfare correlation over time, by three-year birth cohorts.

to have been welfare participants before age twenty-seven, but their parents are more likely to have been welfare participants. This suggests that the intergenerational welfare correlation may be declining over time.

Figure 10.2 shows the trend in the intergenerational correlation estimates for thirteen overlapping or "rolling" groups. Daughters born between 1951 and 1953 form the first group, daughters born between 1952 and 1954 comprise the second group, and so forth, with the last group consisting of daughters born between 1964 and 1966. Note that in these "rolling" groups, two out of three individuals are in the same consecutive groups. Two measures of parental welfare receipt are used: whether the parents received welfare when their daughter was between ages fourteen and sixteen, and whether the parents received welfare when the daughter was sixteen. Table 10.1 demonstrates that the ideal measure of parental welfare receipt would be based on whether the parent ever received welfare during the time that the daughter was at home, but since the length of time over which parental receipt can be observed varies across cohorts I chose not to use this measure. While it is clear that using a measure of parental receipt based on an observation in a single year produces more downward-biased estimates than one based on the three-year window, estimates based on a three-year window cannot be obtained for the oldest cohorts. Both series exhibit a great deal of fluctuation over time but tend to trend downward.

Table 10.3 provides estimated marginal effects (evaluated at sample means) from the simple probit regression:

$$\text{Prob}(Y_{ic} = 1) = \Phi(\alpha + \beta_1 D_{ic} + \beta_2 Year_{ic} + \beta_3 D_{ic} \times Year_{ic}) \qquad (10.3)$$

where $Y_{ic}$ is an indicator for whether daughter $i$ in cohort $c$ ever received welfare, $D_{ic}$ is an indicator variable equal to one if the individual's parents were welfare recipients, and zero if they were not, and $Year_{ic}$ identifies the cohort (year of birth) to which the daughter belongs. The parameter $\beta_3$ indicates the magnitude and direction of the trend in the intergenerational correlation. The two definitions of parental welfare receipt yield similar estimates of $\beta_3$. As can be seen in the first two columns of Table 10.3 these are both negative, but small and not statistically different from zero.[3]

In the remainder of Table 10.3, I consider other factors that might contribute to changes (or the lack of changes) in the relationship between parental welfare receipt and daughters' receipt over time. Specifically, I investigate whether the intergenerational transmission of income and family structure have changed over time, since income and family structure affect eligibility. All of the results in columns 3 through 5 are based on the same sample, whose smaller size results from the omission of observations with missing income data. In column 4, I show the results of a probit regression in which the dependent variable is an indicator variable equal to 1 if the daughter was ever a female head with children prior to age twenty-seven, and the regressors of interest are a dummy variable indicating whether she lived in a female-headed family between ages fifteen and sixteen and an interaction between the

---

[3] Elimination of the 1953 cohort does produce negative, nearly statistically significant, estimates of the trend in the intergenerational correlation when parents' welfare participation is observed over the period their daughters are between the ages of fourteen and sixteen. The coefficient estimate on the interaction is $-0.015$ and the standard error estimate 0.009. When the parents' observation window is limited to the year their daughters turned sixteen, however, eliminating cohorts born before 1954 has no substantive effect on the estimates. One interpretation of the results is that a substantive post 1954 trend exists, but another is that the high correlation estimates for cohorts born in the mid 1950s are simply an anomaly or are driven by noisy data. The fluctuations evident in Figure 10.2 give weight to this possibility.

Table 10.3  Estimated trends in the importance of family background in determining the probability of welfare receipt

| | Sample not limited according to income data availability | | Sample limited to individuals with at least three years of valid data on parental income | | |
| | Daughter's probability of welfare receipt | | Daughter's probability of welfare receipt | Daughter's probability of becoming a female head | Log family income |
| | Mother's welfare receipt when daughters are 14 to 16 years (1) | At 16 years (2) | Mother's welfare receipt when daughters are 14 to 16 years (3) | Parent female head when daughters are 15 to 16 years (4) | Parents' income observed when daughters are 14 to 18 years (5) |
|---|---|---|---|---|---|
| Parent received welfare | 0.347(0.075) | 0.388(0.085) | 0.372(0.077) | | |
| Year | −0.009(0.004) | −0.005(0.003) | −0.009(0.004) | −0.003(0.004) | −0.047(0.090) |
| Parent received welfare × Year | −0.004(0.008) | −0.005(0.008) | −0.009(0.008) | | |
| Daughter lived in female-headed family | | | | 0.083(0.071) | |
| Daughter lived in female-headed family × year | | | | 0.012(0.008) | |
| Log parental income | | | | | 0.377(0.070) |
| Log parental income × year | | | | | 0.005(0.008) |
| Number of observations | 1,628 | 1,849 | 1,502 | 1,502 | 1,502 |

Note: Table entries are marginal effects (evaluated at sample means) derived from probit estimation as described in equation (10.3) of the text, with the exception of column (5) which reports least squares estimates.
Numbers in parentheses ( ) are standard error estimates.

dummy variable and *Year$_{ic}$.*[4] The point estimate on the interaction term suggests that the effect of living in a female-headed family (on the probability of becoming a female head before age twenty-seven) increased by 1.2 percentage points per year. The estimate is statistically different from zero at the 12 percent level and is consistent with McLanahan's (1994) finding that among cohorts born in the 1940s and early 1950s the probability of becoming an unwed teenage mother was unaffected by whether the daughter had lived in a single-parent family, but that among more recent cohorts living in a single-parent family nearly doubles the risk of a non marital teen birth. This trend could reflect changes in the marital status of single mothers. Daughters born more recently are more likely to have grown up in female-headed families in which the mother never married, whereas older cohorts are more likely to have grown up with widowed mothers. The change could also reflect changing social norms. Older cohorts would have been more stigmatized if they had had a non-marital birth, and would usually have married the father before the child was born. Younger cohorts would have felt less pressure to marry if they became pregnant and, within this group, daughters of single mothers may have felt the least pressure of all.

The last column of Table 10.3 presents Least Squares regressions of the log of daughters' family income on the log of family income during childhood, and the interaction between log family income during childhood and *Year$_{ic}$*. Daughters' income is averaged over ages twenty-five to twenty-seven, and parents' income is averaged over the years when the child is fourteen to eighteen. Income is treated as a missing variable in any year it is assigned, and observations with more than two years of missing parental data are dropped. It is important to note that a serious investigation of whether the intergenerational transmission of income has changed over time should not be based on the samples used here, and that the estimates produced by this analysis are not directly

---

[4] I obtain similar results when the variable indicating whether the daughter lived in a female-headed household between ages fifteen and sixteen is replaced with a variable indicating whether she lived in a female-headed household between ages fourteen and sixteen. Estimates based on the latter, however, require elimination of yet another cohort from the sample. Family income and welfare receipt are measured in the year prior to the survey year, whereas family structure is measured in the year of the survey.

comparable to those in Chapter 5. In particular, the income sample is chosen in order to maintain consistency with the welfare sample, which means that the women included in this analysis are young and that their adult incomes will be noisy measures of their permanent income. If parental income has over time become a less important predictor of daughters' income before age twenty-seven then other factors (such as the rising importance of female headship) must explain the constancy of the welfare correlation estimates. In fact, Table 10.3 provides no evidence that the intergenerational income correlation is declining over time: the estimated coefficient on the interaction between log parental income and $Year_{ic}$ is positive and not statistically different from zero.

In sum, Table 10.3 provides no evidence that parental welfare receipt has become a less important determinant of daughters' eventual welfare participation. In addition there does not appear to be a decline over time in the correlation between parents' and daughters' family income. Since program eligibility is largely determined by income level, this finding is not surprising. Table 10.3 does document that family structure during childhood has had an increasingly important effect on daughters' likelihood of becoming female heads as adults. All else being equal, one might expect this change to translate into a larger welfare correlation over time, but, of course, there have been a number of policy changes during this period that may affect both welfare eligibility and take-up, including changes in the AFDC benefit reduction rate, and the introduction of the Earned Income Tax Credit.

## 4 Conclusion

This chapter provides new evidence on the intergenerational correlation in welfare participation. Using more recent data than previous studies, I estimate the intergenerational correlation in welfare participation to be 0.302. Given that the analysis includes more recent cohorts of women (for whom intergenerational correlations appear to be relatively lower) it is somewhat surprising that my estimate is higher than those produced by earlier studies. However, I find that the accuracy of intergenerational welfare correlation estimates is substantively influenced by the age at which individuals' potential welfare receipt is observed and the length of the observation window. This finding echoes the results of other mobility studies showing that income and earnings correlation estimates based on a single year of data substantially

overstate the true level of mobility. The difference between my estimates and those produced by earlier studies may, therefore, reflect
the earlier studies' reliance on short observation windows for young
women.

Given welfare eligibility rules, the intergenerational correlation must
reflect an intergenerational resemblance in income and family structure. Indeed, using the full sample, I estimate that the intergenerational
income correlation is 0.414 and the estimated correlation in female
headship is 0.192. Taken together, these estimates suggest that the
probabilities of experiencing poverty, single motherhood, and welfare
receipt are greatly influenced by family and community background.
Furthermore, I find no evidence that the importance of family and
community background is diminishing over time.

Documenting a substantive relationship between parents' welfare
participation and that of their children is only a first step in help-
ing to inform policy makers. There is a need to know which background factors give rise to the observed correlation, and to what degree
the observed correlation results from the transmission of a welfare
"culture" across generations. It is known that welfare reduces work
effort among adults as the literature review by Moffitt (1992) illustrates, but it is not clear that a causal relationship exists between welfare and family structure or between welfare and attitudes. Even if these
behavioral effects can be confirmed, the paths through which parents
transmit characteristics to their children are not well understood. For
example, it is well known that the incomes of children are highly correlated with those of their parents, but it is not known whether the
intergenerational correlation is due to genetic inheritance, the transmission of values, or parental investments in children's human capital.
Sorting out the causal influences underlying the welfare correlation will
be challenging because of the simultaneous problems of omitted variables, endogeneity, and multicollinearity among the relevant characteristics. Fortunately, the descriptive statistics presented here can still
provide some perspective on these issues. In particular, this chapter
indicates that most women who experienced welfare during childhood
do not become dependent adults. This contradicts the common belief
that welfare dependence is routinely passed across generations. Furthermore, fully 17 percent of women whose parents did not participate will become adult recipients by age twenty-seven, suggesting that
factors other than exposure to welfare in the home play an important
role. Nevertheless, women who experience a spell of welfare receipt

during childhood are almost three times as likely to become welfare participants as are women whose parents did not receive welfare. The magnitude of the intergenerational correlation certainly warrants additional research.

## References

An, Chong-Bum, Robert Haveman, and Barbara Wolfe (1993). "Teen Out-of-Wedlock Births and Welfare Receipt: The Role of Childhood Events and Economic Circumstances." *Review of Economics and Statistics.* Vol. 75, pp. 195–208.

Antel, John J. (1992). "The Intergenerational Transfer of Welfare Dependency: Some Statistical Evidence." *Review of Economics and Statistics.* Vol. 74, no. 3, pp. 467–73.

Borjas, George J., and Glenn T. Sueyoshi (1997). "Ethnicity and the Intergenerational Transmission of Welfare Dependency." National Bureau of Economic Research, Working Paper No. 6175.

Duncan, Greg, Martha Hill, and Saul Hoffman (1988). "Welfare Dependence Within and Across Generations." *Science.* Vol. 29, pp. 467–71.

Gottschalk, Peter (1990). "AFDC Participation Across Generations." *American Economic Review.* Vol. 80, pp. 367–71.

(1992). "The Intergenerational Transmission of Welfare Participation: Facts and Possible Causes." *Journal of Policy Analysis and Management.* Vol. 11, pp. 254–72.

(1996). "Is the Correlation of Welfare Participation across Generations Spurious?" *Journal of Public Economics.* Vol. 63, no. 1, pp. 1–25.

Levine, Phillip B., and David J. Zimmerman (1996). "The Intergenerational Correlation in AFDC Participation: Welfare Trap or Poverty Trap?" Institute for Research on Poverty, Discussion Paper No. 1100–96.

McLanahan, Sara S. (1988). "Family Structure and Dependency: Early Transitions to Female Household Headship." *Demography.* Vol. 25, no. 1, pp. 1–16.

(1994). *Growing Up in a Single Parent Family: What Hurts, What Helps.* Cambridge, MA: Harvard University Press.

Moffitt, Robert (1983). "An Economic Model of Welfare Stigma." *American Economic Review.* Vol. 73, no. 5, pp. 1023–35.

(1992). "The Incentive Effects of the US Welfare System: A Review." *Journal of Economic Literature.* Vol. 30, pp. 1–61.

Rainwater, Lee (1987). "Class, Culture, Poverty and Welfare." Center for Human Resources, Heller Graduate School.

Solon, Gary (1999). "Intergenerational Mobility in the Labor Market." In Orley C. Ashenfelter and David Card (editors) *Handbook of Labor Economics. Volume 3A.* Amsterdam: North-Holland.

Solon, Gary R., Mary Corcoran, Roger Gordon, and Deborah Laren (1988). "Sibling and Intergenerational Correlations in Welfare Participation." *Journal of Human Resources.* Vol. 23, pp. 509–34.

(1991). "A Longitudinal Analysis of Sibling Correlations in Economic Status." *Journal of Human Resources.* Vol. 26, pp. 509–34.

Solon, Gary R., Marianne E. Page, and Greg J. Duncan (2000). "Correlations between Neighboring Children in Their Subsequent Educational Attainment." *Review of Economics and Statistics.* Vol. 82, pp. 383–92.

Wolfe, Barbara, Robert Haveman, and Chong-Bum An (1996). "The 'Window Problem' in Studies of Children's Attainments: A Methodological Exploration." *Journal of the American Statistical Association.* Vol. 91, pp. 970–82.

Wolter, Kirk (1985). *Introduction to Variance Estimation.* New York: Springer-Verlag.

# 11 Intergenerational influences on the receipt of unemployment insurance in Canada and Sweden

MILES CORAK, BJÖRN GUSTAFSSON, AND TORUN ÖSTERBERG

THE objective of this chapter is to examine the extent to which an individual's use of unemployment insurance (UI) as a young adult is influenced by having had a parent who also collected UI. There are a number of competing – but not mutually exclusive – explanations for an intergenerational correlation in the receipt of social programs. These include the intergenerational transmission of information about how programs work, or more generally learning and the formation of habits. But, as Chapter 10 suggests, a major methodological challenge in documenting a causal intergenerational link involves determining the extent to which any observed patterns are due to intergenerational correlation of incomes, occupations, or other (potentially unobservable) factors common to parents and children that influence long-term labor market success. If these factors cannot be controlled for, there is a risk of overstating the causal impact of parental activities on the adult outcomes of their children.

The research summarized in this chapter fits into a number of related literatures dealing with intergenerational dynamics. These are

An earlier version of this chapter was presented to seminars at Statistics Canada, Department of Finance Canada, University of Manitoba, University of Ottawa, Dalhousie University, and Carleton University as well as to the meetings of the European Society for Population Economics, the Canadian Economics Association, and the Centre for the Study of Living Standards conference on Structural Unemployment. Comments from Laura Brown, Seamus Hogan, Stephen Jones, Ted MacDonald, Alice Nakamura, Bill Robson, Christopher Worswick, and three anonymous referees are gratefully acknowledged, as is the help of Sophie Lefebvre in constructing the data. We also thank Timothy Sargent for providing an index of Canadian UI program parameters. The responsibility for the content rests entirely with the authors, and in particular should not be attributed to Statistics Canada.

discussed in more detail in the next section in the context of a schematic overview of the analysis. The empirical work is based upon longitudinal administrative data associated with the Canadian and Swedish income tax systems that have been linked intergenerationally, and focuses on the pattern of UI use by a cohort of young men and how it relates to the UI use of their fathers. These two countries offer a valuable basis for comparative work because their economies display many structural similarities. They have also both directed significant resources toward labor market policy. However, the mix between active and passive labor market measures is rather different. In Canada, the emphasis is almost exclusively on "passive" income support, while in Sweden, significant expenditures are made on "active" measures designed to promote retraining and labor market flexibility. Also, the eligibility rules school leavers must meet to qualify in order to claim benefits differs between the countries: the Canadian program requires a work requirement to be satisfied; the Swedish program requires only a period of joblessness. Attitudes to UI and the consequences for intergenerational transmission may be very different between these two policy regimes.

The nature of the data is discussed in Section 2. An outline of the estimation strategies is also offered in this section. Two alternative approaches are employed. First, event history methods are used to model how long it takes before an individual claims UI for the first time. The methodology proposed by Gottschalk (1996) is employed to estimate the degree to which a father's reliance on UI causes sons to use UI as young adults. This involves using the parent's future UI participation as a control for unobserved heterogeneity. Second, a random effects probit model is used to model the entire history of UI benefit receipt on an annual basis for a twelve to fifteen year period beginning at age sixteen. In this latter model, a distinction is made between "individual" learning and "social" learning in the sense that these terms are used respectively by Lemieux and MacLeod (2000) and Becker (1996). In this way the relative importance of individual learning and family UI history in determining program use is examined.

The results are offered in Section 3. It is found that paternal use of UI plays a role in shortening the time to the first use of this program by the sample of men under study, but only in Canada. The conditional probability of using UI at any age between sixteen and thirty is higher among those whose fathers used UI in the past with the result that only about 24 percent reach the age of thirty without having collected benefits, versus about 32 percent of their counterparts whose parents did not collect. This difference is due in about equal proportions to the role of unobservable factors and to the causal impact of paternal UI use. Furthermore, subsequent UI receipt is governed to a greater degree by parental UI history than by individual learning about the program. In contrast, the intergenerational correlation of first use of UI in Sweden can be entirely accounted for by observable and unobservable influences. Subsequent participation in UI is substantially higher as a result of individual learning about the program. In the concluding section of the paper these findings are related to the differences in the features of UI across the two countries. The design of government policies can influence the nature and extent of the intergenerational transmission of reliance on social programs, and the results call for a closer analysis of the significance of both an active program design, and the eligibility rules facing new labor market entrants for the intergenerational transmission of UI.

## 1 An overview

A comparative analysis of the Canadian and Swedish labor markets is offered in van den Berg, Furåker, and Johansson (1997, chapter 3) who note that, except for possible differences in the relative size of the public and the service sectors, the two economies are remarkably similar. Further, both countries have also had about the same level of expenditure on labor market policies. Throughout the 1970s and early 1980s, the most significant years for the present analysis, this amounted to between 2 and 3 percent of GDP, with Sweden generally spending a bit more in most years than Canada. However, the pattern of expenditure has been very different. In Canada, passive income support through UI accounted for almost 2 percent of GDP, but generally only between 0.5 and 0.75 percent in Sweden. In fact, income support through UI accounted for only about 10 to 15 percent of total Swedish expenditure on labor market policy in the 1970s and about 25 percent during the 1980s. In Canada, on the other hand, this was in the neighborhood of 70 to 80 percent (van den Berg, Furåker, and Johansson 1997, p. 46; Gustafsson and Klevmarken 1993, p. 119; OECD 1994, pp. 93, 101).

The Canadian UI program is administered by the federal government, which holds the responsibility for both collecting contributions and distributing benefits. The benefit structure has its roots in a major reform in 1971. Most paid workers, with the exception of the self-employed, are covered by the program, and are eligible to receive benefits upon becoming unemployed if they had worked a sufficient number of weeks during the qualifying period (generally the previous year). Throughout the 1970s and 1980s, this eligibility rule varied from about ten to fourteen weeks of insured employment depending upon the state of the regional labor market. However, new entrants to the labor market, including school leavers, had a longer work requirement: generally twenty weeks. Benefits could be collected for up to fifty weeks (again depending upon the regional unemployment rate) at 60 to 67 percent of insured earnings. A two week waiting period was also required before benefits could be collected. Generally, up to the 1990s about 70 to 80 percent of the unemployed received benefits. There have been major reforms to the Canadian program during the 1990s, and in fact it is now referred to as "Employment Insurance." These reforms had the effect of reducing the scope of the program to levels before the 1971 reforms. See Sargent (1995) and Canada (1995) for a description of these changes and their impact. Since 1990, the fraction of unemployed receiving benefits has fallen, reaching about 40 percent during the late 1990s.

A reform in the early 1970s also expanded the scope of the Swedish program. UI benefits were not that generous before 1974, covering only those who were members of union-based insurance funds. This amounted to about 60 percent of the employed. In 1974, a reform increased the generosity of benefits for these individuals, but also made the benefits taxable. A second tier of benefits was also introduced and financed by the government – the KAS – for those who were not members of an insurance fund. While the insurance funds are formally union-based, the government determines the most important parameters, including the benefit rate and the eligibility requirements. Thus, to qualify for benefits individuals had, on the one hand, to have been a member of an insurance fund for at least twelve months in the period before the claim, and to have fulfilled a work requirement of at least seventy-five days. (There are also a host of other requirements.) If they were not members of a fund they could qualify for the KAS after meeting the same work requirement. However, in sharp contrast to the Canadian program, school leavers could qualify for benefits after a waiting period of three months, without regard to their actual work experience. Generally, benefits for members of insurance funds lasted about 300 days, and about half of that in the case of KAS. Benefit rates increased during the 1970s and 1980s for those fulfilling the membership requirements – from about 70 percent of average earnings to about 90 percent for those with earnings below a certain ceiling – but were generally much lower for the KAS. Further, coverage increased throughout this period so that the majority of the unemployed were by the mid to late 1980s members of an insurance fund. In 1988, for example, 69 percent of the unemployed received insurance benefits, a further 7 percent KAS, and the remaining 25 percent received no benefits at all. In 1993, the replacement rate was reduced to 80 percent.

The labor market consequences of UI have been the subject of numerous studies. Atkinson and Micklewright (1991) offer a helpful review. But the surveys by Gustafsson and Klevmarken (1993) and Björklund (1991) of the Swedish literature, and by Corak (1994) of the Canadian, are important for present purposes. The general message from these sources is that while the impact of changes in UI generosity on the aggregate unemployment rate remains unclear, there is nonetheless a good deal of evidence suggesting that the behavior of both firms and individuals is influenced. In particular, an increasingly larger and larger fraction of Canadian UI claims are accounted for by individuals who have repeatedly initiated UI claims since the notable liberalization of the program in 1972 (Corak 1993a,b, Lemieux and MacLeod 2000). The OECD (1994, p. 198) suggests that a similar pattern has developed in Sweden, and Ackum Agell, Björklund, and Harkman (1995) offer some evidence suggesting that repeated spells are in fact common.

A schematic overview of the determinants of the incidence of an insured spell of unemployment is offered in Figure 11.1 as a means of organizing the existing literature on this topic, and of offering a framework for a study of the intergenerational influences. A major concern in this literature is the degree to which past use of UI causes future use. This is a form of state dependence that Heckman and Borjas (1980) have termed "occurrence dependence," and is indicated in Figure 11.1 by the solid horizontal arrow connecting the very first spell of UI an individual experiences to subsequent spells. The challenge is to control for other factors that may also determine the onset of an insured unemployment spell. These influences may work directly on the probability of receiving a spell, or just as importantly through the onset of earlier spells. Past spells will appear to cause future spells, when in fact they

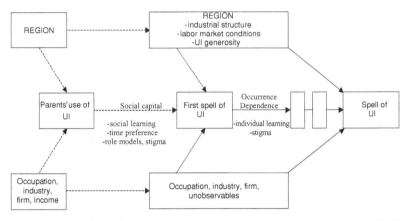

**Figure 11.1**   Schematic overview of the intergenerational transmission of UI status.

really are a signal of other underlying influences. Region of residence is highlighted in the figure as one group of potentially important influences on the incidence of UI, and encompasses factors associated with industrial structure, particularly the seasonality of employment, aggregate labor market conditions, and (since the benefit structure may vary according to the regional unemployment rate) the generosity of the UI program. Other possible influences include the occupation, industry, and even firm of employment (Corak and Chen 2003). Many of these influences will be observable, but some, like the specific employer, will inevitably be unobservable to the analyst.

There seems to be some evidence to suggest that the onset of a UI claim in Canada is caused by the presence of past claims. Lemieux and MacLeod (2000) explicitly address the possibility of occurrence dependence, controlling for a host of observable individual characteristics, and employing econometric methods to control for unobservables. They model the entire sequence of spells experienced over a twenty-year period using random effects probit models and find, in general, that the probability of starting a new UI claim is higher if the individual had a claim in the past. How this pattern of behavior is to be explained remains an issue. Corak (1993b) finds evidence of occurrence dependence in the length of UI spells, each subsequent claim getting longer and longer. He suggests the results are consistent with models in which tastes, habits, or information change as a result of participating in the program. This would also be consistent with the erosion of a stigma to the receipt of government transfers of the kind discussed, for example, in Moffitt (1983) and in the previous chapter. Lemieux and MacLeod are more explicit and view their findings as supporting the idea that individuals learn about the program. They focus on "individual" learning, but note that by implication some of their results also lend support for "social" learning. While their analysis does not directly address the possibility of social learning, they do find that the influence of an individual's past UI use on the probability of future use is lower in regions of the country with a high reliance on UI. The suggestion being that information about the UI program is widespread, and picked up by an individual from family and friends without the need to have actually made a claim.

This is the theme that is built upon here by a focus on the role of paternal UI use in determining the probability of a first spell of UI, and then through it to subsequent spells. The objective of the analysis is to examine the causal influence of parental use of UI on the incidence of a first and subsequent spells of UI, as highlighted by the dashed arrow in Figure 11.1 labeled "social capital." This term is used in the sense of Becker (1996, p. 4) as a catch-all to represent "the influence of past actions by peers and others in an individual's social network . . ." This initial capital stock is an important precondition in the model of rational addiction put forward by Becker and Murphy (1988), but its determinants are left outside of the frame of their analysis. However, the term is sufficiently broad to be consistent with a number of interpretations. It might, for example, be viewed as "social learning" in the sense of Ellison and Fudenberg (1993, 1995) and used by Lemieux and MacLeod if the family is the main locus of information about the labor market; or it could reflect the intergenerational transmission of work ethic as studied by Mulligan (1996); or of time preference as hypothesized by Becker and Mulligan (1997); or most generally as the impact of parents as role models and the erosion of any stigma to the receipt of transfer payments.

The important point, however, is that there does not appear to be any substantive research on this topic in relation to UI programs. O'Neill and Sweetman (1998) and Österbacka (1999) use respectively British and Finnish data to examine intergenerational patterns in unemployment. But they do not make explicit reference to the role of UI. A similar analysis is offered by Soidre (1999) for Sweden. She finds that the unemployment experience of parents influences children by increasing the risk of becoming unemployed, of staying unemployed longer, and of experiencing repeated unemployment spells. Corak and Heisz (1998) use Canadian data to examine the correlates of the intergenerational transmission of income and find that the composition of parental income, not just the level, matters in determining the incomes of the offspring. In particular, children whose parents collected UI end up earning less as adults. They do not have a definitive explanation for this, but suggest that it most likely reflects the intergenerational transmission of occupations. This underscores, once again, the importance of recognizing the role of other familial background variables in order to isolate the true impact of parental UI use. The remaining parts of Figure 11.1 illustrate the possibility that a parent's use of UI will be correlated with a child's future use if there is a tendency for children to work in the same types of jobs as their parents, or in the same industries or firms, or to live in the same regions.

A number of studies dealing with the intergenerational transmission of social assistance (AFDC) in the United States also form the backdrop for the research in this chapter. This literature is concerned with the degree to which a mother's use of social assistance influences a daughter's marital and fertility choices, and causes her to also rely on assistance. The conclusions as to the independent role played by a parent's receipt of transfer payments on the longer-term outcomes of children are varied. Antel (1992, p. 467) finds that "a mother's welfare participation is found to increase her daughter's subsequent welfare dependency." But Levine and Zimmerman (1996, p. 2) find "that at least three-quarters, and perhaps all, of the correlation in welfare participation across generations can be attributed to the expected intergenerational correlation in income and other family characteristics. That is, the correlation in AFDC receipt across generations represents not a welfare trap, but rather a poverty trap." (See Mulligan (1996), Gottschalk (1996), Gottschalk, McLanahan, and Sandefur (1994), but also Beaulieu, Duclos, Fortin, and Rouleau (2002) who use Canadian administrative data for the province of Quebec and Stenberg (2000) who examines Swedish data.) The findings, as many of these analysts are aware and as the results in Chapter 10 make clear, may be influenced by how long and at what point in the life cycle the child's outcomes are observed (parents and children should be observed over as many years as possible in order to develop an accurate picture of their permanent labor market status and use of transfer payments), and the manner in which unobservables are controlled.

In light of the existing literature, the approach adopted in what follows is two-fold. The length of time it takes for an individual to collect UI for the first time is modeled, paying particular attention to the influence of paternal UI receipt and controlling for observable and unobservable influences. The use of event-history methods relies on Gottschalk (1996) and McLanahan (1988), and involves following individuals from the age of sixteen when they first become eligible to work (and therefore to receive UI) until the time of their first claim. In this way individuals are observed for a possibly extended period of time, and the time-varying nature of the co-variates – specifically parental UI use – is incorporated into the model. This could represent the first step in a recursive process that leads to a higher probability of subsequent claims, which may then be influenced both by previous parental UI use (social capital) and by the fact of having had a spell in the past (individual learning). Accordingly, the entire sequence of UI spells experienced over an extended period of time is then modelled in the manner of Lemieux and MacLeod (2000), but with an attempt to discern the relative roles of social and individual learning by including controls for both past parental and individual use of UI.

## 2 Nature of the data and methodology

The analysis is based on administrative records associated with the income tax systems in the two countries. The Canadian data are organized as a panel data set created from the income tax records of a group of men born between 1963 and 1966, who could be linked to a parent when they were between the ages of sixteen and nineteen years. The family linkages are produced as a part of the construction of the T1 Family File (T1FF) by Statistics Canada and require that the individuals file an income tax return at least once while still at home.[1] The

---

[1] A variety of matching strategies are employed to identify family members. Couples (including spouses and common-law couples) are linked using Social Insurance Numbers (SINs) when they are indicated on the T1 form, as well as name and address information. (T1 forms are the main annual tax returns filed by individuals in Canada, and the T1FF incorporates the universe of tax filers.) Children are matched to their parents using name and address fields. See Harris and Lucaciu (1994) for more details on the

first year in which income tax records are available in machine read-
able form is 1978, while the most recently available data at the time
of analysis are for 1997. Information on the children is retained for
the years when they are between fifteen and thirty-one years of age.
Thus, the oldest members of the cohort under study are fifteen in 1978
while the youngest are thirty-one in 1997. Information on the parents
is used as appropriate throughout the 1978 to 1997 period. In order
to ease the computational burden the analysis is based on a randomly
selected one-in-100 sample. In addition, to be included in the sample
individuals must have filed an income tax form at least once between
the ages of twenty-six and thirty-one years. The final analysis sample
consists of 100,795 observations on 6,308 individuals.[2]

The Swedish data are developed in a similar way. A panel data set is
built using a one percent sample from the Register of Total Population
from 1978 to 1995. Parents are identified and matched to children by
means of central registers. These include information for each individual having formal guardianship of a child, usually the biological
parents but also including parents who have adopted. (The Swedish
data also contain information on stepparents, but for the sake of comparability with the Canadian data we consider the stepparent to be the
father if the child is not living with the biological father.) The children
are between fifteen and twenty-nine years of age. Children and parents
are observed each year between 1978 and 1995 even if they have not
paid any income tax in a particular year. The analysis sample consists
of 55,650 observations on 3,835 individuals.

Information on the receipt of UI benefits, either by the parent or
the child, is determined on the basis of whether any UI income is

construction of the T1FF. Versions of the same data used here have also
been employed by Corak and Heisz (1998, 1999), Grawe (2001, 2003),
and Oreopoulos (2002). In particular, Corak and Heisz (1999) explore
some of the data quality and sample selection issues that arise, and also
offer some comparisons to survey data.

[2] The panel is not perfectly balanced because observations for the years in
which some individuals lived in either the Yukon or Northwest Territories
are excluded. This is done because one of the co-variates used in the modeling exercise, the unemployment rate, is not available for these regions
of the country. This involves only thirteen of the 6,308 individuals. Thus
99.48 percent of the sample has observations for each of the sixteen years
between the ages sixteen and thirty-one. The minimum number of years in
which any one individual is observed is four.

Table 11.1 *Correlations in the use of unemployment insurance between fathers and sons: Canada and Sweden*

| | Fathers | | | | | |
| | Did not collect UI | | Collected UI | | Total | |
| Sons | Number | Percent | Number | Percent | Number | Percent |
|---|---|---|---|---|---|---|
| 1. Canada | | | | | | |
| Did not collect UI | 1,064 | 29.7 | 516 | 18.9 | 1,580 | 25.1 |
| Collected UI | 2,519 | 70.3 | 2,209 | 81.1 | 4,728 | 74.9 |
| Total | 3,583 | | 2,725 | | 6,308 | |
| 2. Sweden | | | | | | |
| Did not collect UI | 1,198 | 42.3 | 318 | 31.7 | 1,516 | 39.5 |
| Collected UI | 1,635 | 57.7 | 684 | 68.3 | 2,319 | 60.5 |
| Total | 2,833 | | 1,002 | | 3,835 | |

claimed for the year in question. Binary indicators of the presence of any amount of UI are derived for each year the individual is observed. No distinction is made in the Swedish data between insurance benefits and KAS payments. Table 11.1 offers a rough illustration of the degree of intergenerational correlation of UI receipt in these data by cross-tabulating the sons according to whether they experience UI income at least once at any time with information on their fathers. In Canada, the minority of sons (2,725 out of 6,308 or about 43 percent) had fathers who collected UI benefits at some point. However 81 percent of these individuals relied on UI. In contrast only 70 percent of their counterparts – those whose fathers did not collect UI – did so. This 11 percentage point difference in the incidence of UI across these two groups is the central concern of the modeling exercise. Reliance on UI is not as extensive in Sweden, but the intergenerational correlation of UI receipt is still important. Only about 26 percent of the sample had fathers who used UI. However, slightly more than 68 percent of these individuals received some UI, while about 58 percent of their counterparts did so, implying a 10.6 percentage point difference – a gap comparable to the Canadian.

To model the time to first claim we use discrete time duration models in the manner of Gottschalk (1996) and McLanahan (1988), and as discussed in Jenkins (1995) and Hosmer and Lemeshow (1989, pp. 238–45). If $Y_{it}$ is a binary variable defined to be equal to 0 if individual $i$ does not report receiving UI in year $t$ and 1 if he does, then the hazard rate (the conditional probability that a spell will end at a particular point in time, $t$, given that it has lasted to $t - 1$) is defined as $\lambda_{it} = \mathrm{prob}(Y_{it} = 1 \mid Y_{ik} = 0$ for $k = 1 \ldots t - 1; \mathbf{X}_{it})$ where $i = 1 \ldots \mathrm{N}$ indexes the individuals in the sample, $t = 1 \ldots \mathrm{T}$ the years in which they are observed, and $\mathbf{X}_{it}$ is a vector of co-variates. $Y_{it}$ is a discrete time random variable and the vector of these terms represents the number of years since the age of fifteen that the individual has gone without reporting UI income. The hazard rate is assumed to take the logistic functional form so that $\lambda_{it} (\mathbf{X}_{it}) = \exp\{\mathbf{X}_{it}\beta\}/[1 + \exp\{\mathbf{X}_{it}\beta\}]$ where the $\beta$ is a vector of parameters to be estimated. The vector $\mathbf{X}_{it}$ is assumed to contain both fixed and time-varying co-variates, and in particular contains a set of interval-specific intercept terms.

The path pursued by Gottschalk (1996) is followed to deal with the impact of unobserved influences. This involves using future parental UI participation as an additional co-variate controlling for unobserved heterogeneity. As Gottschalk (1996, p. 4) points out, this requires two assumptions. The first is that timing matters: the probability of the incidence of UI use by the child in any particular year can only be influenced (in a causal sense) by events experienced by the parent in an earlier (or possibly the current) year, but not by events in future years. This would not be the case if, for example, information about the parent's use of the program is conveyed to the child before benefits were actually received. This seems to be an unlikely event in the current context as it would imply that the child would, upon hearing that the parent will be starting a UI claim, have to initiate a claim and receive benefits before the parent actually began receiving benefits. Administrative delays in collecting benefits would preclude such a possibility. The second assumption is that parental behavior influences child behavior, but child behavior does not influence that of the parent. That is, children "learn" from parents, but parents do not learn from children. To some extent this may in fact happen. Or more generally we might recognize that the labor-force decisions of household members are interrelated and made simultaneously in the context of a family utility function. This is more likely to be the case when the children are still living at home.

If these two assumptions hold then the correlation between a child's UI participation and the father's future participation captures the impact of the unobservable influences. The causal impact of the father's UI behaviour is identified from the difference in the coefficients on past and future parental UI use, a larger coefficient on past use indicating that children whose parents rely on UI are also – in a causal sense – more likely to rely on the program. If these coefficients are found not to be statistically different from one another then the entire impact of past parental UI use on the child's probability of receiving UI is due to unobserved heterogeneity. This implies that the violation of the second assumption – that parents do not learn from their children – will lend a conservative bias to our findings. If parents also learn, to some degree, from children this is likely to increase the value of the coefficient associated with future parental use, and thereby make it more difficult to uncover a statistically significant positive difference between the past- and future-use variables.

The models estimated contain two time-varying covariates for parental UI use. The first is a 0–1 binary variable that takes the value of 1 if the father received UI benefits in the current or any previous year; the second is also a binary variable but takes the value of 1 if the father received benefits in any future year. For this reason the child's time to first claim is modelled between the ages of sixteen and thirty for Canada, and sixteen to twenty-eight for Sweden; developments during the age of fifteen and thirty-one, and during fifteen and twenty-nine are used to determine at least one year of the parent's UI status for all periods.

Does the first onset of a UI claim then kick-start a process of repeated future reliance on benefits? To address this possibility the entire sequence of UI participation is modeled, but using a different approach to the control for unobservables. The random effects probit model proposed by Heckman (1981) for discrete panel data is adopted. If $\Phi(.)$ represents the Normal distribution function, then the probability that an individual experiences UI in a given year is:

$$\text{prob}\,(Y_{it} = 1 \mid \gamma_i, Y_{it-1}, \mathbf{y}_{it}, \mathbf{X}_{it}) = \Phi\,(\gamma_i + \beta_1 Y_{it-1} + \mathbf{y}_{it}\beta_2 + \mathbf{X}_{it}\beta_3).$$

In this case $\gamma_i$ is an individual specific unobservable, and $Y_{it-1}$ is the lagged value of the indicator of an individual's UI participation. This latter variable is included in the model since the exact timing of the start and completion of a UI claim is not measured in the administrative files. All that is known is whether UI income is received at any point during the year. In many cases UI claims will be extant at the end

of one year and continue into the next so that a run of two successive
values of 1 does not necessarily mean that two separate claims were
initiated in each year. The vector $y_{it}$ contains three binary variables,
one representing whether the individual collected UI at any time in the
past – a control for individual learning in the sense of Lemieux and
MacLeod (2000) – and another representing whether the individual's
father collected at any time in the past – a control for social capital –
and the final one being their interaction. The relative importance of
the coefficients on these first two variables is the major concern of the
estimation. In particular, it would be interesting to know if individual
learning has any influence independent of social capital in order to
understand more clearly the reasons for occurrence dependence in the
data. It may be that if an individual has a parent who collected UI, his
own use of UI does not offer any further information about the program and hence does not raise the probability of future UI use. Finally,
$X_{it}$ is a vector of observable covariates meant to capture other influences on the incidence of UI use as depicted in Figure 11.1, including
family background variables. In order to obtain an estimable likelihood function, it is assumed that $\gamma_i$ is also distributed normally and
the unconditional probability of observing a particular pattern of UI
receipt is given by integrating over this distribution. If $F(\ )$ is the distribution function of the random effect, the probability of observing a
particular sequence of UI spells over the T years in which an individual
is part of the data set is:

$$\int \prod_{t=1}^{T} \Phi(\gamma_i + \beta_1 Y_{it-1} + y_{it}\beta_2 + X_{it}\beta_3)^{Y_{it}}$$
$$[1 - \Phi(\gamma_i + \beta_1 Y_{it-1} + y_{it}\beta_2 + X_{it}\beta_3)]^{1-Y_{it}} dF(\gamma_i). \quad (11.1)$$

So that the likelihood to be maximized is the sum of the logarithms of
these probabilities over all individuals in the sample.

## 3 Results

The variables actually included in the vector **X**, and the associated
descriptive statistics for both of the models to be estimated, are listed in
Tables 11.2a and 11.2b. Many of these are time varying. They include
a group of contemporaneous individual characteristics as depicted by
the solid arrows in Figure 11.1: age and age-squared (measured in
decades), marital status, an index of the generosity of the UI program,

Table 11.2a    *Descriptive statistics for the analyses of time to first spell and longitudinal patterns in UI use: Canada*

| | Time to first UI spell | | Longitudinal patterns in UI use | |
|---|---|---|---|---|
| | Mean | Standard deviation | Mean | Standard deviation |
| Individual used UI | | | 0.2161 | |
| Individual used UI in past | | | 0.4324 | |
| Father used UI in past | 0.2390 | | 0.3195 | |
| Individual and father used UI in past | | | 0.1838 | |
| Lagged dependent variable | | | 0.2042 | |
| Father used UI in the future | 0.2897 | | | |
| Age (in decades) | | | 2.350 | 0.4610 |
| Age squared | | | 5.734 | 2.175 |
| Married | 0.1323 | | 0.2314 | |
| Provincial UI generosity index | 1.035 | 0.2175 | 0.9855 | 0.2324 |
| Provincial unemployment rate | 9.6 | 2.8 | 9.8 | 2.8 |
| Rural residence | 0.2110 | | 0.2326 | |
| *Region of residence (Toronto Metropolitan as reference case)* | | | | |
| Newfoundland | 0.0167 | | 0.0220 | |
| Nova Scotia | 0.0347 | | 0.0370 | |
| Prince Edward Island | 0.0037 | | 0.0048 | |
| New Brunswick | 0.0251 | | 0.0295 | |
| Quebec East | 0.0706 | | 0.0769 | |
| Montreal Metropolitan | 0.0784 | | 0.0765 | |
| Quebec West | 0.0867 | | 0.1004 | |
| Eastern Ontario | 0.0708 | | 0.0633 | |
| Central Ontario | 0.1226 | | 0.1129 | |
| South-western Ontario | 0.0864 | | 0.0839 | |
| Northern Ontario | 0.0313 | | 0.0319 | |
| Manitoba | 0.0444 | | 0.0425 | |
| Saskatchewan | 0.0400 | | 0.0412 | |
| Alberta | 0.0887 | | 0.0919 | |
| British Columbia | 0.0877 | | 0.0973 | |

*(continued)*

Table 11.2a    (*concluded*)

|  | Time to first UI spell | | Longitudinal patterns in UI use | |
|---|---|---|---|---|
|  | Mean | Standard deviation | Mean | Standard deviation |
| *Family background* | | | | |
| Parental permanent income ($10,000s) | 3.9577 | 7.2931 | 3.4947 | 5.8719 |
| Farming income | 0.0765 | | 0.0774 | |
| Fishing income | 0.00388 | | 0.008532 | |
| Self-employment income | 0.1506 | | 0.1457 | |
| Asset income | 0.6240 | | 0.5877 | |
| Rural residence at age 15 | 0.2386 | | 0.2766 | |
| *Region of residence at age 15 (Toronto Metropolitan as reference case)* | | | | |
| Newfoundland | 0.0180 | | 0.0269 | |
| Nova Scotia | 0.0350 | | 0.0385 | |
| Prince Edward Island | 0.0039 | | 0.0057 | |
| New Brunswick | 0.0266 | | 0.0319 | |
| Quebec East | 0.0733 | | 0.0818 | |
| Montreal Metropolitan | 0.0815 | | 0.0795 | |
| Quebec West | 0.0882 | | 0.0992 | |
| Eastern Ontario | 0.0710 | | 0.0640 | |
| Central Ontario | 0.1119 | | 0.0996 | |
| South-western Ontario | 0.0856 | | 0.0833 | |
| Northern Ontario | 0.0355 | | 0.0356 | |
| Manitoba | 0.0478 | | 0.0468 | |
| Saskatchewan | 0.0435 | | 0.0464 | |
| Alberta | 0.0828 | | 0.0838 | |
| British Columbia | 0.0832 | | 0.0883 | |
| Northwest Territories | 0.0004 | | 0.0003 | |
| Yukon | 0.0001 | | 0.0001 | |
| Number of person-years | 57,208 | | 100,795 | |
| Number of persons | 6,308 | | 6,308 | |

*Notes:* Parental permanent income is measured in constant 1986 dollars, but in the econometric analysis is standardized to have mean zero and standard deviation one. The "Time to first UI spell" analysis also includes a series of age-specific indicator variables. The sample proportions of these are: 16 years, 0.1101; 17 years, 0.1095; 18 years, 0.1075; 19 years, 0.1015; 20 years, 0.0877; 21 years, 0.0741; 22 years, 0.0633; 23 years, 0.0545; 24 years, 0.0486; 25 years, 0.0440; 26 years, 0.0402; 27 years, 0.0364; 28 years, 0.0334; 29 years, 0.0311; 30 years, 0.0295.

**Table 11.2b** *Descriptive Statistics for the Analyses of time to first spell and longitudinal patterns in UI use: Sweden*

| | Time to first UI spell | | Longitudinal patterns in UI use | |
|---|---|---|---|---|
| | Mean | Standard deviation | Mean | Standard deviation |
| Individual used UI | | | 0.161 | |
| Individual used UI in past | | | 0.312 | |
| Father used UI in past | 0.125 | | 0.162 | |
| Individual and father used UI in past | | | 0.076 | |
| Lagged dependent variable | | | 0.144 | |
| Father used UI in the future | 0.148 | | 0.141 | |
| Age (in decades) | | | 2.284 | 0.434 |
| Age squared | | | 5.403 | 2.011 |
| Married | 0.062 | | 0.090 | |
| UI generosity index dummy | 0.132 | | 0.207 | |
| Unemployment rate | 6.887 | 3.640 | 7. 903 | 4.267 |
| *Region of residence* | | | | |
| Stockholm county | 0.219 | | 0.186 | |
| Göteborg county | 0.095 | | 0.090 | |
| Malmöhus county | 0.097 | | 0.097 | |
| Forest counties | 0.132 | | 0.162 | |
| Other counties | 0.456 | | 0.465 | |
| *Family background* | | | | |
| Parental permanent income | 5.1017 | 2.8459 | 4.9034 | 2.6770 |
| Farming income | 0.071 | | 0.069 | |
| Self-employment income | 0.117 | | 0.117 | |
| Positive asset income | 0.233 | | 0.213 | |
| Negative asset income | 0.681 | | 0.698 | |
| *Region of residence at age 15* | | | | |
| Stockholm county | 0.202 | | 0.167 | |
| Göteborg county | 0.093 | | 0.085 | |

(*continued*)

Table 11.2b   (*concluded*)

|  | Time to first UI spell | | Longitudinal patterns in UI use | |
|---|---|---|---|---|
|  | Mean | Standard deviation | Mean | Standard deviation |
| Malmöhus county | 0.095 | | 0.094 | |
| Forest counties | 0.142 | | 0.173 | |
| Other counties | 0.468 | | 0.480 | |
| Number of person years | 38295 | | 55650 | |
| Number of persons | 3835 | | 3835 | |

*Notes:* In the econometric analysis parental permanent income is standardized to have mean zero and standard deviation one. The "Time to first UI sell" analysis also includes a series of age-specific indicator variables. The sample proportions of these are: 16 years, 0.0741; 17 years, 0.0740; 18 years, 0.0742; 19 years, 0.0740; 20 years, 0.0741; 21 years, 0.0740; 22 years, 0.0739; 23 years, 0.0740; 24 years, 0.0739; 25 years, 0.0739; 26 years, 0.0740; 27 years, 0.0741; 28 years, 0.0623.

the provincial/regional unemployment rate, an indicator of whether the individual lived in a rural area (for Canada only), and a series of indicator variables for the region of residence.[3] They also include a group of family background variables as depicted in the dashed arrows of Figure 11.1. These are not time-varying. Parental permanent income is the income earned by both parents averaged over a twenty-year period

[3] In Canada, the UI index varies over time and provinces, and is a function of the number of weeks of work required to establish eligibility, the maximum duration of benefits, and the replacement rate. In Sweden, the index is an indicator variable that takes the value of one beginning in 1993, and reflecting the changes in the replacement rate introduced in that year. The rural residence indicator for Canada is a 0–1 binary variable defined on the basis of the second digit of the postal code. If this digit is zero, the address is considered to be a "rural" postal-delivery route. As such this variable is determined by Canada Post for administrative reasons. As mentioned, years in which the individual lived in the Yukon or the Northwest Territories are excluded from the analysis because an unemployment rate was not available for these regions. Region of residence is based on the first digit of the postal code and offers, in some cases, sub-provincial information. In particular, the metropolitan areas of Toronto and Montreal are distinguished as are various regions in Quebec and Ontario.

in Canada and an eighteen-year period in Sweden. This variable is included to capture the influence of the intergenerational transmission of income status. It is also an important control variable by compensating for the lack of a full set of parental education and occupation indicators. These latter are captured in part, and in the manner most relevant for a study of intergenerational transmission of UI in Canada, by indicators for whether the father reported any income from farming, fishing, and other self-employment for the years during which the son was fifteen and sixteen. If there is an intergenerational transmission of occupation then given that farmers and the self-employed are not eligible for UI, there may be less of a tendency for individuals whose fathers worked in these fields to collect UI. The exception to this are the sons of self-employed fishers, who may be more inclined to receive UI. A self-employment indicator is also used in the Swedish data. However, it should be noted that these variables may not have the same impact in Sweden since the self-employed and farmers are entitled to UI after a three-month qualifying period.

This set of family background variables includes an indicator of whether the father reported any income from assets when the individual was fifteen or sixteen. In Sweden these are subdivided according to whether the asset income is positive or negative during the years in question. Corak and Heisz (1998) find information of this kind to be a very important correlate of the intergenerational transmission of incomes, and suggest that it is a proxy for time preference. Becker and Mulligan (1997) offer a more detailed analysis of this in the context of how time preference is passed on intergenerationally.

The final set of variables control for the possibility that individuals are likely to live in the same regions they grew up in as children: an indicator of rural residence at the age of fifteen and the region of residence. For Canada these are derived from the postal codes of the parents for the appropriate year. There is no indicator of rural residence available in the Swedish data, and only region of residence at fifteen years of age is controlled for.

A summary of the logit estimates of the hazard function is offered in Tables 11.3a and 11.3b for a series of models in which a successively larger and larger set of co-variates is included. Consider, first, the results using the Canadian data in Table 11.3a. The focus is on the estimates of the coefficients associated with parental past and future UI use in the first two rows of the table, and the p-value of the significance test of

Table 11.3a  Time to first UI use for Canadian men: summary of logit estimates of the hazard function

| | (1) | (2) | (3) | (4) | (5) | (6) | (7) | (8) | (9) | (10) | (11) | (12) |
|---|---|---|---|---|---|---|---|---|---|---|---|---|
| Father used UI in the past | 0.410 | 0.338 | 0.340 | 0.334 | 0.327 | 0.313 | 0.321 | 0.245 | 0.246 | 0.244 | 0.245 | 0.248 |
| Father used UI in the future | | 0.172 | 0.173 | 0.155 | 0.149 | 0.151 | 0.153 | 0.139 | 0.137 | 0.137 | 0.137 | 0.135 |
| P-value for test of equality | | 0.009 | 0.009 | 0.005 | 0.005 | 0.011 | 0.009 | 0.104 | 0.093 | 0.102 | 0.102 | 0.085 |
| *Other individual controls* | | | | | | | | | | | | |
| Age | ✓ | ✓ | ✓ | ✓ | ✓ | ✓ | ✓ | ✓ | ✓ | ✓ | ✓ | ✓ |
| Marital status | | | ✓ | ✓ | ✓ | ✓ | ✓ | ✓ | ✓ | ✓ | ✓ | ✓ |
| Provincial UI generosity index | | | | ✓ | ✓ | ✓ | ✓ | ✓ | ✓ | ✓ | ✓ | ✓ |
| Provincial unemployment rate | | | | | ✓ | | | ✓ | ✓ | ✓ | ✓ | ✓ |
| Rural residence | | | | | | ✓ | | ✓ | ✓ | ✓ | ✓ | ✓ |
| Region of residence | | | | | | | ✓ | | | ✓ | ✓ | ✓ |

*Other family background controls*

| | (1) | (2) | (3) | (4) | (5) | (6) | (7) | (8) | (9) | (10) | (11) | (12) |
|---|---|---|---|---|---|---|---|---|---|---|---|---|
| Parental permanent income | | | | | ✓ | ✓ | ✓ | ✓ | | | ✓ | ✓ |
| Sources of father's income | | | | | | | ✓ | ✓ | | | ✓ | ✓ |
| Rural residence at age 15 | | | | | | | | ✓ | | | ✓ | ✓ |
| Region of residence at age 15 | | | | | | | | | | | ✓ | ✓ |
| -log likelihood | 15048.9 | 15038.5 | 15030.3 | 14952.3 | 14929.7 | 14863.8 | 14825.5 | 14743.2 | 14708.9 | 14705.8 | 14691.1 | 14702.8 |

Reported coefficients are from a logit model of the hazard rate to first UI use, and all have a p-value less than 0.001. The standard errors account for clustering across individuals and are robust to heteroscedasticity. Region of residence refers to 16 provincial and sub-provincial regions defined according to the first digit of the postal code. Permanent income refers to the average of total parental income over a twenty-year period, while sources of the father's income include indicator variables for whether the father reported income from farming, fishing, self-employment or asset income when the son was 15 to 16 years of age. A Wald test for the significance of the region of residence indicators in model (11) yields a $\chi^2(15)$ value of 20.7 and an associated p-value of 0.146. A similar test that the coefficients on the controls for region of residence at age 15 are jointly equal to zero yields a $\chi^2(17)$ statistic of 137.6 with a p-value less than 0.0001.

Number of observations is 57,208 representing 6,308 individuals.

their equality in the third row. (All of the estimates of parental past and future UI are statistically significant, having associated p-values of less than 0.001.) The first model estimated includes only controls for father's past UI participation and a series of 0–1 indicators for the age of the son; the second model adds future paternal UI participation to this, namely the control for unobservable factors. The coefficient on past use falls from 0.410 to 0.338 (about 18 percent) when future use is added, but remains statistically different from the coefficient associated with future parental use. These estimates remain essentially unchanged as more and more controls for the contemporaneous characteristics of the individual are included in the model. All of these additional controls are individually statistically significant, with the exception of the UI generosity index, and as a group improve the fit of the model. They do not, however, change the magnitude of the past and future paternal UI coefficient estimates or the relationship between them: in model (2), controlling only for age, past paternal UI use is – at 0.34 – twice the magnitude of future parental UI use; in model (7), with the full set of contemporaneous controls, it remains – at 0.32 – about twice as large. This changes somewhat once variables controlling for family background are included in the model. In particular, the addition of parental permanent income in column (8) lowers the paternal past UI use coefficient to about 0.25 and the future use coefficient slightly to about 0.14, while the addition of the remaining variables in columns (9), (10), and (11) does not lead to any further appreciable changes. The marginal significance level of the t-test of parameter equality rises to about 0.10. All of the additional variables are statistically significant, with the exception of those for the contemporaneous region of residence, many of which seem to lose their significance once region of residence at age fifteen is included in the model.[4] Given that the analysis focuses on time to first spell from the age of sixteen, it is perhaps not surprising that the impact of the region of residence at age fifteen works through the contemporaneous region of residence. There is likely to be a great deal of similarity between these measures for a large fraction of the time the spells are studied. Thus, the results from the preferred

---

[4] A Wald test for the significance of the region of residence indicators in model (10) yields a $\chi^2(15)$ value of 20.7, with an associated p-value of 0.146. A similar test for the joint significance of the region of residence at age 15 variables yields a $\chi^2(17)$ of 137.6 with a p-value of less than 0.0001.

model of this exercise are presented in column (12). It includes all of the available co-variates with the exception of contemporaneous region of residence. In this model, the null hypothesis, that the influence of past and future parental UI use are the same, is incorrectly rejected with a probability of 8.5 percent.

Different results are obtained with the Swedish data (see Table 11.3b). The coefficient associated with the father's past UI use in model (1) has roughly the same general magnitude as that obtained with Canadian data, and falls about 14 percent (from 0.465 to 0.400) when father's future use is added. Even so, in model (2) the two coefficients are statistically different with a p-value of 0.115. With the addition of extra variables this p-value increases slightly to 0.163 in column (7), but jumps markedly – to 0.456 – once parental permanent income is added in column (8). In the full model described in column (11) the coefficients are 0.240 and 0.182, and the marginal significance level for the test of equality is 0.538. Quite clearly, the null hypothesis that the two coefficients are the same cannot be rejected at any reasonable significance level. It remains possible that the impact of paternal UI use on shortening the time to a first UI claim is entirely due to unobservable factors. Further, this impact is to some large degree related to family income.

The complete set of Canadian results for model (12) and Swedish results for model (11) are presented in Tables 11.4a and 11.4b, along with an estimate of the associated marginal impact of each variable.[5] In Canada, being married lowers the probability of starting a spell of UI, while higher provincial unemployment rates and living in a rural area increases it. In Sweden, being married has no statistically significant influence on the probability of starting a UI spell. UI generosity has a statistically significant negative coefficient, but this is the expected sign as it is defined as being equal to one beginning in 1993 when

---

[5] The derivation of the marginal effect of the binary co-variates in this table is approximate and calculated as $\mathcal{L}(X\beta) [1 - \mathcal{L}(X\beta)]\beta$ where $\mathcal{L}(\ )$ represents the logistic probability distribution, $X$ the sample averages of the co-variates (binary co-variates being set to their sample proportions), and $\beta$ the vector of estimated coefficients. This is usually a close approximation to estimating the difference between the probabilities of setting the indicator to one and to zero. See Greene (1997, pp. 875–79). The same caveat applies to the discussion of the marginal effects from the probit model discussed below in the context of Tables 11.7a and 11.7b.

Table 11.3b  *Time to first UI use for Swedish men: summary of logit estimates of the hazard function*

| | (1) | (2) | (3) | (4) | (5) | (6) | (7) | (8) | (9) | (10) | (11) | (12) |
|---|---|---|---|---|---|---|---|---|---|---|---|---|
| Father used UI in the past | 0.465 | 0.400 | 0.399 | 0.390 | 0.320 | | 0.318 | 0.280 | 0.240 | | 0.240 | |
| Father used UI in the future | | 0.245 | 0.247 | 0.257 | 0.184 | | 0.179 | 0.195 | 0.190 | | 0.182 | |
| P-value for test of equality | | 0.115 | 0.121 | 0.159 | 0.170 | | 0.163 | 0.456 | 0.617 | | 0.538 | |
| *Other individual controls* | | | | | | | | | | | | |
| Age | ✓ | ✓ | ✓ | ✓ | ✓ | | ✓ | ✓ | ✓ | | ✓ | |
| Marital status | | ✓ | ✓ | ✓ | ✓ | | ✓ | ✓ | ✓ | | ✓ | |
| UI generosity index | | | ✓ | ✓ | ✓ | | ✓ | ✓ | ✓ | | ✓ | |
| Unemployment rate | | | | ✓ | ✓ | | ✓ | ✓ | ✓ | | ✓ | |
| Rural residence | | | | | | | ✓ | ✓ | ✓ | | | |
| Region of residence | | | | | | | | | | | ✓ | |

*Other family background controls*

| | | | | | | | | |
|---|---|---|---|---|---|---|---|---|
| Permanent income | | | | | | ✓ | | ✓ |
| Sources of father's income | | | | | | ✓ | | ✓ |
| Rural residence at age 15 | | | | | | | | ✓ |
| Region of residence at age 15 | | | | | | | | ✓ |
| -log likelihood | 7844.4 | 7836.5 | 7834.6 | 7829.3 | 7675.4 | 7662.6 | 7639.7 | 7612.4 | 7587.4 |

*Notes:* Reported coefficients are from a logit model of the hazard rate to first UI use. and all have a p-value less than 0.001. Region of Residence refers to five different regions composed of different counties. Permanent income refers to the average of total parental income over a 18-year period, while sources of the father's income include indicator variables for whether the father reported income from farming, self-employment, or asset income when the son was 15 to 16 years of age.

Number of observations is 35,488 representing 3,835 individuals.

Models (6), (10), and (12) are not estimated because rural residence is not available in the Swedish data.

**Table 11.4a** *Logit estimates of the hazard rate governing time to first use of UI: Canada, men aged 16 to 30*

| | Coefficient | Robust standard error | P-value | Marginal effect |
|---|---|---|---|---|
| Father used UI in past | 0.248 | 0.040 | 0.000 | 0.0125 |
| Father used UI in future | 0.135 | 0.039 | 0.000 | 0.0068 |
| Married | −0.248 | 0.062 | 0.000 | −0.0125 |
| Provincial UI generosity index | 0.274 | 0.193 | 0.156 | 0.0138 |
| Provincial unemployment rate | 0.035 | 0.013 | 0.009 | 0.0018 |
| Rural residence | 0.231 | 0.061 | 0.000 | 0.0116 |
| *Family background* | | | | |
| Parental permanent income | −0.344 | 0.059 | 0.000 | −0.0173 |
| Farming income | −0.087 | 0.067 | 0.195 | −0.0044 |
| Fishing income | 0.933 | 0.246 | 0.000 | 0.0470 |
| Self-employment income | 0.072 | 0.046 | 0.111 | 0.0036 |
| Asset income | −0.204 | 0.037 | 0.000 | −0.0103 |
| Rural residence at age 15 | 0.105 | 0.059 | 0.078 | 0.0053 |
| *Region of Residence at Age 15 (Toronto Metropolitan as reference)* | | | | |
| Newfoundland | 0.648 | 0.161 | 0.000 | 0.0326 |
| Nova Scotia | 0.320 | 0.106 | 0.003 | 0.0161 |
| Prince Edward Island | 0.644 | 0.279 | 0.021 | 0.0324 |
| New Brunswick | 0.457 | 0.121 | 0.000 | 0.0230 |
| Quebec East | 0.478 | 0.084 | 0.000 | 0.0241 |
| Montreal Metropolitan | 0.324 | 0.088 | 0.000 | 0.0163 |
| Quebec West | 0.508 | 0.085 | 0.000 | 0.0255 |
| Eastern Ontario | 0.243 | 0.083 | 0.004 | 0.0122 |
| Central Ontario | 0.279 | 0.076 | 0.000 | 0.0140 |
| South-western Ontario | 0.445 | 0.079 | 0.000 | 0.0224 |
| Northern Ontario | 0.417 | 0.105 | 0.000 | 0.0210 |
| Manitoba | 0.379 | 0.097 | 0.000 | 0.0191 |
| Saskatchewan | 0.629 | 0.010 | 0.000 | 0.0316 |
| Alberta | 0.531 | 0.082 | 0.000 | 0.0267 |
| British Columbia | 0.521 | 0.086 | 0.000 | 0.0262 |
| Northwest Territories | −0.746 | 0.939 | 0.427 | −0.0375 |

*(continued)*

Table 11.4a   (*concluded*)

|  | Coefficient | Robust standard error | P-value | Marginal effect |
|---|---|---|---|---|
| Yukon | 1.454 | 0.103 | 0.000 | 0.0732 |
| Constant | −6.444 | 0.227 | 0.000 | |
| -log likelihood | 14,702.82 | | | |
| Number of person-years | 57,208 | | | |

*Notes:* Other controls include a series of indicator variables for each age from 17 to 30 years. The number of observations is 57,208 representing 6,308 individuals. Standard errors are robust to heteroscedasticity and correct for the clustering of observations by individuals. Marginal effects are calculated as $\mathcal{L}(\beta'\mathbf{x})[1 - \mathcal{L}(\beta'\mathbf{x})]\,\beta$ where $\mathcal{L}(\ )$ represents the logistic probability distribution, $\beta$ the vector of estimated coefficients, and $\mathbf{x}$ the sample averages of the co-variates (indicator variables also being set at their sample proportions). As such, these marginal effects are approximations of the impact of the binary co-variates in the model.

the replacement rate declined from 90 percent to 80 percent. Family background variables all seem to work in a plausible way in both countries: higher parental permanent income lowering the chances that a son will experience a first claim; the presence of parental farming, and (positive) asset income doing the same; and the presence of parental fishing income increasing the chances of starting a claim in Canada. The impact of this latter variable is particularly striking. If a father claimed to have income from fishing when the son was fifteen or sixteen, the son's chances of starting a first claim – all other things equal – are almost five percentage points higher.

These results are used to derive estimates of the impact of parental UI use on the hazard rates at the point of sample means from the age of sixteen onward, offered in Figures 11.2a and 11.2b. The overall patterns are roughly the same in the two countries: the hazard rate rises sharply during the teen years and peaks at twenty to twenty-one years of age, then falls and plateaus during the early to mid twenties, before falling during the late twenties. The Canadian estimates typically lie above those for Sweden throughout most of the age period being examined. However, the hazard rate at age eighteen is actually higher in Sweden, an indication that the absence of a work requirement in the eligibility rules for school leavers leads to a quicker transition to UI.

Table 11.4b    *Logit estimates of the hazard rate governing time to first use of UI: Sweden, men aged 16 to 28*

| | Coefficient | Robust standard error | P-value | Marginal effect |
|---|---|---|---|---|
| Father used UI in past | 0.244 | 0.063 | 0.000 | 0.0088 |
| Father used UI in future | 0.182 | 0.063 | 0.004 | 0.0066 |
| Married | 0.075 | 0.118 | 0.528 | 0.0027 |
| UI generosity index | −0.351 | 0.137 | 0.010 | −0.0127 |
| Unemployment rate | 0.113 | 0.012 | 0.000 | 0.0041 |
| *Family background* | | | | |
| Parental permanent income | −0.191 | 0.027 | 0.000 | −0.0069 |
| Farming income | −0.268 | 0.098 | 0.006 | −0.0097 |
| Self-employment income | 0.007 | 0.069 | 0.914 | 0.0002 |
| Positive asset income | −0.248 | 0.094 | 0.008 | −0.0089 |
| Negative asset income | 0.067 | 0.084 | 0.421 | 0.0024 |
| *Region of residence (Stockholm county as reference case)* | | | | |
| Göteborg | 0.668 | 0.219 | 0.002 | 0.0241 |
| Malmö | 0.432 | 0.259 | 0.096 | 0.0156 |
| Forest counties | 0.512 | 0.229 | 0.025 | 0.0185 |
| Other counties | 0.342 | 0.162 | 0.035 | 0.0123 |
| *Region of residence at Age 15 (Stockholm county as reference case)* | | | | |
| Göteborg | −0.646 | 0.228 | 0.005 | −0.0233 |
| Malmöhus | −0.143 | 0.261 | 0.582 | −0.0052 |
| Forest counties | −0.017 | 0.215 | 0.937 | −0.0006 |
| Other counties | −0.068 | 0.157 | 0.666 | −0.0024 |
| Constant | −7.623 | 0.461 | 0.000 | |
| -log likelihood | 7,587.36 | | | |
| Number of person-years | 35,488 | | | |

*Notes:* Other controls include a series of indicator variables for each age from 17 to 28 years. The number of observations is 35,488 representing 3,835 individuals. Standard errors are robust to heteroscedasticity and correct for the clustering of observations by individuals. Marginal effects are calculated as described in the note to Table 11.4a.

By age twenty-eight the hazard rates are about the same in the two countries.

The three lines in these figures refer to the estimated hazard rates when: (1) the indicator variables for past and future parental UI use are both set to zero; (2) when only the future use variable is set to one;

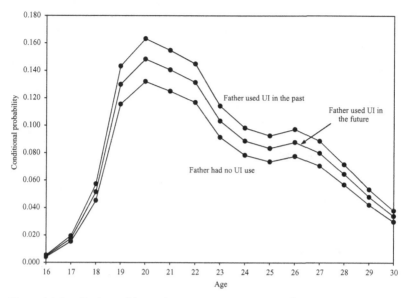

**Figure 11.2a** Estimated hazard rates governing time to first UI use: Canadian men between 16 and 30 years.

(3) and when only the past use variable is set to one. The difference between (1) and (2) represents the impact of unobservables, while that between (2) and (3) represents the causal impact of paternal UI use.

In Canada, the hazard rate associated with having a father who had used UI at any point in the past is higher than that associated with having one who had not used UI at all, the difference being greatest between the ages of nineteen and twenty-two, and peaking at the age of twenty. The conditional probability of beginning a spell of insured unemployment is about three percentage points higher during these years for those whose fathers used UI in the past compared to those whose fathers never used the program, but about half of this is due to unobservable influences. (A model in which the coefficient on father's past UI use is allowed to vary with age was also estimated, but did not lead to statistically significant results.)

Figure 11.2b for Sweden shows an equivalent pattern with the conditional probability of beginning a spell of insured unemployment peaking at twenty to twenty-one years of age. The differences between those whose fathers used UI and those whose fathers didn't are also greatest during these years. However, this difference of about two percentage

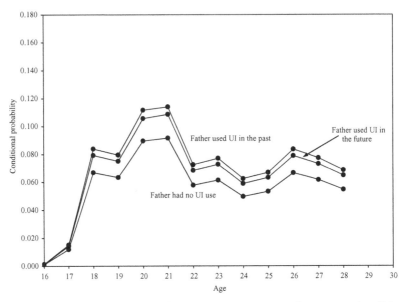

**Figure 11.2b**  Estimated hazard rates governing time to first UI use: Swedish men between 16 and 28 years.

points is almost entirely due to unobservables. In fact, as the results in column (11) of Table 11.3b suggest, the observed difference between the two upper lines is not statistically significant.

These findings are detailed in Table 11.5, where both the hazard and survivor rates associated with model (12) of Table 11.3a for Canada, and model (11) of Table 11.3b for Sweden are presented. The estimates of the survivor function from the Canadian data suggest that only about 24 percent of individuals whose father collected UI at some point in the past will make it to the age of thirty without also collecting UI, while over 32 percent of their counterparts whose fathers did not collect UI do so. This eight percentage point difference is due about equally to unobservables and to the causal influence of parental UI use.

In Sweden, a higher proportion of the sample makes it to the age of twenty-eight without ever collecting UI: 47 percent of those with fathers who did not collect, and 38 percent of those whose fathers did. This nine percentage point difference is due almost entirely to unobservables suggesting that in Sweden the influence of parental UI use does not seem to have a major role in determining the onset of a

Table 11.5 Estimated hazard and survivor rates: time to first UI spell, Canada and Sweden

| Age | Hazard Rates | | | Survivor Rates | | |
| --- | --- | --- | --- | --- | --- | --- |
| | Father did not use UI | Father used UI in future | Father Used UI in past | Father did not use UI | Father used UI in future | Father used UI in past |
| **1. Canada** | | | | | | |
| 16 | 0.0041 | 0.0047 | 0.0052 | 0.9959 | 0.9953 | 0.9948 |
| 17 | 0.0152 | 0.0174 | 0.0194 | 0.9807 | 0.9780 | 0.9754 |
| 18 | 0.0452 | 0.0514 | 0.0572 | 0.9364 | 0.9277 | 0.9196 |
| 19 | 0.1154 | 0.1299 | 0.1432 | 0.8283 | 0.8072 | 0.7879 |
| 20 | 0.1320 | 0.1483 | 0.1631 | 0.7189 | 0.6875 | 0.6594 |
| 21 | 0.1250 | 0.1405 | 0.1546 | 0.6291 | 0.5909 | 0.5575 |
| 22 | 0.1168 | 0.1314 | 0.1448 | 0.5556 | 0.5132 | 0.4767 |
| 23 | 0.0914 | 0.1033 | 0.1142 | 0.5048 | 0.4602 | 0.4223 |
| 24 | 0.0784 | 0.0887 | 0.0983 | 0.4652 | 0.4194 | 0.3808 |
| 25 | 0.0737 | 0.0834 | 0.0925 | 0.4310 | 0.3844 | 0.3456 |
| 26 | 0.0776 | 0.0878 | 0.0973 | 0.3975 | 0.3506 | 0.3119 |
| 27 | 0.0705 | 0.0799 | 0.0886 | 0.3695 | 0.3226 | 0.2843 |
| 28 | 0.0568 | 0.0644 | 0.0716 | 0.3485 | 0.3018 | 0.2640 |
| 29 | 0.0421 | 0.0479 | 0.0533 | 0.3339 | 0.2874 | 0.2499 |
| 30 | 0.0299 | 0.0340 | 0.0379 | 0.3239 | 0.2776 | 0.2404 |
| **2. Sweden** | | | | | | |
| 16 | 0.0011 | 0.0013 | 0.0014 | 0.9989 | 0.9987 | 0.9986 |
| 17 | 0.0119 | 0.0142 | 0.0151 | 0.9870 | 0.9845 | 0.9835 |
| 18 | 0.0670 | 0.0793 | 0.0839 | 0.9209 | 0.9064 | 0.9010 |
| 19 | 0.0635 | 0.0752 | 0.0796 | 0.8624 | 0.8383 | 0.8293 |
| 20 | 0.0896 | 0.1056 | 0.1116 | 0.7851 | 0.7498 | 0.7367 |
| 21 | 0.0916 | 0.1086 | 0.1139 | 0.7132 | 0.6683 | 0.6528 |
| 22 | 0.0578 | 0.0685 | 0.0726 | 0.6720 | 0.6225 | 0.6054 |
| 23 | 0.0615 | 0.0729 | 0.0772 | 0.6306 | 0.5772 | 0.5587 |
| 24 | 0.0497 | 0.0590 | 0.0625 | 0.5993 | 0.5431 | 0.5238 |
| 25 | 0.0533 | 0.0633 | 0.0670 | 0.5674 | 0.5087 | 0.4887 |
| 26 | 0.0667 | 0.0790 | 0.0836 | 0.5295 | 0.4685 | 0.4478 |
| 27 | 0.0617 | 0.0732 | 0.0774 | 0.4968 | 0.4343 | 0.4132 |
| 28 | 0.0547 | 0.0649 | 0.0687 | 0.4697 | 0.4061 | 0.3848 |

*Note:* For Canada, hazard rates are calculated for Model (12) of Table 11.3a at the point of age-specific sample means for the remaining co-variates. For Sweden, hazard rates are calculated for Model (11) of Table 11.3b at the point of age-specific sample means for the remaining co-variates.

first UI spell for the son. (For Canada the comparable figures at age twenty-eight are 35 percent and 26 percent respectively.)

The possibility that a first spell of UI kicks off a long-lasting process by raising the chances of repeated UI use in the future is explored in the random-effects probit model. The central estimates of this model are presented in Tables 11.6a and 11.6b. Once again, a series of models are presented with successively larger sets of co-variates. The model presented in columns (1) contain a single co-variate, the indicator of past individual UI use. For Canada, the estimated probit coefficient of 0.31 falls only slightly, to 0.28, when the indicator of past parental use is added to the model. In this model, individual learning dominates social learning. However, the inclusion of the interaction of these terms in column (3) leads to a finding that can be interpreted to suggest that individual learning is a lot less important and dominated by social learning. Having had a father who collected UI in the past reduces the independent impact of having made a past claim by about half. In other words, the impact of past claims on the probability of future claims is muted by having had a parent who collected. This result is much stronger when controls for age are included in the model. The result in column (4) shows that individual past use in models (1) through (3) is in large part a proxy for age, the coefficient being only a third in magnitude and completely dominated by the interaction term with parental use. In this model, individual learning raises the incidence of UI only if the parent has not received UI. The addition of co-variates associated with the individual's region of residence (the unemployment rate, the UI generosity, and the rural and region controls) lowers the value of the social learning coefficient slightly, but it essentially remains at about 0.23 or 0.24 with the individual learning coefficient about six-tenths to seven-tenths the magnitude.

The addition of familial background controls, most notably the parental permanent income, reduces both coefficients, without changing the relative magnitudes appreciably. In this model, the indicators for the region of residence continue to play a statistically significant role even when the region of residence as a child is entered into the model. In column (13) the results from the complete model are offered. In this model, the null hypothesis that the individual learning and social capital coefficients are equal would be falsely rejected with a probability of 0.0256. The null that the sum of the individual learning and the interaction term are equal to zero has a higher

**Table 11.6a** *The impact of individual learning and social capital on the probability of using UI: summary of estimates from random effects probit models for Canadian men*

| | (1) | (2) | (3) | (4) | (5) | (6) | (7) | (8) | (9) | (10) | (11) | (12) | (13) |
|---|---|---|---|---|---|---|---|---|---|---|---|---|---|
| Individual used UI in the past | 0.310 | 0.277 | 0.331 | 0.113 | 0.116 | 0.149 | 0.148 | 0.162 | 0.164 | 0.148 | 0.146 | 0.140 | 0.134 |
| Father used UI in the past | | 0.200 | 0.294 | 0.269 | 0.270 | 0.238 | 0.238 | 0.229 | 0.230 | 0.197 | 0.195 | 0.193 | 0.193 |
| Individual and Father used UI | | | −0.159 | −0.103 | −0.102 | −0.096 | −0.095 | −0.093 | −0.094 | −0.083 | −0.086 | −0.087 | −0.089 |
| *Individual Characteristics* | | | | | | | | | | | | | |
| Age and age Squared | | | | ✓ | ✓ | ✓ | ✓ | ✓ | ✓ | ✓ | ✓ | ✓ | ✓ |
| Marital status | | | | | ✓ | ✓ | ✓ | ✓ | ✓ | ✓ | ✓ | ✓ | ✓ |
| Provincial unemployment rate | | | | | | ✓ | ✓ | ✓ | ✓ | ✓ | ✓ | ✓ | ✓ |
| Provincial UI generosity | | | | | | | ✓ | ✓ | ✓ | ✓ | ✓ | ✓ | ✓ |
| Rural residence | | | | | | | | ✓ | ✓ | ✓ | ✓ | ✓ | ✓ |
| Region of residence | | | | | | | | | ✓ | ✓ | ✓ | ✓ | ✓ |
| *Family background* | | | | | | | | | | | | | |
| Parental Permanent Income | | | | | | | | | | ✓ | ✓ | ✓ | ✓ |
| Sources of father's income | | | | | | | | | | | ✓ | ✓ | ✓ |
| Rural resident at age 15 | | | | | | | | | | | | ✓ | ✓ |
| Region of residence at age 15 | | | | | | | | | | | | | ✓ |
| -log likelihood | 39,267.3 | 39,153.6 | 39,130.4 | 38,218.7 | 38,185.8 | 37,765.0 | 37,762.0 | 37,668.4 | 37,599.5 | 37,516.3 | 37,450.2 | 37,428.3 | 37,414.2 |

*Notes:* The dependent variable is a 0–1 indicator of whether the individual received income from UI in a particular year. The reported coefficients are from a random effects probit model in which the unobserved individual heterogeneity is assumed to be normally distributed. All reported coefficients have a p-value of less than 0. Number of observations is 100,795 representing annual observations on 6,308 individuals from the ages of 16 to 31.

All models include a lagged value of the dependent variable. Region of residence refers to 16 provincial and sub-provincial regions defined according to the first digit of the postal code. Rural residence is defined on the basis of the second digit of the postal code. Parental permanent income refers to the average of total parental income over a twenty-year period, while sources of the father's income includes four indicator variables for whether the father reported income from farming, fishing, self-employment, or assets when the son was 15 to 16 years of age.

**Table 11.6b** *The impact of individual learning and social capital on the probability of using UI: summary of estimates from random effects probit models for Swedish men*

| | (1) | (2) | (3) | (4) | (5) | (6) | (7) | (8) | (9) | (10) | (11) | (12) | (13) |
|---|---|---|---|---|---|---|---|---|---|---|---|---|---|
| Individual used UI in the past | 0.441 | 0.420 | 0.437 | 0.297 | 0.299 | 0.317 | 0.296 | | 0.290 | 0.275 | 0.261 | | 0.264 |
| Father used UI in the past | | 0.217 | 0.260 | 0.231 | 0.230 | 0.179 | 0.175 | | 0.180 | 0.156 | 0.144 | | 0.145 |
| Individual and father used UI | | | −0.085$^{n.s.}$ | −0.057$^{n.s.}$ | −0.057$^{n.s.}$ | −0.050$^{n.s.}$ | −0.051$^{n.s.}$ | | −0.052$^{n.s.}$ | −0.043$^{n.s.}$ | −0.035$^{n.s.}$ | | −0.041$^{n.s.}$ |
| *Individual characteristics* | | | | | | | | | | | | | |
| Age and age squared | | | | ✓ | ✓ | ✓ | ✓ | | ✓ | ✓ | ✓ | | ✓ |
| Marital status | | | | ✓ | ✓ | ✓ | ✓ | | ✓ | ✓ | ✓ | | ✓ |
| Unemployment rate | | | | | | ✓ | ✓ | | ✓ | ✓ | ✓ | | ✓ |
| UI generosity | | | | | | | ✓ | | ✓ | ✓ | ✓ | | ✓ |
| Rural residence | | | | | | | | | | | | | |
| Region of residence | | | | | | | | | ✓ | ✓ | ✓ | | ✓ |
| *Family background* | | | | | | | | | | | | | |
| Parental permanent income | | | | | | | | | | ✓ | | | ✓ |
| Sources of father's income | | | | | | | | | | | ✓ | | ✓ |
| Rural resident at age 15 | | | | | | | | | | | | | |
| Region of residence at age 15 | | | | | | | | | | | | | ✓ |
| -log likelihood | 15,235.8 | 15,179.9 | 15,177.7 | 15,027.7 | 14,784.6 | 15,021.9 | 14,614.3 | | 14,593.0 | 14,564.9 | 14,533.4 | | 14,487.4 |

*Notes:* The dependent variable is a 0–1 indicator of whether the individual received income from UI in a particular year. The reported coefficients are from a random-effects probit model in which the unobserved individual heterogeneity is assumed to be normally distributed. All reported coefficients have a p-value of less than 0 except those indicated with $^{n.s.}$. Number of observations is 49,133 representing annual observations on 3,835 individuals from the ages of 16 to 28.
All models include a lagged value of the dependent variable. Region of residence refers to five different regions composed of different counties. Permanent income refers to the average of total parental income over a 18-year period, while sources of the father's income include indicator variables for whether the father reported income from farming, self-employment, or asset income when the son was 15 to 16 years of age. Models (8) and (12) are not estimated as there is no information on rural residence in the Swedish data.

associated p-value, 0.0786. It is possible that individual learning continues to raise the probability of experiencing a UI spell in the presence of parental past use but the effect is small, the best estimate of the impact being about 0.04 (that is, 0.134–0.089).

The Swedish results are different: individual learning dominates social learning. The coefficient for individual past use in column (1) at 0.441 is higher than the estimate from the Canadian data, and essentially remains unchanged as controls for the father's past use and the interaction of the two variables are added to the model. Indeed, the interaction term is never statistically significant. Once controls for age are included in the model the estimated coefficient for individual past use is about 0.3, and remains essentially unchanged with the addition of controls for other individual characteristics. At the same time the estimate for father's past use falls with each additional individual characteristic added to the model, taking the value of 0.18 in model (9). Once family background variables are added both coefficients fall in value, the control for individual learning not falling as much as that for social learning. The values of these coefficients in the complete model are 0.264 and 0.145. These are statistically different with a marginal probability level of 0.001.

The complete results from this model as well as the associated marginal effects is presented for both countries in Tables 11.7a and 11.7b. In Canada, individual past use of the program raises the probability of future use by 1.9 percentage points. However, if the father has used UI in the past the probability rises by 2.8 percentage points and leads the impact of individual past use to fall to only about 0.7 percentage points (0.0193–0.0127). In Sweden, on the other hand, individual past use raises the probability of future use by 4.6 percentage points; if the father used the program in the past the probability of future use increases by a further 2.5 percentage points. The remaining results mirror the patterns presented in Tables 11.4a and 11.4b for the time to a first claim. Most notably in Canada, the sons of fishers have a nine percentage point higher chance of collecting UI benefits.

## 4 Conclusion

This chapter offers a comparative analysis of longitudinal patterns in the use of unemployment insurance in Canada and Sweden

Table 11.7a   *Random effect probit estimates of the probability of UI use: Canadian men from the ages of 16 to 31*

| | Coefficient | Robust standard error | P-value | Marginal effect |
|---|---|---|---|---|
| Individual used UI in past | 0.134 | 0.022 | 0.000 | 0.0193 |
| Father used UI in past | 0.193 | 0.021 | 0.000 | 0.0278 |
| Individual and father used UI in past | −0.089 | 0.025 | 0.000 | −0.0127 |
| Lagged dependent variable | 1.196 | 0.015 | 0.000 | 0.1720 |
| Age (in decades) | 7.522 | 0.212 | 0.000 | |
| Age squared | −1.528 | 0.046 | 0.000 | |
| Married | −0.133 | 0.016 | 0.000 | −0.0191 |
| Provincial UI generosity index | 0.030 | 0.060 | 0.612 | 0.0044 |
| Provincial unemployment rate | 0.066 | 0.004 | 0.000 | 0.0095 |
| Rural residence | 0.096 | 0.019 | 0.000 | 0.0138 |
| *Region of residence (Toronto Metropolitan as reference case)* | | | | |
| Newfoundland | −0.290 | 0.090 | 0.001 | −0.0417 |
| Nova Scotia | −0.068 | 0.072 | 0.345 | −0.0098 |
| Prince Edward Island | 0.049 | 0.179 | 0.786 | 0.0070 |
| New Brunswick | 0.023 | 0.084 | 0.782 | 0.0034 |
| Quebec East | 0.110 | 0.078 | 0.157 | 0.0159 |
| Montreal Metropolitan | −0.026 | 0.067 | 0.700 | −0.0037 |
| Quebec West | −0.017 | 0.067 | 0.796 | −0.0025 |
| Eastern Ontario | 0.036 | 0.054 | 0.509 | 0.0051 |
| Central Ontario | 0.021 | 0.039 | 0.591 | 0.0030 |
| South-western Ontario | 0.141 | 0.053 | 0.008 | 0.0202 |
| Northern Ontario | 0.117 | 0.070 | 0.095 | 0.0169 |
| Manitoba | 0.087 | 0.079 | 0.270 | 0.0125 |
| Saskatchewan | 0.305 | 0.076 | 0.000 | 0.0438 |
| Alberta | 0.074 | 0.056 | 0.187 | 0.0106 |
| British Columbia | 0.104 | 0.055 | 0.060 | 0.0149 |
| *Family background* | | | | |
| Parental permanent income | −0.133 | 0.015 | 0.000 | −0.0192 |
| Farming income | −0.011 | 0.030 | 0.712 | −0.0016 |
| Fishing income | 0.632 | 0.080 | 0.000 | 0.0909 |
| Self-employment income | 0.026 | 0.021 | 0.227 | 0.0037 |
| Asset income | −0.117 | 0.016 | 0.000 | −0.0168 |
| Rural residence at age 15 | 0.121 | 0.022 | 0.000 | 0.0175 |

(continued)

Table 11.7a  (*concluded*)

| | Coefficient | Robust standard error | P-value | Marginal effect |
|---|---|---|---|---|
| *Region of residence at age 15 (Toronto Metropolitan as reference case)* | | | | |
| Newfoundland | 0.288 | 0.082 | 0.000 | 0.0414 |
| Nova Scotia | 0.129 | 0.075 | 0.084 | 0.0186 |
| Prince Edward Island | 0.196 | 0.174 | 0.259 | 0.0282 |
| New Brunswick | 0.187 | 0.085 | 0.028 | 0.0269 |
| Quebec East | 0.165 | 0.080 | 0.039 | 0.0238 |
| Montreal Metropolitan | 0.090 | 0.069 | 0.194 | 0.0129 |
| Quebec West | 0.182 | 0.070 | 0.009 | 0.0261 |
| Eastern Ontario | 0.074 | 0.059 | 0.209 | 0.0106 |
| Central Ontario | 0.114 | 0.045 | 0.011 | 0.0163 |
| South-western Ontario | 0.010 | 0.057 | 0.081 | 0.0143 |
| Northern Ontario | 0.139 | 0.073 | 0.055 | 0.0201 |
| Manitoba | 0.074 | 0.080 | 0.352 | 0.0107 |
| Saskatchewan | 0.102 | 0.078 | 0.190 | 0.0147 |
| Alberta | 0.161 | 0.061 | 0.009 | 0.0232 |
| British Columbia | 0.071 | 0.061 | 0.242 | 0.0102 |
| Northwest Territories | −0.754 | 0.492 | 0.126 | −0.1083 |
| Yukon | 0.317 | 0.545 | 0.561 | 0.0456 |
| Constant | −11.1 | 0.238 | 0.000 | |
| $\ln \sigma_v$ | −1.89 | 0.061 | 0.000 | |
| $\sigma_v$ | 0.389 | 0.012 | | |
| $\rho$ | 0.132 | 0.0069 | | |
| -log likelihood | 37,414.2 | | | |

*Notes:* The number of observations is 100,795 representing annual observations on 6,308 individuals from the ages of 16 to 31.

The dependent variable is a 0–1 indicator of whether the individual received income from UI in a particular year. The reported coefficients are from a random-effects probit model in which the unobserved individual heterogeneity is assumed to be normally distributed, with standard deviation $\sigma_v$. The proportion of the total variance contributed by the individual level variance is $\rho = \sigma_v/(1 + \sigma_v)$. A likelihood ratio test of the null hypothesis that $\rho = 0$ yields a $\xi^2(1)$ statistic of 610.5 with an associated p-value of less than 0.0001. Marginal effects are calculated as $\phi(\beta x)\beta$., where $\phi(\ )$ represents the normal probability density function, $\beta$ the vector of estimated coefficients, and x the sample averages of the co-variates (indicator variables also begin set at their sample proportions). As such these marginal effects are approximations of the impact of the binary co-variates in the model. The overall estimated probability of receiving UI (at the point of sample means) is 0.1438.

**Table 11.7b** *Random effect probit estimates of the probability of UI use: Swedish men from the ages of 16 to 28*

| | Coefficient | Robust standard error | P-value | Marginal effect |
|---|---|---|---|---|
| Individual used UI in past | 0.264 | 0.026 | 0.000 | 0.0464 |
| Father used UI in past | 0.145 | 0.030 | 0.000 | 0.0254 |
| Individual and father used UI in past | −0.041 | 0.041 | 0.325 | −0.0072 |
| Lagged dependent variable | 1.440 | 0.026 | 0.000 | 0.2532 |
| Age (in decades) | 6.764 | 0.372 | 0.000 | |
| Age squared | −1.501 | 0.084 | 0.000 | |
| Married | 0.029 | 0.035 | 0.406 | 0.0051 |
| UI generosity index | −0.147 | 0.000 | 0.000 | −0.0258 |
| Unemployment rate | 0.078 | 0.004 | 0.000 | 0.0136 |
| *Family background* | | | | |
| Parental permanent income | −0.080 | 0.010 | 0.000 | −0.0140 |
| Farming income | −0.128 | 0.034 | 0.000 | −0.0225 |
| Self-employment income | −0.032 | 0.026 | 0.206 | −0.0057 |
| Positive asset income | −0.092 | 0.033 | 0.005 | −0.0162 |
| Negative asset income | 0.024 | 0.029 | 0.407 | 0.0042 |
| *Region of residence (Stockholm county as reference case)* | | | | |
| Göteborg | 0.102 | 0.079 | 0.197 | 0.0180 |
| Malmöhus | 0.136 | 0.082 | 0.099 | 0.0239 |
| Forest counties | 0.170 | 0.068 | 0.013 | 0.0298 |
| Other counties | 0.108 | 0.056 | 0.055 | 0.0191 |
| *Region of residence (Stockholm county as reference case)* | | | | |
| Göteborg | −0.141 | 0.082 | 0.086 | −0.0247 |
| Malmöhus | −0.082 | 0.084 | 0.327 | −0.0144 |
| Forest counties | −0.116 | 0.064 | 0.068 | −0.0204 |
| Other counties | −0.090 | 0.055 | 0.104 | −0.0159 |
| Constant | −9.510 | 0.410 | 0.000 | |
| $\ln \sigma_v$ | −1.451 | 0.106 | 0.000 | |
| $\sigma_v$ | 0.438 | 0.023 | | |
| $\rho$ | 1.61 | 0.014 | | |
| -log likelihood | 14,487.4 | | | |

*Note:* The number of observations is 48,920 representing annual observations on 3,818 individuals from the ages of 16 to 28.

The dependent variable is a 0–1 indicator of whether the individual received income from UI in a particular year. The reported coefficients are from a random-effects probit model in which the unobserved individual heterogeneity is assumed to be normally distributed, with standard deviation $\sigma_v$. The proportion of the total variance contributed by the individual level variance is $\rho = \sigma_v/(1 + \sigma_v)$. A likelihood ratio test of the null hypothesis that $\rho = 0$ yields a $\chi^2(1)$ statistic of 197.5 with an associated p-value of less than 0.0001. Marginal effects are calculated as $\phi(\beta x)\beta$, where $\phi(\ )$ represents the normal probability density function, $\beta$ the vector of estimated coefficients, and $\mathbf{x}$ the sample averages of the co-variates (indicator variables also begin set at their sample proportions). As such, these marginal effects are approximations of the impact of the binary co-variates in the model. The overall estimated probability of receiving UI (at the point of sample means) is 0.1002.

in two parts. First, discrete time duration models are used to examine the time to a first UI spell paying particular attention to the influence of father's UI use, and controlling for unobservable influences by relying on the timing of the father's UI spells. Second, the entire sequence of UI use over a twelve to fifteen year period (beginning in the late 1970s) is modeled using random effects probit models, and focusing upon the relative role of paternal and individual past use in determining the probability of receiving UI. In this way, the analysis addresses both the degree to which parental UI background launches individuals down a path of repeated interaction with UI and the relative importance of past individual interaction with the program.

The results suggest, firstly, that the incidence of UI use is high among young adult men in both Canada and Sweden. About 75 percent of young Canadian men rely on the program at least once by the age of thirty; slightly more than 60 percent of Swedes do so. However, there are substantial differences in these proportions between those whose fathers used UI at some point, and those whose fathers did not: over 80 percent of young Canadian men whose fathers collected UI also collected, versus about 70 percent of those whose fathers did not; in Sweden the comparable figures are about 70 percent and 58 percent. The major objective is to examine the extent to which these differences reflect a correlation in characteristics (both observed and unobserved) between father and son that influence UI use, and the extent to which they reflect a relationship in which a father's use of UI somehow influences the son's probability of relying on the program.

In Canada, the incidence of a first UI claim is influenced by family UI background. Young men whose fathers collected UI in the past generally begin their first UI claim sooner. Paternal UI history also heightens the chances of repeated UI use regardless of individual past history. Individual learning about the program is significant only if the individual has no family background of UI use. In Sweden, the first experience is not influenced in a causal way by family background. However, once the individual relies on the program – and those from lower-income families are more likely to do so – individual learning becomes an important influence on the probability of experiencing another claim. The probability of beginning a claim after about the age of twenty-five, conditional on not having used it up to that time, is about the same in the two countries, but generally young Swedish men are less likely to begin a UI claim than Canadian men. The only exception to this occurs at about the age of eighteen when they are more likely to do so. Individual learning – not social learning – is the dominant influence in determining repeated interaction with the Swedish program.

These differences may reflect differences in the design and underlying philosophies of UI in the two countries. The Canadian program is for the most part viewed as an insurance program offering income support to those experiencing a job loss; the Swedish program is an element of labor market adjustment policy meant to facilitate the retraining of individuals and thereby promote long-term employment. It may be that these different philosophies have different intergenerational consequences. In a "passive" program of income support, children with parents who have received UI may be learning that labor market earnings are legitimately and possibly not uncommonly supplemented with UI benefits. They may not require their own interaction with the program to become familiar with it if their parent's interaction is readily observable. In an "active" program geared toward retraining, children will observe parents engaged in other activities associated with skills development and there may be less of a tendency to associate UI solely as a source of income support. They are less likely to fully understand the workings of UI from parental behavior, and their understanding of what exactly it entails would be more likely to come from their own interaction with it.

This supposition leaves the effectiveness of "active" measures in promoting long-term employment and lowering subsequent reliance on UI very much open. Both Canada and Sweden have high rates of repeat reliance on UI. This would be consistent with the hypothesis that in Canada some individuals cycle between periods of short-term employment and spells of UI receipt, while in Sweden they cycle between periods of retraining and UI receipt: neither short-term jobs on the one hand, nor labor market retraining on the other leading to long-term employment. The difference is that parental UI use may play a more important role in kick-starting this process in Canada. At the same time, other features of program design may kick-start the process of individual learning in Sweden. The requirement that first time labor market entrants experience only a period of joblessness to qualify for UI is consistent with the philosophy of UI as a retraining program: failure to obtain a job being evidence of a need for re-skilling. But the evidence in this chapter seems to be consistent with the possibility that this leads to a sharp rise in the chances of receiving UI for 18-year-olds, so that individual learning about UI starts sooner in Sweden. If the retraining aspects of the program are not effective in promoting stable employment this will also lead to high rates of repeated reliance on UI in the future, particularly since participation in active programs can be used to support future claims. The result is that repeat use of UI is also high in Sweden but it comes about in a different way.

This explanation of the results should not obscure the finding that other variables also play a role in influencing the propensity to receive UI. Most notably, parental income plays a particularly important inter-generational role in conditioning the labor market success of children. The major point of this chapter is that how parental income is obtained, not just its level, may also be an aspect of intergenerational dynamics, and that the structure and design of government income transfer policies may influence this.

## References

Ackum Agell, Susanne, Anders Björklund, and Anders Harkman (1995). "Unemployment Insurance, Labour Market Programmes and Repeated Unemployment in Sweden." *Swedish Economic Policy Review*. Vol. 2, pp. 101–28.

Antel, John J. (1992). "The Intergenerational Transfer of Welfare Dependency: Some Statistical Evidence." *Review of Economics and Statistics*. Vol. 74, no. 3, pp. 467–73.

Atkinson, A. B., and John Micklewright (1991). "Unemployment Compensation and Labour Market Transitions: A Critical Review." *Journal of Economic Literature*. Vol. 29, pp. 1679–727.

Beaulieu, Nicolas, Jean-Yves Duclos, Bernard Fortin, and Manon Rouleau (2002). "The Intergenerational Reliance on Social Assistance: Evidence from Canada." Laval University: unpublished.

Becker, Gary S. (1996). *Accounting for Tastes*. Cambridge, MA: Harvard University Press.

Becker, Gary S., and Casey B. Mulligan (1997). "The Endogenous Determination of Time Preference." *Quarterly Journal of Economics*. Vol. 112, no. 3, pp. 729–58.

Becker, Gary S. and Kevin M. Murphy (1988). "A Theory of Rational Addiction." *Journal of Political Economy*. Vol. 96, no. 4, pp. 675–700. Reprinted as Chapter 3 in Becker (1996).

van den Berg, Axel, Bengt Furåker, and Leif Johansson (1997). *Labour Market Regimes and Patterns of Flexibility: A Sweden-Canada Comparison.* Lund: Arkiv förlag.

Björklund, A. (1991). "The Economics of Unemployment Insurance: The Case of Sweden." In A. Björklund et al. (editors). *Labour Market Policy and Unemployment Insurance.* Oxford: Clarendon Press.

Canada (1995). Human Resources Development Canada. *A 21st Century Employment System for Canada: Guide to the Employment Insurance Legislation.* Ottawa: Minister of Supply and Services Canada.

Corak, Miles (1993a). "Unemployment Insurance Once Again: The Incidence of Repeat Participation in the Canadian UI Program." *Canadian Public Policy.* Vol. 19, no. 2, pp. 162–76.

(1993b). "Is Unemployment Insurance Addictive? Evidence from the Benefit Durations of Repeat Users." *Industrial and Labor Relations Review.* Vol. 47, no. 1, pp. 62–72.

(1994). "Unemployment Insurance, Work Disincentives, and the Canadian Labor Market: An Overview." In Christopher Green, Fred Lazar, Miles Corak, and Dominique M. Gross. *Unemployment Insurance: How to Make it Work.* Toronto: C. D. Howe Institute.

Corak, Miles, and Wen-Hao Chen (2003). "Firms, Industries, and Unemployment Insurance: An Analysis using Employer-Employee Data." Statistics Canada, Analytical Studies Research Paper, in print.

Corak, Miles, and Andrew Heisz (1998). "How to Get Ahead in Life: Some Correlates of Intergenerational Income Mobility in Canada." In Miles Corak (editor). *Labour Markets, Social Institutions, and the Future of Canada's Children.* Ottawa: Statistics Canada, Catalogue No. 89–553-xpb.

(1999). "The Intergenerational Earnings and Income Mobility of Canadian Men: Evidence from Longitudinal Income Tax Data." *Journal of Human Resources.* Vol. 34, no. 3, pp. 504–33.

Ellison, Glenn, and Drew Fudenberg (1993). "Rules of Thumb for Social Learning." *Journal of Political Economy.* Vol. 101, pp. 612–43.

(1995). "Word-of-Mouth Communication and Social Learning." *Quarterly Journal of Economics.* Vol. 110, no. 1, pp. 93–126.

Gottschalk, Peter (1996). "Is the Correlation in Welfare Participation Across Generations Spurious?" *Journal of Public Economics.* Vol. 63, no. 1, pp. 1–25.

Gottschalk, Peter, Sara McLanahan, and Gary D. Sandefur (1994). "The Dynamics and Intergenerational Transmission of Poverty and Welfare Participation." In Sheldon H. Danziger, Gary D. Sandefur, and Daniel H. Weinberg (editors). *Confronting Poverty: Prescriptions for Change.* Cambridge MA: Harvard University Press and Russell Sage.

Grawe, Nathan D. (2001). "In Search of Intergenerational Credit Constraints Among Canadian Men: Quantile Versus Mean Regression Tests for Binding Credit Constraints." Family and Labour Studies, Analytical Studies Branch Research Paper No. 158. Ottawa: Statistics Canada.

(2003). "Life Cycle Bias in the Estimation of Intergenerational Earnings Persistence." Family and Labour Studies, Analytical Studies Branch Research Paper No. 207. Ottawa: Statistics Canada.

Greene, William H. (1997). *Econometric Analysis*. Third Edition. Upper Saddle River, NJ: Prentice-Hall.

Gustafsson, Björn, and N. Anders Klevmarken (1993). "Taxes and Transfers in Sweden: Incentive Effects on Labour Supply." In *Welfare and Work Incentives*. New York: Oxford University Press.

Harris, Shelly, and Daniela Lucaciu (1994). "An Overview of the T1FF Creation." LAD Reports, Reference Number 94-24-01 v1.2. Small Areas and Administrative Data Division. Ottawa: Statistics Canada.

Heckman, James J. (1981). "Statistical Models for Discrete Panel Data." In Charles F. Manski and Daniel McFadden (editors). *Structural Analysis of Discrete Data with Economic Applications*. Cambridge MA: The MIT Press.

Heckman, James J, and George Borjas (1980). "Does Unemployment Cause Future Unemployment? Definitions, Questions, and Answers from a Continuous Time Model of Heterogeneity and State Dependence." *Economica*. Vol. 47, no. 187, pp. 247–83.

Hosmer, David W., and Stanley Lemeshow (1989). *Applied Logistic Regression*. New York: John Wiley & Sons.

Jenkins, Stephen P. (1995). "Easy Estimation Methods for Discrete-Time Duration Models." *Oxford Bulletin of Economics and Statistics*. Vol. 57, no. 1, pp. 129–38.

Lemieux, Thomas, and W. Bentley MacLeod. (2000). "Supply Side Hysteresis: The Case of the Canadian Unemployment Insurance System." *Journal of Public Economics*. Vol. 78, pp. 139–70.

Levine, Phillip B., and David J. Zimmerman (1996). "The Intergenerational Correlation in AFDC Participation: Welfare Trap or Poverty Trap?" Institute for Research on Poverty, Discussion Paper no. 1100–96.

McLanahan, Sara S. (1988). "Family Structure and Dependency: Early Transitions to Female Household Headship." *Demography*. Vol. 25, no. 1, pp. 1–16.

Moffitt, Robert (1983). "An Economic Model of Welfare Stigma." *American Economic Review*. Vol. 73, no. 5, pp. 1023–35.

Mulligan, Casey B. (1996). "Work Ethic and Family Background: Some Evidence." University of Chicago: unpublished.

OECD (1994). *The OECD Jobs Study: Evidence and Explanations, Part II The Adjustment Potential of the Labour Market.* Paris: Organisation for Economic Cooperation and Development.

O'Neill, Donal, and Olive Sweetman (1998). "Intergenerational Mobility in Britain: Evidence from Unemployment Patterns." *Oxford Bulletin of Economics and Statistics.* Vol. 60, no. 4, pp. 431–47.

Oreopoulos, Philip (2002). "Do Neighbourhoods Influence Long-Term Labour Market Success? A Comparison of Adults Who Grew Up in Different Public Housing Projects." Statistics Canada, Analytical Studies Research Paper No. 185. Forthcoming in *Quarterly Journal of Economics.*

Österbacka, Eva (1999). "The Connection Between Unemployment Among Relatives in Finland." Paper presented to the meetings of the European Society for Population Economics, Turin, Italy.

Sargent, Timothy C. (1995). "An Index of Unemployment Insurance Disincentives." Economic and Fiscal Policy Branch, Working Paper No. 95–10. Ottawa: Department of Finance.

Soidre, Tiiu (1999). "Arbetslöshet och generation – unga kvinnor och män och dera föräldrar." *Arbetsmarknad & Arbetsliv.* Vol. 5, no. 2, pp. 127–44.

Stenberg, Sten-Åke (2000). "Inheritance of Welfare Recipiency: An Intergenerational Study of Social Assistance Recipiency in Post-War Sweden." *Journal of Marriage and the Family.* Vol. 62, no. 1, pp. 228–39.

# 12 Unequal opportunities and the mechanisms of social inheritance

GØSTA ESPING-ANDERSEN

I DEOLOGY and myth do not die easily, and certainly not at the hands of social scientists. Even with decades of systematic and cumulative social scientific evidence to the contrary, in many public policy circles it is still widely believed that North Americans and Europeans live in the land of equal opportunities. Yet the evidence, including the chapters of this book, demonstrates that, notwithstanding a half century of educational expansion and social reform, life chances remain powerfully determined by social origins. This is certainly worrisome if policy makers care about social justice, but it is also problematic if they are concerned with the future. If a large share of today's youth fails to realize its full productive potential, tomorrow's retirees will be less well off.

In this chapter, I shall try to bring together what sociologists and economists know, or at least need to know, about social inheritance and life chances. The bad news is that the constancy of social inheritance dominates our findings. The good news is that recent research has uncovered instances in which it has diminished importantly. If we can identify the precise mechanisms at work this might help governments devise policies to more effectively ensure equal opportunities. To anticipate my conclusions I am, first of all, sceptical of the usual assumption that generational inheritance is primarily driven by investments in education. Instead, there is good reason to believe that the decisive mechanisms lie in the "cultural capital" of families, and furthermore that it is in early childhood that parental transmission is key. This would indicate that research needs to be refocused, and that government policy needs to be rethought.

## 1 The economics and sociology of social inheritance

A superficial reading of the two disciplinary literatures might conclude that economists and sociologists pursue quite different aims,

I would like to thank Miles Corak for his useful comments on an earlier draft and Josep Mestres for research assistance.

even if they appear to be studying a similar issue. To sociologists, intergenerational transmission is of central importance because it tells us something about social divisions and ascriptive processes in the opportunity structure. The key concern is with life chances. Economists also worry about equal opportunities, but their concern is market imperfections, and the degree of intergenerational mobility is interpreted as telling us something about how the labor market functions. In addition, economic analysis is in the first instance concerned with earnings and incomes, while sociologists mainly examine educational, occupational, or social-class attainment. Methods also appear to diverge. Economists prefer linear estimation, often because theory is framed in terms of an "average" individual, and other times in recognition that data limitations prevent the use of more refined approaches. Sociologists are driven towards non-linear analysis, largely because they start out seeing the world in terms of discrete classes and categories. They prefer the household as their unit of analysis so as to capture the embeddedness of the individual in social collectivities.

A closer look suggests, however, that convergence overwhelms diversity. The main mobility variables – earnings to economists, occupational class to sociologists – are pretty much two sides of the same coin. Indeed, the early socio-economic status (or prestige) measures that sociologists constructed, Duncan's (1961) SEI scores, were a weighted composite of occupation-specific earnings and the educational profile of jobs. Earnings and occupational status are very highly correlated (Erickson and Goldthorpe 1992), and this holds also for Marxian-inspired class categories (Wright 1979).[1]

---

[1] The mobility studies that ensued from Duncan's SEI variable, as well as those more recently associated with Treiman's (1976) occupational prestige variable, typically adopt linear modeling approaches, a fact that seems to contradict the idea that sociologists favor categorical, non-linear methods. There are two important circumstances to note here. First, the transformation of class into monotonic SEI, or social prestige scores, that underpinned Blau and Duncan's (1967) and other work was in large part a second-best solution to simple computation problems. Second, as Treiman's and other recent work indicates, sociological interest in social prestige continues to thrive in its own right. Nonetheless, most sociologists studying social mobility have abandoned the linear SEI or prestige approach. For general overviews, see Featherman and Hauser (1976), Erickson and Goldthorpe (1992), Hauser and Warren (1997) and Sorensen (2001).

The two disciplines also converge in viewing education as the chief mediating variable in intergenerational mobility. To be sure, the theoretical underpinnings differ, both in terms of formalization and of substantive interpretation. Human capital theory permits formal modeling to an extent that is not possible (or even desired) in sociology. Following Becker (1964) and Becker and Tomes (1979, 1986) it is possible to construct strong and elegant theoretical prediction from few variables. Solon does as much in Chapter 2 of this volume: child's income is correlated with parental income because parents invest in their offspring's education. The elasticity between earnings across the generations may diminish if government investment in education is of more benefit to lower-income families. Economists would posit a similar intergenerational correlation everywhere and at any time unless there is a change in either or both of two parameters: the distribution of inter-household income and public educational subsidies. In any case, the causal chain is exclusively money driven: money of the parents → investment in children → money of the children.

In order to establish whether observed variations in mobility are nontrivial we need to accurately know *a priori* the elasticity between parent and child earnings. Not surprisingly, this is a key objective in many of the studies of this book. As the reader will have noted, the search for the true value of the intergenerational elasticity is wrought with difficulties, in particular because parent–child correlations are very sensitive to when (and for how long) we monitor parental and offspring outcomes. Earnings usually rise with age and can fluctuate substantially from year to year. Hence, information on permanent income is desirable, and analysts would be best off with income data at a similar stage in the parent's and child's life cycle. Recent advances in the availability of panel and longitudinally linked administrative data has made the task of estimating the elasticity much easier, and it can reasonably be assumed that the findings presented in this volume are more robust than previous (and generally lower) estimates.

These findings coalesce into an interesting set of conclusions. First, there does seem to be substantial support for a core elasticity in the neighbourhood of 0.4, at least for the United States. Second, there is credible support for the prediction that changes in income distribution and in government investment in education will affect this elasticity. Diachronic comparisons, such as Mayer and Lopoo (Chapter 5) and Harding et al. (forthcoming) demonstrate a change over time in the

US elasticity that is related to both government expenditure and to declining household income dispersion during the 1960s and 1970s. Interestingly, rising inequalities thereafter produce a reversal. Comparisons with other countries are, of course, better suited to test the effects of differing educational policies. In Chapter 4, Grawe offers an extensive comparative analysis of nine countries, both developed and developing. Björklund and Jäntti (1997) compare Sweden and the United States and find substantially greater intergenerational income mobility in the former. In their analysis of the United Kingdom, the authors of Chapter 6 show that government policy may easily reinforce, rather than weaken, the social origins effect if the expansion of higher education were to be mainly to the benefit of the privileged classes.

Providing a first link to prevailing sociological research, two chapters come to the conclusion that researchers should be more sensitive to non-linear (or asymmetric) effects: that is, the intergenerational earnings elasticity may diverge considerably across social (or income) classes. Ermisch and Francesconi suggest in Chapter 7 that downward mobility from the top of the class structure is far less likely than upward mobility from the bottom. Couch and Lillard in Chapter 8 find that immobility among sons of high-income fathers is more prevalent in the United States than in Germany. In contrast, they also find that children of poor parents are more likely to move up the income hierarchy in the United States than in Germany. Unfortunately, it is not easy to ascertain how such non-linearities are brought about. As Ermisch and Francesconi suggest, the inter-class differences in mobility run counter to standard economic theory. Since such differences indicate class closure, this is exactly what sociologists would predict, namely that there exist inbuilt barriers to mobility between distinct social strata. Can sociology help find answers?

A quick read of standard sociological treatments of social stratification would probably not help much. Sociologists take their clues from an age-old debate on where modern society is heading. In a nutshell, the issue is whether modernization – economic growth and industrialization – will in the long run reproduce or undo the old class divide? The key hypothesis that guided post-war mobility research was that modernization expands individual mobility and hence produces a less class-ridden society. A subsequent revision of this thesis argued that rising mobility would mainly occur in the initial stages of industrialization, after which mobility flows would stabilize (Featherman, Jones, and Hauser 1975, Grusky and Hauser 1984). It was assumed, rather than demonstrated, that the United States as the vanguard of economic development boasted substantially more social fluidity than elsewhere. And it was predicted that Europe, and even Third World nations, would eventually exhibit similarly high mobility rates once the economic catch-up process caught on. In practice, the modernization hypothesis that guided sociological mobility research has a close kinship to the thesis in economics that earnings begin to regress to the mean as countries become rich (Solon 1999, p. 1779).

Mobility research over the past decades has given this thesis the death-knell, not least because comparative data indicate that the United States may be less mobile than other countries (Solon 1999). The new consensus, as far as long-run historical evolution is concerned, is best captured by Erickson and Goldthorpe's (1992) notion of the constant flux. That is, the correlation between social origins and achievement appears extraordinarily stable and trend-less over even very long historical periods.[2] This holds for occupational class mobility, as in Erickson and Goldthorpe's (1992) research, and for educational attainment, as in Shavit and Blossfeld (1993). Yet, these very same studies identify exceptions to the constant flux. In the former, it is found that intergenerational class mobility has increased among the youngest cohorts in Sweden, and arguably also in the Netherlands. The latter study arrives at a very similar conclusion: there is a clear decline in the social inheritance effect on educational attainment in Sweden and apparently also in the Netherlands. Subsequent analyses corroborate this (Erickson and Jonsson, 1996).

The upshot is that it is necessary to look elsewhere than economic development for any explanation of mobility behavior. Like in economics, sociological mobility research also assumes education to be the main locus of intergenerational transmission. But this seems increasingly doubtful considering that intergenerational education correlations echo intergenerational occupational correlations, both over time and across nations. Not unlike economists, sociologists typically find that the direct effect of education on later earnings or occupation

---

[2] It is important to note here that we are referring to net mobility rates, that is net of changes in the marginals of parent–child mobility matrices.

is modest at best, and that it gradually declines as careers progress (Warren, Hauser, and Sheridan 2002).[3]

As I discuss in the next section, sociological mobility research has always been preoccupied with the mechanisms that connect social origins with destinations, especially with those that may jointly explain both educational and job inheritance. Hence, most sociologists will interpret intergenerational mobility correlations in terms of two main kinds of social interactions: first, the social milieu of the family during childhood and youth (such as family stability, poverty, or cultural resources), and second, the characteristics of the social community (neighborhood, class, or race segregation, or social networks).[4] In effect, sociologists would advocate going beyond any straightforward money → investment → money model. When confronting recent mobility research in economics with its sociological counterparts, one is struck by the consistency of empirical results. The emerging consensus around a core "inheritance elasticity" among economists has its counterpart in the sociologists' "constant flux." Moreover, both disciplines are discovering significant and seemingly important deviations from the core elasticity, both across time and nations. If "money" is not everything what can help us understand both the constant flux and its deviations?

## 2 The mechanisms of intergenerational transmission

The assumption that education is the chief mechanism through which origins are linked to destinations has been broadly shared by postwar social reformers. Indeed, the expansion and democratization of schooling in the postwar era were launched in the name of meritocracy and equality. From what is now known, the promise largely failed, and this requires explanation. To begin with, we must remember that the

---

[3] Very similar to intergenerational earnings estimates in economics, sociologists show that correlations are very sensitive to the age at which we monitor the achievements of offspring. Warren, Hauser, and Sheridan (2002) use siblings data to show that the effect of education declines across the life course. This is not the case for alternative human capital measures, such as cognitive abilities.

[4] Economic analysis has moved in similar directions. See Borjas (1995) and Corcoran et al. (1992). I will not address community effects mainly because they are empirically less salient than family effects.

explanatory nature of "education" changes, depending on whether we focus on micro processes (i.e., individual behaviour) or on societal level differences. In the former case, the system is treated as given and the concern is with the processes of social selection within that system. In the latter, as in cross-national mobility comparisons, the concern is with education systems and with whether one model promotes more or less opportunity than another.

Some of the studies in this volume lean towards the latter type of interpretation, and come to puzzling results when comparing, for example, Germany and the United States. Indeed, Couch and Lillard's finding that upward mobility from the bottom is greater in the United States would seem to contradict the money → investment → money model outright: first because Germany's household income distribution is more egalitarian, and second because public investment in education differs very little between the two countries. More generally, the results from comparative educational attainment research suggest that differences in public educational spending matter very little (Shavit and Blossfeld 1993, Erickson and Jonsson 1996, OECD 2001b). The two exceptions to the constant flux of educational attainment, Sweden and the Netherlands, cannot be explained in terms of extraordinary levels of public investment in education. Public expenditure on education is actually a couple of percentage points higher in Sweden than the OECD average, but the Dutch spend less. The United States lies almost exactly at the mean, and Germany a bit below (OECD 2000, Tables B1–B2).

System design might conceivably be of greater importance. For example, it is an established fact that early tracking in schools reinforces social inequalities. The Swedish comprehensive-school reform was explicitly designed to augment equal opportunities. Some of the findings in this volume give credence to a systems-explanation. Indeed, the finding in Chapter 8 that upward mobility from the bottom in Germany is limited squares better with sociological research than with economic theory. As Blossfeld (1993) and Blossfeld *et al.* (1993) show, the heavy skill-biased credentialism that is built into the German dual system implies that those who fail to pursue either academic or vocational training will have foreclosed, practically for ever, any chances of upward mobility.

Educational-system characteristics (such as tracking, or the mix of public and private schools) may help account for group-specific mobility patterns, but they generally fail to explain overall mobility differences. Hence, the constant flux of occupational mobility or educational attainment prevails in countries with distinctly different educational systems, such as the United States, Germany, Italy, and the United Kingdom. These four countries pretty much represent the global diversity in education systems. This is corroborated in OECD (2001b), which shows that variations in the educational and cognitive performance of fifteen year olds are predominantly related to family-of-origin variables. National differences in school systems, or even intra-national variations in the quality of teachers and schools, make very little difference. Nor is it easy to explain the two deviant cases by reference to system attributes. Dutch education is quite similar to the German dual system while Sweden (since the 1960s) boasts an unusually comprehensive school system.[5]

When we move to micro-analyses the education variable comes closer to the individualized investment-logic driving economic theory. The prevalence of a stable income elasticity in economics and a constant flux in sociology, coupled with significant deviations (like the Dutch and Swedish cases), raises the question of how this transmission occurs. If there is doubt that it is all money-driven, analysts need to broaden their search for the smoking gun. In fact, education hardly ever explains more than a fifth of the variation in log-earnings (Card 1999).

Sociologists generally prefer to study educational attainment in terms of transitions rather than years of education (Mare 1993). This is so for two principal reasons. First, the social-origins effect is not monotonic and linear by years of schooling. It is stronger at earlier key transitions (in particular transitions into secondary education) and tapers off later on. Put differently, if "poor" children make it through the hurdles their performance is more on par with "rich" kids. There is a potential problem of selection bias when we measure education simply in terms of years of schooling. Second, the important selections occur at the moment youth face transitions because it is at these points that

---

[5] As Erickson and Jonsson (1996) suggest, it is possible that the comprehensive Swedish system has helped create more educational equality. Yet they remain quite skeptical as to whether this is what accounts for the declining social-inheritance effects found for Sweden. In fact, as will be shown below, Denmark and Norway (previously unstudied) exhibit a similar and very strong declining inheritance effect, and their education systems are not of the comprehensive type. Echoing the growing consensus in the literature, it is necessary to look elsewhere for explanations.

they (and their parents) will calculate the potential gains, risks, and opportunity costs associated with additional schooling (Breen 2001). The risk calculus is likely to vary with the mechanisms (income, social networks, or cultural resources) that link social origins to educational outcomes. What, then, determines educational choices and outcomes?

An important clue comes from research on remedial education (Heckman 1999). One solid finding is that attempts to correct for skills deficiencies later in life are ineffective if people do not already possess adequate motivational or cognitive resources to begin with. This begins in early childhood, in particular between birth and six years of age. Developmental psychologists have established that the basic abilities for learning are most intensely developed during this period (Danziger and Waldfogel 2000, Duncan and Brooks-Gunn 1997). The analysis of the black–white score gap by Jencks and Phillips (1998) also highlights the decisiveness of early childhood. This said, one would therefore predict that family effects overshadow community or neighborhood effects, the latter being more likely to assert their influence at later stages. There is now substantial and consistent evidence that the family milieu during early childhood is decisive for later achievement, such as educational attainment, earnings, and careers, and also for later social problems, such as dropping out of school and criminality. One factor that has been studied extensively is the impact of family poverty, and more generally of family resources (Duncan et al. 1998, Duncan and Brooks-Gunn 1997, Machin 1998, McCulloch and Joshi 2002). Indeed, the effects can be very powerful, as illustrated by estimates showing that, in the United States, poverty during childhood is associated with an average of two years less schooling and substantially lower adult earnings (Mayer 1997, Duncan et al. 1998). There is also strong evidence that family instability, parental unemployment, and alcoholism seriously impair children's educational attainment. But there is no evidence that mothers' employment *per se* harms children's development, rather just the contrary (Duncan and Brooks-Gunn 1997).

Admittedly, many of these family characteristics are correlated with parental income and will as a result be captured in the money → investment → money model. Financial security within the family is, for example, key to Breen's (2001) rational choice theory of transition decisions: the perceived risks associated with continuing education are likely to be more intense in families feeling financially insecure. But other characteristics are not necessarily correlated with income.

Inspired by Bourdieu's (1983) emphasis on "cultural capital," there is a growing literature suggesting that: (a) social skills, personality traits, and cultural resources may be as important as educational certificates in hiring and promotion decisions or, more broadly, in dictating who gets ahead (Jencks et al. 1972, DiMaggio 1982, DiMaggio and Mohr 1985, De Graaf 1998, Bowles et al. 2001); and (b) that the cultural and educational resources of parents are vital for children's cognitive development and subsequent school performance (OECD 2001b).

"Cultural capital" refers to both formal (highbrow) and everyday cultural consumption and interchange (such as reading literature or discussing cultural issues). Bourdieu's thesis is that familiarity with, and the ability to use, cultural symbols and meaning is essential for getting ahead in the school system – not least because the education system (especially at higher levels) is, itself, biased in favour of middle- and upper-class cultural norms. It is, furthermore, argued that schools do not help correct for inadequate cultural skills among children. In brief, it is believed that cultural skills are mainly transmitted from parents to children, and that they are crucial for the nurturing of children's cognitive abilities, too. Cultural resources may also be decisive in allowing parents to better "navigate" the educational system in the best interests of their offspring (Erickson and Jonsson 1996).

That cognitive skills compete with education in dictating life chances is fairly well established. What comes as a surprise is that the two are only weakly correlated. Data from the International Adult Literacy Survey (IALS) suggests that the simple bi-variate correlation hovers between 0.4 and 0.5 depending upon the country. This implies that they capture different dimensions of human capital. There is evidence that cognitive abilities affect life chances independent of the influence of educational attainment. Bowles *et al.* (2001, p. 1154) review the econometric evidence from twenty-four studies and conclude that "a standard deviation difference in cognitive performance is associated with something less than a ten percent increase in wages, and is in this respect roughly equivalent to a year of schooling." Green and Riddell (2001) find that cognitive abilities account for about a third of the "returns to education" in earnings equations. There is strong support for the possibility that a good part of the intergenerational class inheritance of earnings, education, and occupational outcomes is mediated via parents' impact on children's cognitive development. If that is so, researchers need to examine a broader menu of parental characteristics, and also need to focus more on what happens before children even start

school. Economists have taken some steps to study more dimensions of
parents' status. Solon (1992) instruments parental income with father's
education, and Mulligan's (1997) analyses of intergenerational mobility include a host of conceivably relevant family characteristics, such as
parents' occupation, race, and education. Sociologists have routinely
controlled for these (and other) variables in their mobility studies. Some
recent work has deepened the family context considerably by including
direct information on cultural assets, such as literature, reading, and
cultural consumption (de Graaf 1998, OECD 2001b).

We might better understand the "constant flux" of educational
attainment if, indeed, cognitive abilities and education measure distinct
attributes, and to the extent that the former are largely developed during pre-school ages. In large part, the selection mechanisms that occur
in school systems are prefigured in that cognitively strong children will
profit far more from any given curriculum and teaching than will their
weaker counterparts, regardless of what kind of school system prevails
or of how well it is financed. This is also the main conclusion of OECD
(2001b), an analysis that includes detailed information on children's
cognitive performance, knowledge, and social background as well as
on the schools and on "neighborhood effects." In other words, if we
want to identify the smoking gun behind the constant flux, parental
influence on cognitive development may be a good place to start.

The International Adult Literacy Survey can be used to arrive at a
first approximation. Ideally, the analysis would correlate cognitive performance with both social origins and with career outcomes. Unfortunately these data furnish no information on parents' income, and
children's earnings data are available only for a handful countries.
The survey does, however, give information on parents' education.
As a first approximation, offspring's cognitive performance (and educational attainment) can be regressed on parents' educational level.
Regression estimates of the impact of fathers' education are presented
in Table 12.1. To arrive at a more accurate estimate of father–child
education correlations, the coefficients are adjusted for differing generational distributions in educational attainment (see note to Table 12.1).
The analysis is based upon eight countries representing both the country comparisons undertaken in the previous chapters and the diversity of educational systems within advanced countries. All estimations
control for gender and for immigrant status and pertain only to those
thirty to thirty-nine years of age. The analysis is restricted to this age
group so that the vast majority of respondents will have completed

Table 12.1   *The impact of father's education on the educational attainment and on cognitive performance of children in eight countries*

|  | Child's years of education | | Child's cognitive score | |
|---|---|---|---|---|
|  | Estimated coefficient | Standardized coefficient | Estimated coefficient | Standardized coefficient |
| Canada | 0.080 | 0.423 | 5.06 | 0.411 |
| United States | 0.206 | 0.424 | 10.30 | 0.364 |
| United Kingdom | 0.489 | 0.331 | 11.30 | 0.284 |
| Sweden | 0.085 | 0.339 | 6.20 | 0.338 |
| Norway | 0.105 | 0.328 | 6.06 | 0.286 |
| Denmark | 0.277 | 0.259 | 4.40 | 0.204 |
| Germany | 0.803 | 0.403 | 4.05 | 0.105 |
| Netherlands | 0.319 | 0.377 | 4.99 | 0.251 |

*Notes:* All estimates are significant at the 0.001 level of significance or better. The cognitive performance variable is defined as the mean individual score on the three literacy items tested in the International Adult Literacy Survey (document, prose, and quantitative abilities). The analysis is restricted to those 30 to 39 years of age for all countries except Canada, where the age range is 25 to 35 years. All estimations also control for gender and immigration status.

The standardized coefficient refers to the adjustment of the estimated coefficient for differing variances in father and child outcomes, derived as the estimated coefficient multiplied by the ratio of the variance of father outcomes to child outcomes.

*Source:* Calculations by the author using the International Adult Literacy Survey, second wave microdata as provided by Statistics Canada.

formal education, and because this is the age range employed in most studies of generational income mobility.

The results confirm much of what is already known. In particular, an unusually modest parental impact on children's education and on their cognitive performance is evident in Scandinavia (although the education elasticity is rather strong in Denmark). In addition the Dutch results contradict the conclusions from earlier research, at least as far as educational attainment is concerned.[6] The United Kingdom and especially Germany show unusually strong elasticities as far as

[6] In reality, these and earlier estimates are not strictly comparable given that the correlations presented here are based on years of education and not on educational transitions, as in Shavit and Blossfeld (1993) or Erickson and Jonsson (1996).

educational attainment is concerned. Further, the United Kingdom and the United States stand out in terms of very strong parental effects on cognitive performance.[7] A coefficient of 10.3 for the United States suggests that fathers with five more years of schooling than average will push their offspring roughly one quintile up in the distribution of cognitive skills. The standardized coefficients serve to compare across the two human capital dimensions. As signaled, cognitive abilities and educational attainment are both powerfully and rather similarly driven by social origins.

The two measures tap distinct human capital attributes, yet both are strongly related to social origins. Considering the modest amount of information available on the parental milieu, it is not easy to go from here to a deeper understanding of whether this is chiefly "money-driven," or alternatively if there is a need to worry about "culture." Fortunately, the recently released Programme for International Student Assessment (PISA) data allow identification of factors more directly related to family and parenting factors, and to some extent permit differentiation of these from money factors. The PISA study is an international OECD-sponsored study of the scholastic and cognitive aptitudes of fifteen and sixteen year olds, and is described in OECD (2001b). The PISA does not include information on parental income, but does include a "wealth" variable based on a composite of information on the size, standards, and quality of the parental home, arguably a fairly good proxy for permanent income. It also includes a variable describing the socio-economic status of parents, information on father's and mother's education, and a battery of variables that tap the family's cultural milieu.

Least Squares regressions of children's scholastic-cognitive aptitudes (in reading) on wealth, cultural capital, father's education, and household's socio-economic status are presented in Table 12.2. The socio-economic status variable is an updated variant of the old Blau–Duncan occupational prestige index. Like its progenitor, it offers a weighted score for the educational and income profile of occupational groups. In the following analyses, the socio-economic index scores that pertain to the household (the highest of either of the parents) are used.

---

[7] The German (and probably also Dutch) education coefficients are likely overstated due to measurement problems. Transforming educational levels into their year-equivalents is especially difficult for these two countries.

**Table 12.2** *Least Squares regression results of the impact of family background on the cognitive performance of children in six countries*

|  | Germany | France | Denmark | Sweden | Canada | United Kingdom | United States |
|---|---|---|---|---|---|---|---|
| Cultural Capital | **0.296** | **0.307** | **0.297** | **0.255** | **0.272** | **0.317** | **0.259** |
| Father's education | **0.118** | 0.003 | **0.157** | 0.002 | **0.080** | 0.023 | 0.047 |
| Socio-economic status | **0.178** | **0.213** | **0.126** | **0.190** | **0.145** | **0.212** | **0.172** |
| Household wealth | −0.020 | 0.033 | −0.031 | −0.011 | −0.001 | 0.042 | 0.057 |
| $R^2$ | 0.213 | 0.198 | 0.177 | 0.131 | 0.142 | 0.193 | 0.163 |
| Sample size | 4,164 | 3,774 | 3,572 | 3,970 | 26,735 | 7,752 | 2,732 |

*Note*: The dependent variable in all regression is the mean test score on tests of reading ability, comprehension, and interpretation. **Boldface** indicates statistically significant estimates at the .001 level of confidence.

*Source*: Calculations by the author using OECD, Programme for International Student Assessment, microdata.

Also, as in the earlier regressions, only father's education is used. The "culture" variable derives from factor analysis which yields a strong and unique "culture" factor based on three variables: a measure of the quantity of books possessed by the family, a measure of "high" culture (classical music, theatre), and a measure of cultural communication within the family (like frequency of discussing literature or the like). Note that the "quantity of books" variable is, by far, the most strongly associated with outcomes. OECD (2001b) offers details on variable measurement. Wealth is albeit an indirect measure of income, but the household socio-economic index score – as in Ermisch and Francesconi's analysis in Chapter 7 – should also help capture family income.[8] With these qualifiers in mind, it is nonetheless evident that children's cognitive performance at age fifteen is far more powerfully related to the family's cultural capital than to its material wealth, or alternatively to its socio-economic status. Indeed, the wealth variable (household amenities) is systematically weak and not statistically significant in several cases. The socio-economic status variable performs everywhere much better (with estimates in the neighborhood of 0.170 to 0.200), but it is the culture variable that dominates. This also seems quite robust when it is noted that the culture effect is consistent across such very different countries. In other words, for whatever these analyses are worth there does seem to be a fairly good case for a family culture explanation that is distinct from money effects. This is not to say that parents do not invest in their children, only that arguably very decisive kinds of investment are not of the monetary kind, and furthermore do not seem to correlate strongly with money. The simple correlation between wealth and our culture factor is generally about 0.15, the correlation between household socio-economic status and the culture factor is around 0.4.

As mentioned, it is more difficult to correlate "the other way," that is connecting cognitive abilities and education to earnings in adult life.

---

[8] In reality, the two variables are not correlated very strongly. The correlation is strongest in the United States (0.36) and hovers around 0.25 in Western European countries with, unsurprisingly, Sweden being the lowest (0.13). Note that there are no problems of multi-colinearity in any of the regressions. However, the surprisingly modest effects of father's education on child's cognitive performance is, no doubt, partly attributable to the socio-economic status variable (the bi-variate correlation hovers between 0.4 and 0.5).

In this regard, the important issue concerns their relative importance for life chances. The standard "money" assumptions behind inter-generational earnings models can be questioned further if these two influences tap uniquely different aspects of human capital – while at the same time being powerfully correlated with family origins – and if earnings are strongly related to cognitive abilities. The PISA data do not help in this regard since they observe children still in school. The IALS data furnishes full annual earnings information for the United States and Sweden. Table 12.3 presents regressions of cognitive perfor-mance, educational attainment (measured in years), and experience on log (annual) earnings. As earlier, controls are also used for gender and immigrant status. The analysis compares Sweden and the United States which are, without doubt, the two most orthogonal cases in terms of earnings distribution.

The results for the United States are very similar to those obtained for Canada by Green and Riddell (2001, Table 12.1). The inclusion of the cognitive variable leads to a 30 percent decline in the education elasticity (and eliminates the immigrant effect). Since the experience coefficients remain unchanged, it is evident that work experience does not have much of an influence on cognitive performance. A compar-ison of the results in Model 2 (not shown) suggests that the relative weight of education and cognitive ability is just about the same (0.305 for education and 0.298 for cognitive score). The Swedish story is very different, mainly because earnings are far less related to any observ-able individual attribute. This is hardly surprising considering Sweden's uniquely compressed wage structure. Hence, in Model 1 the education elasticity is only one-third that of the United States, and the inclusion of cognitive score in Model 2 contributes very little as well.

When these results are held up against the findings in Table 12.1 it is clear that there are very different contours to life chances. On the one hand, parental inheritance is far more powerful in the United States than in Sweden, be it for educational attainment or for cogni-tive skills. On the other hand, the very same educational and cognitive attributes play a far greater role in dictating adult life chances (in this case earnings) in the United States than in Sweden. In any case, the transmission mechanisms are fairly similar across all countries; the money-investment model does not offer a very complete account of how intergenerational correlations come about. If anything, the cul-tural capital of families appears rather more decisive. As Mayer (1997)

Table 12.3 *Least Squares regression estimates of the impact of education and cognitive ability on annual earnings in the United States and Sweden*

|  | United States | | Sweden | |
|---|---|---|---|---|
|  | *(1)* | *(2)* | *(1)* | *(2)* |
| Female | **−0.369** | **−0.364** | **−0.244** | **−0.241** |
| Foreign born | −0.164 | 0.005 | −0.104 | −0.079 |
| Experience | 0.046 | 0.046 | 0.030 | 0.030 |
| Experience$^2$ | −0.0007 | −0.0007 | −0.0004 | −0.0004 |
| Education in years | 0.096 | 0.063 | 0.033 | 0.030 |
| Cognitive ability |  | 0.003 |  | 0.001 |
| Constant | 8.54 | 8.12 | 11.4 | 11.2 |
| R$^2$ | 0.322 | 0.370 | 0.136 | 0.139 |
| Sample size | 1,133 | 1,133 | 1,096 | 1,096 |

*Note:* The dependent variable in all regressions is the natural logarithm of annual earnings and all models are based on full-time full-year workers aged 20 to 60. **Boldface** indicates statistically significant estimates at the 0.001 level of significance.
*Source:* Derivations by the author using second-wave microdata from the International Adult Literacy Survey as provided by Statistics Canada.

has argued, money alone cannot buy equal opportunities. One overriding puzzle remains: why is the social inheritance of life chances so much stronger in some countries than in others? And why does it also vary over time? Since family culture seems to play a key role in the process of transmission, the money–investment–money thesis has shortcomings. What, in other words, have countries like Sweden done to diminish the intergenerational correlation of incomes?

# 3 Public policy and equality of opportunity

Since it would be difficult to explain Sweden's egalitarianism in terms of public investment in education, an alternative economic explanation might lie in Sweden's extraordinarily compressed wage distribution, which implies that earnings are only weakly linked to human capital or gender. The United States has one of the OECD's most unequal wage distributions: wage setting is extremely decentralized and it would be expected that skills or other worker attributes play a far greater role in dictating individual earnings. No doubt there is some truth in this account. Yet it fails to explain the fact that Sweden is also more egalitarian in terms of educational attainment, occupational mobility, and cognitive development. In fact, there is a danger of explaining all this tautologically: very inegalitarian societies beget very inegalitarian results. But the tautology disappears when we add to this that very inegalitarian societies also beget more ascription and less mobility. Corak (2001) has also argued that intergenerational correlations will be higher in more unequal societies, stressing the centrality of non-monetary factors, such as parenting styles and skills. This runs counter to prevailing thought, which continues to insist that unequal income distributions (such as in the United States) are offset by greater individual mobility. Indeed, the standard assumption is that income inequality stimulates incentives for mobility. From sociological research it is known that educational and occupational attainment is less correlated with social origins in Sweden and other fairly egalitarian societies. It is also known from economic research that this is also the case for earnings and incomes. Therefore it may be that the old "mobility myth" is simply false. Rather, there is a good argument to be made that mobility is negatively related to levels of overall inequality.

The evidence seems supportive if this hypothesis is tackled cross-nationally. Take the case of cognitive abilities that I have emphasized so much. These are distributed far more unequally in some countries than in others. Using test-score data from the IALS it is possible to compute national "cognitive" Gini coefficients. In a large sample of advanced societies, the Gini ranges from 0.08 in Denmark to 0.158 in the United States, and is substantially higher in countries like Poland and Chile. The telling point is that the cognitive Ginis are very powerfully correlated not only with national income Ginis, but also with the elasticity of father's education on child's cognitive performance and educational attainment. The $R^2$ for 15 countries is 0.68.

This does not reveal anything about causal direction, only that unequal societies also boast more social inheritance. Why this is so is the great challenge for policy makers. This challenge can motivate two kinds of strategies. The first, and classic one, is to pursue more equality by reforming key institutions. Indeed, the foremost strategy over the past half century has been educational expansion and reform: delaying or abolishing tracking, affirmative action for underprivileged children, standardizing curricula, school facilities, and so forth. There is certainly evidence that institutional changes can yield positive results, at least at the margin. Head Start is clearly a success in the United States, albeit limited to severely disadvantaged children (Currie 2001). But the pervasive sociological finding that differences in education system explain little in terms of the constant flux suggests that policy makers might turn their attention elsewhere. The second strategy is more attentive to the micro-processes of social transmission. If, as so much data suggest, the real selection process begins prior to school age, then the focus needs to be shifted from schools to families. This is all the more so when consideration is given to what is known about adult remedial programs, namely that they only work well for those who already possess a strong motivational and cognitive base. Erickson and Goldthorpe (1992) speculate that the diminished impact of origins in Sweden may be related to the equalization of family resources – including the virtual eradication of child poverty – brought about by the welfare state.

Equalizing household incomes via transfer programs is arguably one important pre-condition for more equality of opportunity. Income-poor families are less resourceful, less able to plan ahead and "navigate the school system," and poor parents are more likely to spur their children to abandon school in favor of a job. After all, it is well known that child poverty is strongly correlated with inferior educational and job attainment later on. Yet, there is a huge amount of research showing that social transfers to the poor can cut both ways. As discussed in Chapter 10, it is possible that welfare policy in the United States (AFDC in particular) inadvertently helped to reproduce intergenerational welfare dependence. The point is that money is possibly less neutral than commonly believed; social transfers may have second-order distributional effects that depend very much on how a transfer program is designed. In fact, this is also the underlying argument in Chapter 11 with reference to unemployment insurance in Canada and Sweden. As Korpi and Palme (1998) argue, the universal nature of the Scandinavian social-transfer system yields far more effective redistribution than does an American-style system that narrowly targets the poor. Perhaps most importantly, targeted benefits to the poor, as in the United States, are far more likely to produce poverty and welfare dependency traps that are counterproductive for mobility. This suggests the standard money-investment model needs to be amended by information on the nature of the money in question. This becomes all the more evident when the reasons for so little child poverty in Scandinavia are examined.

In fact, the abolition of poverty and material want in Scandinavian families with children is due far less to public income transfers than to public social service provision. Universal access to affordable day care explains why virtually all mothers are employed and it is this, in turn, that explains the absence of poverty (Esping-Andersen 2002, Chapter 2). This is especially evident in the case of Swedish lone mothers, whose employment rate is near 80 percent and whose poverty rate is only 4 percent. American mothers are now typically employed and use day care, but here the similarities end. More unequal wages mean that low-educated American mothers will have greater difficulty raising their families above the poverty line. The rate of child poverty in the United States stood at 19.3 percent in 1995, and in excess of 50 percent for lone mother households (Esping-Andersen 2002). Furthermore, day care in the United States is almost exclusively privately provided, and quality care is simply priced out of the market for low-income families (Blau 2001). Scandinavian day care is basically of uniform, high pedagogical standards, meaning that children from disadvantaged families will benefit disproportionately. Day care in the United States is of extremely uneven quality, and children from disadvantaged families are likely to find themselves concentrated at the low end. Additionally, it is common practice in the Nordic countries for school-age children to remain in schools after classes in organized "after-hours" activities. This implies fewer hours parked in front of the family television.

The upshot is that the uneven distribution of cultural capital among families is greatly neutralized in the Nordic countries, simply because much of the cognitive stimulus has been shifted from the parents to centers that do not replicate social class differences. As Waldfogel's (2002) review of both American and European research shows, child-care programs that are intensive, intervene early, and that promote high pedagogical standards contribute very effectively to the raising of the cognitive performance of children from disadvantaged milieux. In turn, this helps children start and proceed on a much more equal footing once they enter formal education. Although there is precious little longitudinal research, what evidence there is suggests that early quality care continues to exert positive emotional and cognitive results throughout childhood (Waldfogel 2002, p. 539).

All this said, care is needed not to throw the baby out with the bath-water. "Money" is decisive, and perhaps most important of all is long-term financial security. This emerges clearly from sociological research on educational transitions. Gifted or not, children from financially strained families are far more likely to stop their studies and seek employment at the decisive educational transitions for two reasons: the family may need additional income; and, as emphasized by Breen (2001), the family's risk calculus is powerfully related to its financial status. That social origins matter less for life chances in Scandinavia may very well have something to do with *de facto* universal welfare state guarantees that reduce perceived risks to a minimum.

The last word is certainly not in, but there is evidence (perhaps circumstantial) that both sociological and economic studies of social inheritance have been barking up the wrong explanatory tree. True enough, the parental effect on children's life chances is mediated through education. Social inheritance remains as pervasive as ever in large part because education systems largely reproduce pre-existing inequalities. Where public policy has gone wrong, for almost half a century now, has been in making the assumption that formal education could completely undo these inequalities, either by redistributive investment (as in the Becker tradition) or by system reform. If cultural capital rivals money, and if the decisive moment of social inheritance pre-dates formal education, the standard money-investment model must be re-thought. Yet, such a re-thinking should not provoke despair among those who believe in money. Public investment in early-childhood development will undoubtedly help neutralize the uneven distribution of cultural capital in families. It is not wholly utopian to believe that if Head Start were expanded to cover say a third of all American children, then the opportunity structure in the United States might look more Scandinavian. In addition, I think it can be fairly safely hypothesized that the key lies in how "money" and "culture" interact. A policy single-mindedly aimed at rectifying deficiencies in cultural capital, say through early child development, is unlikely to be sufficient if the risk of premature school-exit is continuous throughout youth. Likewise, a one-dimensional "money" strategy, say through income redistribution in favor of low-income families, will most likely fail unless it somehow also helps correct for cultural inequalities.

## 4 Conclusion

To conclude, one promising avenue for future research is to refine the money–investment–money model so that it can better differentiate

"types" of money and to deepen the model so that it better captures
money–culture interactions. And considering what is now known from
economics and sociology, there are some clear directions toward which
policy might fruitfully move. First, notwithstanding their contemporary popularity, "activation" policy and "life-long learning" may be
worthy of pursuit for other aims, but they are very unlikely to correct
for socially inherited disadvantages. Remedial programs are very cost-
ineffective. Second, educational system reform may be very desirable
but it is by now evident that it is unrealistic to expect that even the
most egalitarian-looking blueprint will deliver much more equality of
opportunity. Since it is pretty evident that school systems by and large
reproduce prevailing social inequalities, policy needs to be redirected
at those institutions which, in the first place, produce the inequalities.
A lot of what is now known suggests that the family is key. This leads
me to the third, and final, policy conclusion: the pressing need for a
new family policy. I have elaborated these arguments in much greater
detail in Esping-Andersen (2002). Suffice it to say that most advanced
welfare states have proceeded on the assumption that families require
little public support. On the one hand, it is still commonly believed
that parental, namely fathers', earnings suffice to ensure adequate economic welfare. This, of course, is belied by rising child poverty rates.
On the other hand, governments rarely worry about early childhood
development or care, assuming this to be the domain of the mother.
Yet, the housewife is rapidly becoming extinct. The irony, as far as
policy is concerned, is that the most effective remedy against child
poverty and arguably also an effective strategy of equalizing children's
cultural capital is to support working mothers by either providing or
subsidizing quality care for small children across the board. It appears,
additionally, to be a policy that increases the well-being of some without reducing the well-being of others because the individual gains that
many children and families will reap will also yield a substantial col-
lective dividend, not least for those among us who will retire in the
coming decades.

### References

Becker, Gary S. (1964). *Human Capital: A Theoretical and Empirical Anal-
    ysis*. New York: Columbia University Press.
Becker, Gary S., and  Nigel Tomes (1979). "An Equilibrium Theory of
    the Distribution of Income and Intergenerational Mobility." *Journal
    of Political Economy*. Vol. 87, no. 6, pp. 1153–89.

(1986). "Human Capital and the Rise and Fall of Families." *Journal of Labor Economics*. Vol. 4, no. 3, pp. S1–S39.

Björklund, Anders, and Markus Jäntti (1997). "Intergenerational Income Mobility in Sweden Compared to the United States." *American Economic Review*. Vol. 87, pp. 1009–18.

Blau, D. (2001). *The Childcare Problem*. New York: Russell Sage.

Blau, P, and O. D. Duncan (1967). *The American Occupational Structure*. New York: John Wiley.

Blossfeld, H. P. (1993). "Changes in Educational Opportunity in the Federal Republic of Germany: A Longitudinal Comparison of Cohorts Born between 1916 and 1965." In Y. Shavit and H. P. Blossfeld (editors). *Persistent Inequality*. Boulder, CO: Westview Press.

Blossfeld, H. P., G. Gianelli, and K. U. Mayer (1993). "Is There a New Service Proletariat? The Tertiary Sector and Social Inequality in Germany." In G. Esping-Andersen (editor). *Changing Classes. Stratification and Mobility in Postindustrial Societies*. London: Sage.

Borjas, G. (1995). "Ethnicity, Neighborhoods, and Human Capital Externalities." *American Economic Review*. Vol. 85, pp. 365–90.

Bourdieu, P. (1983). "The Forms of Capital." In J. Richardson (editor). *Handbook of Theory and Research in the Sociology of Education*. Westport, CT: Greenwood.

Bowles, Samuel, Herbert Gintis, and M. Osborne (2001). "The Determinants of Earnings: A Behavioural Approach." *Journal of Economic Literature*. Vol. 39, pp. 1137–76.

Breen, R. (2001). "A Rational Choice Model of Educational Inequality." *Instituto Juan March Working Paper*. Vol. 166, pp. 1–29.

Card, David (1999). "The Causal Effect of Education on Earnings." In Orley C. Ashenfelter and David Card (editors). *Handbook of Labor Economics, Volume 3A*. Amsterdam: North-Holland.

Corak, Miles (2001). "Are the Kids All Right? Intergenerational Mobility and Child Well-Being in Canada." In Keith Banting, Andrew Sharpe, and France St. Hilaire (editors). *The Review of Economic Performance and Social Progress, The Longest Decade; Canada in the 1990s*. Montreal: McGill-Queen's Press, and Statistics Canada Analytical Studies Branch Research Paper No. 171.

Corcoran, Mary, Roger Gordon, Deboroh Laren, and Gary R. Solon (1992). "The Association Between Men's Economic Status and Their Family and Community Origins." *Journal of Human Resources*. Vol. 27, pp. 575–601.

Currie, J. (2001). "Early Childhood Intervention Programs." *Journal of Economic Perspectives*. Vol. 15, pp. 213–38.

Danziger, S., and J. Waldfogel (2000). *Securing the Future. Investing in Children from Birth to College*. New York: Russell Sage.

De Graaf, P. (1998). "Parents' Financial and Cultural Resources, Grades, and Transitions to Secondary School." *European Sociological Review.* Vol. 4, pp. 209–21.

DiMaggio, P. (1982). "Cultural Capital and School Success." *American Sociological Review.* Vol. 47, pp. 189–201.

DiMaggio, P., and J. Mohr (1985). "Cultural Capital, Educational Attainment and Marital Selection." *American Journal of Sociology.* Vol. 90, pp. 1231–61.

Duncan, O. D. (1961). "A Socio-Economic Index for All Occupations." In A. J. Reiss (editor). *Occupations and Social Status.* New York: Free Press.

Duncan, G., and J. Brooks-Gunn (1997). *Consequences of Growing up Poor.* New York: Russell Sage.

Duncan, G., W. Jean Yeung, J. Brooks-Gunn, and J. Smith (1998). "The Effects of Childhood Poverty on the Life Chances of Children." *American Sociological Review.* Vol. 63, pp. 406–23.

Erickson, R., and J. Goldthorpe (1992). *The Constant Flux: A Study of Class Mobility in Industrial Societies.* Oxford: Clarendon Press.

Erickson, R., and J. Jonsson (1996). *Can Education be Equalized? The Swedish Case in Comparative Perspective.* Boulder, CO: Westview Press.

Esping-Andersen, G. (2002). *Why We Need a New Welfare State.* Oxford: Oxford University Press.

Featherman, D. L., and R. M. Hauser (1976). "Prestige or Socio-Economic Scales in the Study of Occupational Achievement." *Sociological Methods and Research*, Vol. 4, pp. 403–22.

Featherman, D., F. Jones, and R. Hauser (1975). "Assumptions of Social Mobility Research in The United States: The Case of Occupational Status." *Social Science Research.* Vol. 4, pp. 329–60.

Green, David A., and W. Craig Riddell (2001). "Literacy, Numeracy and Labour Market Outcomes in Canada." Ottawa: Statistics Canada, Catalogue No. 89-552-MIE, No. 8.

Grusky, David and R. M. Hauser (1984). "Comparative Social Mobility Revisited." *American Sociological Review.* Vol. 49, pp. 19–38.

Harding, David J., Christopher Jencks, Leonard M. Lopoo, and Susan E. Mayer (forthcoming). "The Changing Effects of Family Background on the Incomes of American Adults." In S. Bowles, H. Gintis, and M. Osborne (editors). *Family Background and Economic Success.* New York: Russell Sage.

Hauser, R., and J. R. Warren (1997). "Socioeconomic Indexes for Occupations: A Review, Update, and Critique." *Sociological Methodology.* Vol. 27, pp. 177–298.

Haveman, R., and B. Wolfe (1995). *Succeeding Generations. On the Effects of Investments in Children.* New York: Russell Sage.

Heckman, James J. (1999). "Doing it Right: Job Training and Education." *The Public Interest.* Spring, pp. 86–106.

Jencks, C., M. Smith, H. Acland, M. J. Bane, D. Cohen, H. Gintis, B. Heyns, and S. Michelson (1972). *Inequality: A Reassessment of Family and Schooling in America.* New York: Basic Books.

Jencks, C. and M. Phillips (1998). *The Black-White Test Score Gap.* New York: Russell Sage.

Korpi, W., and J. Palme (1998). "The Paradox of Redistribution and Strategies of Equality." *American Sociological Review.* Vol. 63, pp. 661–87.

Machin, S. (1998). "Childhood Disadvantage and Intergenerational Transmissions of Economic Status." In A. Atkinson and J. Hills (editors). *Exclusion, Employment and Opportunity.* London: London School of Economics.

Mare, R. (1993). "Educational Stratification and Observed and Unobserved Components of Family Background." In Y. Shavit and H. P. Blossfeld (editors). *Persistent Inequality.* Boulder, CO: Westview Press.

Mayer, Susan E. (1997). *What Money Can't Buy: Family Income and children's life chances.* Cambridge, MA: Harvard University Press.

McCulloch, A., and H. Joshi (2002). 'Child Development and Family Resources: Evidence from the Second Generation of the 1958 British Birth Cohort'. *Journal of Population Economics*, Vol. 15, No. 2, pp. 283–304.

Mulligan, Casey B. (1997). *Parental Priorities and Economic Inequality.* Chicago: University of Chicago Press.

OECD (2000). *Literacy in the Knowledge Society.* Paris: OECD.

OECD (2001a). *Education at a Glance.* Paris: OECD.

OECD (2001b). *Knowledge and Skills for Life.* Paris: OECD.

Shavit, Y., and H. P. Blossfeld (1993). *Persistent Inequality.* Boulder, CO: Westview Press.

Sieben, I., J. Huinink, and P. de Graaf (2001). "Family Background and Sibling Resemblance in Educational Attainment." *European Sociological Review.* Vol. 17, pp. 401–30.

Solon, Gary (1992). "Intergenerational Income Mobility in the United States." *American Economic Review.* Vol. 82, no. 3, pp. 393–408.

(1999). "Intergenerational Mobility in the Labor Market." In Orley C. Ashenfelter and David Card (editors). *Handbook of Labor Economics, Volume 3A.* Amsterdam: North-Holland.

Sorensen, A. B. (2001). "The Basic Concepts of Stratification: Class, Status and Power." In D. Grusky (editor). *Social Stratification.* Boulder, CO: Westview Press.

Treiman, D. (1976). *Occupational Prestige in Comparative Perspective.* New York: Academic Press.

Waldfogel, J. (2002). "Child Care, Women's Employment, and Child Outcomes." *Journal of Population Economics.* Vol. 15, pp. 527–48.

Warren, J., R. Hauser, and J. Sheridan (2002). "Occupational Stratification Across the Life Course." *American Sociological Review.* Vol. 67, pp. 432–55.

Wright, E. O. (1979). *Class Structure and Income Determination.* New York: Academic Press.

# Index

Printed in the United States
By Bookmasters